SECOND EDITION

Laravel: Up & Running
A Framework for Building Modern PHP Apps

Matt Stauffer

Beijing · Boston · Farnham · Sebastopol · Tokyo

Laravel: Up & Running

by Matt Stauffer

Published by O'Reilly Media, Inc., 1005 Gravenstein Highway North, Sebastopol, CA 95472.

O'Reilly books may be purchased for educational, business, or sales promotional use. Online editions are also available for most titles (*http://oreilly.com*). For more information, contact our corporate/institutional sales department: 800-998-9938 or *corporate@oreilly.com*.

Editor: Alicia Young
Production Editor: Christopher Faucher
Copyeditor: Rachel Head
Proofreader: Amanda Kersey

Indexer: WordCo Indexing Services, Inc.
Interior Designer: David Futato
Cover Designer: Karen Montgomery
Illustrator: Rebecca Demarest

December 2016:   First Edition
April 2019:   Second Edition

Revision History for the Second Edition
2019-04-01:   First Release

33614081413303

See *http://oreilly.com/catalog/errata.csp?isbn=9781492041214* for release details.

978-1-492-04121-4

[LSI]

This book is dedicated to my family.
Mia, my little princess and bundle of joy and energy.
Malachi, my little prince and adventurer and empath.
Tereva, my inspiration, encourager, upgrader, pusher, rib.

Table of Contents

Preface. xvii

1. Why Laravel?. 1
   Why Use a Framework?   1
      "I'll Just Build It Myself"   2
      Consistency and Flexibility   2
   A Short History of Web and PHP Frameworks   2
      Ruby on Rails   2
      The Influx of PHP Frameworks   3
      The Good and the Bad of CodeIgniter   3
      Laravel 1, 2, and 3   3
      Laravel 4   4
      Laravel 5   4
   What's So Special About Laravel?   4
      The Philosophy of Laravel   5
      How Laravel Achieves Developer Happiness   5
      The Laravel Community   6
   How It Works   7
   Why Laravel?   9

2. Setting Up a Laravel Development Environment. 11
   System Requirements   11
   Composer   12
   Local Development Environments   12
      Laravel Valet   12
      Laravel Homestead   13
   Creating a New Laravel Project   14
      Installing Laravel with the Laravel Installer Tool   14

Installing Laravel with Composer's create-project Feature   14
Lambo: Super-Powered "Laravel New"   14
Laravel's Directory Structure   15
The Folders   16
The Loose Files   17
Configuration   18
The .env File   19
Up and Running   21
Testing   21
TL;DR   22

3. Routing and Controllers. 23
A Quick Introduction to MVC, the HTTP Verbs, and REST   23
What Is MVC?   23
The HTTP Verbs   24
What Is REST?   25
Route Definitions   26
Route Verbs   28
Route Handling   28
Route Parameters   29
Route Names   31
Route Groups   33
Middleware   34
Path Prefixes   36
Fallback Routes   36
Subdomain Routing   37
Namespace Prefixes   37
Name Prefixes   38
Signed Routes   38
Signing a Route   39
Modifying Routes to Allow Signed Links   40
Views   40
Returning Simple Routes Directly with Route::view()   41
Using View Composers to Share Variables with Every View   42
Controllers   42
Getting User Input   45
Injecting Dependencies into Controllers   46
Resource Controllers   47
API Resource Controllers   49
Single Action Controllers   49
Route Model Binding   50
Implicit Route Model Binding   50

Custom Route Model Binding	51
Route Caching	52
Form Method Spoofing	52
HTTP Verbs in Laravel	52
HTTP Method Spoofing in HTML Forms	53
CSRF Protection	53
Redirects	55
redirect()->to()	56
redirect()->route()	56
redirect()->back()	57
Other Redirect Methods	57
redirect()->with()	57
Aborting the Request	59
Custom Responses	60
response()->make()	60
response()->json() and ->jsonp()	60
response()->download(), ->streamDownload(), and ->file()	60
Testing	61
TL;DR	62

4. Blade Templating. **63**

Echoing Data	64
Control Structures	65
Conditionals	65
Loops	65
Template Inheritance	68
Defining Sections with @section/@show and @yield	68
Including View Partials	70
Using Stacks	72
Using Components and Slots	73
View Composers and Service Injection	75
Binding Data to Views Using View Composers	76
Blade Service Injection	79
Custom Blade Directives	80
Parameters in Custom Blade Directives	81
Example: Using Custom Blade Directives for a Multitenant App	82
Easier Custom Directives for "if" Statements	83
Testing	83
TL;DR	84

5. Databases and Eloquent. **87**

Configuration	87

Database Connections	88
Other Database Configuration Options	89
Defining Migrations	90
Running Migrations	97
Seeding	98
Creating a Seeder	98
Model Factories	99
Query Builder	105
Basic Usage of the DB Facade	105
Raw SQL	106
Chaining with the Query Builder	107
Transactions	116
Introduction to Eloquent	117
Creating and Defining Eloquent Models	119
Retrieving Data with Eloquent	120
Inserts and Updates with Eloquent	122
Deleting with Eloquent	126
Scopes	128
Customizing Field Interactions with Accessors, Mutators, and Attribute Casting	131
Eloquent Collections	135
Eloquent Serialization	137
Eloquent Relationships	139
Child Records Updating Parent Record Timestamps	152
Eloquent Events	154
Testing	155
TL;DR	157

6. Frontend Components. 159

Laravel Mix	159
Mix Folder Structure	161
Running Mix	161
What Does Mix Provide?	162
Frontend Presets and Auth Scaffolding	169
Frontend Presets	169
Auth Scaffolding	170
Pagination	170
Paginating Database Results	170
Manually Creating Paginators	171
Message Bags	172
Named Error Bags	174
String Helpers, Pluralization, and Localization	174

    The String Helpers and Pluralization   174
    Localization   175
  Testing   179
    Testing Message and Error Bags   179
    Translation and Localization   179
  TL;DR   180

7. Collecting and Handling User Data. **181**
  Injecting a Request Object   181
    $request->all()   182
    $request->except() and $request->only()   182
    $request->has()   183
    $request->input()   183
    $request->method() and ->isMethod()   184
    Array Input   184
    JSON Input (and $request->json())   185
  Route Data   186
    From Request   186
    From Route Parameters   186
  Uploaded Files   187
  Validation   189
    validate() on the Request Object   189
    Manual Validation   192
    Custom Rule Objects   192
    Displaying Validation Error Messages   193
  Form Requests   194
    Creating a Form Request   194
    Using a Form Request   195
  Eloquent Model Mass Assignment   196
  {{ Versus {!!   197
  Testing   197
  TL;DR   199

8. Artisan and Tinker. **201**
  An Introduction to Artisan   201
  Basic Artisan Commands   202
    Options   203
    The Grouped Commands   203
  Writing Custom Artisan Commands   206
    A Sample Command   208
    Arguments and Options   209
    Using Input   211

Prompts   213
Output   214
Writing Closure-Based Commands   215
Calling Artisan Commands in Normal Code   216
Tinker   217
Laravel Dump Server   218
Testing   219
TL;DR   219

9. User Authentication and Authorization. 221
The User Model and Migration   222
Using the auth() Global Helper and the Auth Facade   225
The Auth Controllers   226
  RegisterController   226
  LoginController   227
  ResetPasswordController   229
  ForgotPasswordController   229
  VerificationController   229
Auth::routes()   229
The Auth Scaffold   231
"Remember Me"   232
Manually Authenticating Users   233
Manually Logging Out a User   233
  Invalidating Sessions on Other Devices   233
Auth Middleware   234
Email Verification   235
Blade Authentication Directives   236
Guards   236
  Changing the Default Guard   237
  Using Other Guards Without Changing the Default   237
  Adding a New Guard   237
  Closure Request Guards   238
  Creating a Custom User Provider   238
  Custom User Providers for Nonrelational Databases   239
Auth Events   239
Authorization (ACL) and Roles   240
  Defining Authorization Rules   240
  The Gate Facade (and Injecting Gate)   241
  Resource Gates   242
  The Authorize Middleware   243
  Controller Authorization   243
  Checking on the User Instance   245

      Blade Checks   246

Blade Checks 246

Intercepting Checks 246

Policies 247

Testing 249

TL;DR 252

10. Requests, Responses, and Middleware. **253**

Laravel's Request Lifecycle 253

Bootstrapping the Application 254

Service Providers 255

The Request Object 257

Getting a Request Object in Laravel 257

Getting Basic Information About a Request 258

The Response Object 262

Using and Creating Response Objects in Controllers 263

Specialized Response Types 264

Laravel and Middleware 269

An Introduction to Middleware 269

Creating Custom Middleware 270

Binding Middleware 272

Passing Parameters to Middleware 275

Trusted Proxies 276

Testing 277

TL;DR 278

11. The Container. **279**

A Quick Introduction to Dependency Injection 279

Dependency Injection and Laravel 281

The app() Global Helper 281

How the Container Is Wired 282

Binding Classes to the Container 283

Binding to a Closure 283

Binding to Singletons, Aliases, and Instances 284

Binding a Concrete Instance to an Interface 285

Contextual Binding 286

Constructor Injection in Laravel Framework Files 287

Method Injection 287

Facades and the Container 289

How Facades Work 289

Real-Time Facades 291

Service Providers 291

Testing 292

TL;DR   293

12. Testing.... **295**
   Testing Basics   296
   Naming Tests   300
   The Testing Environment   301
   The Testing Traits   301
      RefreshDatabase   302
      WithoutMiddleware   302
      DatabaseMigrations   302
      DatabaseTransactions   302
   Simple Unit Tests   303
   Application Testing: How It Works   304
      TestCase   304
   HTTP Tests   305
      Testing Basic Pages with $this->get() and Other HTTP Calls   305
      Testing JSON APIs with $this->getJson() and Other JSON HTTP Calls 306
      Assertions Against $response   306
      Authenticating Responses   309
      A Few Other Customizations to Your HTTP Tests   310
      Handling Exceptions in Application Tests   310
   Database Tests   311
      Using Model Factories in Tests   312
      Seeding in Tests   312
   Testing Other Laravel Systems   312
      Event Fakes   312
      Bus and Queue Fakes   314
      Mail Fakes   315
      Notification Fakes   316
      Storage Fakes   317
   Mocking   318
      A Quick Introduction to Mocking   318
      A Quick Introduction to Mockery   318
      Faking Other Facades   321
   Testing Artisan Commands   322
      Asserting Against Artisan Command Syntax   322
   Browser Tests   323
      Choosing a Tool   324
      Testing with Dusk   324
   TL;DR   335

13. Writing APIs. 337
    The Basics of REST-Like JSON APIs   337
    Controller Organization and JSON Returns   339
    Reading and Sending Headers   342
        Sending Response Headers in Laravel   343
        Reading Request Headers in Laravel   343
    Eloquent Pagination   344
    Sorting and Filtering   345
        Sorting Your API Results   346
        Filtering Your API Results   347
    Transforming Results   348
        Writing Your Own Transformer   349
        Nesting and Relationships with Custom Transformers   350
    API Resources   352
        Creating a Resource Class   352
        Resource Collections   354
        Nesting Relationships   355
        Using Pagination with API Resources   356
        Conditionally Applying Attributes   357
        More Customizations for API Resources   357
    API Authentication with Laravel Passport   357
        A Brief Introduction to OAuth 2.0   358
        Installing Passport   358
        Passport's API   360
        Passport's Available Grant Types   360
        Managing Clients and Tokens with the Passport API and Vue Components 368
        Passport Scopes   371
        Deploying Passport   373
    API Token Authentication   373
    Customizing 404 Responses   374
        Triggering the Fallback Route   374
    Testing   374
        Testing Passport   375
    TL;DR   375

14. Storage and Retrieval. 377
    Local and Cloud File Managers   377
        Configuring File Access   377
        Using the Storage Facade   378
        Adding Additional Flysystem Providers   380
    Basic File Uploads and Manipulation   380
    Simple File Downloads   382

Sessions   382
    Accessing the Session   383
    Methods Available on Session Instances   383
    Flash Session Storage   385
Cache   386
    Accessing the Cache   386
    Methods Available on Cache Instances   387
Cookies   388
    Cookies in Laravel   388
    Accessing the Cookie Tools   389
Logging   392
    When and Why to Use Logs   392
    Writing to the Logs   393
    Log Channels   393
Full-Text Search with Laravel Scout   396
    Installing Scout   396
    Marking Your Model for Indexing   397
    Searching Your Index   397
    Queues and Scout   398
    Performing Operations Without Indexing   398
    Conditionally Indexing Models   398
    Manually Triggering Indexing via Code   398
    Manually Triggering Indexing via the CLI   399
Testing   399
    File Storage   399
    Session   401
    Cache   402
    Cookies   402
    Log   403
    Scout   404
TL;DR   404

15. Mail and Notifications. 405
Mail   405
    "Classic" Mail   406
    Basic "Mailable" Mail Usage   406
    Mail Templates   409
    Methods Available in build()   410
    Attachments and Inline Images   410
    Markdown Mailables   411
    Rendering Mailables to the Browser   413
    Queues   414

Local Development   415
Notifications   416
Defining the via() Method for Your Notifiables   419
Sending Notifications   419
Queueing Notifications   420
Out-of-the-Box Notification Types   421
Testing   424
Mail   425
Notifications   425
TL;DR   426

16. **Queues, Jobs, Events, Broadcasting, and the Scheduler.** **427**
Queues   427
Why Queues?   428
Basic Queue Configuration   428
Queued Jobs   428
Controlling the Queue   435
Queues Supporting Other Functions   436
Laravel Horizon   436
Events   437
Firing an Event   437
Listening for an Event   439
Broadcasting Events over WebSockets, and Laravel Echo   442
Configuration and Setup   443
Broadcasting an Event   443
Receiving the Message   446
Advanced Broadcasting Tools   448
Laravel Echo (the JavaScript Side)   452
Scheduler   457
Available Task Types   457
Available Time Frames   458
Defining Time Zones for Scheduled Commands   459
Blocking and Overlap   460
Handling Task Output   460
Task Hooks   461
Testing   461
TL;DR   463

17. **Helpers and Collections.** **465**
Helpers   465
Arrays   465
Strings   467

Application Paths   469
URLs   470
Miscellaneous   472
Collections   475
The Basics   475
A Few Methods   477
TL;DR   481

18. The Laravel Ecosystem. **483**
Tools Covered in This Book   483
Valet   483
Homestead   484
The Laravel Installer   484
Mix   484
Dusk   484
Passport   484
Horizon   484
Echo   485
Tools Not Covered in This Book   485
Forge   485
Envoyer   485
Cashier   486
Socialite   486
Nova   486
Spark   487
Lumen   487
Envoy   487
Telescope   488
Other Resources   488

Glossary. **489**

Index. **497**

Preface

The story of how I got started with Laravel is a common one: I had written PHP for years, but I was on my way out the door, pursuing the power of Rails and other modern web frameworks. Rails in particular had a lively community, a perfect combination of opinionated defaults and flexibility, and the power of Ruby Gems to leverage prepackaged common code.

Something kept me from jumping ship, and I was glad for that when I found Laravel. It offered everything I was drawn to in Rails, but it wasn't just a Rails clone; this was an innovative framework with incredible documentation, a welcoming community, and clear influences from many languages and frameworks.

Since that day I've been able to share my journey of learning Laravel through blogging, podcasting, and speaking at conferences; I've written dozens of apps in Laravel for work and side projects; and I've met thousands of Laravel developers online and in person. I have plenty of tools in my development toolkit, but I am honestly happiest when I sit down in front of a command line and type `laravel new projectName`.

What This Book Is About

This is not the first book about Laravel, and it won't be the last. I don't intend for this to be a book that covers every line of code or every implementation pattern. I don't want this to be the sort of book that goes out of date when a new version of Laravel is released. Instead, its primary purpose is to provide developers with a high-level overview and concrete examples to learn what they need to work in any Laravel codebase with any and every Laravel feature and subsystem. Rather than mirroring the docs, I want to help you understand the foundational concepts behind Laravel.

Laravel is a powerful and flexible PHP framework. It has a thriving community and a wide ecosystem of tools, and as a result it's growing in appeal and reach. This book is for developers who already know how to make websites and applications and want to learn how to do so well in Laravel.

Laravel's documentation is thorough and excellent. If you find that I don't cover any particular topic deeply enough for your liking, I encourage you to visit the online documentation (*https://laravel.com/docs*) and dig deeper into that particular topic.

I think you will find the book a comfortable balance between high-level introduction and concrete application, and by the end you should feel comfortable writing an entire application in Laravel, from scratch. And, if I did my job well, you'll be excited to try.

Who This Book Is For

This book assumes knowledge of basic object-oriented programming practices, PHP (or at least the general syntax of C-family languages), and the basic concepts of the Model–View–Controller (MVC) pattern and templating. If you've never made a website before, you may find yourself in over your head. But as long as you have some programming experience, you don't have to know anything about Laravel before you read this book—we'll cover everything you need to know, from the simplest "Hello, world!"

Laravel can run on any operating system, but there will be some bash (shell) commands in the book that are easiest to run on Linux/macOS. Windows users may have a harder time with these commands and with modern PHP development, but if you follow the instructions to get Homestead (a Linux virtual machine) running, you'll be able to run all of the commands from there.

How This Book Is Structured

This book is structured in what I imagine to be a chronological order: if you're building your first web app with Laravel, the early chapters cover the foundational components you'll need to get started, and the later chapters cover less foundational or more esoteric features.

Each section of the book can be read on its own, but for someone new to the framework, I've tried to structure the chapters so that it's actually very reasonable to start from the beginning and read until the end.

Where applicable, each chapter will end with two sections: "Testing" and "TL;DR." If you're not familiar, "TL;DR" means "too long; didn't read." These final sections will show you how to write tests for the features covered in each chapter and will give a high-level overview of what was covered.

The book is written for Laravel 5.8, but will cover features and syntax changes back to Laravel 5.1.

About the Second Edition

The first edition of *Laravel: Up & Running* came out in November 2016 and covered Laravel versions 5.1 to 5.3. This second edition adds coverage for 5.4 to 5.8 and Laravel Dusk and Horizon, and adds an 18th chapter about community resources and other non-core Laravel packages that weren't covered in the first 17 chapters.

Conventions Used in This Book

The following typographical conventions are used in this book:

Italic
: Indicates new terms, URLs, email addresses, filenames, and file extensions.

`Constant width`
: Used for program listings, as well as within paragraphs to refer to program elements such as variable or function names, databases, data types, environment variables, statements, and keywords.

`Constant width bold`
: Shows commands or other text that should be typed literally by the user.

`Constant width italic`
: Shows code text that should be replaced with user-supplied values or by values determined by context.

{Italic in braces}
: Shows file names or file pathways that should be replaced with user-supplied values or by values determined by context.

This element signifies a tip or suggestion.

This element signifies a general note.

This element indicates a warning or caution.

5.x Because this book covers Laravel from versions 5.1 to 5.8, you'll find markers throughout the book indicating version-specific comments. Generally speaking, the indicator is showing the version of Laravel a feature was introduced in (so you'll see a 5.3 next to a feature that's only accessible in Laravel 5.3 and higher).

O'Reilly Online Learning

 For almost 40 years, *O'Reilly Media* has provided technology and business training, knowledge, and insight to help companies succeed.

Our unique network of experts and innovators share their knowledge and expertise through books, articles, conferences, and our online learning platform. O'Reilly's online learning platform gives you on-demand access to live training courses, indepth learning paths, interactive coding environments, and a vast collection of text and video from O'Reilly and 200+ other publishers. For more information, please visit *http://oreilly.com*.

How to Contact Us

Please address comments and questions concerning this book to the publisher:

O'Reilly Media, Inc.
1005 Gravenstein Highway North
Sebastopol, CA 95472
800-998-9938 (in the United States or Canada)
707-829-0515 (international or local)
707-829-0104 (fax)

We have a web page for this book, where we list errata, examples, and any additional information. You can access this page at *http://bit.ly/laravel-up-and-running-2e*.

To comment or ask technical questions about this book, send email to *bookquestions@oreilly.com*.

For more information about our books, courses, conferences, and news, see our website at *http://www.oreilly.com*.

Find us on Facebook: *http://facebook.com/oreilly*

Follow us on Twitter: *http://twitter.com/oreillymedia*

Watch us on YouTube: *http://www.youtube.com/oreillymedia*

Acknowledgments for the First Edition

This book would not have happened without the gracious support of my amazing wife, Tereva, or the understanding ("Daddy's writing, buddy!") of my son Malachi. And while she wasn't explicitly aware of it, my daughter Mia was around for almost the entire creation of the book, so this book is dedicated to the whole family. There were many, many long evening hours and weekend Starbucks trips that took me away from them, and I couldn't be more grateful for their support and also their presence just making my life awesome.

Additionally, the entire Tighten family has supported and encouraged me through the writing of the book, several colleagues even editing code samples (Keith Damiani, editor extraordinaire) and helping me with challenging ones (Adam Wathan, King of the Collection Pipeline). Dan Sheetz, my partner in Tighten crime, has been gracious enough to watch me while away many a work hour cranking on this book and was nothing but supportive and encouraging; and Dave Hicking, our operations manager, helped me arrange my schedule and work responsibilities around writing time.

Taylor Otwell deserves thanks and honor for creating Laravel—and therefore creating so many jobs and helping so many developers love our lives that much more. He deserves appreciation for how he's focused on developer happiness and how hard he's worked to have empathy for developers and to build a positive and encouraging community. But I also want to thank him for being a kind, encouraging, and challenging friend. Taylor, you're a boss.

Thanks to Jeffrey Way, who is one of the best teachers on the internet. He originally introduced me to Laravel and introduces more people every day. He's also, unsurprisingly, a fantastic human being whom I'm glad to call a friend.

Thank you to Jess D'Amico, Shawn McCool, Ian Landsman, and Taylor for seeing value in me as a conference speaker early on and giving me a platform to teach from. Thanks to Dayle Rees for making it so easy for so many to learn Laravel in the early days.

Thanks to every person who put their time and effort into writing blog posts about Laravel, especially early on: Eric Barnes, Chris Fidao, Matt Machuga, Jason Lewis, Ryan Tablada, Dries Vints, Maks Surguy, and so many more.

And thanks to the entire community of friends on Twitter, IRC, and Slack who've interacted with me over the years. I wish I could name every name, but I would miss some and then feel awful about missing them. You all are brilliant, and I'm honored to get to interact with you on a regular basis.

Thanks to my O'Reilly editor, Ally MacDonald, and all of my technical editors: Keith Damiani, Michael Dyrynda, Adam Fairholm, and Myles Hyson.

And, of course, thanks to the rest of my family and friends, who supported me directly or indirectly through this process—my parents and siblings, the Gainesville community, other business owners and authors, other conference speakers, and the inimitable DCB. I need to stop writing because by the time I run out of space here I'll be thanking my Starbucks baristas.

Acknowledgments for the Second Edition

The second edition is very similar to the first, so all of the previous acknowledgments are still valid. But I've gotten help from a few new people this time around. My technical proofreaders have been Tate Peñaranda, Andy Swick, Mohamed Said, and Samantha Geitz, and my new O'Reilly editor has been Alicia Young, who's kept me on task through a lot of changes in my life and the Laravel community over the last year. Matt Hacker on the Atlas team answered all my stupid AsciiDoc formatting questions, including about the surprisingly difficult formatting for the __() method.

And I couldn't have made it through the process of writing a second edition without the help of my research assistant, Wilbur Powery. Wilbur was willing to sift through the last several years' worth of changelogs and pull requests and announcements and match each feature up with the current structure of the book, and he even tested every single code example in the book in Laravel 5.7 (and then, later, 5.8) so that I could focus my limited time and energy on writing the new and updated segments.

Also, my daughter, Mia, is out of her mama's belly now. So, let's just add her joy and energy and love and cuteness and adventurous spirit to my list of sources of inspiration.

## CHAPTER 1

Why Laravel?

In the early days of the dynamic web, writing a web application looked a lot different than it does today. Developers then were responsible for writing the code for not just the unique business logic of our applications, but also each of the components that are so common across sites—user authentication, input validation, database access, templating, and more.

Today, programmers have dozens of application development frameworks and thousands of components and libraries easily accessible. It's a common refrain among programmers that, by the time you learn one framework, three newer (and purportedly better) frameworks have popped up intending to replace it.

"Just because it's there" might be a valid justification for climbing a mountain, but there are better reasons to choose to use a specific framework—or to use a framework at all. It's worth asking the question, why frameworks? More specifically, why Laravel?

Why Use a Framework?

It's easy to see why it's beneficial to use the individual components, or packages, that are available to PHP developers. With packages, someone else is responsible for developing and maintaining an isolated piece of code that has a well-defined job, and in theory that person has a deeper understanding of this single component than you have time to have.

Frameworks like Laravel—and Symfony, Lumen, and Slim—prepackage a collection of third-party components together with custom framework "glue" like configuration files, service providers, prescribed directory structures, and application bootstraps. So, the benefit of using a framework in general is that someone has made decisions not just about individual components for you, but also about *how those components should fit together*.

"I'll Just Build It Myself"

Let's say you start a new web app without the benefit of a framework. Where do you begin? Well, it should probably route HTTP requests, so you now need to evaluate all of the HTTP request and response libraries available and pick one. Then you'll have to pick a router. Oh, and you'll probably need to set up some form of routes configuration file. What syntax should it use? Where should it go? What about controllers? Where do they live, and how are they loaded? Well, you probably need a dependency injection container to resolve the controllers and their dependencies. But which one?

Furthermore, if you do take the time to answer all those questions and successfully create your application, what's the impact on the next developer? What about when you have four such custom framework–based applications, or a dozen, and you have to remember where the controllers live in each, or what the routing syntax is?

Consistency and Flexibility

Frameworks address this issue by providing a carefully considered answer to the question "Which component should we use here?" and ensuring that the particular components chosen work well together. Additionally, frameworks provide conventions that reduce the amount of code a developer new to the project has to understand—if you understand how routing works in one Laravel project, for example, you understand how it works in all Laravel projects.

When someone prescribes rolling your own framework for each new project, what they're really advocating is the ability to *control* what does and doesn't go into your application's foundation. That means the best frameworks will not only provide you with a solid foundation, but also give you the freedom to customize to your heart's content. And this, as I'll show you in the rest of this book, is part of what makes Laravel so special.

A Short History of Web and PHP Frameworks

An important part of being able to answer the question "Why Laravel?" is understanding Laravel's history—and understanding what came before it. Prior to Laravel's rise in popularity, there were a variety of frameworks and other movements in PHP and other web development spaces.

Ruby on Rails

David Heinemeier Hansson released the first version of Ruby on Rails in 2004, and it's been hard to find a web application framework since then that hasn't been influenced by Rails in some way.

Rails popularized MVC, RESTful JSON APIs, convention over configuration, Active-Record, and many more tools and conventions that had a profound influence on the way web developers approached their applications—especially with regard to rapid application development.

The Influx of PHP Frameworks

It was clear to most developers that Rails and similar web application frameworks were the wave of the future, and PHP frameworks, including those admittedly imitating Rails, started popping up quickly.

CakePHP was the first in 2005, and it was soon followed by Symfony, CodeIgniter, Zend Framework, and Kohana (a CodeIgniter fork). Yii arrived in 2008, and Aura and Slim in 2010. 2011 brought FuelPHP and Laravel, both of which were not quite CodeIgniter offshoots, but instead proposed as alternatives.

Some of these frameworks were more Rails-y, focusing on database object-relational mappers (ORMs), MVC structures, and other tools targeting rapid development. Others, like Symfony and Zend, focused more on enterprise design patterns and ecommerce.

The Good and the Bad of CodeIgniter

CakePHP and CodeIgniter were the two early PHP frameworks that were most open about how much their inspiration was drawn from Rails. CodeIgniter quickly rose to fame and by 2010 was arguably the most popular of the independent PHP frameworks.

CodeIgniter was simple, easy to use, and boasted amazing documentation and a strong community. But its use of modern technology and patterns advanced slowly; and as the framework world grew and PHP's tooling advanced, CodeIgniter started falling behind in terms of both technological advances and out-of-the-box features. Unlike many other frameworks, CodeIgniter was managed by a company, and it was slow to catch up with PHP 5.3's newer features like namespaces and the moves to GitHub and later Composer. It was in 2010 that Taylor Otwell, Laravel's creator, became dissatisfied enough with CodeIgniter that he set off to write his own framework.

Laravel 1, 2, and 3

The first beta of Laravel 1 was released in June 2011, and it was written completely from scratch. It featured a custom ORM (Eloquent); closure-based routing (inspired by Ruby Sinatra); a module system for extension; and helpers for forms, validation, authentication, and more.

Early Laravel development moved quickly, and Laravel 2 and 3 were released in November 2011 and February 2012, respectively. They introduced controllers, unit testing, a command-line tool, an inversion of control (IoC) container, Eloquent relationships, and migrations.

Laravel 4

With Laravel 4, Taylor rewrote the entire framework from the ground up. By this point Composer, PHP's now-ubiquitous package manager, was showing signs of becoming an industry standard, and Taylor saw the value of rewriting the framework as a collection of components, distributed and bundled together by Composer.

Taylor developed a set of components under the code name *Illuminate* and, in May 2013, released Laravel 4 with an entirely new structure. Instead of bundling the majority of its code as a download, Laravel now pulled in the majority of its components from Symfony (another framework that released its components for use by others) and the Illuminate components through Composer.

Laravel 4 also introduced queues, a mail component, facades, and database seeding. And because Laravel was now relying on Symfony components, it was announced that Laravel would be mirroring (not exactly, but soon after) the six-monthly release schedule Symfony follows.

Laravel 5

Laravel 4.3 was scheduled to release in November 2014, but as development progressed it became clear that the significance of its changes merited a major release, and Laravel 5 was released in February 2015.

Laravel 5 featured a revamped directory structure, removal of the form and HTML helpers, the introduction of the contract interfaces, a spate of new views, Socialite for social media authentication, Elixir for asset compilation, Scheduler to simplify cron, dotenv for simplified environment management, form requests, and a brand new REPL (read–evaluate–print loop). Since then it's grown in features and maturity, but there have been no major changes like in previous versions.

What's So Special About Laravel?

So what is it that sets Laravel apart? Why is it worth having more than one PHP framework at any time? They all use components from Symfony anyway, right? Let's talk a bit about what makes Laravel "tick."

The Philosophy of Laravel

You only need to read through the Laravel marketing materials and READMEs to start seeing its values. Taylor uses light-related words like "Illuminate" and "Spark." And then there are these: "Artisans." "Elegant." Also, these: "Breath of fresh air." "Fresh start." And finally: "Rapid." "Warp speed."

The two most strongly communicated values of the framework are to increase developer speed and developer happiness. Taylor has described the "Artisan" language as intentionally contrasting against more utilitarian values. You can see the genesis of this sort of thinking in his 2011 question on StackExchange (*http://bit.ly/2dT5kmS*) in which he stated, "Sometimes I spend ridiculous amounts of time (hours) agonizing over making code 'look pretty'"—just for the sake of a better experience of looking at the code itself. And he's often talked about the value of making it easier and quicker for developers to take their ideas to fruition, getting rid of unnecessary barriers to creating great products.

Laravel is, at its core, about equipping and enabling developers. Its goal is to provide clear, simple, and beautiful code and features that help developers quickly learn, start, and develop, and write code that's simple, clear, and lasting.

The concept of targeting developers is clear across Laravel materials. "Happy developers make the best code" is written in the documentation. "Developer happiness from download to deploy" was the unofficial slogan for a while. Of course, any tool or framework will say it wants developers to be happy. But having developer happiness as a *primary* concern, rather than secondary, has had a huge impact on Laravel's style and decision-making progress. Where other frameworks may target architectural purity as their primary goal, or compatibility with the goals and values of enterprise development teams, Laravel's primary focus is on serving the individual developer. That doesn't mean you can't write architecturally pure or enterprise-ready applications in Laravel, but it won't have to be at the expense of the readability and comprehensibility of your codebase.

How Laravel Achieves Developer Happiness

Just saying you want to make developers happy is one thing. Doing it is another, and it requires you to question what in a framework is most likely to make developers unhappy and what is most likely to make them happy. There are a few ways Laravel tries to make developers' lives easier.

First, Laravel is a rapid application development framework. That means it focuses on a shallow (easy) learning curve and on minimizing the steps between starting a new app and publishing it. All of the most common tasks in building web applications, from database interactions to authentication to queues to email to caching, are made simpler by the components Laravel provides. But Laravel's components aren't just great on their own; they provide a consistent API and predictable structures across the entire framework. That means that, when you're trying something new in Laravel, you're more than likely going to end up saying, "… and it just works."

This doesn't end with the framework itself, either. Laravel provides an entire ecosystem of tools for building and launching applications. You have Homestead and Valet for local development, Forge for server management, and Envoyer for advanced deployment. And there's a suite of add-on packages: Cashier for payments and subscriptions, Echo for WebSockets, Scout for search, Passport for API authentication, Dusk for frontend testing, Socialite for social login, Horizon for monitoring queues, Nova for building admin panels, and Spark to bootstrap your SaaS. Laravel is trying to take the repetitive work out of developers' jobs so they can do something unique.

Next, Laravel focuses on "convention over configuration"—meaning that if you're willing to use Laravel's defaults, you'll have to do much less work than with other frameworks that require you to declare all of your settings even if you're using the recommended configuration. Projects built on Laravel take less time than those built on most other PHP frameworks.

Laravel also focuses deeply on simplicity. It's possible to use dependency injection and mocking and the Data Mapper pattern and repositories and Command Query Responsibility Segregation and all sorts of other more complex architectural patterns with Laravel, if you want. But while other frameworks might suggest using those tools and structures on every project, Laravel and its documentation and community lean toward starting with the simplest possible implementation—a global function here, a facade there, ActiveRecord over there. This allows developers to create the simplest possible application to solve for their needs, without limiting its usefulness in complex environments.

An interesting source of how Laravel is different from other PHP frameworks is that its creator and its community are more connected to and inspired by Ruby and Rails and functional programming languages than by Java. There's a strong current in modern PHP to lean toward verbosity and complexity, embracing the more Java-esque aspects of PHP. But Laravel tends to be on the other side, embracing expressive, dynamic, and simple coding practices and language features.

The Laravel Community

If this book is your first exposure to the Laravel community, you have something special to look forward to. One of the distinguishing elements of Laravel, which has contributed to its growth and success, is the welcoming, teaching community that surrounds it. From Jeffrey Way's Laracasts (*https://laracasts.com/*) video tutorials to Laravel News (*https://laravel-news.com/*) to Slack and IRC and Discord channels, from Twitter friends to bloggers to podcasts to the Laracon conferences, Laravel has a rich and vibrant community full of folks who've been around since day one and folks who are just starting their own "day one." And this isn't an accident:

> From the very beginning of Laravel, I've had this idea that all people want to feel like they are part of something. It's a natural human instinct to want to belong and be accepted into a group of other like-minded people. So, by injecting personality into a web framework and being really active with the community, that type of feeling can grow in the community.
>
> —Taylor Otwell, *Product and Support interview*

Taylor understood from the early days of Laravel that a successful open source project needed two things: good documentation and a welcoming community. And those two things are now hallmarks of Laravel.

How It Works

Up until now, everything I've shared here has been entirely abstract. What about the code, you ask? Let's dig into a simple application (Example 1-1) so you can see what working with Laravel day to day is actually like.

Example 1-1. "Hello, World" in routes/web.php

```php
<?php

Route::get('/', function () {
    return 'Hello, World!';
});
```

The simplest possible action you can take in a Laravel application is to define a route and return a result any time someone visits that route. If you initialize a brand new Laravel application on your machine, define the route in Example 1-1, and then serve the site from the *public* directory, you'll have a fully functioning "Hello, World" example (see Figure 1-1).

Figure 1-1. Returning "Hello, World!" with Laravel

It looks very similar with controllers, as you can see in Example 1-2.

Example 1-2. "Hello, World" with controllers

```php
// File: routes/web.php
<?php

Route::get('/', 'WelcomeController@index');

// File: app/Http/Controllers/WelcomeController.php
<?php

namespace App\Http\Controllers;

class WelcomeController extends Controller
{
    public function index()
    {
        return 'Hello, World!';
    }
}
```

And if you're storing your greetings in a database, it'll also look pretty similar (see Example 1-3).

Example 1-3. Multigreeting "Hello, World" with database access

```php
// File: routes/web.php
<?php

use App\Greeting;

Route::get('create-greeting', function () {
    $greeting = new Greeting;
    $greeting->body = 'Hello, World!';
    $greeting->save();
});

Route::get('first-greeting', function () {
    return Greeting::first()->body;
});

// File: app/Greeting.php
<?php

namespace App;

use Illuminate\Database\Eloquent\Model;

class Greeting extends Model
{
    //
}
```

```
// File: database/migrations/2015_07_19_010000_create_greetings_table.php
<?php

use Illuminate\Database\Schema\Blueprint;
use Illuminate\Database\Migrations\Migration;

class CreateGreetingsTable extends Migration
{
    public function up()
    {
        Schema::create('greetings', function (Blueprint $table) {
            $table->bigIncrements('id');
            $table->string('body');
            $table->timestamps();
        });
    }

    public function down()
    {
        Schema::dropIfExists('greetings');
    }
}
```

Example 1-3 might be a bit overwhelming, and if so, just skip over it. You'll learn about everything that's happening here in later chapters, but you can already see that with just a few lines of code, you can set up database migrations and models and pull records out. It's just that simple.

Why Laravel?

So—why Laravel?

Because Laravel helps you bring your ideas to reality with no wasted code, using modern coding standards, surrounded by a vibrant community, with an empowering ecosystem of tools.

And because you, dear developer, deserve to be happy.

## CHAPTER 2

Setting Up a Laravel Development Environment

Part of PHP's success has been because it's hard to find a web server that *can't* serve PHP. However, modern PHP tools have stricter requirements than those of the past. The best way to develop for Laravel is to ensure a consistent local and remote server environment for your code, and thankfully, the Laravel ecosystem has a few tools for this.

System Requirements

Everything we'll cover in this chapter is possible with Windows machines, but you'll need dozens of pages of custom instructions and caveats. I'll leave those instructions and caveats to actual Windows users, so the examples here and in the rest of the book will focus on Unix/Linux/macOS developers.

Whether you choose to serve your website by installing PHP and other tools on your local machine, serve your development environment from a virtual machine via Vagrant or Docker, or rely on a tool like MAMP/WAMP/XAMPP, your development environment will need to have all of the following installed in order to serve Laravel sites:

- PHP >= 7.1.3 for Laravel versions 5.6 to 5.8, PHP >= 7.0.0 for version 5.5, PHP >= 5.6.4 for version 5.4, PHP between 5.6.4 and 7.1.* for version 5.3, or PHP >= 5.5.9 for versions 5.2 and 5.1
- OpenSSL PHP extension
- PDO PHP extension
- Mbstring PHP extension

- Tokenizer PHP extension
- XML PHP extension (Laravel 5.3 and higher)
- Ctype PHP extension (Laravel 5.6 and higher)
- JSON PHP extension (Laravel 5.6 and higher)
- BCMath PHP extension (Laravel 5.7 and higher)

Composer

Whatever machine you're developing on will need to have Composer (*https://getcom poser.org/*) installed globally. If you're not familiar with Composer, it's a tool that's at the foundation of most modern PHP development. Composer is a dependency manager for PHP, much like NPM for Node or RubyGems for Ruby. But like NPM, Composer is also the foundation of much of our testing, local script loading, installation scripts, and much more. You'll need Composer to install Laravel, update Laravel, and bring in external dependencies.

Local Development Environments

For many projects, hosting your development environment using a simpler toolset will be enough. If you already have MAMP or WAMP or XAMPP installed on your system, that will likely be fine to run Laravel. You can also just run Laravel with PHP's built-in web server, assuming your system PHP is the right version.

All you really need to get started is the ability to run PHP. Everything past that is up to you.

However, Laravel offers two tools for local development, Valet and Homestead, and we'll cover both briefly. If you're unsure of which to use, I'd recommend using Valet and just becoming briefly familiar with Homestead; however, both tools are valuable and worth understanding.

Laravel Valet

If you want to use PHP's built-in web server, your simplest option is to serve every site from a *localhost* URL. If you run `php -S localhost:8000 -t public` from your Laravel site's root folder, PHP's built-in web server will serve your site at *http://localhost:8000/*. You can also run `php artisan serve` once you have your application set up to easily spin up an equivalent server.

But if you're interested in tying each of your sites to a specific development domain, you'll need to get comfortable with your operating system's hosts file and use a tool like dnsmasq (*http://bit.ly/2eNPJ5T*). Let's instead try something simpler.

If you're a Mac user (there are also unofficial forks for Windows and Linux), Laravel Valet takes away the need to connect your domains to your application folders. Valet installs dnsmasq and a series of PHP scripts that make it possible to type `laravel new myapp && open myapp.test` and for it to *just work*. You'll need to install a few tools using Homebrew, which the documentation will walk you through, but the steps from initial installation to serving your apps are few and simple.

Install Valet—see the docs (*http://bit.ly/2U7uy7b*) for the latest installation instructions—and point it at one or more directories where your sites will live. I ran `valet park` from my *~/Sites* directory, which is where I put all of my under-development apps. Now, you can just add *.test* to the end of the directory name and visit it in your browser.

Valet makes it easy to serve all folders in a given folder as *{foldername}.test* using `valet park`, to serve just a single folder using `valet link`, to open the Valet-served domain for a folder using `valet open`, to serve the Valet site with HTTPS using `valet secure`, and to open an ngrok tunnel so you can share your site with others with `valet share`.

Laravel Homestead

Homestead is another tool you might want to use to set up your local development environment. It's a configuration tool that sits on top of Vagrant (which is a tool for managing virtual machines) and provides a preconfigured virtual machine image that is perfectly set up for Laravel development *and* mirrors the most common production environment that many Laravel sites run on. Homestead is also likely the best local development environment for developers running Windows machines.

The Homestead docs (*http://bit.ly/2FwQ7EZ*) are robust and kept constantly up to date, so I'll just refer you to them if you want to learn how it works and how to get it set up.

Vessel

It's not an official Laravel project, but Chris Fidao of Servers for Hackers (*https://serversforhackers.com/*) and Shipping Docker (*https://shippingdocker.com/*) has created a simple tool for creating Docker environments for Laravel development called Vessel (*https://vessel.shippingdocker.com/*). Take a look at the Vessel documentation to learn more.

Creating a New Laravel Project

There are two ways to create a new Laravel project, but both are run from the command line. The first option is to globally install the Laravel installer tool (using Composer); the second is to use Composer's `create-project` feature.

You can learn about both options in greater detail on the Installation documentation page (*http://bit.ly/2HFzBFY*), but I'd recommend the Laravel installer tool.

Installing Laravel with the Laravel Installer Tool

If you have Composer installed globally, installing the Laravel installer tool is as simple as running the following command:

```
composer global require "laravel/installer"
```

Once you have the Laravel installer tool installed, spinning up a new Laravel project is simple. Just run this command from your command line:

```
laravel new projectName
```

This will create a new subdirectory of your current directory named *{projectName}* and install a bare Laravel project in it.

Installing Laravel with Composer's create-project Feature

Composer also offers a feature called `create-project` for creating new projects with a particular skeleton. To use this tool to create a new Laravel project, issue the following command:

```
composer create-project laravel/laravel projectName
```

Just like the installer tool, this will create a subdirectory of your current directory named *{projectName}* that contains a skeleton Laravel install, ready for you to develop.

Lambo: Super-Powered "Laravel New"

Because I often take the same series of steps after creating a new Laravel project, I made a simple script called Lambo (*http://bit.ly/2TCcQo8*) that automates those steps every time I create a new project.

Lambo runs `laravel new` and then commits your code to Git, sets up your *.env* credentials with reasonable defaults, opens the project in a browser, and (optionally) opens it in your editor and takes a few other helpful build steps.

You can install Lambo using Composer's `global require`:

```
composer global require tightenco/lambo
```

And you can use it just like `laravel new`:

```
cd Sites
lambo my-new-project
```

Laravel's Directory Structure

When you open up a directory that contains a skeleton Laravel application, you'll see the following files and directories:

```
app/
bootstrap/
config/
public/
resources/
routes/
storage/
tests/
vendor/
.editorconfig
.env
.env.example
.gitattributes
.gitignore
artisan
composer.json
composer.lock
package.json
phpunit.xml
readme.md
server.php
webpack.mix.js
```

Different Build Tools in Laravel Prior to 5.4

In projects created prior to Laravel 5.4, you'll likely see a *gulpfile.js* instead of *webpack.mix.js*; this shows the project is running Laravel Elixir (*http://bit.ly/2JCToYp*) instead of Laravel Mix (*http://bit.ly/2U4X09P*).

Let's walk through them one by one to get familiar.

The Folders

The root directory contains the following folders by default:

app
> Where the bulk of your actual application will go. .Models, controllers, commands, and your PHP domain code all go in here.

bootstrap
> Contains the files that the Laravel framework uses to boot every time it runs.

config
> Where all the configuration files live.

database
> Where database migrations, seeds, and factories live.

public
> The directory the server points to when it's serving the website. This contains *index.php*, which is the front controller that kicks off the bootstrapping process and routes all requests appropriately. It's also where any public-facing files like images, stylesheets, scripts, or downloads go.

resources
> Where files that are needed for other scripts live. Views, language files, and (optionally) Sass/Less/source CSS and source JavaScript files live here.

routes
> Where all of the route definitions live, both for HTTP routes and "console routes," or Artisan commands.

storage
> Where caches, logs, and compiled system files live.

tests
> Where unit and integration tests live.

vendor
> Where Composer installs its dependencies. It's Git-ignored (marked to be excluded from your version control system), as Composer is expected to run as a part of your deploy process on any remote servers.

The Loose Files

The root directory also contains the following files:

.editorconfig
>   Gives your IDE/text editor instructions about Laravel's coding standars (e.g., the size of indents, the charset, and whether to trim trailing whitespace). You'll see this in any Laravel apps running 5.5 and later.

.env and .env.example
>   Dictate the environment variables (variables that are expected to be different in each environment and are therefore not committed to version control). *.env.example* is a template that each environment should duplicate to create its own *.env* file, which is Git-ignored.

.gitignore and .gitattributes
>   Git configuration files.

artisan
>   Allows you to run Artisan commands (see Chapter 8) from the command line.

composer.json and composer.lock
>   Configuration files for Composer; *composer.json* is user-editable and *composer.lock* is not. These files share some basic information about the project and also define its PHP dependencies.

package.json
>   Like *composer.json* but for frontend assets and dependencies of the build system; it instructs NPM on which JavaScript-based dependencies to pull in.

phpunit.xml
>   A configuration file for PHPUnit, the tool Laravel uses for testing out of the box.

readme.md
>   A Markdown file giving a basic introduction to Laravel. You won't see this file if you use the Laravel installer.

server.php
>   A backup server that tries to allow less-capable servers to still preview the Laravel application.

webpack.mix.js
>   The (optional) configuration file for Mix. If you're using Elixir, you'll instead see *gulpfile.js*. These files are for giving your build system directions on how to compile and process your frontend assets.

Configuration

The core settings of your Laravel application—database connection settings, queue and mail settings, etc.—live in files in the *config* folder. Each of these files returns a PHP array, and each value in the array is accessible by a config key that is comprised of the filename and all descendant keys, separated by dots (.).

So, if you create a file at *config/services.php* that looks like this:

```
// config/services.php
<?php
return [
    'sparkpost' => [
        'secret' => 'abcdefg',
    ],
];
```

you can access that config variable using `config('services.sparkpost.secret')`.

Any configuration variables that should be distinct for each environment (and therefore not committed to source control) will instead live in your *.env* files. Let's say you want to use a different Bugsnag API key for each environment. You'd set the config file to pull it from *.env*:

```
// config/services.php
<?php
return [
    'bugsnag' => [
        'api_key' => env('BUGSNAG_API_KEY'),
    ],
];
```

This `env()` helper function pulls a value from your *.env* file with that same key. So now, add that key to your *.env* (settings for this environment) and *.env.example* (template for all environments) files:

```
# In .env
BUGSNAG_API_KEY=oinfp9813410942

# In .env.example
BUGSNAG_API_KEY=
```

Your *.env* file will already contain quite a few environment-specific variables needed by the framework, like which mail driver you'll be using and what your basic database settings are.

Using env() Outside of Config Files

Certain features in Laravel, including some caching and optimization features, aren't available if you use env() calls anywhere outside of config files.

The best way to pull in environment variables is to set up config items for anything you want to be environment-specific. Have those config items read the environment variables, and then reference the config variables anywhere within your app:

```php
// config/services.php
return [
    'bugsnag' => [
        'key' => env('BUGSNAG_API_KEY'),
    ],
];

// In controller, or whatever
$bugsnag = new Bugsnag(config('services.bugsnag.key'));
```

The .env File

Let's take a quick look at the default contents of the *.env* file. The exact keys will vary depending on which version of Laravel you're using, but take a look at Example 2-1 to see what they look like in 5.8.

Example 2-1. The default environment variables in Laravel 5.8

```
APP_NAME=Laravel
APP_ENV=local
APP_KEY=
APP_DEBUG=true
APP_URL=http://localhost

LOG_CHANNEL=stack

DB_CONNECTION=mysql
DB_HOST=127.0.0.1
DB_PORT=3306
DB_DATABASE=homestead
DB_USERNAME=homestead
DB_PASSWORD=secret

BROADCAST_DRIVER=log
CACHE_DRIVER=file
QUEUE_CONNECTION=sync
SESSION_DRIVER=file
SESSION_LIFETIME=120

REDIS_HOST=127.0.0.1
```

```
REDIS_PASSWORD=null
REDIS_PORT=6379

MAIL_DRIVER=smtp
MAIL_HOST=smtp.mailtrap.io
MAIL_PORT=2525
MAIL_USERNAME=null
MAIL_PASSWORD=null
MAIL_ENCRYPTION=null

AWS_ACCESS_KEY_ID=
AWS_SECRET_ACCESS_KEY=

PUSHER_APP_ID=
PUSHER_APP_KEY=
PUSHER_APP_SECRET=
PUSHER_APP_CLUSTER=mt1

MIX_PUSHER_APP_KEY="${PUSHER_APP_KEY}"
MIX_PUSHER_APP_CLUSTER="${PUSHER_APP_CLUSTER}"
```

I won't go into all of them, because quite a few are just groups of authentication infor‐
mation for various services (Pusher, Redis, DB, Mail). Here are two important envi‐
ronment variables you should know about, though:

APP_KEY

> A randomly generated string that's used to encrypt data. If this is ever empty, you
> may run into the error "No application encryption key has been specified." In
> that case, just run php artisan key:generate and Laravel will generate one for
> you.

APP_DEBUG

> A Boolean determining whether the users of this instance of your application
> should see debug errors—great for local and staging environments, terrible for
> production.

The rest of the non-authentication settings (BROADCAST_DRIVER, QUEUE_CONNECTION,
etc.) are given default values that work with as little reliance on external services as
possible, which is perfect for when you're getting started.

When you start your first Laravel app, the only change you'll likely want to make for
most projects is to the database configuration settings. I use Laravel Valet, so I change
DB_DATABASE to the name of my project, DB_USERNAME to root, and DB_PASSWORD to
an empty string:

```
DB_DATABASE=myProject
DB_USERNAME=root
DB_PASSWORD=
```

Then, I create a database with the same name as my project in my favorite MySQL client, and I'm ready to go.

Up and Running

You're now up and running with a bare Laravel install. Run `git init`, commit the bare files with `git add .` and `git commit`, and you're ready to start coding. That's it! And if you're using Valet, you can run the following commands and instantly see your site live in your browser:

```
laravel new myProject && cd myProject && valet open
```

Every time I start a new project, these are the steps I take:

```
laravel new myProject
cd myProject
git init
git add .
git commit -m "Initial commit"
```

I keep all of my sites in a *~/Sites* folder, which I have set up as my primary Valet directory, so in this case I'd instantly have *myProject.test* accessible in my browser with no added work. I can edit *.env* and point it to a particular database, add that database in my MySQL app, and I'm ready to start coding. And remember, if you use Lambo, all of these steps are already taken for you.

Testing

In every chapter after this, the "Testing" section at the end of the chapter will show you how to write tests for the feature or features that were covered. Since this chapter doesn't cover a testable feature, let's talk tests quickly. (To learn more about writing and running tests in Laravel, head over to Chapter 12.)

Out of the box, Laravel brings in PHPUnit as a dependency and is configured to run the tests in any file in the *tests* directory whose name ends with *Test.php* (for example, *tests/UserTest.php*).

So, the simplest way to write tests is to create a file in the *tests* directory with a name that ends with *Test.php*. And the easiest way to run them is to run `./vendor/bin/phpunit` from the command line (in the project root).

If any tests require database access, be sure to run your tests from the machine where your database is hosted—so if you're hosting your database in Vagrant, make sure to `ssh` into your Vagrant box to run your tests from there. Again, you can learn about this and much more in Chapter 12.

Also, some of the testing sections will use testing syntax and features that you will not be familiar with yet if you're reading the book for the first time. If code in any of the testing sections is confusing, just skip it and come back to it after you've had a chance to read the testing chapter.

TL;DR

Since Laravel is a PHP framework, it's very simple to serve it locally. Laravel also provides two tools for managing your local development: a simpler tool called Valet that uses your local machine to provide your dependencies, and a preconfigured Vagrant setup named Homestead. Laravel relies on and can be installed by Composer and comes out of the box with a series of folders and files that reflect both its conventions and its relationship with other open source tools.

## CHAPTER 3

Routing and Controllers

The essential function of any web application framework is to take requests from a user and deliver responses, usually via HTTP(S). This means defining an application's routes is the first and most important project to tackle when learning a web framework; without routes, you have little to no ability to interact with the end user.

In this chapter we will examine routes in Laravel; you'll see how to define them, how to point them to the code they should execute, and how to use Laravel's routing tools to handle a diverse array of routing needs.

A Quick Introduction to MVC, the HTTP Verbs, and REST

Most of what we'll talk about in this chapter references how Model–View–Controller (MVC) applications are structured, and many of the examples we'll be looking at use REST-ish route names and verbs, so let's take a quick look at both.

What Is MVC?

In MVC, you have three primary concepts:

model
> Represents an individual database table (or a record from that table)—think "Company" or "Dog."

view
> Represents the template that outputs your data to the end user—think "the login page template with this given set of HTML and CSS and JavaScript."

controller

Like a traffic cop, takes HTTP requests from the browser, gets the right data out of the database and other storage mechanisms, validates user input, and eventually sends a response back to the user.

In Figure 3-1, you can see that the end user will first interact with the controller by sending an HTTP request using their browser. The controller, in response to that request, may write data to and/or pull data from the model (database). The controller will then likely send data to a view, and then the view will be returned to the end user to display in their browser.

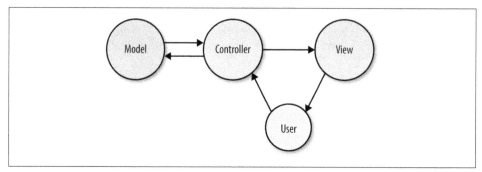

Figure 3-1. A basic illustration of MVC

We'll cover some use cases for Laravel that don't fit this relatively simplistic way of looking at application architecture, so don't get hung up on MVC, but this will at least get you ready to approach the rest of this chapter as we talk about views and controllers.

The HTTP Verbs

The most common HTTP verbs are GET and POST, followed by PUT and DELETE. There are also HEAD, OPTIONS, and PATCH, and two others that are pretty much never used in normal web development, TRACE and CONNECT.

Here's a quick rundown:

GET

Request a resource (or a list of resources).

HEAD

Ask for a headers-only version of the GET response.

POST

Create a resource.

PUT
> Overwrite a resource.

PATCH
> Modify a resource.

DELETE
> Delete a resource.

OPTIONS
> Ask the server which verbs are allowed at this URL.

Table 3-1 shows the actions available on a resource controller (more on these in "Resource Controllers" on page 47). Each action expects you to call a specific URL pattern using a specific verb, so you can get a sense of what each verb is used for.

Table 3-1. The methods of Laravel's resource controllers

Verb	URL	Controller method	Name	Description
GET	tasks	index()	tasks.index	Show all tasks
GET	tasks/create	create()	tasks.create	Show the create task form
POST	tasks	store()	tasks.store	Accept form submission from the create task form
GET	tasks/{task}	show()	tasks.show	Show one task
GET	tasks/{task}/edit	edit()	tasks.edit	Edit one task
PUT/PATCH	tasks/{task}	update()	tasks.update	Accept form submission from the edit task form
DELETE	tasks/{task}	destroy()	tasks.destroy	Delete one task

What Is REST?

We'll cover REST in greater detail in "The Basics of REST-Like JSON APIs" on page 337, but as a brief introduction, it's an architectural style for building APIs. When we talk about REST in this book, we'll mainly be referencing a few characteristics, such as:

- Being structured around one primary resource at a time (e.g., tasks)
- Consisting of interactions with predictable URL structures using HTTP verbs (as seen in Table 3-1)
- Returning JSON and often being requested with JSON

There's more to it, but usually "RESTful" as it'll be used in this book will mean "patterned after these URL-based structures so we can make predictable calls like GET /tasks/14/edit for the edit page." This is relevant (even when not building APIs) because Laravel's routing structures are based around a REST-like structure, as you can see in Table 3-1.

REST-based APIs follow mainly this same structure, except they don't have a *create* route or an *edit* route, since APIs just represent actions, not pages that prep for the actions.

Route Definitions

In a Laravel application, you will define your web routes in *routes/web.php* and your API routes in *routes/api.php*. Web routes are those that will be visited by your end users; API routes are those for your API, if you have one. For now, we'll primarily focus on the routes in *routes/web.php*.

 Routes File Location in Laravel Prior to 5.3

In projects running versions of Laravel prior to 5.3, there will be only one routes file, located at *app/Http/routes.php*.

The simplest way to define a route is to match a path (e.g., /) with a closure, as seen in Example 3-1.

Example 3-1. Basic route definition

```
// routes/web.php
Route::get('/', function () {
    return 'Hello, World!';
});
```

What's a Closure?

Closures are PHP's version of anonymous functions. A closure is a function that you can pass around as an object, assign to a variable, pass as a parameter to other functions and methods, or even serialize.

You've now defined that if anyone visits / (the root of your domain), Laravel's router should run the closure defined there and return the result. Note that we return our content and don't echo or print it.

A Quick Introduction to Middleware

You might be wondering, "Why am I returning 'Hello, World!' instead of echoing it?"

There are quite a few answers, but the simplest is that there are a lot of wrappers around Laravel's request and response cycle, including something called *middleware*. When your route closure or controller method is done, it's not time to send the output to the browser yet; returning the content allows it to continue flowing through the response stack and the middleware before it is returned back to the user.

Many simple websites could be defined entirely within the web routes file. With a few simple GET routes combined with some templates, as illustrated in Example 3-2, you can serve a classic website easily.

Example 3-2. Sample website

```
Route::get('/', function () {
    return view('welcome');
});

Route::get('about', function () {
    return view('about');
});

Route::get('products', function () {
    return view('products');
});

Route::get('services', function () {
    return view('services');
});
```

Static Calls

If you have much experience developing with PHP, you might be surprised to see static calls on the Route class. This is not actually a static method per se, but rather service location using Laravel's facades, which we'll cover in Chapter 11.

If you prefer to avoid facades, you can accomplish these same definitions like this:

```
$router->get('/', function () {
    return 'Hello, World!';
});
```

Route Verbs

You might've noticed that we've been using `Route::get()` in our route definitions. This means we're telling Laravel to only match for these routes when the HTTP request uses the `GET` action. But what if it's a form `POST`, or maybe some JavaScript sending `PUT` or `DELETE` requests? There are a few other options for methods to call on a route definition, as illustrated in Example 3-3.

Example 3-3. Route verbs

```
Route::get('/', function () {
    return 'Hello, World!';
});

Route::post('/', function () {
    // Handle someone sending a POST request to this route
});

Route::put('/', function () {
    // Handle someone sending a PUT request to this route
});

Route::delete('/', function () {
    // Handle someone sending a DELETE request to this route
});

Route::any('/', function () {
    // Handle any verb request to this route
});

Route::match(['get', 'post'], '/', function () {
    // Handle GET or POST requests to this route
});
```

Route Handling

As you've probably guessed, passing a closure to the route definition is not the only way to teach it how to resolve a route. Closures are quick and simple, but the larger your application gets, the clumsier it becomes to put all of your routing logic in one file. Additionally, applications using route closures can't take advantage of Laravel's route caching (more on that later), which can shave up to hundreds of milliseconds off of each request.

The other common option is to pass a controller name and method as a string in place of the closure, as in Example 3-4.

Example 3-4. Routes calling controller methods

```
Route::get('/', 'WelcomeController@index');
```

This is telling Laravel to pass requests to that path to the `index()` method of the `App\Http\Controllers\WelcomeController` controller. This method will be passed the same parameters and treated the same way as a closure you might've alternatively put in its place.

Laravel's Controller/Method Reference Syntax

Laravel has a convention for how to refer to a particular method in a given controller: *ControllerName@methodName*. Sometimes this is just a casual communication convention, but it's also used in real bindings, like in Example 3-4. Laravel parses what's before and after the @ and uses those segments to identify the controller and method. Laravel 5.7 also introduced the "tuple" syntax (`Route::get('/', [WelcomeControl ler::class, 'index'])`) but it's still common to use *ControllerName@methodName* to describe a method in written communication.

Route Parameters

If the route you're defining has parameters—segments in the URL structure that are variable—it's simple to define them in your route and pass them to your closure (see Example 3-5).

Example 3-5. Route parameters

```
Route::get('users/{id}/friends', function ($id) {
    //
});
```

You can also make your route parameters optional by including a question mark (?) after the parameter name, as illustrated in Example 3-6. In this case, you should also provide a default value for the route's corresponding variable.

Example 3-6. Optional route parameters

```
Route::get('users/{id?}', function ($id = 'fallbackId') {
    //
});
```

And you can use regular expressions (regexes) to define that a route should only match if a parameter meets particular requirements, as in Example 3-7.

Example 3-7. Regular expression route constraints

```
Route::get('users/{id}', function ($id) {
    //
})->where('id', '[0-9]+');

Route::get('users/{username}', function ($username) {
    //
})->where('username', '[A-Za-z]+');

Route::get('posts/{id}/{slug}', function ($id, $slug) {
    //
})->where(['id' => '[0-9]+', 'slug' => '[A-Za-z]+']);
```

As you've probably guessed, if you visit a path that matches a route string but the regex doesn't match the parameter, it won't be matched. Since routes are matched top to bottom, `users/abc` would skip the first closure in Example 3-7, but it would be matched by the second closure, so it would get routed there. On the other hand, `posts/abc/123` wouldn't match any of the closures, so it would return a 404 (Not Found) error.

The Naming Relationship Between Route Parameters and Closure/Controller Method Parameters

As you can see in Example 3-5, it's most common to use the same names for your route parameters (`{id}`) and the method parameters they inject into your route definition (`function ($id)`). But is this necessary?

Unless you're using route model binding, discussed later in this chapter, no. The only thing that defines which route parameter matches with which method parameter is their order (left to right), as you can see here:

```
Route::get('users/{userId}/comments/{commentId}', function (
    $thisIsActuallyTheUserId,
    $thisIsReallyTheCommentId
    ) {
    //
});
```

That having been said, just because you *can* make them different doesn't mean you *should*. I recommend keeping them the same for the sake of future developers, who could get tripped up by inconsistent naming.

Route Names

The simplest way to refer to these routes elsewhere in your application is just by their path. There's a url() global helper to simplify that linking in your views, if you need it; see Example 3-8 for an example. The helper will prefix your route with the full domain of your site.

Example 3-8. The url() helper

```
<a href="<?php echo url('/'); ?>">
// Outputs <a href="http://myapp.com/">
```

However, Laravel also allows you to name each route, which enables you to refer to it without explicitly referencing the URL. This is helpful because it means you can give simple nicknames to complex routes, and also because linking them by name means you don't have to rewrite your frontend links if the paths change (see Example 3-9).

Example 3-9. Defining route names

```
// Defining a route with name() in routes/web.php:
Route::get('members/{id}', 'MembersController@show')->name('members.show');

// Linking the route in a view using the route() helper:
<a href="<?php echo route('members.show', ['id' => 14]); ?>">
```

This example illustrates a few new concepts. First, we're using fluent route definition to add the name, by chaining the name() method after the get() method. This method allows us to name the route, giving it a short alias to make it easier to reference elsewhere.

Defining Custom Routes in Laravel 5.1

Fluent route definitions don't exist in Laravel 5.1. You'll need to instead pass an array to the second parameter of your route definition; check the Laravel docs (*http://bit.ly/2UZm1Aw*) to see more about how this works. Here's Example 3-9 in Laravel 5.1:

```
Route::get('members/{id}', [
    'as' => 'members.show',
    'uses' => 'MembersController@show',
]);
```

In our example, we've named this route members.show; *resourcePlural.action* is a common convention within Laravel for route and view names.

This example also introduced the `route()` helper. Just like `url()`, it's intended to be used in views to simplify linking to a named route. If the route has no parameters, you can simply pass the route name (`route('members.index')`) and receive a route string (`http://myapp.com/members`). If it has parameters, pass them in as an array as the second parameter like we did in Example 3-9.

In general, I recommend using route names instead of paths to refer to your routes, and therefore using the `route()` helper instead of the `url()` helper. Sometimes it can get a bit clumsy—for example, if you're working with multiple subdomains—but it provides an incredible level of flexibility to later change the application's routing structure without major penalty.

Option 3:

```
route('users.comments.show', ['commentId' => 2, 'userId' => 1])
// http://myapp.com/users/1/comments/2
```

Option 4:

```
route('users.comments.show', ['userId' => 1, 'commentId' => 2, 'opt' => 'a'])
// http://myapp.com/users/1/comments/2?opt=a
```

As you can see, nonkeyed array values are assigned in order; keyed array values are matched with the route parameters matching their keys, and anything left over is added as a query parameter.

Route Groups

Often a group of routes share a particular characteristic—a certain authentication requirement, a path prefix, or perhaps a controller namespace. Defining these shared characteristics again and again on each route not only seems tedious but also can muddy up the shape of your routes file and obscure some of the structures of your application.

Route groups allow you to group several routes together and apply any shared configuration settings once to the entire group, to reduce this duplication. Additionally, route groups are visual cues to future developers (and to your own brain) that these routes are grouped together.

To group two or more routes together, you "surround" the route definitions with a route group, as shown in Example 3-10. In reality, you're actually passing a closure to the group definition, and defining the grouped routes within that closure.

Example 3-10. Defining a route group

```
Route::group(function () {
    Route::get('hello', function () {
        return 'Hello';
    });
    Route::get('world', function () {
        return 'World';
    });
});
```

By default, a route group doesn't actually do anything. There's no difference between using the group in Example 3-10 and separating a segment of your routes with code comments.

Middleware

Probably the most common use for route groups is to apply middleware to a group of routes. You'll learn more about middleware in Chapter 10, but, among other things, they're what Laravel uses for authenticating users and restricting guest users from using certain parts of a site.

In Example 3-11, we're creating a route group around the dashboard and account views and applying the auth middleware to both. In this example, this means users have to be logged in to the application to view the dashboard or the account page.

Example 3-11. Restricting a group of routes to logged-in users only

```
Route::middleware('auth')->group(function() {
    Route::get('dashboard', function () {
        return view('dashboard');
    });
    Route::get('account', function () {
        return view('account');
    });
});
```

Modifying Route Groups Prior to Laravel 5.4

Just like fluent route definition didn't exist in Laravel prior to 5.2, fluently applying modifiers like middleware, prefixes, domains, and more to route groups wasn't possible prior to 5.4.

Here's Example 3-11 in Laravel 5.3 and prior:

```
Route::group(['middleware' => 'auth'], function () {
    Route::get('dashboard', function () {
        return view('dashboard');
    });
    Route::get('account', function () {
        return view('account');
    });
});
```

Applying middleware in controllers

Often it's clearer and more direct to attach middleware to your routes in the controller instead of at the route definition. You can do this by calling the middleware() method in the constructor of your controller. The string you pass to the middleware() method is the name of the middleware, and you can optionally chain modifier methods (only() and except()) to define which methods will receive that middleware:

```
class DashboardController extends Controller
{
    public function __construct()
    {
        $this->middleware('auth');

        $this->middleware('admin-auth')
            ->only('editUsers');

        $this->middleware('team-member')
            ->except('editUsers');
    }
}
```

Note that if you're doing a lot of "only" and "except" customizations, that's often a sign that you should break out a new controller for the exceptional routes.

Rate limiting

If you need to limit users to only accessing any give route(s) a certain number of times in a given time frame (called *rate limiting*, and most common with APIs), there's an out-of-the-box middleware for that in version 5.2 and above. Apply the throttle middleware, which takes two parameters: the first is the number of tries a user is permitted and the second is the number of minutes to wait before resetting the attempt count. Example 3-12 demonstrates its use.

Example 3-12. Applying the rate limiting middleware to a route

```
Route::middleware('auth:api', 'throttle:60,1')->group(function () {
    Route::get('/profile', function () {
        //
    });
});
```

Dynamic rate limiting. If you'd like to differentiate one user's rate limit from another's, you can instruct the throttle middleware to pull the tries count (its first parameter) from the user's Eloquent model. Instead of passing a tries count as the first parameter of throttle, instead pass the name of an attribute on the Eloquent model, and that attribute will be used to calculate whether the user has passed their rate limit.

So, if your user model has a plan_rate_limit attribute on it, you could use the middleware with throttle:plan_rate_limit,1.

> ## A Brief Introduction to Eloquent
>
> We'll be covering Eloquent, database access, and Laravel's query builder in depth in Chapter 5, but there will be a few references between now and then that will make a basic understanding useful.
>
> Eloquent is Laravel's ActiveRecord database object-relational mapper (ORM), which makes it easy to relate a `Post` class (model) to the `posts` database table and get all records with a call like `Post::all()`.
>
> The query builder is the tool that makes it possible to make calls like `Post::where('active', true)->get()` or even `DB::table('users')->all()`. You're *building* a query by chaining methods one after another.

Path Prefixes

If you have a group of routes that share a segment of their path—for example, if your site's dashboard is prefixed with `/dashboard`—you can use route groups to simplify this structure (see Example 3-13).

Example 3-13. Prefixing a group of routes

```
Route::prefix('dashboard')->group(function () {
    Route::get('/', function () {
        // Handles the path /dashboard
    });
    Route::get('users', function () {
        // Handles the path /dashboard/users
    });
});
```

Note that each prefixed group also has a / route that represents the root of the prefix —in Example 3-13 that's `/dashboard`.

Fallback Routes

In Laravel prior to 5.6, you could define a "fallback route" (which you need to define at the end of your routes file) to catch all unmatched paths:

```
Route::any('{anything}', 'CatchAllController')->where('anything', '*');
```

5.6 In Laravel 5.6+, you can use the `Route::fallback()` method instead:

```
Route::fallback(function () {
    //
});
```

Subdomain Routing

Subdomain routing is the same as route prefixing, but it's scoped by subdomain instead of route prefix. There are two primary uses for this. First, you may want to present different sections of the application (or entirely different applications) to different subdomains. Example 3-14 shows how you can achieve this.

Example 3-14. Subdomain routing

```
Route::domain('api.myapp.com')->group(function () {
    Route::get('/', function () {
        //
    });
});
```

Second, you might want to set part of the subdomain as a parameter, as illustrated in Example 3-15. This is most often done in cases of multitenancy (think Slack or Harvest, where each company gets its own subdomain, like *tighten.slack.co*).

Example 3-15. Parameterized subdomain routing

```
Route::domain('{account}.myapp.com')->group(function () {
    Route::get('/', function ($account) {
        //
    });
    Route::get('users/{id}', function ($account, $id) {
        //
    });
});
```

Note that any parameters for the group get passed into the grouped routes' methods as the first parameter(s).

Namespace Prefixes

When you're grouping routes by subdomain or route prefix, it's likely their controllers have a similar PHP namespace. In the dashboard example, all of the dashboard routes' controllers might be under a `Dashboard` namespace. By using the route group namespace prefix, as shown in Example 3-16, you can avoid long controller references in groups like `"Dashboard/UsersController@index"` and `"Dashboard/PurchasesController@index"`.

Example 3-16. Route group namespace prefixes

```
// App\Http\Controllers\UsersController
Route::get('/', 'UsersController@index');

Route::namespace('Dashboard')->group(function () {
    // App\Http\Controllers\Dashboard\PurchasesController
    Route::get('dashboard/purchases', 'PurchasesController@index');
});
```

Name Prefixes

The prefixes don't stop there. It's common that route names will reflect the inheritance chain of path elements, so users/comments/5 will be served by a route named users.comments.show. In this case, it's common to use a route group around all of the routes that are beneath the users.comments resource.

Just like we can prefix URL segments and controller namespaces, we can also prefix strings to the route name. With route group name prefixes, we can define that every route within this group should have a given string prefixed to its name. In this context, we're prefixing "users." to each route name, then "comments." (see Example 3-17).

Example 3-17. Route group name prefixes

```
Route::name('users.')->prefix('users')->group(function () {
    Route::name('comments.')->prefix('comments')->group(function () {
        Route::get('{id}', function () {

        })->name('show');
    });
});
```

Signed Routes

Many applications regularly send notifications about one-off actions (resetting a password, accepting an invitation, etc.) and provide simple links to take those actions. Let's imagine sending an email confirming the recipient was willing to be added to a mailing list.

There are three ways to send that link:

1. Make that URL public and hope no one else discovers the approval URL or modifies their own approval URL to approve someone else.

2. Put the action behind authentication, link to the action, and require the user to log in if they're not logged in yet (which, in this case, may be impossible, as many mailing list recipients likely won't be users).

3. "Sign" the link so that it uniquely proves that the user received the link from your email, without them having to log in; something like *http://myapp.com/invitations/5816/yes?signature=030ab0ef6a8237bd86a8b8*.

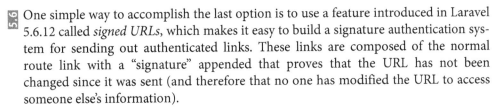 One simple way to accomplish the last option is to use a feature introduced in Laravel 5.6.12 called *signed URLs*, which makes it easy to build a signature authentication system for sending out authenticated links. These links are composed of the normal route link with a "signature" appended that proves that the URL has not been changed since it was sent (and therefore that no one has modified the URL to access someone else's information).

Signing a Route

In order to build a signed URL to access a given route, the route must have a name:

```
Route::get('invitations/{invitation}/{answer}', 'InvitationController')
    ->name('invitations');
```

To generate a normal link to this route you would use the route() helper, as we've already covered, but you could also use the URL facade to do the same thing: URL::route('invitations', ['invitation' => 12345, 'answer' => 'yes']). To generate a *signed* link to this route, simply use the signedRoute() method instead. And if you want to generate a signed route with an expiration, use temporarySigned Route():

```
// Generate a normal link
URL::route('invitations', ['invitation' => 12345, 'answer' => 'yes']);

// Generate a signed link
URL::signedRoute('invitations', ['invitation' => 12345, 'answer' => 'yes']);

// Generate an expiring (temporary) signed link
URL::temporarySignedRoute(
    'invitations',
    now()->addHours(4),
    ['invitation' => 12345, 'answer' => 'yes']
);
```

Using the now() Helper

Since version 5.5 Laravel has offered a now() helper that's the equivalent of Carbon::now(); it returns a Carbon object representative of today, right at this second. If you're working with Laravel prior to 5.5, you can replace any instance of now() in this book with Carbon::now().

Carbon, if you're not familiar with it, is a datetime library that's included with Laravel.

Modifying Routes to Allow Signed Links

Now that you've generated a link to your signed route, you need to protect against any unsigned access. The easiest option is to apply the signed middleware (which, if it's not in your $routeMiddleware array in *app/Http/Kernel.php*, should be, backed by Illuminate\Routing\Middleware\ValidateSignature):

```
Route::get('invitations/{invitation}/{answer}', 'InvitationController')
    ->name('invitations')
    ->middleware('signed');
```

If you'd prefer, you can manually validate using the hasValidSignature() method on the Request object instead of using the signed middleware:

```
class InvitationController
{
    public function __invoke(Invitation $invitation, $answer, Request $request)
    {
        if (! $request->hasValidSignature()) {
            abort(403);
        }

        //
    }
}
```

Views

In a few of the route closures we've looked at so far, we've seen something along the lines of return view('account'). What's going on here?

In the MVC pattern (Figure 3-1), *views* (or templates) are files that describe what some particular output should look like. You might have views for JSON or XML or emails, but the most common views in a web framework output HTML.

In Laravel, there are two formats of view you can use out of the box: plain PHP, or Blade templates (see Chapter 4). The difference is in the filename: *about.php* will

---

be rendered with the PHP engine, and *about.blade.php* will be rendered with the Blade engine.

Three Ways to Load a View

There are three different ways to return a view. For now, just concern yourself with `view()`, but if you ever see `View::make()`, it's the same thing, or you could inject the `Illuminate\View\ViewFactory` if you prefer.

Once you've "loaded" a view with the `view()` helper, you have the option to simply return it (as in Example 3-18), which will work fine if the view doesn't rely on any variables from the controller.

Example 3-18. Simple view() usage

```
Route::get('/', function () {
    return view('home');
});
```

This code looks for a view in *resources/views/home.blade.php* or *resources/views/home.php*, and loads its contents and parses any inline PHP or control structures until you have just the view's output. Once you return it, it's passed on to the rest of the response stack and eventually returned to the user.

But what if you need to pass in variables? Take a look at Example 3-19.

Example 3-19. Passing variables to views

```
Route::get('tasks', function () {
    return view('tasks.index')
        ->with('tasks', Task::all());
});
```

This closure loads the *resources/views/tasks/index.blade.php* or *resources/views/tasks/index.php* view and passes it a single variable named `tasks`, which contains the result of the `Task::all()` method. `Task::all()` is an Eloquent database query you'll learn about in Chapter 5.

Returning Simple Routes Directly with Route::view()

 Because it's so common for a route to just return a view with no custom data, Laravel 5.5+ allows you to define a route as a "view" route without even passing the route definition a closure or a controller/method reference, as you can see in Example 3-20.

Example 3-20. Route::view()

```
// Returns resources/views/welcome.blade.php
Route::view('/', 'welcome');

// Passing simple data to Route::view()
Route::view('/', 'welcome', ['User' => 'Michael']);
```

Using View Composers to Share Variables with Every View

Sometimes it can become a hassle to pass the same variables over and over. There may be a variable that you want accessible to every view in the site, or to a certain class of views or a certain included subview—for example, all views related to tasks, or the header partial.

It's possible to share certain variables with every template or just certain templates, like in the following code:

```
view()->share('variableName', 'variableValue');
```

To learn more, check out "View Composers and Service Injection" on page 75.

Controllers

I've mentioned controllers a few times, but until now most of the examples have shown route closures. In the MVC pattern, controllers are essentially classes that organize the logic of one or more routes together in one place. Controllers tend to group similar routes together, especially if your application is structured in a traditionally CRUD-like format; in this case, a controller might handle all the actions that can be performed on a particular resource.

What is CRUD?

CRUD stands for *create, read, update, delete,* which are the four primary operations that web applications most commonly provide on a resource. For example, you can create a new blog post, you can read that post, you can update it, or you can delete it.

It may be tempting to cram all of the application's logic into the controllers, but it's better to think of controllers as the traffic cops that route HTTP requests around your application. Since there are other ways requests can come into your application —cron jobs, Artisan command-line calls, queue jobs, etc.—it's wise to not rely on controllers for much behavior. This means a controller's primary job is to capture the intent of an HTTP request and pass it on to the rest of the application.

So, let's create a controller. One easy way to do this is with an Artisan command, so from the command line run the following:

```
php artisan make:controller TasksController
```

 Artisan and Artisan Generators

Laravel comes bundled with a command-line tool called Artisan. Artisan can be used to run migrations, create users and other database records manually, and perform many other manual, one-time tasks.

Under the make namespace, Artisan provides tools for generating skeleton files for a variety of system files. That's what allows us to run php artisan make:controller.

To learn more about this and other Artisan features, see Chapter 8.

This will create a new file named *TasksController.php* in *app/Http/Controllers*, with the contents shown in Example 3-21.

Example 3-21. Default generated controller

```php
<?php

namespace App\Http\Controllers;

use Illuminate\Http\Request;

class TasksController extends Controller
{
    //
}
```

Modify this file as shown in Example 3-22, creating a new public method called index(). We'll just return some text there.

Example 3-22. Simple controller example

```php
<?php

namespace App\Http\Controllers;

class TasksController extends Controller
{
    public function index()
    {
        return 'Hello, World!';
```

```
        }
}
```

Then, like we learned before, we'll hook up a route to it, as shown in Example 3-23.

Example 3-23. Route for the simple controller

```
// routes/web.php
<?php

Route::get('/', 'TasksController@index');
```

That's it. Visit the / route and you'll see the words "Hello, World!"

Controller Namespacing

In Example 3-23 we referenced a controller that has the fully qualified class name of `App\Http\Controllers\TasksController`, but we only used the class name. This isn't because we can simply reference controllers by their class name. Rather, we can ignore the `App\Http\Controllers\` when we reference controllers; by default, Laravel is configured to look for controllers within that namespace.

This means that if you have a controller with the fully qualified class name of `App\Http\Controllers\API\ExercisesController`, you'd reference it in a route definition as `API\ExercisesController`.

The most common use of a controller method, then, will be something like Example 3-24, which provides the same functionality as our route closure in Example 3-19.

Example 3-24. Common controller method example

```
// TasksController.php
...
public function index()
{
    return view('tasks.index')
        ->with('tasks', Task::all());
}
```

This controller method loads the *resources/views/tasks/index.blade.php* or *resources/views/tasks/index.php* view and passes it a single variable named `tasks`, which contains the result of the `Task::all()` Eloquent method.

Generating Resource Controllers

🔲 If you ever used php artisan make:controller in Laravel
5.3 prior to 5.3, you might be expecting it to autogenerate methods
for all of the basic resource routes like create() and update(). You
can bring this behavior back in Laravel 5.3+ by passing the
--resource flag when you create the controller:

```
php artisan make:controller TasksController --resource
```

Getting User Input

The second most common action to perform in a controller method is to take input
from the user and act on it. That introduces a few new concepts, so let's take a look at
a bit of sample code and walk through the new pieces.

First, let's bind our route; see Example 3-25.

Example 3-25. Binding basic form actions

```
// routes/web.php
Route::get('tasks/create', 'TasksController@create');
Route::post('tasks', 'TasksController@store');
```

Notice that we're binding the GET action of tasks/create (which shows a form for
creating a new task) and the POST action of tasks/ (which is where our form will
POST to when we're creating a new task). We can assume the create() method in our
controller just shows a form, so let's look at the store() method in Example 3-26.

Example 3-26. Common form input controller method

```
// TasksController.php
...
public function store()
{
    Task::create(request()->only(['title', 'description']));

    return redirect('tasks');
}
```

This example makes use of Eloquent models and the redirect() functionality, and
we'll talk about them more later, but for now let's talk quickly about how we're getting
our data here.

We're using the request() helper to represent the HTTP request (more on that later)
and using its only() method to pull just the title and description fields the user
submitted.

We're then passing that data into the `create()` method of our `Task` model, which creates a new instance of the `Task` with `title` set to the passed-in title and `description` set to the passed-in description. Finally, we redirect back to the page that shows all tasks.

There are a few layers of abstraction at work here, which we'll cover in a second, but know that the data coming from the `only()` method comes from the same pool of data all common methods used on the `Request` object draw from, including `all()` and `get()`. The set of data each of these methods is pulling from represents all user-provided data, whether from query parameters or `POST` values. So, our user filled out two fields on the "add task" page: "title" and "description."

To break down the abstraction a bit, `request()->only()` takes an associative array of input names and returns them:

```
request()->only(['title', 'description']);
// returns:
[
    'title' => 'Whatever title the user typed on the previous page',
    'description' => 'Whatever description the user typed on the previous page',
]
```

And `Task::create()` takes an associative array and creates a new task from it:

```
Task::create([
    'title' => 'Buy milk',
    'description' => 'Remember to check the expiration date this time, Norbert!',
]);
```

Combining them together creates a task with just the user-provided "title" and "description" fields.

Injecting Dependencies into Controllers

Laravel's facades and global helpers present a simple interface to the most useful classes in Laravel's codebase. You can get information about the current request and user input, the session, caches, and much more.

But if you prefer to inject your dependencies, or if you want to use a service that doesn't have a facade or a helper, you'll need to find some way to bring instances of these classes into your controller.

This is our first exposure to Laravel's service container. For now, if this is unfamiliar, you can think about it as a little bit of Laravel magic; or, if you want to know more about how it's actually functioning, you can skip ahead to Chapter 11.

All controller methods (including the constructors) are resolved out of Laravel's container, which means anything you typehint that the container knows how to resolve will be automatically injected.

As a nice example, what if you'd prefer having an instance of the Request object
instead of using the global helper? Just typehint Illuminate\Http\Request in your
method parameters, like in Example 3-27.

Example 3-27. Controller method injection via typehinting

```
// TasksController.php
...
public function store(\Illuminate\Http\Request $request)
{
    Task::create($request->only(['title', 'description']));

    return redirect('tasks');
}
```

So, you've defined a parameter that must be passed into the store() method. And
since you typehinted it, and since Laravel knows how to resolve that class name,
you're going to have the Request object ready for you to use in your method with no
work on your part. No explicit binding, no anything else—it's just there as the
$request variable.

And, as you can tell from comparing Example 3-26 and Example 3-27, the request()
helper and the Request object behave exactly the same.

Resource Controllers

Sometimes naming the methods in your controllers can be the hardest part of writing
a controller. Thankfully, Laravel has some conventions for all of the routes of a traditional REST/CRUD controller (called a "resource controller" in Laravel); additionally,
it comes with a generator out of the box and a convenience route definition that
allows you to bind an entire resource controller at once.

To see the methods that Laravel expects for a resource controller, let's generate a new
controller from the command line:

```
php artisan make:controller MySampleResourceController --resource
```

Now open *app/Http/Controllers/MySampleResourceController.php*. You'll see it comes prefilled with quite a few methods. Let's walk over what each represents. We'll use a `Task` as an example.

The methods of Laravel's resource controllers

Remember the table from earlier? Table 3-1 shows the HTTP verb, the URL, the controller method name, and the name for each of these default methods that are generated in Laravel's resource controllers.

Binding a resource controller

So, we've seen that these are the conventional route names to use in Laravel, and also that it's easy to generate a resource controller with methods for each of these default routes. Thankfully, you don't have to generate routes for each of these controller methods by hand, if you don't want to. There's a trick for that, called *resource controller binding*. Take a look at Example 3-28.

Example 3-28. Resource controller binding

```
// routes/web.php
Route::resource('tasks', 'TasksController');
```

This will automatically bind all of the routes listed in Table 3-1 for this resource to the appropriate method names on the specified controller. It'll also name these routes appropriately; for example, the `index()` method on the `tasks` resource controller will be named `tasks.index()`.

artisan route:list

If you ever find yourself in a situation where you're wondering what routes your current application has available, there's a tool for that: from the command line, run `php artisan route:list` and you'll get a listing of all of the available routes (see Figure 3-2).

Figure 3-2. artisan route:list

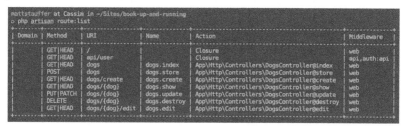

API Resource Controllers

When you're working with RESTful APIs, the list of potential actions on a resource is not the same as it is with an HTML resource controller. For example, you can send a POST request to an API to create a resource, but you can't really "show a create form" in an API.

 Laravel 5.6 introduced a new way to generate an *API resource controller*, which has the same structure as a resource controller except it excludes the *create* and *edit* actions. We can generate API resource controllers by passing the `--api` flag when creating a controller:

```
php artisan make:controller MySampleResourceController --api
```

Binding an API resource controller

To bind an API resource controller, use the `apiResource()` method instead of the `resource()` method, as shown in Example 3-29.

Example 3-29. API resource controller binding

```
// routes/web.php
Route::apiResource('tasks', 'TasksController');
```

Single Action Controllers

There will be times in your applications when a controller should only service a single route. You may find yourself wondering how to name the controller method for that route. Thankfully, you can point a single route at a single controller without concerning yourself with naming the one method.

As you may already know, the `__invoke()` method is a PHP magic method that allows you to "invoke" an instance of a class, treating it like a function and calling it. This is the tool Laravel's *single action controllers* use to allow you to point a route to a single controller, as you can see in Example 3-30.

Example 3-30. Using the __invoke() method

```
// \App\Http\Controllers\UpdateUserAvatar.php
public function __invoke(User $user)
{
    // Update the user's avatar image
}

// routes/web.php
Route::post('users/{user}/update-avatar', 'UpdateUserAvatar');
```

Route Model Binding

One of the most common routing patterns is that the first line of any controller method tries to find the resource with the given ID, like in Example 3-31.

Example 3-31. Getting a resource for each route

```
Route::get('conferences/{id}', function ($id) {
    $conference = Conference::findOrFail($id);
});
```

Laravel provides a feature that simplifies this pattern called *route model binding*. This allows you to define that a particular parameter name (e.g., {conference}) will indicate to the route resolver that it should look up an Eloquent database record with that ID and then pass it in as the parameter *instead* of just passing the ID.

There are two kinds of route model binding: implicit and custom (or explicit).

Implicit Route Model Binding

The simplest way to use route model binding is to name your route parameter something unique to that model (e.g., name it $conference instead of $id), then typehint that parameter in the closure/controller method and use the same variable name there. It's easier to show than to describe, so take a look at Example 3-32.

Example 3-32. Using an implicit route model binding

```
Route::get('conferences/{conference}', function (Conference $conference) {
    return view('conferences.show')->with('conference', $conference);
});
```

Because the route parameter ({conference}) is the same as the method parameter ($conference), and the method parameter is typehinted with a Conference model (Conference $conference), Laravel sees this as a route model binding. Every time this route is visited, the application will assume that whatever is passed into the URL in place of {conference} is an ID that should be used to look up a Conference, and then that resulting model instance will be passed in to your closure or controller method.

Customizing the Route Key for an Eloquent Model

Any time an Eloquent model is looked up via a URL segment (usually because of route model binding), the default column Eloquent will look it up by is its primary key (ID).

To change the column your Eloquent model uses for URL lookups, add a method to your model named getRouteKeyName():

```
public function getRouteKeyName()
{
    return 'slug';
}
```

Now, a URL like conferences/{conference} will expect to get an entry from the slug column instead of the ID, and will perform its lookups accordingly.

Implicit route model binding was added in Laravel 5.2, so you won't have access to it in 5.1.

Custom Route Model Binding

To manually configure route model bindings, add a line like the one in Example 3-33 to the boot() method in App\Providers\RouteServiceProvider.

Example 3-33. Adding a route model binding

```
public function boot()
{
    // Just allows the parent's boot() method to still run
    parent::boot();

    // Perform the binding
    Route::model('event', Conference::class);
}
```

You've now specified that whenever a route has a parameter in its definition named {event}, as demonstrated in Example 3-34, the route resolver will return an instance of the Conference class with the ID of that URL parameter.

Example 3-34. Using an explicit route model binding

```
Route::get('events/{event}', function (Conference $event) {
    return view('events.show')->with('event', $event);
});
```

Route Caching

If you're looking to squeeze every millisecond out of your load time, you may want to take a look at route caching. One of the pieces of Laravel's bootstrap that can take anywhere from a few dozen to a few hundred milliseconds is parsing the *routes/** files, and route caching speeds up this process dramatically.

To cache your routes file, you need to be using all controller, redirect, view, and resource routes (no route closures). If your app isn't using any route closures, you can run php artisan route:cache and Laravel will serialize the results of your *routes/** files. If you want to delete the cache, run php artisan route:clear.

Here's the drawback: Laravel will now match routes against that cached file instead of your actual *routes/** files. You can make endless changes to your routes files, and they won't take effect until you run route:cache again. This means you'll have to recache every time you make a change, which introduces a lot of potential for confusion.

Here's what I would recommend instead: since Git ignores the route cache file by default anyway, consider only using route caching on your production server, and run the php artisan route:cache command every time you deploy new code (whether via a Git post-deploy hook, a Forge deploy command, or as a part of whatever other deploy system you use). This way you won't have confusing local development issues, but your remote environment will still benefit from route caching.

Form Method Spoofing

Sometimes you need to manually define which HTTP verb a form should send as. HTML forms only allow for GET or POST, so if you want any other sort of verb, you'll need to specify that yourself.

HTTP Verbs in Laravel

As we've seen already, you can define which verbs a route will match in the route definition using Route::get(), Route::post(), Route::any(), or Route::match(). You can also match with Route::patch(), Route::put(), and Route::delete().

But how does one send a request other than GET with a web browser? First, the method attribute in an HTML form determines its HTTP verb: if your form has a method of "GET", it will submit via query parameters and a GET method; if the form has a method of "POST", it will submit via the post body and a POST method.

JavaScript frameworks make it easy to send other requests, like DELETE and PATCH. But if you find yourself needing to submit HTML forms in Laravel with verbs other than GET or POST, you'll need to use *form method spoofing*, which means spoofing the HTTP method in an HTML form.

HTTP Method Spoofing in HTML Forms

To inform Laravel that the form you're currently submitting should be treated as something other than a `POST`, add a hidden variable named `_method` with the value of either `"PUT"`, `"PATCH"`, or `"DELETE"`, and Laravel will match and route that form submission as if it were actually a request with that verb.

The form in Example 3-35, since it's passing Laravel the method of `"DELETE"`, will match routes defined with `Route::delete()` but not those with `Route::post()`.

Example 3-35. Form method spoofing

```
<form action="/tasks/5" method="POST">
    <input type="hidden" name="_method" value="DELETE">
    <!-- or: -->
    @method('DELETE')
</form>
```

CSRF Protection

If you've tried to submit a form in a Laravel application already, including the one in Example 3-35, you've likely run into the dreaded `TokenMismatchException`.

By default, all routes in Laravel except "read-only" routes (those using `GET`, `HEAD`, or `OPTIONS`) are protected against cross-site request forgery (CSRF) attacks by requiring a token, in the form of an input named `_token`, to be passed along with each request. This token is generated at the start of every session, and every non–read-only route compares the submitted `_token` against the session token.

What is CSRF?

A cross-site request forgery is when one website pretends to be another. The goal is for someone to hijack your users' access to your website, by submitting forms from *their* website to *your* website via the logged-in user's browser.

The best way around CSRF attacks is to protect all inbound routes —POST, DELETE, etc.—with a token, which Laravel does out of the box.

You have two options for getting around this CSRF error. The first, and preferred, method is to add the `_token` input to each of your submissions. In HTML forms, that's simple; look at Example 3-36.

Example 3-36. CSRF tokens

```
<form action="/tasks/5" method="POST">
    <?php echo csrf_field(); ?>
    <!-- or: -->
    <input type="hidden" name="_token" value="<?php echo csrf_token(); ?>">
    <!-- or: -->
    @csrf
</form>
```

CSRF Helpers in Laravel Prior to 5.6

The @csrf Blade directive is not available in projects running versions of Laravel prior to 5.6. Instead, you'll need to use the csrf_field() helper function.

In JavaScript applications, it takes a bit more work, but not much. The most common solution for sites using JavaScript frameworks is to store the token on every page in a <meta> tag like this one:

```
<meta name="csrf-token" content="<?php echo csrf_token(); ?>" id="token">
```

Storing the token in a <meta> tag makes it easy to bind it to the correct HTTP header, which you can do once globally for all requests from your JavaScript framework, like in Example 3-37.

Example 3-37. Globally binding a header for CSRF

```
// In jQuery:
$.ajaxSetup({
    headers: {
        'X-CSRF-TOKEN': $('meta[name="csrf-token"]').attr('content')
    }
});

// With Axios:
window.axios.defaults.headers.common['X-CSRF-TOKEN'] =
    document.head.querySelector('meta[name="csrf-token"]');
```

Laravel will check the X-CSRF-TOKEN on every request, and valid tokens passed there will mark the CSRF protection as satisfied.

Note that the Vue syntax for CSRF in this example is not necessary if you're working with the default Vue bootstrap in a Laravel installation; it already does this work for you.

Binding CSRF Tokens with Vue Resource

In projects running Laravel 5.3 and earlier and Vue, you may be relying on a library called Vue Resource (*http://bit.ly/2UbVkLz*) to make Ajax calls. Bootstrapping the CSRF token into Vue Resource looks a bit different than it does for Laravel; see the Vue Resource docs for examples.

Redirects

So far the only things we've explicitly talked about returning from a controller method or route definition have been views. But there are a few other structures we can return to give the browser instructions on how to behave.

First, let's cover the *redirect*. You've already seen a few of these in other examples. There are two common ways to generate a redirect; we'll use the `redirect()` global helper here, but you may prefer the facade. Both create an instance of `Illuminate\Http\RedirectResponse`, perform some convenience methods on it, and then return it. You can also do this manually, but you'll have to do a little more work yourself. Take a look at Example 3-38 to see a few ways you can return a redirect.

Example 3-38. Different ways to return a redirect

```
// Using the global helper to generate a redirect response
Route::get('redirect-with-helper', function () {
    return redirect()->to('login');
});

// Using the global helper shortcut
Route::get('redirect-with-helper-shortcut', function () {
    return redirect('login');
});

// Using the facade to generate a redirect response
Route::get('redirect-with-facade', function () {
    return Redirect::to('login');
});

// Using the Route::redirect shortcut in Laravel 5.5+
Route::redirect('redirect-by-route', 'login');
```

Note that the `redirect()` helper exposes the same methods as the `Redirect` facade, but it also has a shortcut; if you pass parameters directly to the helper instead of chaining methods after it, it's a shortcut to the `to()` redirect method.

Also note that the (optional) third parameter for the `Route::redirect()` route helper can be the status code (e.g., 302) for your redirect.

redirect()->to()

The method signature for the `to()` method for redirects looks like this:

```
function to($to = null, $status = 302, $headers = [], $secure = null)
```

`$to` is a valid internal path, `$status` is the HTTP status (defaulting to 302), `$headers` allows you to define which HTTP headers to send along with your redirect, and `$secure` allows you to override the default choice of `http` versus `https` (which is normally set based on your current request URL). Example 3-39 shows an example of its use.

Example 3-39. redirect()->to()

```
Route::get('redirect', function () {
    return redirect()->to('home');

    // Or same, using the shortcut:

    return redirect('home');
});
```

redirect()->route()

The `route()` method is the same as the `to()` method, but rather than pointing to a particular path, it points to a particular route name (see Example 3-40).

Example 3-40. redirect()->route()

```
Route::get('redirect', function () {
    return redirect()->route('conferences.index');
});
```

Note that, since some route names require parameters, its parameter order is a little different. `route()` has an optional second parameter for the route parameters:

```
function route($to = null, $parameters = [], $status = 302, $headers = [])
```

So, using it might look a little like Example 3-41.

Example 3-41. redirect()->route() with parameters

```
Route::get('redirect', function () {
    return redirect()->route('conferences.show', ['conference' => 99]);
});
```

redirect()->back()

Because of some of the built-in conveniences of Laravel's session implementation, your application will always have knowledge of what the user's previously visited page was. That opens up the opportunity for a `redirect()->back()` redirect, which simply redirects the user to whatever page they came from. There's also a global shortcut for this: `back()`.

Other Redirect Methods

The redirect service provides other methods that are less commonly used, but still available:

`home()`
> Redirects to a route named `home`. `refresh()`::Redirects to the same page the user is currently on. `away()`::Allows for redirecting to an external URL without the default URL validation.

`secure()`
> Like `to()` with the `secure` parameter set to `"true"`.

`action()`
> Allows you to link to a controller and method in one of two ways: as a string (`redirect()->action('MyController@myMethod')`) or as a tuple (`redirect()->action([MyController::class, 'myMethod'])`).

`guest()`
> Used internally by the authentification system (discussed in Chapter 9); when a user visits a route they're not authenticated for, this captures the "intended" route and then redirects the user (usually to a login page).

`intended()`
> Also used internally by the auth system; after a successful authentication, this grabs the "intended" URL stored by the `guest()` method and redirects the user there.

redirect()->with()

While it is structured similarly to the other methods you can call on `redirect()`, `with()` is different in that it doesn't define where you're redirecting to, but what data you're passing along with the redirect. When you're redirecting users to different pages, you often want to pass certain data along with them. You could manually flash the data to the session, but Laravel has some convenience methods to help you with that.

Most commonly, you can pass along either an array of keys and values or a single key and value using with(), like in Example 3-42. This saves your with() data to the session just for the next page load.

Example 3-42. Redirect with data

```
Route::get('redirect-with-key-value', function () {
    return redirect('dashboard')
        ->with('error', true);
});

Route::get('redirect-with-array', function () {
    return redirect('dashboard')
        ->with(['error' => true, 'message' => 'Whoops!']);
});
```

 Chaining Methods on Redirects

As with many other facades, most calls to the Redirect facade can accept fluent method chains, like the with() calls in Example 3-42. You'll learn more about fluency in "What Is a Fluent Interface?" on page 105.

You can also use withInput(), as in Example 3-43, to redirect with the user's form input flashed; this is most common in the case of a validation error, where you want to send the user back to the form they just came from.

Example 3-43. Redirect with form input

```
Route::get('form', function () {
    return view('form');
});

Route::post('form', function () {
    return redirect('form')
        ->withInput()
        ->with(['error' => true, 'message' => 'Whoops!']);
});
```

The easiest way to get the flashed input that was passed with withInput() is using the old() helper, which can be used to get all old input (old()) or just the value for a particular key as shown in the following example, with the second parameter as the default if there is no old value). You'll commonly see this in views, which allows this HTML to be used both on the "create" and the "edit" view for this form:

```
<input name="username" value="<?=
    old('username', 'Default username instructions here');
?>">
```

Speaking of validation, there is also a useful method for passing errors along with a redirect response: `withErrors()`. You can pass it any "provider" of errors, which may be an error string, an array of errors, or, most commonly, an instance of the Illuminate `Validator`, which we'll cover in Chapter 10. Example 3-44 shows an example of its use.

Example 3-44. Redirect with errors

```
Route::post('form', function (Illuminate\Http\Request $request) {
    $validator = Validator::make($request->all(), $this->validationRules);

    if ($validator->fails()) {
        return back()
            ->withErrors($validator)
            ->withInput();
    }
});
```

`withErrors()` automatically shares an `$errors` variable with the views of the page it's redirecting to, for you to handle however you'd like.

The validate() Method on Requests

Don't like how Example 3-44 looks? There's a simple and powerful tool that will make it easy for you to clean up that code. Read more in "validate() on the Request Object" on page 189.

Aborting the Request

Aside from returning views and redirects, the most common way to exit a route is to abort. There are a few globally available methods (`abort()`, `abort_if()`, and `abort_unless()`), which optionally take HTTP status codes, a message, and a headers array as parameters.

As Example 3-45 shows, `abort_if()` and `abort_unless()` take a first parameter that is evaluated for its truthiness and perform the abort depending on the result.

Example 3-45. 403 Forbidden aborts

```
Route::post('something-you-cant-do', function (Illuminate\Http\Request $request) {
    abort(403, 'You cannot do that!');
    abort_unless($request->has('magicToken'), 403);
```

```
    abort_if($request->user()->isBanned, 403);
});
```

Custom Responses

There are a few other options available for us to return, so let's go over the most common responses after views, redirects, and aborts. Just like with redirects, you can run
these methods on either the response() helper or the Response facade.

response()->make()

If you want to create an HTTP response manually, just pass your data into the first
parameter of response()->make(): for example, return response()->make(*Hello,
World!*). Once again, the second parameter is the HTTP status code and the third is
your headers.

response()->json() and ->jsonp()

To create a JSON-encoded HTTP response manually, pass your JSON-able content
(arrays, collections, or whatever else) to the json() method: for example return
response()->json(User::all()). It's just like make(), except it +json_encode+s
your content and sets the appropriate headers.

response()->download(), ->streamDownload(), and ->file()

To send a file for the end user to download, pass either an SplFileInfo instance or a
string filename to download(), with an optional second parameter of the download
filename: for   example,   return   response()->download('file501751.pdf',
'myFile.pdf'), which would send a file that's at *file501751.pdf* and rename it, as it's
sent, *myFile.pdf*.

To display the same file in the browser (if it's a PDF or an image or something else
the browser can handle), use response()->file() instead, which takes the same
parameters as response->download().

If you want to make some content from an external service available as a download
without having to write it directly to your server's disk, you can stream the download
using response()->streamDownload(). This method expects as parameters a closure
that echoes a string, a filename, and optionally an array of headers; see Example 3-46.

Example 3-46. Streaming downloads from external servers

```
return response()->streamDownload(function () {
    echo DocumentService::file('myFile')->getContent();
}, 'myFile.pdf');
```

Testing

In some other communities the idea of unit-testing controller methods is common, but within Laravel (and most of the PHP community) it's typical to rely on *application testing* to test the functionality of routes.

For example, to verify that a POST route works correctly, we can write a test like Example 3-47.

Example 3-47. Writing a simple POST route test

```
// tests/Feature/AssignmentTest.php
public function test_post_creates_new_assignment()
{
    $this->post('/assignments', [
        'title' => 'My great assignment',
    ]);

    $this->assertDatabaseHas('assignments', [
        'title' => 'My great assignment',
    ]);
}
```

Did we directly call the controller methods? No. But we ensured that the goal of this route—to receive a POST and save its important information to the database—was met.

You can also use similar syntax to visit a route and verify that certain text shows up on the page, or that clicking certain buttons does certain things (see Example 3-48).

Example 3-48. Writing a simple GET route test

```
// AssignmentTest.php
public function test_list_page_shows_all_assignments()
{
    $assignment = Assignment::create([
        'title' => 'My great assignment',
    ]);

    $this->get('/assignments')
        ->assertSee('My great assignment');
}
```

Different Names for Testing Methods Prior to Laravel 5.4

In projects running versions of Laravel prior to 5.4 `assertDatabaseHas()` should be replaced by `seeInDatabase()`, and `get()` and `assertSee()` should be replaced by `visit()` and `see()`.

TL;DR

Laravel's routes are defined in *routes/web.php* and *routes/api.php*. You can define the expected path for each route, which segments are static and which are parameters, which HTTP verbs can access the route, and how to resolve it. You can also attach middleware to routes, group them, and give them names.

What is returned from the route closure or controller method dictates how Laravel responds to the user. If it's a string or a view, it's presented to the user; if it's other sorts of data, it's converted to JSON and presented to the user; and if it's a redirect, it forces a redirect.

Laravel provides a series of tools and conveniences to simplify common routing-related tasks and structures. These include resource controllers, route model binding, and form method spoofing.

## CHAPTER 4

Blade Templating

Compared to most other backend languages, PHP actually functions relatively well as a templating language. But it has its shortcomings, and it's also just ugly to be using <?php inline all over the place, so you can expect most modern frameworks to offer a templating language.

Laravel offers a custom templating engine called *Blade*, which is inspired by .NET's Razor engine. It boasts a concise syntax, a shallow learning curve, a powerful and intuitive inheritance model, and easy extensibility.

For a quick look at what writing Blade looks like, check out Example 4-1.

Example 4-1. Blade samples

```
<h1>{{ $group->title }}</h1>
{!! $group->heroImageHtml() !!}

@forelse ($users as $user)
    • {{ $user->first_name }} {{ $user->last_name }}<br>
@empty
    No users in this group.
@endforelse
```

As you can see, Blade uses curly braces for its "echo" and introduces a convention in which its custom tags, called "directives," are prefixed with an @. You'll use directives for all of your control structures and also for inheritance and any custom functionality you want to add.

Blade's syntax is clean and concise, so at its core it's just more pleasant and tidy to work with than the alternatives. But the moment you need anything of any complexity in your templates—nested inheritance, complex conditionals, or recursion—Blade starts to really shine. Just like the best Laravel components, it takes complex application requirements and makes them easy and accessible.

Additionally, since all Blade syntax is compiled into normal PHP code and then cached, it's fast and it allows you to use native PHP in your Blade files if you want. However, I'd recommend avoiding usage of PHP if at all possible—usually if you need to do anything that you can't do with Blade or a custom Blade directive, it doesn't belong in the template.

Using Twig with Laravel

Unlike many other Symfony-based frameworks, Laravel doesn't use Twig by default. But if you're just in love with Twig, there's a Twig Bridge (*http://bit.ly/2U8dFt0*) package that makes it easy to use Twig instead of Blade.

Echoing Data

As you can see in Example 4-1, {{ and }} are used to wrap sections of PHP that you'd like to echo. {{ $variable }} is similar to <?= $variable ?> in plain PHP.

It's different in one way, however, and you might've guessed this already: Blade escapes all echoes by default using PHP's htmlentities() to protect your users from malicious script insertion. That means {{ $variable }} is functionally equivalent to <?= htmlentities($variable) ?>. If you want to echo without the escaping, use {!! and !!} instead.

{{ and }} When Using a Frontend Templating Framework

You might've noticed that the echo syntax for Blade ({{ }}) is similar to the echo syntax for many frontend frameworks. So how does Laravel know when you're writing Blade versus Handlebars?

Blade will ignore any {{ that's prefaced with an @. So, it will parse the first of the following examples, but the second will be echoed out directly:

```
// Parsed as Blade; the value of $bladeVariable is echoed to the view
{{ $bladeVariable }}

// @ is removed and "{{ handlebarsVariable }}" echoed to the view directly
@{{ handlebarsVariable }}
```

You can also wrap any large sections of script content with the @verbatim directive (*http://bit.ly/2OnrPRP*).

Control Structures

Most of the control structures in Blade will be very familiar. Many directly echo the name and structure of the same tag in PHP.

There are a few convenience helpers, but in general, the control structures just look cleaner than they would in PHP.

Conditionals

First, let's take a look at the control structures that allow for logic.

@if

Blade's `@if ($condition)` compiles to `<?php if ($condition): ?>`. `@else`, `@elseif`, and `@endif` also compile to the exact same style of syntax in PHP. Take a look at Example 4-2 for some examples.

Example 4-2. @if, @else, @elseif, and @endif

```
@if (count($talks) === 1)
    There is one talk at this time period.
@elseif (count($talks) === 0)
    There are no talks at this time period.
@else
    There are {{ count($talks) }} talks at this time period.
@endif
```

Just like with the native PHP conditionals, you can mix and match these how you want. They don't have any special logic; there's literally a parser looking for something with the shape of `@if ($condition)` and replacing it with the appropriate PHP code.

@unless and @endunless

`@unless`, on the other hand, is a new syntax that doesn't have a direct equivalent in PHP. It's the direct inverse of `@if`. `@unless ($condition)` is the same as `<?php if (!$condition)`. You can see it in use in Example 4-3.

Example 4-3. @unless and @endunless

```
@unless ($user->hasPaid())
    You can complete your payment by switching to the payment tab.
@endunless
```

Loops

Next, let's take a look at the loops.

@for, @foreach, and @while

@for, @foreach, and @while work the same in Blade as they do in PHP; see Examples 4-4, 4-5, and 4-6.

Example 4-4. @for and @endfor

```
@for ($i = 0; $i < $talk->slotsCount(); $i++)
    The number is {{ $i }}<br>
@endfor
```

Example 4-5. @foreach and @endforeach

```
@foreach ($talks as $talk)
    • {{ $talk->title }} ({{ $talk->length }} minutes)<br>
@endforeach
```

Example 4-6. @while and @endwhile

```
@while ($item = array_pop($items))
    {{ $item->orSomething() }}<br>
@endwhile
```

@forelse and @endforelse

@forelse is a @foreach that also allows you to program in a fallback if the object you're iterating over is empty. We saw it in action at the start of this chapter; Example 4-7 shows another example.

Example 4-7. @forelse

```
@forelse ($talks as $talk)
    • {{ $talk->title }} ({{ $talk->length }} minutes)<br>
@empty
    No talks this day.
@endforelse
```

$loop Within @foreach and @forelse

The @foreach and @forelse directives (introduced in Laravel 5.3) add one feature that's not available in PHP foreach loops: the $loop variable. When used within a @foreach or @forelse loop, this variable will return a stdClass object with these properties:

index
> The 0-based index of the current item in the loop; 0 would mean "first item"

iteration
> The 1-based index of the current item in the loop; 1 would mean "first item"

remaining
> How many items remain in the loop

count
> The count of items in the loop

first
> A Boolean indicating whether this is the first item in the loop

last
> A Boolean indicating whether this is the last item in the loop

depth
> How many "levels" deep this loop is: 1 for a loop, 2 for a loop within a loop, etc.

parent
> A reference to the $loop variable for the parent loop item if this loop is within another @foreach loop; otherwise, null

Here's an example of how to use it:

```
<ul>
@foreach ($pages as $page)
    <li>{{ $loop->iteration }}: {{ $page->title }}
        @if ($page->hasChildren())
        <ul>
        @foreach ($page->children() as $child)
            <li>{{ $loop->parent->iteration }}
                .{{ $loop->iteration }}:
                {{ $child->title }}</li>
        @endforeach
        </ul>
        @endif
    </li>
@endforeach
</ul>
```

Template Inheritance

Blade provides a structure for template inheritance that allows views to extend, modify, and include other views.

Let's take a look at how inheritance is structured with Blade.

Defining Sections with @section/@show and @yield

Let's start with a top-level Blade layout, like in Example 4-8. This is the definition of a generic page wrapper that we'll later place page-specific content into.

Example 4-8. Blade layout

```
<!-- resources/views/layouts/master.blade.php -->
<html>
    <head>
        <title>My Site | @yield('title', 'Home Page')</title>
    </head>
    <body>
        <div class="container">
            @yield('content')
        </div>
        @section('footerScripts')
            <script src="app.js"></script>
        @show
    </body>
</html>
```

This looks a bit like a normal HTML page, but you can see we've *yielded* in two places (title and content) and we've defined a *section* in a third (footerScripts). We have three Blade directives here: @yield('content') alone, @yield('title', 'Home Page') with a defined default, and @section/@show with actual content in it.

While they each look a little different, *all three function essentially the same.* All three are defining that there's a section with a given name (the first parameter) that can be extended later, and all three are defining what to do if the section isn't extended. They do this either by providing a string fallback ('Home Page'), no fallback (which will just not show anything if it's not extended), or an entire block fallback (in this case, <script src="app.js"></script>).

What's different? Well, clearly, @yield('content') has no default content. But additionally, the default content in @yield('title') will *only* be shown if it's never extended. If it is extended, its child sections will not have programmatic access to the default value. @section/@show, on the other hand, is both defining a default *and* doing so in such a way that its default contents will be available to its children, through @parent.

Once you have a parent layout like this, you can extend it in a new template file like in Example 4-9.

Example 4-9. Extending a Blade layout

```
<!-- resources/views/dashboard.blade.php -->
@extends('layouts.master')

@section('title', 'Dashboard')

@section('content')
    Welcome to your application dashboard!
@endsection

@section('footerScripts')
    @parent
    <script src="dashboard.js"></script>
@endsection
```

@show Versus @endsection

You may have noticed that Example 4-8 uses @section/@show, but Example 4-9 uses @section/@endsection. What's the difference?

Use @show when you're defining the place for a section, in the parent template. Use @endsection when you're defining the content for a template in a child template.

This child view allows us to cover a few new concepts in Blade inheritance.

@extends

In Example 4-9, with @extends('layouts.master'), we define that this view should not be rendered on its own but that it instead *extends* another view. That means its role is to define the content of various sections, but not to stand alone. It's almost more like a series of buckets of content, rather than an HTML page. This line also defines that the view it's extending lives at *resources/views/layouts/master.blade.php*.

Each file should only extend one other file, and the @extends call should be the first line of the file.

@section and @endsection

With @section('title', 'Dashboard'), we provide our content for the first section, title. Since the content is so short, instead of using @section and @end section, we're just using a shortcut. This allows us to pass the content in as the second parameter of @section and then move on. If it's a bit disconcerting to see @section without @endsection, you could just use the normal syntax.

With @section('content') and on, we use the normal syntax to define the contents of the content section. We'll just throw a little greeting in for now. Note, however, that when you're using @section in a child view, you end it with @endsection (or its alias @stop), instead of @show, which is reserved for defining sections in parent views.

@parent

Finally, with @section('footerScripts') and on, we use the normal syntax to define the contents of the footerScripts section.

But remember, we actually defined that content (or, at least, its "default") already in the master layout. So this time, we have two options: we can either *overwrite* the content from the parent view, or we can *add* to it.

You can see that we have the option to include the content from the parent by using the @parent directive within the section. If we didn't, the content of this section would entirely overwrite anything defined in the parent for this section.

Including View Partials

Now that we've established the basics of inheritance, there are a few more tricks we can perform.

@include

What if we're in a view and want to pull in another view? Maybe we have a call-to-action "Sign up" button that we want to reuse around the site. And maybe we want to customize the button text every time we use it. Take a look at Example 4-10.

Example 4-10. Including view partials with @include

```
<!-- resources/views/home.blade.php -->
<div class="content" data-page-name="{{ $pageName }}">
    <p>Here's why you should sign up for our app: <strong>It's Great.</strong></p>

    @include('sign-up-button', ['text' => 'See just how great it is'])
</div>

<!-- resources/views/sign-up-button.blade.php -->
<a class="button button--callout" data-page-name="{{ $pageName }}">
    <i class="exclamation-icon"></i> {{ $text }}
</a>
```

@include pulls in the partial and, optionally, passes data into it. Note that not only can you *explicitly* pass data to an include via the second parameter of @include, but you can also reference any variables within the included file that are available to the including view ($pageName, in this example). Once again, you can do whatever you want, but I would recommend you consider always explicitly passing every variable that you intend to use, just for clarity.

You also use the @includeIf, @includeWhen, and @includeFirst directives, as shown in Example 4-11.

Example 4-11. Conditionally including views

```
{{-- Include a view if it exists --}}
@includeIf('sidebars.admin', ['some' => 'data'])

{{-- Include a view if a passed variable is truth-y --}}
@includeWhen($user->isAdmin(), 'sidebars.admin', ['some' => 'data'])

{{-- Include the first view that exists from a given array of views --}}
@includeFirst(['customs.header', 'header'], ['some' => 'data'])
```

@each

You can probably imagine some circumstances in which you'd need to loop over an array or collection and @include a partial for each item. There's a directive for that: @each.

Let's say we have a sidebar composed of modules, and we want to include multiple modules, each with a different title. Take a look at Example 4-12.

Example 4-12. Using view partials in a loop with @each

```
<!-- resources/views/sidebar.blade.php -->
<div class="sidebar">
    @each('partials.module', $modules, 'module', 'partials.empty-module')
</div>

<!-- resources/views/partials/module.blade.php -->
<div class="sidebar-module">
    <h1>{{ $module->title }}</h1>
</div>

<!-- resources/views/partials/empty-module.blade.php -->
<div class="sidebar-module">
    No modules :(
</div>
```

Consider that @each syntax. The first parameter is the name of the view partial. The second is the array or collection to iterate over. The third is the variable name that each item (in this case, each element in the $modules array) will be passed to the view as. And the optional fourth parameter is the view to show if the array or collection is empty (or, optionally, you can pass a string in here that will be used as your template).

Using Stacks

 One common pattern that can be difficult to manage using basic Blade includes is when each view in a Blade include hierarchy needs to add something to a certain section—almost like adding an entry to an array.

The most common situation for this is when certain pages (and sometimes, more broadly, certain sections of a website) have specific unique CSS and JavaScript files they need to load. Imagine you have a site-wide "global" CSS file, a "jobs section" CSS file, and an "apply for a job" page CSS file.

Blade's *stacks* are built for exactly this situation. In your parent template, define a stack, which is just a placeholder. Then, in each child template you can "push" entries onto that stack with @push/@endpush, which adds them to the bottom of the stack in the final render. You can also use @prepend/@endprepend to add them to the top of the stack. Example 4-13 illustrates.

Example 4-13. Using Blade stacks

```
<!-- resources/views/layouts/app.blade.php -->
<html>
<head><!-- the head --></head>
<body>
    <!-- the rest of the page -->
    <script src="/css/global.css"></script>
    <!-- the placeholder where stack content will be placed -->
    @stack('scripts')
</body>
</html>

<!-- resources/views/jobs.blade.php -->
@extends('layouts.app')

@push('scripts')
    <!-- push something to the bottom of the stack -->
    <script src="/css/jobs.css"></script>
@endpush

<!-- resources/views/jobs/apply.blade.php -->
@extends('jobs')

@prepend('scripts')
```

```
<!-- push something to the top of the stack -->
<script src="/css/jobs--apply.css"></script>
@endprepend
```

These generate the following result:

```
<html>
<head><!-- the head --></head>
<body>
    <!-- the rest of the page -->
    <script src="/css/global.css"></script>
    <!-- the placeholder where stack content will be placed -->
    <script src="/css/jobs--apply.css"></script>
    <script src="/css/jobs.css"></script>
</body>
</html>
```

Using Components and Slots

Laravel offers another pattern for including content between views, which was introduced in 5.4: *components* and *slots*. Components make the most sense in contexts when you find yourself using view partials and passing large chunks of content into them as variables. Take a look at Example 4-14 for an example of a model, or popover, that might alert the user in response to an error or other action.

Example 4-14. A modal as an awkward view partial

```
<!-- resources/views/partials/modal.blade.php -->
<div class="modal">
    <div>{{ $content }}</div>
    <div class="close button etc">...</div>
</div>

<!-- in another template -->
@include('partials.modal', [
    'body' => '<p>The password you have provided is not valid. Here are the rules
    for valid passwords: [...]</p><p><a href="#">...</a></p>'
])
```

This is too much for this variable, and it's the perfect fit for a component.

Components with slots are view partials that are explicitly designed to have big chunks ("slots") that are meant to get content from the including template. Take a look at Example 4-15 to see how to refactor Example 4-14 with components and slots.

Example 4-15. A modal as a more appropriate component with slots

```
<!-- resources/views/partials/modal.blade.php -->
<div class="modal">
```

```
    <div>{{ $slot }}</div>
    <div class="close button etc">...</div>
</div>

<!-- in another template -->
@component('partials.modal')
    <p>The password you have provided is not valid.
    Here are the rules for valid passwords: [...]</p>

    <p><a href="#">...</a></p>
@endcomponent
```

As you can see in Example 4-15, the @component directive allows us to pull our HTML out of a cramped variable string and back into the template space. The $slot variable in our component template receives whatever content is passed in the @compo nent directive.

Multiple slots

The method we used in Example 4-15 is called the "default" slot; whatever you pass in between @component and @endcomponent is passed to the $slot variable. But you can also have more than just the default slot. Let's imagine a modal with a title, like in Example 4-16.

Example 4-16. A modal view partial with two variables

```
<!-- resources/views/partials/modal.blade.php -->
<div class="modal">
    <div class="modal-header">{{ $title }}</div>
    <div>{{ $slot }}</div>
    <div class="close button etc">...</div>
</div>
```

You can use the @slot directive in your @component calls to pass content to slots other than the default, as you can see in Example 4-17.

Example 4-17. Passing more than one slot to a component

```
@component('partials.modal')
    @slot('title')
        Password validation failure
    @endslot

    <p>The password you have provided is not valid.
    Here are the rules for valid passwords: [...]</p>

    <p><a href="#">...</a></p>
@endcomponent
```

And if you have other variables in your view that don't make sense as a slot, you can still pass an array of content as the second parameter to @component, just like you can with @include. Take a look at Example 4-18.

Example 4-18. Passing data to a component without slots

```
@component('partials.modal', ['class' => 'danger'])
    ...
@endcomponent
```

Aliasing a component to be a directive

There's a clever trick you can use to make your components even easier to call: aliasing. Simply call Blade::component() on the Blade facade—the most common location is the boot() method of the AppServiceProvider—and pass it first the location of the component and second the name of your desired directive, as shown in Example 4-19.

Example 4-19. Aliasing a component to be a directive

```
// AppServiceProvider@boot
Blade::component('partials.modal', 'modal');

<!-- in a template -->
@modal
    Modal content here
@endmodal
```

Importing Facades

This is our first time working with a facade in a namespaced class. We'll cover them in more depth later, but just know that if you use facades in namespaced classes, which is most classes in recent versions of Laravel, you might find errors showing that the facade cannot be found. This is because facades are just normal classes with normal namespaces, but Laravel does a bit of trickery to make them available from the root namespace.

So, in Example 4-19, we'd need to import the Illuminate\Support\Facades\Blade facade at the top of the file.

View Composers and Service Injection

As we covered in Chapter 3, it's simple to pass data to our views from the route definition (see Example 4-20).

Example 4-20. Reminder of how to pass data to views

```
Route::get('passing-data-to-views', function () {
    return view('dashboard')
        ->with('key', 'value');
});
```

There may be times, however, when you find yourself passing the same data over and over to multiple views. Or you might find yourself using a header partial or something similar that requires some data; will you have to pass that data in from every route definition that might ever load that header partial?

Binding Data to Views Using View Composers

Thankfully, there's a simpler way. The solution is called a *view composer*, and it allows you to define that *any time a particular view loads, it should have certain data passed to it*—without the route definition having to pass that data in explicitly.

Let's say you have a sidebar on every page, which is defined in a partial named `partials.sidebar` (*resources/views/partials/sidebar.blade.php*) and then included on every page. This sidebar shows a list of the last seven posts that were published on your site. If it's on every page, every route definition would normally have to grab that list and pass it in, like in Example 4-21.

Example 4-21. Passing sidebar data in from every route

```
Route::get('home', function () {
    return view('home')
        ->with('posts', Post::recent());
});

Route::get('about', function () {
    return view('about')
        ->with('posts', Post::recent());
});
```

That could get annoying quickly. Instead, we're going to use view composers to "share" that variable with a prescribed set of views. We can do this a few ways, so let's start simple and move up.

Sharing a variable globally

First, the simplest option: just globally "share" a variable with every view in your application like in Example 4-22.

Example 4-22. Sharing a variable globally

```
// Some service provider
public function boot()
{
    ...
    view()->share('recentPosts', Post::recent());
}
```

If you want to use `view()->share()`, the best place would be the `boot()` method of a service provider so that the binding runs on every page load. You can create a custom `ViewComposerServiceProvider` (see Chapter 11 for more about service providers), but for now just put it in `App\Providers\AppServiceProvider` in the `boot()` method.

Using `view()->share()` makes the variable accessible to every view in the entire application, however, so it might be overkill.

View-scoped view composers with closures

The next option is to use a closure-based view composer to share variables with a single view, like in Example 4-23.

Example 4-23. Creating a closure-based view composer

```
view()->composer('partials.sidebar', function ($view) {
    $view->with('recentPosts', Post::recent());
});
```

As you can see, we've defined the name of the view we want it shared with in the first parameter (`partials.sidebar`) and then passed a closure to the second parameter; in the closure we've used `$view->with()` to share a variable, but only with a specific view.

View Composers for Multiple Views

Anywhere a view composer is binding to a particular view (like in Example 4-23, which binds to `partials.sidebar`), you can pass an array of view names instead to bind to multiple views.

You can also use an asterisk in the view path, as in `partials.*` or `tasks.*`:

```
view()->composer(
    ['partials.header', 'partials.footer'],
    function () {
        $view->with('recentPosts', Post::recent());
    }
);
```

```
view()->composer('partials.*', function () {
    $view->with('recentPosts', Post::recent());
});
```

View-scoped view composers with classes

Finally, the most flexible but also most complex option is to create a dedicated class for your view composer.

First, let's create the view composer class. There's no formally defined place for view composers to live, but the docs recommend App\Http\ViewComposers. So, let's create App\Http\ViewComposers\RecentPostsComposer like in Example 4-24.

Example 4-24. A view composer

```php
<?php

namespace App\Http\ViewComposers;

use App\Post;
use Illuminate\Contracts\View\View;

class RecentPostsComposer
{
    public function compose(View $view)
    {
        $view->with('recentPosts', Post::recent());
    }
}
```

As you can see, when this composer is called, it runs the compose() method, in which we bind the posts variable to the result of running the Post model's recent() method.

Like the other methods of sharing variables, this view composer needs to have a binding somewhere. Again, you'd likely create a custom ViewComposerServiceProvider, but for now, as seen in Example 4-25, we'll just put it in the boot() method of App\Providers\AppServiceProvider.

Example 4-25. Registering a view composer in AppServiceProvider

```php
public function boot()
{
    view()->composer(
        'partials.sidebar',
        \App\Http\ViewComposers\RecentPostsComposer::class
```

```
    );
}
```

Note that this binding is the same as a closure-based view composer, but instead of passing a closure, we're passing the class name of our view composer. Now, every time Blade renders the `partials.sidebar` view, it'll automatically run our provider and pass the view a `recentPosts` variable set to the results of the `recent()` method on our `Post` model.

Blade Service Injection

There are three primary types of data we're most likely to inject into a view: collections of data to iterate over, single objects that we're displaying on the page, and services that generate data or views.

With a service, the pattern will most likely look like Example 4-26, where we inject an instance of our analytics service into the route definition by typehinting it in the route's method signature, and then pass it into the view.

Example 4-26. Injecting services into a view via the route definition constructor

```
Route::get('backend/sales', function (AnalyticsService $analytics) {
    return view('backend.sales-graphs')
        ->with('analytics', $analytics);
});
```

Just as with view composers, Blade's service injection offers a convenient shortcut to reduce duplication in your route definitions. Normally, the content of a view using our analytics service might look like Example 4-27.

Example 4-27. Using an injected navigation service in a view

```
<div class="finances-display">
    {{ $analytics->getBalance() }} / {{ $analytics->getBudget() }}
</div>
```

Blade service injection makes it easy to inject an instance of a class from the container directly from the view, like in Example 4-28.

Example 4-28. Injecting a service directly into a view

```
@inject('analytics', 'App\Services\Analytics')

<div class="finances-display">
    {{ $analytics->getBalance() }} / {{ $analytics->getBudget() }}
</div>
```

As you can see, this @inject directive has actually made an $analytics variable available, which we're using later in our view.

The first parameter of @inject is the name of the variable you're injecting, and the second parameter is the class or interface that you want to inject an instance of. This is resolved just like when you typehint a dependency in a constructor elsewhere in Laravel; if you're unfamiliar with how that works, check out Chapter 11 to learn more.

Just like view composers, Blade service injection makes it easy to make certain data or functionality available to every instance of a view, without having to inject it via the route definition every time.

Custom Blade Directives

All of the built-in syntax of Blade that we've covered so far—@if, @unless, and so on—are called *directives*. Each Blade directive is a mapping between a pattern (e.g., @if ($condition)) and a PHP output (e.g., <?php if ($condition): ?>).

Directives aren't just for the core; you can actually create your own. You might think directives are good for making little shortcuts to bigger pieces of code—for example, using @button('buttonName') and having it expand to a larger set of button HTML. This isn't a *terrible* idea, but for simple code expansion like this you might be better off including a view partial.

Custom directives tend to be the most useful when they simplify some form of repeated logic. Say we're tired of having to wrap our code with @if (auth()->guest()) (to check if a user is logged in or not) and we want a custom @ifGuest directive. As with view composers, it might be worth having a custom service provider to register these, but for now let's just put it in the boot() method of App\Providers\AppServiceProvider. Take a look at Example 4-29 to see what this binding will look like.

Example 4-29. Binding a custom Blade directive in a service provider

```
public function boot()
{
    Blade::directive('ifGuest', function () {
        return "<?php if (auth()->guest()): ?>";
    });
}
```

We've now registered a custom directive, @ifGuest, which will be replaced with the PHP code <?php if (auth()->guest()): ?>.

This might feel strange. You're writing a *string* that will be returned and then executed as PHP. But what this means is that you can now take the complex, or ugly, or unclear, or repetitive aspects of your PHP templating code and hide them behind clear, simple, and expressive syntax.

Custom Directive Result Caching

You might be tempted to do some logic to make your custom directive faster by performing an operation *in* the binding and then embedding the result within the returned string:

```
Blade::directive('ifGuest', function () {
    // Antipattern! Do not copy.
    $ifGuest = auth()->guest();
    return "<?php if ({$ifGuest}): ?>";
});
```

The problem with this idea is that it assumes this directive will be recreated on every page load. However, Blade caches aggressively, so you're going to find yourself in a bad spot if you try this.

Parameters in Custom Blade Directives

What if you want to accept parameters in your custom logic? Check out Example 4-30.

Example 4-30. Creating a Blade directive with parameters

```
// Binding
Blade::directive('newlinesToBr', function ($expression) {
    return "<?php echo nl2br({$expression}); ?>";
});

// In use
<p>@newlinesToBr($message->body)</p>
```

The $expression parameter received by the closure represents whatever's within the parentheses. As you can see, we then generate a valid PHP code snippet and return it.

$expression Parameter Scoping Before Laravel 5.3

Before Laravel 5.3, the $expression parameter also included *the parentheses themselves*. So, in Example 4-30, $expression (which is $message->body in Laravel 5.3 and later) would have instead been ($message->body), and we would've had to write <?php echo nl2br{$expression}; ?>.

If you find yourself constantly writing the same conditional logic over and over, you should consider a Blade directive.

Example: Using Custom Blade Directives for a Multitenant App

Let's imagine we're building an application that supports *multitenancy*, which means users might be visiting the site from *www.myapp.com*, *client1.myapp.com*, *client2.myapp.com*, or elsewhere.

Suppose we have written a class to encapsulate some of our multitenancy logic and named it Context. This class will capture information and logic about the context of the current visit, such as who the authenticated user is and whether the user is visiting the public website or a client subdomain.

We'll probably frequently resolve that Context class in our views and perform conditionals on it, like in Example 4-31. app('context') is a shortcut to get an instance of a class from the container, which we'll learn more about in Chapter 11.

Example 4-31. Conditionals on context without a custom Blade directive

```
@if (app('context')->isPublic())
    &copy; Copyright MyApp LLC
@else
    &copy; Copyright {{ app('context')->client->name }}
@endif
```

What if we could simplify @if (app('context')->isPublic()) to just @ifPublic? Let's do it. Check out Example 4-32.

Example 4-32. Conditionals on context with a custom Blade directive

```
// Binding
Blade::directive('ifPublic', function () {
    return "<?php if (app('context')->isPublic()): ?>";
});

// In use
@ifPublic
    &copy; Copyright MyApp LLC
@else
    &copy; Copyright {{ app('context')->client->name }}
@endif
```

Since this resolves to a simple if statement, we can still rely on the native @else and @endif conditionals. But if we wanted, we could also create a custom @elseIfClient directive, or a separate @ifClient directive, or really whatever else we want.

Easier Custom Directives for "if" Statements

 While custom Blade directives are powerful, the most common use for them is if statements. So there's a simpler way to create custom "if" directives: `Blade::if()`. Example 4-33 shows how we could refactor Example 4-32 using the `Blade::if()` method:

Example 4-33. Defining a custom "if" Blade directive

```
// Binding
Blade::if('ifPublic', function () {
    return (app('context'))->isPublic();
});
```

You'll use the directives exactly the same way, but as you can see, defining them is a bit simpler. Instead of having to manually type out PHP braces, you can just write a closure that returns a Boolean.

Testing

The most common method of testing views is through application testing, meaning that you're actually calling the route that displays the views and ensuring the views have certain content (see Example 4-34). You can also click buttons or submit forms and ensure that you are redirected to a certain page, or that you see a certain error. (You'll learn more about testing in Chapter 12.)

Example 4-34. Testing that a view displays certain content

```
// EventsTest.php
public function test_list_page_shows_all_events()
{
    $event1 = factory(Event::class)->create();
    $event2 = factory(Event::class)->create();

    $this->get('events')
        ->assertSee($event1->title)
        ->assertSee($event2->title);
}
```

You can also test that a certain view has been passed a particular set of data, which, if it accomplishes your testing goals, is less fragile than checking for certain text on the page. Example 4-35 demonstrates this approach.

Example 4-35. Testing that a view was passed certain content

```
// EventsTest.php
public function test_list_page_shows_all_events()
{
    $event1 = factory(Event::class)->create();
    $event2 = factory(Event::class)->create();

    $response = $this->get('events');

    $response->assertViewHas('events', Event::all());
    $response->assertViewHasAll([
        'events' => Event::all(),
        'title' => 'Events Page',
    ]);
    $response->assertViewMissing('dogs');
}
```

Different Names for Testing Methods Prior to Laravel 5.4

In projects running versions of Laravel prior to 5.4, get() and assertSee() should be replaced by visit() and see().

In 5.3 we gained the ability to pass a closure to assertViewHas(), meaning we can customize how we want to check more complex data structures. Example 4-36 illustrates how we might use this.

Example 4-36. Passing a closure to assertViewHas()

```
// EventsTest.php
public function test_list_page_shows_all_events()
{
    $event1 = factory(Event::class)->create();

    $response = $this->get("events/{ $event->id }");

    $response->assertViewHas('event', function ($event) use ($event1) {
        return $event->id === $event1->id;
    });
}
```

TL;DR

Blade is Laravel's templating engine. Its primary focus is a clear, concise, and expressive syntax with powerful inheritance and extensibility. Its "safe echo" brackets are {{ and }}, its unprotected echo brackets are {!! and !!}, and it has a series of custom tags called directives that all begin with @ (@if and @unless, for example).

You can define a parent template and leave "holes" in it for content using `@yield` and `@section`/`@show`. You can then teach its child views to extend it using `@extends('parent.view')`, and define their sections using `@section`/`@endsection`. You use `@parent` to reference the content of the block's parent.

View composers make it easy to define that, every time a particular view or subview loads, it should have certain information available to it. And service injection allows the view itself to request data straight from the application container.

## CHAPTER 5

Databases and Eloquent

Laravel provides a suite of tools for interacting with your application's databases, but the most notable is Eloquent, Laravel's ActiveRecord ORM (object-relational mapper).

Eloquent is one of Laravel's most popular and influential features. It's a great example of how Laravel is different from the majority of PHP frameworks; in a world of Data-Mapper ORMs that are powerful but complex, Eloquent stands out for its simplicity. There's one class per table, which is responsible for retrieving, representing, and persisting data in that table.

Whether or not you choose to use Eloquent, however, you'll still get a ton of benefit from the other database tools Laravel provides. So, before we dig into Eloquent, we'll start by covering the basics of Laravel's database functionality: migrations, seeders, and the query builder.

Then we'll cover Eloquent: defining your models; inserting, updating, and deleting; customizing your responses with accessors, mutators, and attribute casting; and finally relationships. There's a lot going on here, and it's easy to get overwhelmed, but if we take it one step at a time we'll make it through.

Configuration

Before we get into how to use Laravel's database tools, let's pause for a second and go over how to configure your database credentials and connections.

The configuration for database access lives in *config/database.php* and *.env*. Like many other configuration areas in Laravel, you can define multiple "connections" and then decide which the code will use by default.

Database Connections

By default, there's one connection for each of the drivers, as you can see in Example 5-1.

Example 5-1. The default database connections list

```
'connections' => [

    'sqlite' => [
        'driver' => 'sqlite',
        'database' => env('DB_DATABASE', database_path('database.sqlite')),
        'prefix' => '',
    ],

    'mysql' => [
        'driver' => 'mysql',
        'host' => env('DB_HOST', '127.0.0.1'),
        'port' => env('DB_PORT', '3306'),
        'database' => env('DB_DATABASE', 'forge'),
        'username' => env('DB_USERNAME', 'forge'),
        'password' => env('DB_PASSWORD', ''),
        'unix_socket' => env('DB_SOCKET', ''),
        'charset' => 'utf8',
        'collation' => 'utf8_unicode_ci',
        'prefix' => '',
        'strict' => false,
        'engine' => null,
    ],

    'pgsql' => [
        'driver' => 'pgsql',
        'host' => env('DB_HOST', '127.0.0.1'),
        'port' => env('DB_PORT', '5432'),
        'database' => env('DB_DATABASE', 'forge'),
        'username' => env('DB_USERNAME', 'forge'),
        'password' => env('DB_PASSWORD', ''),
        'charset' => 'utf8',
        'prefix' => '',
        'schema' => 'public',
        'sslmode' => 'prefer',
    ],

    'sqlsrv' => [
        'driver' => 'sqlsrv',
        'host' => env('DB_HOST', 'localhost'),
        'port' => env('DB_PORT', '1433'),
        'database' => env('DB_DATABASE', 'forge'),
        'username' => env('DB_USERNAME', 'forge'),
        'password' => env('DB_PASSWORD', ''),
        'charset' => 'utf8',
```

```
            'prefix' => '',
        ],

    ]
```

Nothing is stopping you from deleting or modifying these named connections or creating your own. You can create new named connections, and you'll be able to set the drivers (MySQL, Postgres, etc.) in them. So, while there's one connection per driver by default, that's not a constraint; you could have five different connections, all with the mysql driver, if you wanted.

Each connection allows you to define the properties necessary for connecting to and customizing each connection type.

There are a few reasons for the idea of multiple drivers. To start with, the "connections" section as it comes out of the box is a simple template that makes it easy to start apps that use any of the supported database connection types. In many apps, you can pick the database connection you'll be using, fill out its information, and even delete the others if you'd like. I usually just keep them all there, in case I might eventually use them.

But there are also some cases where you might need multiple connections within the same application. For example, you might use different database connections for two different types of data, or you might read from one and write to another. Support for multiple connections makes this possible.

Other Database Configuration Options

The *config/database.php* configuration section has quite a few other configuration settings. You can configure Redis access, customize the table name used for migrations, determine the default connection, and toggle whether non-Eloquent calls return stdClass or array instances.

With any service in Laravel that allows connections from multiple sources—sessions can be backed by the database or file storage, the cache can use Redis or Memcached, databases can use MySQL or PostgreSQL—you can define multiple connections and also choose that a particular connection will be the "default," meaning it will be used any time you don't explicitly ask for a particular connection. Here's how you ask for a specific connection, if you want to:

```
$users = DB::connection('secondary')->select('select * from users');
```

[role="less_space pagebreak-before"]' === Migrations

Modern frameworks like Laravel make it easy to define your database structure with code-driven migrations. Every new table, column, index, and key can be defined in code, and any new environment can be brought from bare database to your app's perfect schema in seconds.

Defining Migrations

A migration is a single file that defines two things: the modifications desired when running this migration *up* and, optionally, the modifications desired when running this migration *down*.

"Up" and "Down" in Migrations

Migrations are always run in order by date. Every migration file is named something like this: *2018_10_12_000000_create_users_table.php*. When a new system is migrated, the system grabs each migration, starting at the earliest date, and runs its up() method—you're migrating it "up" at this point. But the migration system also allows you to "roll back" your most recent set of migrations. It'll grab each of them and run its down() method, which should undo whatever changes the up migration made.

So, the up() method of a migration should "do" its migration, and the down() method should "undo" it.

Example 5-2 shows what the default "create users table" migration that comes with Laravel looks like.

Example 5-2. Laravel's default "create users table" migration

```php
<?php

use Illuminate\Database\Schema\Blueprint;
use Illuminate\Database\Migrations\Migration;

class CreateUsersTable extends Migration
{
    /**
     * Run the migrations.
     *
     * @return void
     */
    public function up()
    {
        Schema::create('users', function (Blueprint $table) {
            $table->bigIncrements('id');
            $table->string('name');
            $table->string('email')->unique();
            $table->timestamp('email_verified_at')->nullable();
            $table->string('password');
            $table->rememberToken();
```

```
            $table->timestamps();
        });
    }

    /**
     * Reverse the migrations.
     *
     * @return void
     */
    public function down()
    {
        Schema::dropIfExists('users');
    }
}
```

Email Verification

The email_verified_at column is only present in apps built in
Laravel 5.7 and later. It stores a timestamp indicating when the
user verified their email address.

As you can see, we have an up() method and a down() method. up() tells the migration to create a new table named users with a few fields, and down() tells it to drop the users table.

Creating a migration

As you will see in Chapter 8, Laravel provides a series of command-line tools you can use to interact with your app and generate boilerplate files. One of these commands allows you to create a migration file. You can run it using php artisan make:migration, and it has a single parameter, which is the name of the migration. For example, to create the table we just covered, you would run php artisan make:migration create_users_table.

There are two flags you can optionally pass to this command. --create=*table_name* prefills the migration with code designed to create a table named *table_name*, and --table=*table_name* just prefills the migration for modifications to an existing table. Here are a few examples:

```
php artisan make:migration create_users_table
php artisan make:migration add_votes_to_users_table --table=users
php artisan make:migration create_users_table --create=users
```

Creating tables

We already saw in the default create_users_table migration that our migrations depend on the Schema facade and its methods. Everything we can do in these migrations will rely on the methods of Schema.

To create a new table in a migration, use the create() method—the first parameter is the table name, and the second is a closure that defines its columns:

```
Schema::create('users', function (Blueprint $table) {
    // Create columns here
});
```

Creating columns

To create new columns in a table, whether in a create table call or a modify table call, use the instance of Blueprint that's passed into your closure:

```
Schema::create('users', function (Blueprint $table) {
    $table->string('name');
});
```

Let's look at the various methods available on Blueprint instances for creating columns. I'll describe how they work in MySQL, but if you're using another database, Laravel will just use the closest equivalent.

The following are the simple field Blueprint methods:

integer(*colName*), tinyInteger(*colName*), smallInteger(*colName*), mediumInteger(*colName*), bigInteger(*colName*)
  Adds an INTEGER type column, or one of its many variations

string(*colName, length*)
  Adds a VARCHAR type column with an optional length

binary(*colName*)
  Adds a BLOB type column

boolean(*colName*)
  Adds a BOOLEAN type column (a TINYINT(1) in MySQL)

char(*colName, length*)
  Adds a CHAR column with an optional length

datetime(*colName*)
  Adds a DATETIME column

decimal(*colName, precision, scale*)
  Adds a DECIMAL column, with precision and scale—for example, decimal('*amount*', *5, 2*) specifies a precision of 5 and a scale of 2

double(*colName, total digits, digits after decimal*)
  Adds a DOUBLE column—for example, double('*tolerance*', *12, 8*) specifies 12 digits long, with 8 of those digits to the right of the decimal place, as in 7204.05691739

enum(*colName*, [*choiceOne*, *choiceTwo*])
> Adds an ENUM column, with provided choices

float(*colName*, *precision*, *scale*)
> Adds a FLOAT column (same as double in MySQL)

json(*colName*) *and* jsonb(*colName*)
> Adds a JSON or JSONB column (or a TEXT column in Laravel 5.1)

text(*colName*), mediumText(*colName*), longText(*colName*)
> Adds a TEXT column (or its various sizes)

time(*colName*)
> Adds a TIME column

timestamp(*colName*)
> Adds a TIMESTAMP column

uuid(*colName*)
> Adds a UUID column (CHAR(36) in MySQL)

And these are the special (joined) Blueprint methods:

increments(*colName*) *and* bigIncrements(*colName*)
> Add an unsigned incrementing INTEGER or BIG INTEGER primary key ID

timestamps() *and* nullableTimestamps()
> Adds created_at and updated_at timestamp columns

rememberToken()
> Adds a remember_token column (VARCHAR(100)) for user "remember me" tokens

softDeletes()
> Adds a deleted_at timestamp for use with soft deletes

morphs(*colName*)
> For a provided *colName*, adds an integer colName_id and a string colName_type (e.g., morphs(tag) adds integer tag_id and string tag_type); for use in polymorphic relationships

Building extra properties fluently

Most of the properties of a field definition—its length, for example—are set as the second parameter of the field creation method, as we saw in the previous section. But there are a few other properties that we'll set by chaining more method calls after the creation of the column. For example, this email field is nullable and will be placed (in MySQL) right after the last_name field:

```
Schema::table('users', function (Blueprint $table) {
    $table->string('email')->nullable()->after('last_name');
});
```

The following methods are used to set additional properties of a field:

nullable()
> Allows NULL values to be inserted into this column

default('*default content*')
> Specifies the default content for this column if no value is provided

unsigned()
> Marks integer columns as unsigned (not negative or positive, but just an integer)

first() *(MySQL only)*
> Places the column first in the column order

after(*colName*) *(MySQL only)*
> Places the column after another column in the column order

unique()
> Adds a UNIQUE index

primary()
> Adds a primary key index

index()
> Adds a basic index

Note that unique(), primary(), and index() can also be used outside of the fluent column building context, which we'll cover later.

Dropping tables

If you want to drop a table, there's a dropIfExists() method on Schema that takes one parameter, the table name:

```
Schema::dropIfExists('contacts');
```

Modifying columns

To modify a column, just write the code you would write to create the column as if it were new, and then append a call to the change() method after it.

Required Dependency Before Modifying Columns

Before you modify any columns (or drop any columns in SQLite), you'll need to run composer require doctrine/dbal.

So, if we have a string column named name that has a length of 255 and we want to change its length to 100, this is how we would write it:

```
Schema::table('users', function (Blueprint $table) {
    $table->string('name', 100)->change();
});
```

The same is true if we want to adjust any of its properties that aren't defined in the method name. To make a field nullable, we do this:

```
Schema::table('contacts', function (Blueprint $table) {
    $table->string('deleted_at')->nullable()->change();
});
```

Here's how we rename a column:

```
Schema::table('contacts', function (Blueprint $table)
{
    $table->renameColumn('promoted', 'is_promoted');
});
```

And this is how we drop a column:

```
Schema::table('contacts', function (Blueprint $table)
{
    $table->dropColumn('votes');
});
```

Modifying Multiple Columns at Once in SQLite

If you try to drop or modify multiple columns within a single migration closure and you are using SQLite, you'll run into errors.

In Chapter 12 I recommend that you use SQLite for your testing database, so even if you're using a more traditional database, you may want to consider this a limitation for testing purposes.

However, you don't have to create a new migration for each. Instead, just create multiple calls to Schema::table() within the up() method of your migration:

```
public function up()
{
    Schema::table('contacts', function (Blueprint $table)
    {
        $table->dropColumn('is_promoted');
    });

    Schema::table('contacts', function (Blueprint $table)
    {
        $table->dropColumn('alternate_email');
    });
}
```

Indexes and foreign keys

We've covered how to create, modify, and delete columns. Let's move on to indexing and relating them.

If you're not familiar with indexes, your databases can survive if you just never use them, but they're pretty important for performance optimization and for some data integrity controls with regard to related tables. I'd recommend reading up on them, but if you absolutely must, you can skip this section for now.

Adding indexes. Check out Example 5-3 for examples of how to add indexes to your column.

Example 5-3. Adding column indexes in migrations

```
// After columns are created...
$table->primary('primary_id'); // Primary key; unnecessary if used increments()
$table->primary(['first_name', 'last_name']); // Composite keys
$table->unique('email'); // Unique index
$table->unique('email', 'optional_custom_index_name'); // Unique index
$table->index('amount'); // Basic index
$table->index('amount', 'optional_custom_index_name'); // Basic index
```

Note that the first example, `primary()`, is not necessary if you're using the `increments()` or `bigIncrements()` methods to create your index; this will automatically add a primary key index for you.

Removing indexes. We can remove indexes as shown in Example 5-4.

Example 5-4. Removing column indexes in migrations

```
$table->dropPrimary('contacts_id_primary');
$table->dropUnique('contacts_email_unique');
$table->dropIndex('optional_custom_index_name');

// If you pass an array of column names to dropIndex, it will
// guess the index names for you based on the generation rules
$table->dropIndex(['email', 'amount']);
```

Adding and removing foreign keys. To add a foreign key that defines that a particular column references a column on another table, Laravel's syntax is simple and clear:

```
$table->foreign('user_id')->references('id')->on('users');
```

Here we're adding a `foreign` index on the `user_id` column, showing that it references the `id` column on the `users` table. Couldn't get much simpler.

If we want to specify foreign key constraints, we can do that too, with onDelete() and onUpdate(). For example:

```
$table->foreign('user_id')
    ->references('id')
    ->on('users')
    ->onDelete('cascade');
```

To drop a foreign key, we can either delete it by referencing its index name (which is automatically generated by combining the names of the columns and tables being referenced):

```
$table->dropForeign('contacts_user_id_foreign');
```

or by passing it an array of the fields that it's referencing in the local table:

```
$table->dropForeign(['user_id']);
```

Running Migrations

Once you have your migrations defined, how do you run them? There's an Artisan command for that:

```
php artisan migrate
```

This command runs all "outstanding" migrations (by running the up() method on each). Laravel keeps track of which migrations you have run and which you haven't. Every time you run this command, it checks whether you've run all available migrations, and if you haven't, it'll run any that remain.

There are a few options in this namespace that you can work with. First, you can run your migrations *and* your seeds (which we'll cover next):

```
php artisan migrate --seed
```

You can also run any of the following commands:

migrate:install
> Creates the database table that keeps track of which migrations you have and haven't run; this is run automatically when you run your migrations, so you can basically ignore it.

migrate:reset
> Rolls back every database migration you've run on this instance.

migrate:refresh
> Rolls back every database migration you've run on this instance, and then runs every migration available. It's the same as running migrate:reset and then migrate, one after the other.

migrate:fresh

Drops all of your tables and runs every migration again. It's the same as refresh but doesn't bother with the "down" migrations—it just deletes the tables and then runs the "up" migrations again.

migrate:rollback

Rolls back *just* the migrations that ran the last time you ran migrate, or, with the added option --step=*n*, rolls back the number of migrations you specify.

migrate:status

Shows a table listing every migration, with a Y or N next to each showing whether or not it has run yet in this environment.

 Migrating with Homestead/Vagrant

If you're running migrations on your local machine and your *.env* file points to a database in a Vagrant box, your migrations will fail. You'll need to ssh into your Vagrant box and then run the migrations from there. The same is true for seeds and any other Artisan commands that affect or read from the database.

Seeding

Seeding with Laravel is so simple, it has gained widespread adoption as a part of normal development workflows in a way it hasn't in previous PHP frameworks. There's a *database/seeds* folder that comes with a DatabaseSeeder class, which has a run() method that is called when you call the seeder.

There are two primary ways to run the seeders: along with a migration, or separately.

To run a seeder along with a migration, just add --seed to any migration call:

```
php artisan migrate --seed
php artisan migrate:refresh --seed
```

And to run it independently:

```
php artisan db:seed
php artisan db:seed --class=VotesTableSeeder
```

This will call the run() method of the DatabaseSeeder by default, or the seeder class specified by --class.

Creating a Seeder

To create a seeder, use the make:seeder Artisan command:

```
php artisan make:seeder ContactsTableSeeder
```

You'll now see a `ContactsTableSeeder` class show up in the *database/seeds* directory. Before we edit it, let's add it to the `DatabaseSeeder` class, as shown in Example 5-5, so it will run when we run our seeders.

Example 5-5. Calling a custom seeder from DatabaseSeeder.php

```
// database/seeds/DatabaseSeeder.php
...
    public function run()
    {
        $this->call(ContactsTableSeeder::class);
    }
```

Now let's edit the seeder itself. The simplest thing we can do there is manually insert a record using the DB facade, as illustrated in Example 5-6.

Example 5-6. Inserting database records in a custom seeder

```php
<?php

use Illuminate\Database\Seeder;
use Illuminate\Database\Eloquent\Model;

class ContactsTableSeeder extends Seeder
{
    public function run()
    {
        DB::table('contacts')->insert([
            'name' => 'Lupita Smith',
            'email' => 'lupita@gmail.com',
        ]);
    }
}
```

This will get us a single record, which is a good start. But for truly functional seeds, you'll likely want to loop over some sort of random generator and run this `insert()` many times, right? Laravel has a feature for that.

Model Factories

Model factories define one (or more) patterns for creating fake entries for your database tables. By default each factory is named after an Eloquent class, but you can also just name them after the table if you're not going to work with Eloquent. Example 5-7 shows the same factory set up both ways.

Example 5-7. Defining model factories with Eloquent class and table name keys

```
$factory->define(User::class, function (Faker\Generator $faker) {
    return [
        'name' => $faker->name,
    ];
});

$factory->define('users', function (Faker\Generator $faker) {
    return [
        'name' => $faker->name,
    ];
});
```

Theoretically you can name these factories anything you like, but naming the factory after your Eloquent class is the most idiomatic approach.

Creating a model factory

 Model factories are located in *database/factories*. In Laravel 5.5 and later each factory is usually defined in its own class, with a key (name) and a closure defining how to create a new instance of the defined class. The `$factory->define()` method takes the factory name as the first parameter and a closure that's run for each generation as the second parameter.

 The Model Factory File in Laravel 5.4 and Earlier

In Laravel prior to 5.5, all factories should be defined in *database/factories/ModelFactory.php*. There are no separate classes for each factory until 5.5.

To generate a new factory class, use the Artisan `make:factory` command; just like with naming the factory keys, it's also most common to name factory classes after the Eloquent models they're meant to generate instances of:

```
php artisan make:factory ContactFactory
```

This will generate a new file within the *database/factories* directory called *ContactFactory.php*. The simplest factory we could define for a contact might look something like Example 5-8:

Example 5-8. The simplest possible factory definition

```
$factory->define(Contact::class, function (Faker\Generator $faker) {
    return [
        'name' => 'Lupita Smith',
        'email' => 'lupita@gmail.com',
```

```
    ];
});
```

Now we can use the `factory()` global helper to create an instance of `Contact` in our seeding and testing:

```
// Create one
$contact = factory(Contact::class)->create();

// Create many
factory(Contact::class, 20)->create();
```

However, if we used that factory to create 20 contacts, all 20 would have the same information. That's less useful.

We will get even more benefit from model factories when we take advantage of the instance of `Faker` (*http://bit.ly/2FtyJRr*) that's passed into the closure; `Faker` makes it easy to randomize the creation of structured fake data. The previous example now turns into Example 5-9.

Example 5-9. A simple factory, modified to use Faker

```
$factory->define(Contact::class, function (Faker\Generator $faker) {
    return [
        'name' => $faker->name,
        'email' => $faker->email,
    ];
});
```

Now, every time we create a fake contact using this model factory, all of our properties will be randomly generated.

Guaranteeing the Uniqueness of Randomly Generated Data

If you want to guarantee that the randomly generated values of any given entry are unique compared to the other randomly generated values during that PHP process, you can use Faker's `unique()` method:

```
return ['email' => $faker->unique()->email];
```

Using a model factory

There are two primary contexts in which we'll use model factories: testing, which we'll cover in Chapter 12, and seeding, which we'll cover here. Let's write a seeder using a model factory; take a look at Example 5-10.

Example 5-10. Using model factories

```
factory(Post::class)->create([
    'title' => 'My greatest post ever',
]);

// Pro-level factory; but don't get overwhelmed!
factory(User::class, 20)->create()->each(function ($u) use ($post) {
    $post->comments()->save(factory(Comment::class)->make([
        'user_id' => $u->id,
    ]));
});
```

To create an object, we use the factory() global helper and pass it the name of the factory—which, as we just saw, is the name of the Eloquent class we're generating an instance of. That returns the factory, and then we can run one of two methods on it: make() or create().

Both methods generate an instance of this specified model, using the definition in the factory file. The difference is that make() creates the instance but doesn't (yet) save it to the database, whereas create() saves it to the database instantly. You can see both in use in the two examples in Example 5-10.

The second example will make more sense once we cover relationships in Eloquent later in this chapter.

Overriding properties when calling a model factory. If you pass an array to either make() or create(), you can override specific keys from the factory, like we did in Example 5-10 to set the user_id on the comment and to manually set the title of our post.

Generating more than one instance with a model factory. If you pass a number as the second parameter to the factory() helper, you can specify that you're creating more than one instance. Instead of returning a single instance, it'll return a collection of instances. This means you can treat the result like an array, you can associate each of its instances with another entity, or you can use other entity methods on each instance—like we used each() in Example 5-10 to add a comment from each newly created user.

Pro-level model factories

Now that we've covered the most common uses for and arrangements of model factories, let's dive into some of the more complicated ways we can use them.

Attaching relationships when defining model factories. Sometimes you need to create a related item along with the item you're creating. You can use a closure on that property to create a related item and pull its ID, as shown in Example 5-11.

Example 5-11. Creating a related term item in a seeder

```
$factory->define(Contact::class, function (Faker\Generator $faker) {
    return [
        'name' => 'Lupita Smith',
        'email' => 'lupita@gmail.com',
        'company_id' => function () {
            return factory(App\Company::class)->create()->id;
        },
    ];
});
```

Each closure is passed a single parameter, which contains the array form of the generated item up until that point. This can be used in other ways, as demonstrated in Example 5-12.

Example 5-12. Using values from other parameters in a seeder

```
$factory->define(Contact::class, function (Faker\Generator $faker) {
    return [
        'name' => 'Lupita Smith',
        'email' => 'lupita@gmail.com',
        'company_id' => function () {
            return factory(App\Company::class)->create()->id;
        },
        'company_size' => function ($contact) {
            // Uses the "company_id" property generated above
            return App\Company::find($contact['company_id'])->size;
        },
    ];
});
```

Defining and accessing multiple model factory states. Let's go back to *ContactFactory.php* (from Example 5-8 and Example 5-9) for a second. We have a base `Contact` factory defined:

```
$factory->define(Contact::class, function (Faker\Generator $faker) {
    return [
        'name' => $faker->name,
        'email' => $faker->email,
    ];
});
```

But sometimes you need more than one factory for a class of object. What if we need to be able to add some contacts who are very important people (VIPs)? We can use the `state()` method to define a second factory state for this, as seen in Example 5-13. The first parameter to `state()` is still the name of the entity you're generating, the second is the name of your state, and the third is an array of any attributes you want to specifically set for this state.

Example 5-13. Defining multiple factory states for the same model

```
$factory->define(Contact::class, function (Faker\Generator $faker) {
    return [
        'name' => $faker->name,
        'email' => $faker->email,
    ];
});

$factory->state(Contact::class, 'vip', [
    'vip' => true,
]);
```

If the modified attributes require more than a simple static value, you can pass a closure instead of an array as the second parameter and then return an array of the attributes you want to modify, like in Example 5-14.

Example 5-14. Specifying a factory state with a closure

```
$factory->state(Contact::class, 'vip', function (Faker\Generator $faker) {
    return [
        'vip' => true,
        'company' => $faker->company,
    ];
});
```

Now, let's make an instance of a specific state:

```
$vip = factory(Contact::class, 'vip')->create();

$vips = factory(Contact::class, 'vip', 3)->create();
```

Factory States Prior to Laravel 5.3

In projects running versions of Laravel prior to 5.3, factory states were called factory types, and you'll want to use `$factory->defineAs()` instead of `$factory->state()`. You can learn more about this in the 5.2 docs (*http://bit.ly/2Fmnaew*).

Whew. That was a lot. Don't worry if that was tough to follow—the last bit was definitely higher-level stuff. Let's get back down to the basics and talk about the core of Laravel's database tooling: the query builder.

Query Builder

Now that you're connected and you've migrated and seeded your tables, let's get started with how to use the database tools. At the core of every piece of Laravel's database functionality is the query builder, a fluent interface for interacting with several different types of databases with a single clear API.

What Is a Fluent Interface?

A fluent interface is one that primarily uses method chaining to provide a simpler API to the end user. Rather than expecting all of the relevant data to be passed into either a constructor or a method call, fluent call chains can be built gradually, with consecutive calls. Consider this comparison:

```
// Non-fluent:
$users = DB::select(['table' => 'users', 'where' => ['type' => 'donor']]);

// Fluent:
$users = DB::table('users')->where('type', 'donor')->get();
```

Laravel's database architecture can connect to MySQL, Postgres, SQLite, and SQL Server through a single interface, with just the change of a few configuration settings.

If you've ever used a PHP framework, you've likely used a tool that allows you to run "raw" SQL queries with basic escaping for security. The query builder is that, with a lot of convenience layers and helpers on top. So, let's start with some simple calls.

Basic Usage of the DB Facade

Before we get into building complex queries with fluent method chaining, let's take a look at a few sample query builder commands. The DB facade is used both for query builder chaining and for simpler raw queries, as illustrated in Example 5-15.

Example 5-15. Sample raw SQL and query builder usage

```
// Basic statement
DB::statement('drop table users');

// Raw select, and parameter binding
DB::select('select * from contacts where validated = ?', [true]);
```

```
// Select using the fluent builder
$users = DB::table('users')->get();

// Joins and other complex calls
DB::table('users')
    ->join('contacts', function ($join) {
        $join->on('users.id', '=', 'contacts.user_id')
            ->where('contacts.type', 'donor');
    })
    ->get();
```

Raw SQL

As you saw in Example 5-15, it's possible to make any raw call to the database using the DB facade and the `statement()` method: `DB::statement('SQL statement here')`.

But there are also specific methods for various common actions: `select()`, `insert()`, `update()`, and `delete()`. These are still raw calls, but there are differences. First, using `update()` and `delete()` will return the number of rows affected, whereas `statement()` won't; second, with these methods it's clearer to future developers exactly what sort of statement you're making.

Raw selects

The simplest of the specific DB methods is `select()`. You can run it without any additional parameters:

```
$users = DB::select('select * from users');
```

This will return a collection of `stdClass` objects.

Illuminate Collections

Prior to Laravel 5.3, the DB facade returned a `stdClass` object for methods that return only one row (like `first()`) and an array for any that return multiple rows (like `all()`). In Laravel 5.3+, the DB facade, like Eloquent, returns a collection for any method that returns (or can return) multiple rows. The DB facade returns an instance of `Illuminate\Support\Collection` and Eloquent returns an instance of `Illuminate\Database\Eloquent\Collection`, which extends `Illuminate\Support\Collection` with a few Eloquent-specific methods.

`Collection` is like a PHP array with superpowers, allowing you to run `map()`, `filter()`, `reduce()`, `each()`, and much more on your data. You can learn more about collections in Chapter 17.

Parameter bindings and named bindings

Laravel's database architecture allows for the use of PDO parameter binding, which protects your queries from potential SQL attacks. Passing a parameter to a statement is as simple as replacing the value in your statement with a ?, then adding the value to the second parameter of your call:

```
$usersOfType = DB::select(
    'select * from users where type = ?',
    [$type]
);
```

You can also name those parameters for clarity:

```
$usersOfType = DB::select(
    'select * from users where type = :type',
    ['type' => $userType]
);
```

Raw inserts

From here, the raw commands all look pretty much the same. Raw inserts look like this:

```
DB::insert(
    'insert into contacts (name, email) values (?, ?)',
    ['sally', 'sally@me.com']
);
```

Raw updates

Updates look like this:

```
$countUpdated = DB::update(
    'update contacts set status = ? where id = ?',
    ['donor', $id]
);
```

Raw deletes

And deletes look like this:

```
$countDeleted = DB::delete(
    'delete from contacts where archived = ?',
    [true]
);
```

Chaining with the Query Builder

Up until now, we haven't actually used the query builder, per se. We've just used simple method calls on the DB facade. Let's actually build some queries.

The query builder makes it possible to chain methods together to, you guessed it, *build a query*. At the end of your chain you'll use some method—likely `get()`—to trigger the actual execution of the query you've just built.

Let's take a look at a quick example:

```
$usersOfType = DB::table('users')
    ->where('type', $type)
    ->get();
```

Here, we built our query—users table, `$type` type—and then we executed the query and got our result.

Let's take a look at what methods the query builder allows you to chain. The methods can be split up into what I'll call constraining methods, modifying methods, conditional methods, and ending/returning methods.

Constraining methods

These methods take the query as it is and constrain it to return a smaller subset of possible data:

`select()`

Allows you to choose which columns you're selecting:

```
$emails = DB::table('contacts')
    ->select('email', 'email2 as second_email')
    ->get();
// Or
$emails = DB::table('contacts')
    ->select('email')
    ->addSelect('email2 as second_email')
    ->get();
```

`where()`

Allows you to limit the scope of what's being returned using WHERE. By default, the signature of the `where()` method is that it takes three parameters—the column, the comparison operator, and the value:

```
$newContacts = DB::table('contact')
    ->where('created_at', '>', now()->subDay())
    ->get();
```

However, if your comparison is =, which is the most common comparison, you can drop the second operator:

```
$vipContacts = DB::table('contacts')->where('vip',true)->get();
```

If you want to combine `where()` statements, you can either chain them after each other, or pass an array of arrays:

```
$newVips = DB::table('contacts')
    ->where('vip', true)
    ->where('created_at', '>', now()->subDay());
// Or
$newVips = DB::table('contacts')->where([
    ['vip', true],
    ['created_at', '>', now()->subDay()],
]);
```

orWhere()

Creates simple OR WHERE statements:

```
$priorityContacts = DB::table('contacts')
    ->where('vip', true)
    ->orWhere('created_at', '>', now()->subDay())
    ->get();
```

To create a more complex OR WHERE statement with multiple conditions, pass orWhere() a closure:

```
$contacts = DB::table('contacts')
    ->where('vip', true)
    ->orWhere(function ($query) {
        $query->where('created_at', '>', now()->subDay())
            ->where('trial', false);
    })
    ->get();
```

Potential Confusion with Multiple where() and orWhere() Calls

If you are using orWhere() calls in conjunction with multiple where() calls, you need to be very careful to ensure the query is doing what you think it is. This isn't because of any fault with Laravel, but because a query like the following might not do what you expect:

```
$canEdit = DB::table('users')
    ->where('admin', true)
    ->orWhere('plan', 'premium')
    ->where('is_plan_owner', true)
    ->get();

SELECT * FROM users
    WHERE admin = 1
    OR plan = 'premium'
    AND is_plan_owner = 1;
```

If you want to write SQL that says "if this OR (this and this)," which is clearly the intention in the previous example, you'll want to pass a closure into the orWhere() call:

```
$canEdit = DB::table('users')
    ->where('admin', true)
    ->orWhere(function ($query) {
        $query->where('plan', 'premium')
            ->where('is_plan_owner', true);
    })
    ->get();

SELECT * FROM users
    WHERE admin = 1
    OR (plan = 'premium' AND is_plan_owner = 1);
```

whereBetween(*colName*, [*low, high*])

Allows you to scope a query to return only rows where a column is between two values (inclusive of the two values):

```
$mediumDrinks = DB::table('drinks')
    ->whereBetween('size', [6, 12])
    ->get();
```

The same works for whereNotBetween(), but it will select the inverse.

whereIn(*colName*, [*1, 2, 3*])

Allows you to scope a query to return only rows where a column value is in an explicitly provided list of options:

```
$closeBy = DB::table('contacts')
    ->whereIn('state', ['FL', 'GA', 'AL'])
    ->get();
```

The same works for whereNotIn(), but it will select the inverse.

whereNull(*colName*) *and* whereNotNull(*colName*)

Allow you to select only rows where a given column is NULL or is NOT NULL, respectively.

whereRaw()

Allows you to pass in a raw, unescaped string to be added after the WHERE statement:

```
$goofs = DB::table('contacts')->whereRaw('id = 12345')->get()
```

Beware of SQL Injection!

Any SQL queries passed to whereRaw() will not be escaped. Use this method carefully and infrequently; this is a prime opportunity for SQL injection attacks in your app.

whereExists()

Allows you to select only rows that, when passed into a provided subquery, return at least one row. Imagine you only want to get those users who have left at least one comment:

```
$commenters = DB::table('users')
    ->whereExists(function ($query) {
        $query->select('id')
            ->from('comments')
            ->whereRaw('comments.user_id = users.id');
    })
    ->get();
```

distinct()

Selects only rows where the selected data is unique when compared to the other rows in the returned data. Usually this is paired with select(), because if you use a primary key, there will be no duplicated rows:

```
$lastNames = DB::table('contacts')->select('city')->distinct()->get();
```

Modifying methods

These methods change the way the query's results will be output, rather than just limiting its results:

orderBy(*colName, direction*)

Orders the results. The second parameter may be either asc (the default, ascending order) or desc (descending order):

```
$contacts = DB::table('contacts')
    ->orderBy('last_name', 'asc')
    ->get();
```

`groupBy()` *and* `having()` *or* `havingRaw()`

Groups your results by a column. Optionally, `having()` and `havingRaw()` allow you to filter your results based on properties of the groups. For example, you could look for only cities with at least 30 people in them:

```
$populousCities = DB::table('contacts')
    ->groupBy('city')
    ->havingRaw('count(contact_id) > 30')
    ->get();
```

`skip()` *and* `take()`

Most often used for pagination, these allow you to define how many rows to return and how many to skip before starting the return—like a page number and a page size in a pagination system:

```
// returns rows 31-40
$page4 = DB::table('contacts')->skip(30)->take(10)->get();
```

`latest(`*colName*`)` *and* `oldest(`*colName*`)`

Sort by the passed column (or `created_at` if no column name is passed) in descending (`latest()`) or ascending (`oldest()`) order.

`inRandomOrder()`

Sorts the result randomly.

Conditional methods

There are two methods, available in Laravel 5.2 and later, that allow you to condition-ally apply their "contents" (a closure you pass to them) based on the Boolean state of a value you pass in:

`when()`

Given a truthy first parameter, applies the query modification contained in the closure; given a falsy first parameter, it does nothing. Note that the first parame-ter could be a Boolean (e.g., `$ignoreDrafts`, set to `true` or `false`), an optional value (`$status`, pulled from user input and defaulting to `null`), or a closure that returns either; what matters is that it evaluates to truthy or falsy. For example:

```
$status = request('status'); // Defaults to null if not set

$posts = DB::table('posts')
    ->when($status, function ($query) use ($status) {
        return $query->where('status', $status);
    })
    ->get();

// Or
$posts = DB::table('posts')
```

```
    ->when($ignoreDrafts, function ($query) {
        return $query->where('draft', false);
    })
    ->get();
```

You can also pass a third parameter, another closure, which will only be applied if the first parameter is falsy.

unless()

The exact inverse of when(). If the first parameter is falsy, it will run the second closure.

Ending/returning methods

These methods stop the query chain and trigger the execution of the SQL query. Without one of these at the end of the query chain, your return will always just be an instance of the query builder; chain one of these onto a query builder and you'll actually get a result:

get()

Gets all results for the built query:

```
$contacts = DB::table('contacts')->get();
$vipContacts = DB::table('contacts')->where('vip', true)->get();
```

first() *and* firstOrFail()

Get only the first result—like get(), but with a LIMIT 1 added:

```
$newestContact = DB::table('contacts')
    ->orderBy('created_at', 'desc')
    ->first();
```

first() fails silently if there are no results, whereas firstOrFail() will throw an exception.

If you pass an array of column names to either method, it will return the data for just those columns instead of all columns.

find(*id*) *and* findOrFail(*id*)

Like first(), but you pass in an ID value that corresponds to the primary key to look up. find() fails silently if a row with that ID doesn't exist, while findOrFail() will throw an exception:

```
$contactFive = DB::table('contacts')->find(5);
```

value()

Plucks just the value from a single field from the first row. Like first(), but if you only want a single column:

```
$newestContactEmail = DB::table('contacts')
    ->orderBy('created_at', 'desc')
    ->value('email');
```

count()

Returns an integer count of all of the matching results:

```
$countVips = DB::table('contacts')
    ->where('vip', true)
    ->count();
```

min() *and* max()

Return the minimum or maximum value of a particular column:

```
$highestCost = DB::table('orders')->max('amount');
```

sum() *and* avg()

Return the sum or average of all of the values in a particular column:

```
$averageCost = DB::table('orders')
    ->where('status', 'completed')
    ->avg('amount');
```

Writing raw queries inside query builder methods with DB::raw

You've already seen a few custom methods for raw statements—for example, select() has a selectRaw() counterpart that allows you to pass in a string for the query builder to place after the WHERE statement.

You can also, however, pass in the result of a DB::raw() call to almost any method in the query builder to achieve the same result:

```
$contacts = DB::table('contacts')
    ->select(DB::raw('*, (score * 100) AS integer_score'))
    ->get();
```

Joins

Joins can sometimes be a pain to define, and there's only so much a framework can do to make them simpler, but the query builder does its best. Let's look at a sample:

```
$users = DB::table('users')
    ->join('contacts', 'users.id', '=', 'contacts.user_id')
    ->select('users.*', 'contacts.name', 'contacts.status')
    ->get();
```

The join() method creates an inner join. You can also chain together multiple joins one after another, or use leftJoin() to get a left join.

Finally, you can create more complex joins by passing a closure into the join() method:

```
DB::table('users')
    ->join('contacts', function ($join) {
        $join
            ->on('users.id', '=', 'contacts.user_id')
            ->orOn('users.id', '=', 'contacts.proxy_user_id');
    })
    ->get();
```

Unions

You can union two queries (join their results together into one result set) by creating
them first and then using the union() or unionAll() method:

```
$first = DB::table('contacts')
    ->whereNull('first_name');

$contacts = DB::table('contacts')
    ->whereNull('last_name')
    ->union($first)
    ->get();
```

Inserts

The insert() method is pretty simple. Pass it an array to insert a single row or an
array of arrays to insert multiple rows, and use insertGetId() instead of insert() to
get the autoincrementing primary key ID back as a return:

```
$id = DB::table('contacts')->insertGetId([
    'name' => 'Abe Thomas',
    'email' => 'athomas1987@gmail.com',
]);

DB::table('contacts')->insert([
    ['name' => 'Tamika Johnson', 'email' => 'tamikaj@gmail.com'],
    ['name' => 'Jim Patterson', 'email' => 'james.patterson@hotmail.com'],
]);
```

Updates

Updates are also simple. Create your update query and, instead of get() or first(),
just use update() and pass it an array of parameters:

```
DB::table('contacts')
    ->where('points', '>', 100)
    ->update(['status' => 'vip']);
```

You can also quickly increment and decrement columns using the increment() and
decrement() methods. The first parameter of each is the column name, and the sec‐
ond (optional) is the number to increment/decrement by:

```
DB::table('contacts')->increment('tokens', 5);
DB::table('contacts')->decrement('tokens');
```

Deletes

Deletes are even simpler. Build your query and then end it with `delete()`:

```
DB::table('users')
    ->where('last_login', '<', now()->subYear())
    ->delete();
```

You can also truncate the table, which deletes every row and also resets the autoincrementing ID:

```
DB::table('contacts')->truncate();
```

JSON operations

If you have JSON columns, you can update or select rows based on aspects of the JSON structure by using the arrow syntax to traverse children:

```
// Select all records where the "isAdmin" property of the "options"
// JSON column is set to true
DB::table('users')->where('options->isAdmin', true)->get();

// Update all records, setting the "verified" property
// of the "options" JSON column to true
DB::table('users')->update(['options->isVerified', true]);
```

 This is a new feature since Laravel 5.3.

Transactions

If you're not familiar with database transactions, they're a tool that allows you to wrap up a series of database queries to be performed in a batch, which you can choose to roll back, undoing the entire series of queries. Transactions are often used to ensure that *all* or *none*, but not *some*, of a series of related queries are performed—if one fails, the ORM will roll back the entire series of queries.

With the Laravel query builder's transaction feature, if any exceptions are thrown at any point within the transaction closure, all the queries in the transaction will be rolled back. If the transaction closure finishes successfully, all the queries will be committed and not rolled back.

Let's take a look at the sample transaction in Example 5-16.

Example 5-16. A simple database transaction

```
DB::transaction(function () use ($userId, $numVotes) {
    // Possibly failing DB query
    DB::table('users')
        ->where('id', $userId)
        ->update(['votes' => $numVotes]);
```

```
// Caching query that we don't want to run if the above query fails
DB::table('votes')
    ->where('user_id', $userId)
    ->delete();
});
```

In this example, we can assume we had some previous process that summarized the number of votes from the votes table for a given user. We want to cache that number in the users table and then wipe those votes from the votes table. But, of course, we don't want to wipe the votes *until* the update to the users table has run successfully. And we don't want to keep the updated number of votes in the users table if the votes table deletion fails.

If anything goes wrong with either query, the other won't be applied. That's the magic of database transactions.

Note that you can also manually begin and end transactions—and this applies both for query builder queries and for Eloquent queries. Start with DB::beginTransaction(), end with DB::commit(), and abort with DB::rollBack():

```
DB::beginTransaction();

// Take database actions

if ($badThingsHappened {
    DB::rollBack();
}

// Take other database actions

DB::commit();
```

Introduction to Eloquent

Now that we've covered the query builder, let's talk about Eloquent, Laravel's flagship database tool that's built on the query builder.

Eloquent is an ActiveRecord ORM, which means it's a database abstraction layer that provides a single interface to interact with multiple database types. "ActiveRecord" means that a single Eloquent class is responsible for not only providing the ability to interact with the table as a whole (e.g., User::all() gets all users), but also representing an individual table row (e.g., $sharon = new User). Additionally, each instance is capable of managing its own persistence; you can call $sharon->save() or $sharon->delete().

Eloquent has a primary focus on simplicity, and like the rest of the framework, it relies on "convention over configuration" to allow you to build powerful models with minimal code.

For example, you can perform all of the operations in Example 5-18 with the model defined in Example 5-17.

Example 5-17. The simplest Eloquent model

```php
<?php

use Illuminate\Database\Eloquent\Model;

class Contact extends Model {}
```

Example 5-18. Operations achievable with the simplest Eloquent model

```php
// In a controller
public function save(Request $request)
{
    // Create and save a new contact from user input
    $contact = new Contact();
    $contact->first_name = $request->input('first_name');
    $contact->last_name = $request->input('last_name');
    $conatct->email = $request->input('email');
    $contact->save();

    return redirect('contacts');
}

public function show($contactId)
{
    // Return a JSON representation of a contact based on a URL segment;
    // if the contact doesn't exist, throw an exception
    return Contact::findOrFail($contactId);
}

public function vips()
{
    // Unnecessarily complex example, but still possible with basic Eloquent
    // class; adds a "formalName" property to every VIP entry
    return Contact::where('vip', true)->get()->map(function ($contact) {
        $contact->formalName = "The exalted {$contact->first_name} of the
          {$contact->last_name}s";

        return $contact;
    });
}
```

How? Convention. Eloquent assumes the table name (`Contact` becomes `contacts`), and with that you have a fully functional Eloquent model.

Let's cover how we work with Eloquent models.

Creating and Defining Eloquent Models

First, let's create a model. There's an Artisan command for that:

```
php artisan make:model Contact
```

This is what we'll get, in *app/Contact.php*:

```php
<?php

namespace App;

use Illuminate\Database\Eloquent\Model;

class Contact extends Model
{
    //
}
```

Creating a Migration Along with Your Model

If you want to automatically create a migration when you create
your model, pass the -m or --migration flag:

```
php artisan make:model Contact --migration
```

Table name

The default behavior for table names is that Laravel "snake cases" and pluralizes your
class name, so SecondaryContact would access a table named secondary_contacts.
If you'd like to customize the name, set the $table property explicitly on the model:

```
protected $table = 'contacts_secondary';
```

Primary key

Laravel assumes, by default, that each table will have an autoincrementing integer primary key, and it will be named id.

If you want to change the name of your primary key, change the $primaryKey prop-
erty:

```
protected $primaryKey = 'contact_id';
```

And if you want to set it to be nonincrementing, use:

```
public $incrementing = false;
```

Timestamps

Eloquent expects every table to have `created_at` and `updated_at` timestamp columns. If your table won't have them, disable the `$timestamps` functionality:

```
public $timestamps = false;
```

You can customize the format Eloquent uses to store your timestamps to the database by setting the `$dateFormat` class property to a custom string. The string will be parsed using PHP's `date()` syntax, so the following example will store the date as seconds since the Unix epoch:

```
protected $dateFormat = 'U';
```

Retrieving Data with Eloquent

Most of the time you pull data from your database with Eloquent, you'll use static calls on your Eloquent model.

Let's start by getting everything:

```
$allContacts = Contact::all();
```

That was easy. Let's filter it a bit:

```
$vipContacts = Contact::where('vip', true)->get();
```

We can see that the `Eloquent` facade gives us the ability to chain constraints, and from there the constraints get very familiar:

```
$newestContacts = Contact::orderBy('created_at', 'desc')
    ->take(10)
    ->get();
```

It turns out that once you move past the initial facade name, you're just working with Laravel's query builder. You can do a lot more—we'll cover that soon—but everything you can do with the query builder on the `DB` facade you can do on your Eloquent objects.

Get one

Like we covered earlier in the chapter, you can use `first()` to return only the first record from a query, or `find()` to pull just the record with the provided ID. For either, if you append "OrFail" to the method name, it will throw an exception if there are no matching results. This makes `findOrFail()` a common tool for looking up an entity by a URL segment (or throwing an exception if a matching entity doesn't exist), like you can see in Example 5-19.

Example 5-19. Using an Eloquent OrFail() method in a controller method

```
// ContactController
public function show($contactId)
{
    return view('contacts.show')
        ->with('contact', Contact::findOrFail($contactId));
}
```

Any method intended to return a single record (`first()`, `firstOrFail()`, `find()`, or `findOrFail()`) will return an instance of the Eloquent class. So, `Contact::first()` will return an instance of the class `Contact` with the data from the first row in the table filling it out.

Exceptions

As you can see in Example 5-19, we don't need to catch Eloquent's model not found exception (`Illuminate\Database\Eloquent\ModelNotFoundException`) in our controllers; Laravel's routing system will catch it and throw a 404 for us.

You could, of course, catch that particular exception and handle it, if you'd like.

Get many

`get()` works with Eloquent just like it does in normal query builder calls—build a query and call `get()` at the end to get the results:

```
$vipContacts = Contact::where('vip', true)->get();
```

However, there is an Eloquent-only method, `all()`, which you'll often see people use when they want to get an unfiltered list of all data in the table:

```
$contacts = Contact::all();
```

Using get() Instead of all()

Any time you can use `all()`, you could use `get()`. `Contact::get()` has the same response as `Contact::all()`. However, the moment you start modifying your query—adding a `where()` filter, for example—`all()` will no longer work, but `get()` will continue working.

So, even though `all()` is very common, I'd recommend using `get()` for everything, and ignoring the fact that `all()` even exists.

The other thing that's different about Eloquent's `get()` method (versus `all()`) is that, prior to Laravel 5.3, it returned an array of models instead of a collection. In 5.3 and later, they both return collections.

Chunking responses with chunk()

If you've ever needed to process a large amount (thousands or more) of records at a time, you may have run into memory or locking issues. Laravel makes it possible to break your requests into smaller pieces (chunks) and process them in batches, keeping the memory load of your large request smaller. Example 5-20 illustrates the use of chunk() to split a query into "chunks" of 100 records each.

Example 5-20. Chunking an Eloquent query to limit memory usage

```
Contact::chunk(100, function ($contacts) {
    foreach ($contacts as $contact) {
        // Do something with $contact
    }
});
```

Aggregates

The aggregates that are available on the query builder are available on Eloquent queries as well. For example:

```
$countVips = Contact::where('vip', true)->count();
$sumVotes = Contact::sum('votes');
$averageSkill = User::avg('skill_level');
```

Inserts and Updates with Eloquent

Inserting and updating values is one of the places where Eloquent starts to diverge from normal query builder syntax.

Inserts

There are two primary ways to insert a new record using Eloquent.

First, you can create a new instance of your Eloquent class, set your properties manually, and call save() on that instance, like in Example 5-21.

Example 5-21. Inserting an Eloquent record by creating a new instance

```
$contact = new Contact;
$contact->name = 'Ken Hirata';
$contact->email = 'ken@hirata.com';
$contact->save();

// or

$contact = new Contact([
    'name' => 'Ken Hirata',
    'email' => 'ken@hirata.com',
```

```
]);
$contact->save();

// or

$contact = Contact::make([
    'name' => 'Ken Hirata',
    'email' => 'ken@hirata.com',
]);
$contact->save();
```

Until you save(), this instance of Contact represents the contact fully—except it has never been saved to the database. That means it doesn't have an id, if the application quits it won't persist, and it doesn't have its created_at and updated_at values set.

You can also pass an array to Model::create(), as shown in Example 5-22. Unlike make(), create() saves the instance to the database as soon as it's called.

Example 5-22. Inserting an Eloquent record by passing an array to create()

```
$contact = Contact::create([
    'name' => 'Keahi Hale',
    'email' => 'halek481@yahoo.com',
]);
```

Also be aware that in any context where you are passing an array (to new Model(), Model::make(), Model::create(), or Model::update()), every property you set via Model::create() has to be approved for "mass assignment," which we'll cover shortly. This is not necessary with the first example in Example 5-21, where you assign each property individually.

Note that if you're using Model::create(), you don't need to save() the instance—that's handled as a part of the model's create() method.

Updates

Updating records looks very similar to inserting. You can get a specific instance, change its properties, and then save, or you can make a single call and pass an array of updated properties. Example 5-23 illustrates the first approach.

Example 5-23. Updating an Eloquent record by updating an instance and saving

```
$contact = Contact::find(1);
$contact->email = 'natalie@parkfamily.com';
$contact->save();
```

Since this record already exists, it will already have a `created_at` timestamp and an `id`, which will stay the same, but the `updated_at` field will be changed to the current date and time. Example 5-24 illustrates the second approach.

Example 5-24. Updating one or more Eloquent records by passing an array to the update() method

```
Contact::where('created_at', '<', now()->subYear())
    ->update(['longevity' => 'ancient']);

// or

$contact = Contact::find(1);
$contact->update(['longevity' => 'ancient']);
```

This method expects an array where each key is the column name and each value is the column value.

Mass assignment

We've looked at a few examples of how to pass arrays of values into Eloquent class methods. However, none of these will actually work until you define which fields are "fillable" on the model.

The goal of this is to protect you from (possibly malicious) user input accidentally setting new values on fields you don't want changed. Consider the common scenario in Example 5-25.

Example 5-25. Updating an Eloquent model using the entirety of a request's input

```
// ContactController
public function update(Contact $contact, Request $request)
{
    $contact->update($request->all());
}
```

If you're not familiar with the Illuminate `Request` object, Example 5-25 will take every piece of user input and pass it to the `update()` method. That `all()` method includes things like URL parameters and form inputs, so a malicious user could easily add some things in there, like `id` and `owner_id`, that you likely don't want updated.

Thankfully, that won't actually work until you define your model's fillable fields. You can either whitelist the fillable fields, or blacklist the "guarded" fields to determine which fields can or cannot be edited via "mass assignment"—that is, by passing an array of values into either `create()` or `update()`. Note that nonfillable properties can

still be changed by direct assignment (e.g., $contact->password = 'abc';).
Example 5-26 shows both approaches.

Example 5-26. Using Eloquent's fillable or guarded properties to define mass-assignable fields

```
class Contact
{
    protected $fillable = ['name', 'email'];

    // or

    protected $guarded = ['id', 'created_at', 'updated_at', 'owner_id'];
}
```

Using Request::only() with Eloquent Mass Assignment

In Example 5-25, we needed Eloquent's mass assignment guard because we were using the all() method on the Request object to pass in the *entirety* of the user input.

Eloquent's mass assignment protection is a great tool here, but there's also a helpful trick to keep you from accepting any old input from the user.

The Request class has an only() method that allows you to pluck only a few keys from the user input. So now you can do this:

```
Contact::create($request->only('name', 'email'));
```

firstOrCreate() and firstOrNew()

Sometimes you want to tell your application, "Get me an instance with these properties, or if it doesn't exist, create it." This is where the firstOr*() methods come in.

The firstOrCreate() and firstOrNew() methods take an array of keys and values as their first parameter:

```
$contact = Contact::firstOrCreate(['email' => 'luis.ramos@myacme.com']);
```

They'll both look for and retrieve the first record matching those parameters, and if there are no matching records, they'll create an instance with those properties; firstOrCreate() will persist that instance to the database and then return it, while firstOrNew() will return it without saving it.

If you pass an array of values as the second parameter, those values will be added to the created entry (if it's created) but *won't* be used to look up whether the entry exists.

Deleting with Eloquent

Deleting with Eloquent is very similar to updating with Eloquent, but with (optional) soft deletes, you can archive your deleted items for later inspection or even recovery.

Normal deletes

The simplest way to delete a model record is to call the `delete()` method on the instance itself:

```
$contact = Contact::find(5);
$contact->delete();
```

However, if you only have the ID, there's no reason to look up an instance just to delete it; you can pass an ID or an array of IDs to the model's `destroy()` method to delete them directly:

```
Contact::destroy(1);
// or
Contact::destroy([1, 5, 7]);
```

Finally, you can delete all of the results of a query:

```
Contact::where('updated_at', '<', now()->subYear())->delete();
```

Soft deletes

Soft deletes mark database rows as deleted without actually deleting them from the database. This gives you the ability to inspect them later, to have records that show more than "no information, deleted" when displaying historic information, and to allow your users (or admins) to restore some or all data.

The hard part about handcoding an application with soft deletes is that *every query* you ever write will need to exclude the soft-deleted data. Thankfully, if you use Eloquent's soft deletes, every query you ever make will be scoped to ignore soft deletes by default, unless you explicitly ask to bring them back.

Eloquent's soft delete functionality requires a `deleted_at` column to be added to the table. Once you enable soft deletes on that Eloquent model, every query you ever write (unless you explicitly include soft-deleted records) will be scoped to ignore soft-deleted rows.

When Should I Use Soft Deletes?

Just because a feature exists, it doesn't mean you should always use it. Many folks in the Laravel community default to using soft deletes on every project just because the feature is there. There are real costs to soft deletes, though. It's pretty likely that, if you view your database directly in a tool like Sequel Pro, you'll forget to check the deleted_at column at least once. And if you don't clean up old soft-deleted records, your databases will get larger and larger.

Here's my recommendation: don't use soft deletes by default. Instead, use them when you need them, and when you do, clean out old soft deletes as aggressively as you can using a tool like Quicksand (*https://github.com/tightenco/quicksand*). The soft delete feature is a powerful tool, but not worth using unless you need it.

Enabling soft deletes. You enable soft deletes by doing three things: adding the deleted_at column in a migration, importing the SoftDeletes trait in the model, and adding the deleted_at column to your $dates property. There's a softDeletes() method available on the schema builder to add the deleted_at column to a table, as you can see in Example 5-27. And Example 5-28 shows an Eloquent model with soft deletes enabled.

Example 5-27. Migration to add the soft delete column to a table

```
Schema::table('contacts', function (Blueprint $table) {
    $table->softDeletes();
});
```

Example 5-28. An Eloquent model with soft deletes enabled

```
<?php

use Illuminate\Database\Eloquent\Model;
use Illuminate\Database\Eloquent\SoftDeletes;

class Contact extends Model
{
    use SoftDeletes; // use the trait

    protected $dates = ['deleted_at']; // mark this column as a date
}
```

Once you make these changes, every delete() and destroy() call will now set the deleted_at column on your row to be the current date and time instead of deleting that row. And all future queries will exclude that row as a result.

Querying with soft deletes. So, how do we get soft-deleted items?

First, you can add soft-deleted items to a query:

```
$allHistoricContacts = Contact::withTrashed()->get();
```

Next, you can use the `trashed()` method to see if a particular instance has been soft-deleted:

```
if ($contact->trashed()) {
    // do something
}
```

Finally, you can get *only* soft-deleted items:

```
$deletedContacts = Contact::onlyTrashed()->get();
```

Restoring soft-deleted entities. If you want to restore a soft-deleted item, you can run `restore()` on an instance or a query:

```
$contact->restore();

// or

Contact::onlyTrashed()->where('vip', true)->restore();
```

Force-deleting soft-deleted entities. You can delete a soft-deleted entity by calling `forceDelete()` on an entity or query:

```
$contact->forceDelete();

// or

Contact::onlyTrashed()->forceDelete();
```

Scopes

We've covered "filtered" queries, meaning any query where we're not just returning every result for a table. But every time we've written them so far in this chapter, it's been a manual process using the query builder.

Local and global scopes in Eloquent allow you to define prebuilt "scopes" (filters) that you can use either every time a model is queried ("global") or every time you query it with a particular method chain ("local").

Local scopes

Local scopes are the simplest to understand. Let's take this example:

```
$activeVips = Contact::where('vip', true)->where('trial', false)->get();
```

First of all, if we write this combination of query methods over and over, it will get tedious. But additionally, the *knowledge* of how to define someone being an "active VIP" is now spread around our application. We want to centralize that knowledge. What if we could just write this?

```
$activeVips = Contact::activeVips()->get();
```

We can—it's called a local scope. And it's easy to define on the Contact class, as you can see in Example 5-29.

Example 5-29. Defining a local scope on a model

```
class Contact
{
    public function scopeActiveVips($query)
    {
        return $query->where('vip', true)->where('trial', false);
    }
}
```

To define a local scope, we add a method to the Eloquent class that begins with "scope" and then contains the title-cased version of the scope name. This method is passed a query builder and needs to return a query builder, but of course you can modify the query before returning—that's the whole point.

You can also define scopes that accept parameters, as shown in Example 5-30.

Example 5-30. Passing parameters to scopes

```
class Contact
{
    public function scopeStatus($query, $status)
    {
        return $query->where('status', $status);
    }
}
```

And you use them in the same way, just passing the parameter to the scope:

```
$friends = Contact::status('friend')->get();
```

Global scopes

Remember how we talked about soft deletes only working if you scope *every query* on the model to ignore the soft-deleted items? That's a global scope. And we can define our own global scopes, which will be applied on every query made from a given model.

There are two ways to define a global scope: using a closure or using an entire class. In each, you'll register the defined scope in the model's boot() method. Let's start with the closure method, illustrated in Example 5-31.

Example 5-31. Adding a global scope using a closure

```
...
class Contact extends Model
{
```

```
protected static function boot()
{
    parent::boot();

    static::addGlobalScope('active', function (Builder $builder) {
        $builder->where('active', true);
    });
}
```

That's it. We just added a global scope named `active`, and now every query on this model will be scoped to only rows with `active` set to `true`.

Next, let's try the longer way, as shown in Example 5-32. Create a class that implements `Illuminate\Database\Eloquent\Scope`, which means it will have an `apply()` method that takes an instance of a query builder and an instance of the model.

Example 5-32. Creating a global scope class

```php
<?php

namespace App\Scopes;

use Illuminate\Database\Eloquent\Scope;
use Illuminate\Database\Eloquent\Model;
use Illuminate\Database\Eloquent\Builder;

class ActiveScope implements Scope
{
    public function apply(Builder $builder, Model $model)
    {
        return $builder->where('active', true);
    }
}
```

To apply this scope to a model, once again override the parent's `boot()` method and call `addGlobalScope()` on the class using `static`, as shown in Example 5-33.

Example 5-33. Applying a class-based global scope

```php
<?php

use App\Scopes\ActiveScope;
use Illuminate\Database\Eloquent\Model;

class Contact extends Model
{
    protected static function boot()
    {
        parent::boot();
```

```
        static::addGlobalScope(new ActiveScope);
    }
}
```

 Contact with No Namespace

You may have noticed that several of these examples have used the class `Contact`, with no namespace. This is abnormal, and I've only done this to save space in the book. Normally even your top-level models would live at something like `App\Contact`.

Removing global scopes. There are three ways to remove a global scope, and all three use the `withoutGlobalScope()` or `withoutGlobalScopes()` methods. If you're removing a closure-based scope, the first parameter of that scope's `addGlobalScope()` registration will be the key you used to enable it:

```
$allContacts = Contact::withoutGlobalScope('active')->get();
```

If you're removing a single class-based global scope, you can pass the class name to `withoutGlobalScope()` or `withoutGlobalScopes()`:

```
Contact::withoutGlobalScope(ActiveScope::class)->get();
```

```
Contact::withoutGlobalScopes([ActiveScope::class, VipScope::class])->get();
```

Or, you can just disable all global scopes for a query:

```
Contact::withoutGlobalScopes()->get();
```

Customizing Field Interactions with Accessors, Mutators, and Attribute Casting

Now that we've covered how to get records into and out of the database with Eloquent, let's talk about decorating and manipulating the individual attributes on your Eloquent models.

Accessors, mutators, and attribute casting all allow you to customize the way individual attributes of Eloquent instances are input or output. Without using any of these, each attribute of your Eloquent instance is treated like a string, and you can't have any attributes on your models that don't exist on the database. But we can change that.

Accessors

Accessors allow you to define custom attributes on your Eloquent models for when you are *reading* data from the model instance. This may be because you want to change how a particular column is output, or because you want to create a custom attribute that doesn't exist in the database table at all.

You define an accessor by writing a method on your model with the following structure: `get{PascalCasedPropertyName}Attribute`. So, if your property name is `first_name`, the accessor method would be named `getFirstNameAttribute`.

Let's try it out. First, we'll decorate a preexisting column (Example 5-34).

Example 5-34. Decorating a preexisting column using Eloquent accessors

```
// Model definition:
class Contact extends Model
{
    public function getNameAttribute($value)
    {
        return $value ?: '(No name provided)';
    }
}

// Accessor usage:
$name = $contact->name;
```

But we can also use accessors to define attributes that never existed in the database, as seen in Example 5-35.

Example 5-35. Defining an attribute with no backing column using Eloquent accessors

```
// Model definition:
class Contact extends Model
{
    public function getFullNameAttribute()
    {
        return $this->first_name . ' ' . $this->last_name;
    }
}

// Accessor usage:
$fullName = $contact->full_name;
```

Mutators

Mutators work the same way as accessors, except they're for determining how to process *setting* the data instead of *getting* it. Just like with accessors, you can use them to modify the process of writing data to existing columns, or to allow for setting columns that don't exist in the database.

You define a mutator by writing a method on your model with the following structure: `set{PascalCasedPropertyName}Attribute`. So, if your property name is `first_name`, the mutator method would be named `setFirstNameAttribute`.

Let's try it out. First, we'll add a constraint to updating a preexisting column (Example 5-36).

Example 5-36. Decorating setting the value of an attribute using Eloquent mutators

```
// Defining the mutator
class Order extends Model
{
    public function setAmountAttribute($value)
    {
        $this->attributes['amount'] = $value > 0 ? $value : 0;
    }
}

// Using the mutator
$order->amount = '15';
```

This reveals that the way mutators are expected to "set" data on the model is by setting it in `$this->attributes` with the column name as the key.

Now let's add a proxy column for setting, as shown in Example 5-37.

Example 5-37. Allowing for setting the value of a nonexistent attribute using Eloquent mutators

```
// Defining the mutator
class Order extends Model
{
    public function setWorkgroupNameAttribute($workgroupName)
    {
        $this->attributes['email'] = "{$workgroupName}@ourcompany.com";
    }
}

// Using the mutator
$order->workgroup_name = 'jstott';
```

As you can probably guess, it's relatively uncommon to create a mutator for a nonexistent column, because it can be confusing to set one property and have it change a different column—but it is possible.

Attribute casting

You can probably imagine writing accessors to cast all of your integer-type fields as integers, encode and decode JSON to store in a TEXT column, or convert TINYINT 0 and 1 to and from Boolean values.

Thankfully, there's a system for that in Eloquent already. It's called *attribute casting*, and it allows you to define that any of your columns should always be treated, both on read and on write, as if they are of a particular data type. The options are listed in Table 5-1.

Table 5-1. Possible attribute casting column types

Type	Description
int|integer	Casts with PHP (int)
real|float|double	Casts with PHP (float)
string	Casts with PHP (string)
bool|boolean	Casts with PHP (bool)
object	Parses to/from JSON, as a stdClass object
array	Parses to/from JSON, as an array
collection	Parses to/from JSON, as a collection
date|datetime	Parses from database DATETIME to Carbon, and back
timestamp	Parses from database TIMESTAMP to Carbon, and back

Example 5-38 shows how you use attribute casting in your model.

Example 5-38. Using attribute casting on an Eloquent model

```
class Contact
{
    protected $casts = [
        'vip' => 'boolean',
        'children_names' => 'array',
        'birthday' => 'date',
    ];
}
```

Date mutators

You can choose for particular columns to be mutated as `timestamp` columns by adding them to the `dates` array, as seen in Example 5-39.

Example 5-39. Defining columns to be mutated as timestamps

```
class Contact
{
    protected $dates = [
        'met_at',
    ];
}
```

By default, this array contains `created_at` and `updated_at`, so adding entries to `dates` just adds them to the list.

However, there's no difference between adding columns to this list and adding them to $this->casts as timestamp, so this is becoming a bit of an unnecessary feature now that attribute casting can cast timestamps (new since Laravel 5.2).

Eloquent Collections

When you make any query call in Eloquent that has the potential to return multiple rows, instead of an array they'll come packaged in an Eloquent collection, which is a specialized type of collection. Let's take a look at collections and Eloquent collections, and what makes them better than plain arrays.

Introducing the base collection

Laravel's Collection objects (Illuminate\Support\Collection) are a little bit like arrays on steroids. The methods they expose on array-like objects are so helpful that, once you've been using them for a while, you'll likely want to pull them into non-Laravel projects—which you can, with the Tightenco/Collect (*https://github.com/tightenco/collect*) package.

The simplest way to create a collection is to use the collect() helper. Either pass an array in, or use it without arguments to create an empty collection and then push items into it later. Let's try it:

```
$collection = collect([1, 2, 3]);
```

Now let's say we want to filter out any even numbers:

```
$odds = $collection->reject(function ($item) {
    return $item % 2 === 0;
});
```

Or what if we want to get a version of the collection where each item is multiplied by 10? We can do that as follows:

```
$multiplied = $collection->map(function ($item) {
    return $item * 10;
});
```

We can even get only the even numbers, multiply them all by 10, and reduce them to a single number by sum():

```
$sum = $collection
    ->filter(function ($item) {
        return $item % 2 == 0;
    })->map(function ($item) {
        return $item * 10;
    })->sum();
```

As you can see, collections provide a series of methods, which can optionally be chained, to perform functional operations on your arrays. They provide the same functionality as native PHP methods like `array_map()` and `array_reduce()`, but you don't have to memorize PHP's unpredictable parameter order, and the method chaining syntax is infinitely more readable.

There are more than 60 methods available on the `Collection` class, including methods like `max()`, `whereIn()`, `flatten()`, and `flip()`, and there's not enough space to cover them all here. We'll talk about more in Chapter 17, or you can check out the Laravel collections docs (*https://laravel.com/docs/master/collections*) to see all of the methods.

Collections in the Place of Arrays

Collections can also be used in any context (except typehinting) where you can use arrays; they allow for iteration, so you can pass them to `foreach`, and they allow for array access, so if they're keyed you can try `$a = $collection['a']`.

What Eloquent collections add

Each Eloquent collection is a normal collection, but extended for the particular needs of a collection of Eloquent results.

Once again, there's not enough room here to cover all of the additions, but they're centered around the unique aspects of interacting with a collection not just of generic objects, but objects meant to represent database rows.

For example, every Eloquent collection has a method called `modelKeys()` that returns an array of the primary keys of every instance in the collection. `find($id)` looks for an instance that has the primary key of `$id`.

One additional feature available here is the ability to define that any given model should return its results wrapped in a specific class of collection. So, if you want to add specific methods to any collection of objects of your `Order` model—possibly related to summarizing the financial details of your orders—you could create a custom `OrderCollection` that extends `Illuminate\Database\Eloquent\Collection`, and then register it in your model, as shown in Example 5-40.

Example 5-40. Custom Collection classes for Eloquent models

```
...
class OrderCollection extends Collection
{
    public function sumBillableAmount()
    {
        return $this->reduce(function ($carry, $order) {
            return $carry + ($order->billable ? $order->amount : 0);
        }, 0);
```

```
    }
}

...
class Order extends Model
{
    public function newCollection(array $models = [])
    {
        return new OrderCollection($models);
    }
}
```

Now, any time you get back a collection of Orders (e.g., from Order::all()), it'll actually be an instance of the OrderCollection class:

```
$orders = Order::all();
$billableAmount = $orders->sumBillableAmount();
```

Eloquent Serialization

Serialization is what happens when you take something complex—an array, or an object—and convert it to a string. In a web-based context, that string is often JSON, but it could take other forms as well.

Serializing complex database records can be, well, complex, and this is one of the places many ORMs fall short. Thankfully, you get two powerful methods for free with Eloquent: toArray() and toJson(). Collections also have toArray() and toJson(), so all of these are valid:

```
$contactArray = Contact::first()->toArray();
$contactJson = Contact::first()->toJson();
$contactsArray = Contact::all()->toArray();
$contactsJson = Contact::all()->toJson();
```

You can also cast an Eloquent instance or collection to a string ($string = (string) $contact;), but both models and collections will just run toJson() and return the result.

Returning models directly from route methods

Laravel's router eventually converts everything routes return to a string, so there's a clever trick you can use. If you return the result of an Eloquent call in a controller, it will be automatically cast to a string, and therefore returned as JSON. That means a JSON-returning route can be as simple as either of the ones in Example 5-41.

Example 5-41. Returning JSON from routes directly

```
// routes/web.php
Route::get('api/contacts', function () {
    return Contact::all();
```

```
});

Route::get('api/contacts/{id}', function ($id) {
    return Contact::findOrFail($id);
});
```

Hiding attributes from JSON

It's very common to use JSON returns in APIs, and it's very common to want to hide certain attributes in these contexts, so Eloquent makes it easy to hide any attributes every time you cast to JSON.

You can either blacklist attributes, hiding the ones you list:

```
class Contact extends Model
{
    public $hidden = ['password', 'remember_token'];
```

or whitelist attributes, showing only the ones you list:

```
class Contact extends Model
{
    public $visible = ['name', 'email', 'status'];
```

This also works for relationships:

```
class User extends Model
{
    public $hidden = ['contacts'];

    public function contacts()
    {
        return $this->hasMany(Contact::class);
    }
```

 Loading the Contents of a Relationship

By default, the contents of a relationship are not loaded when you get a database record, so it doesn't matter whether you hide them or not. But, as you'll learn shortly, it's possible to get a record *with* its related items, and in this context, those items will not be included in a serialized copy of that record if you choose to hide that relationship.

In case you're curious now, you can get a User with all contacts—assuming you've set up the relationship correctly—with the following call:

```
$user = User::with('contacts')->first();
```

There might be times when you want to make an attribute visible just for a single call. That's possible, with the Eloquent method makeVisible():

```
$array = $user->makeVisible('remember_token')->toArray();
```

Adding a Generated Column to Array and JSON Output

If you have created an accessor for a column that doesn't exist—for example, our full_name column from Example 5-35—add it to the $appends array on the model to add it to the array and JSON output:

```
class Contact extends Model
{
    protected $appends = ['full_name'];

    public function getFullNameAttribute()
    {
        return "{$this->first_name} {$this->last_name}";
    }
}
```

Eloquent Relationships

In a relational database model, it's expected that you will have tables that are *related* to each other—hence the name. Eloquent provides simple and powerful tools to make the process of relating your database tables easier than ever before.

Many of our examples in this chapter have been centered around a *user* who has many *contacts*, a relatively common situation.

In an ORM like Eloquent, you would call this a *one-to-many* relationship: the one user *has many* contacts.

If it was a CRM where a contact could be assigned to many users, then this would be a *many-to-many* relationship: many users can be related to one contact, and each user can be related to many contacts. A user *has and belongs to many* contacts.

If each contact can have many phone numbers, and a user wanted a database of every phone number for their CRM, you would say the user *has many* phone numbers *through* contacts—that is, a user *has many* contacts, and the contact *has many* phone numbers, so the contact is sort of an intermediary.

And what if each contact has an address, but you're only interested in tracking one address? You could have all the address fields on the Contact, but you might also create an Address model—meaning the contact *has one* address.

Finally, what if you want to be able to star (favorite) contacts, but also events? This would be a *polymorphic* relationship, where a user *has many* stars, but some may be contacts and some may be events.

So, let's dig into how to define and access these relationships.

One to one

Let's start simple: a Contact *has one* PhoneNumber. This relationship is defined in Example 5-42.

Example 5-42. Defining a one-to-one relationship

```
class Contact extends Model
{
    public function phoneNumber()
    {
        return $this->hasOne(PhoneNumber::class);
    }
}
```

As you can tell, the methods defining relationships are on the Eloquent model itself ($this->hasOne()) and take, at least in this instance, the fully qualified class name of the class that you're relating them to.

How should this be defined in your database? Since we've defined that the Contact has one PhoneNumber, Eloquent expects that the table supporting the PhoneNumber class (likely phone_numbers) has a contact_id column on it. If you named it something different (for instance, owner_id), you'll need to change your definition:

```
    return $this->hasOne(PhoneNumber::class, 'owner_id');
```

Here's how we access the PhoneNumber of a Contact:

```
    $contact = Contact::first();
    $contactPhone = $contact->phoneNumber;
```

Notice that we define the method in Example 5-42 with phoneNumber(), but we access it with ->phoneNumber. That's the magic. You could also access it with ->phone_number. This will return a full Eloquent instance of the related PhoneNumber record.

But what if we want to access the Contact from the PhoneNumber? There's a method for that, too (see Example 5-43).

Example 5-43. Defining a one-to-one relationship's inverse

```
class PhoneNumber extends Model
{
    public function contact()
    {
        return $this->belongsTo(Contact::class);
    }
}
```

Then we access it the same way:

```
    $contact = $phoneNumber->contact;
```

Inserting Related Items

Each relationship type has its own quirks for how to relate models, but here's the core of how it works: pass an instance to save(), or an array of instances to saveMany(). You can also pass properties to create() or createMany() and they'll make new instances for you:

```
$contact = Contact::first();

$phoneNumber = new PhoneNumber;
$phoneNumber->number = 8008675309;
$contact->phoneNumbers()->save($phoneNumber);

// or

$contact->phoneNumbers()->saveMany([
    PhoneNumber::find(1),
    PhoneNumber::find(2),
]);

// or

$contact->phoneNumbers()->create([
    'number' => '+13138675309',
]);

// or

$contact->phoneNumbers()->createMany([
    ['number' => '+13138675309'],
    ['number' => '+15556060842'],
]);
```

The createMany() method is only available in Laravel 5.4 and later.

One to many

The one-to-many relationship is by far the most common. Let's take a look at how to define that our User *has many* Contacts (Example 5-44).

Example 5-44. Defining a one-to-many relationship

```
class User extends Model
{
    public function contacts()
    {
        return $this->hasMany(Contact::class);
    }
}
```

Once again, this expects that the Contact model's backing table (likely contacts) has a user_id column on it. If it doesn't, override it by passing the correct column name as the second parameter of hasMany().

We can get a User's Contacts as follows:

```
$user = User::first();
$usersContacts = $user->contacts;
```

Just like with one to one, we use the name of the relationship method and call it as if it were a property instead of a method. However, this method returns a collection instead of a model instance. And this is a normal Eloquent collection, so we can have all sorts of fun with it:

```
$donors = $user->contacts->filter(function ($contact) {
    return $contact->status == 'donor';
});

$lifetimeValue = $contact->orders->reduce(function ($carry, $order) {
    return $carry + $order->amount;
}, 0);
```

Just like with one to one, we can also define the inverse (Example 5-45).

Example 5-45. Defining a one-to-many relationship's inverse

```
class Contact extends Model
{
    public function user()
    {
        return $this->belongsTo(User::class);
    }
}
```

And just like with one to one, we can access the User from the Contact:

```
$userName = $contact->user->name;
```

Attaching and Detaching Related Items from the Attached Item

Most of the time we attach an item by running `save()` on the parent and passing in the related item, as in `$user->contacts()->save($contact)`. But if you want to perform these behaviors on the attached ("child") item, you can use `associate()` and `dissociate()` on the method that returns the `belongsTo` relationship:

```
$contact = Contact::first();

$contact->user()->associate(User::first());
$contact->save();

// and later

$contact->user()->dissociate();
$contact->save();
```

Using relationships as query builders.   Until now, we've taken the method name (e.g., `contacts()`) and called it as if were a property (e.g., `$user->contacts`). What happens if we call it as a method? Instead of processing the relationship, it will return a pre-scoped query builder.

So if you have `User 1`, and you call its `contacts()` method, you will now have a query builder prescoped to "all contacts that have a field `user_id` with the value of 1." You can then build out a functional query from there:

```
$donors = $user->contacts()->where('status', 'donor')->get();
```

Selecting only records that have a related item.   You can choose to select only records that meet particular criteria with regard to their related items using `has()`:

```
$postsWithComments = Post::has('comments')->get();
```

You can also adjust the criteria further:

```
$postsWithManyComments = Post::has('comments', '>=', 5)->get();
```

You can nest the criteria:

```
$usersWithPhoneBooks = User::has('contacts.phoneNumbers')->get();
```

And finally, you can write custom queries on the related items:

```
// Gets all contacts with a phone number containing the string "867-5309"
$jennyIGotYourNumber = Contact::whereHas('phoneNumbers', function ($query) {
    $query->where('number', 'like', '%867-5309%');
});
```

Has many through

`hasManyThrough()` is really a convenience method for pulling in relationships of a relationship. Think of the example I gave earlier, where a `User` has many `Contacts` and each `Contact` has many `PhoneNumbers`. What if you want to get a user's list of contact phone numbers? That's has-many-through relation.

This structure assumes that your `contacts` table has a `user_id` to relate the contacts to the users and the `phone_numbers` table has a `contact_id` to relate it to the contacts. Then, we define the relationship on the `User` as in Example 5-46.

Example 5-46. Defining a has-many-through relationship

```
class User extends Model
{
    public function phoneNumbers()
    {
        return $this->hasManyThrough(PhoneNumber::class, Contact::class);
    }
}
```

You'd access this relationship using `$user->phone_numbers`, and as always you can customize the relationship key on the intermediate model (with the third parameter of `hasManyThrough()`) and the relationship key on the distant model (with the fourth parameter).

Has one through

`hasOneThrough()` is just like `hasManyThrough()`, but instead of accessing many related items through intermediate items, you're only accessing a single related item through a single intermediate item.

What if each user belonged to a company, and that company had a single phone number, and you wanted to be able to get a user's phone number by pulling their company's phone number? That's `hasOneThrough()`.

Example 5-47. Defining a has-one-through relationship

```
class User extends Model
{
    public function phoneNumber()
    {
        return $this->hasOneThrough(PhoneNumber::class, Company::class);
    }
}
```

Many to many

This is where things start to get complex. Let's take our example of a CRM that allows a User to have many Contacts, and each Contact to be related to multiple Users.

First, we define the relationship on the User as in Example 5-48.

Example 5-48. Defining a many-to-many relationship

```
class User extends Model
{
    public function contacts()
    {
        return $this->belongsToMany(Contact::class);
    }
}
```

And since this is many to many, the inverse looks exactly the same (Example 5-49).

Example 5-49. Defining a many-to-many relationship's inverse

```
class Contact extends Model
{
    public function users()
    {
        return $this->belongsToMany(User::class);
    }
}
```

Since a single Contact can't have a user_id column and a single User can't have a contact_id column, many-to-many relationships rely on a pivot table that connects the two. The conventional naming of this table is done by placing the two singular table names together, ordered alphabetically, and separating them by an underscore.

So, since we're linking users and contacts, our pivot table should be named contacts_users (if you'd like to customize the table name, pass it as the second parameter to the belongsToMany() method). It needs two columns: contact_id and user_id.

Just like with hasMany(), we get access to a collection of the related items, but this time it's from both sides (Example 5-50).

Example 5-50. Accessing the related items from both sides of a many-to-many relationship

```
$user = User::first();

$user->contacts->each(function ($contact) {
```

```
    // do something
});

$contact = Contact::first();

$contact->users->each(function ($user) {
    // do something
});

$donors = $user->contacts()->where('status', 'donor')->get();
```

Getting data from the pivot table.   One thing that's unique about many to many is that it's our first relationship that has a pivot table. The less data you have in a pivot table, the better, but there are some cases where it's valuable to store information in your pivot table—for example, you might want to store a created_at field to see when this relationship was created.

In order to store these fields, you have to add them to the relationship definition, like in Example 5-51. You can define specific fields using withPivot() or add created_at and updated_at timestamps using withTimestamps().

Example 5-51. Adding fields to a pivot record

```
public function contacts()
{
    return $this->belongsToMany(Contact::class)
        ->withTimestamps()
        ->withPivot('status', 'preferred_greeting');
}
```

When you get a model instance through a relationship, it will have a pivot property on it, which will represent its place in the pivot table you just pulled it from. So, you can do something like Example 5-52.

Example 5-52. Getting data from a related item's pivot entry

```
$user = User::first();

$user->contacts->each(function ($contact) {
    echo sprintf(
        'Contact associated with this user at: %s',
        $contact->pivot->created_at
    );
});
```

If you'd like, you can customize the pivot key to have a different name using the as() method, as shown in Example 5-53.

Example 5-53. Customizing the pivot attribute name

```
// User model
public function groups()
{
    return $this->belongsToMany(Group::class)
        ->withTimestamps()
        ->as('membership');
}

// Using this relationship:
User::first()->groups->each(function ($group) {
    echo sprintf(
        'User joined this group at: %s',
        $group->membership->created_at
    );
});
```

Unique Aspects of Attaching and Detaching Many-to-Many Related Items

Since your pivot table can have its own properties, you need to be able to set those properties when you're attaching a many-to-many related item. You can do that by passing an array as the second parameter to save():

```
$user = User::first();
$contact = Contact::first();
$user->contacts()->save($contact, ['status' => 'donor']);
```

Additionally, you can use attach() and detach() and, instead of passing in an instance of a related item, you can just pass an ID. They work just the same as save() but can also accept an array of IDs without you needing to rename the method to something like attachMany():

```
$user = User::first();
$user->contacts()->attach(1);
$user->contacts()->attach(2, ['status' => 'donor']);
$user->contacts()->attach([1, 2, 3]);
$user->contacts()->attach([
    1 => ['status' => 'donor'],
    2,
    3,
]);

$user->contacts()->detach(1);
$user->contacts()->detach([1, 2]);
$user->contacts()->detach(); // Detaches all contacts
```

If your goal is not to attach or detach, but instead just to invert whatever the current attachment state is, you want the toggle() method. When you use toggle(), if the given ID is currently attached, it will be detached; and if it is currently detached, it will be attached:

```
$user->contacts()->toggle([1, 2, 3]);
```

You can also use updateExistingPivot() to make changes just to the pivot record:

```
$user->contacts()->updateExistingPivot($contactId, [
    'status' => 'inactive',
]);
```

And if you'd like to replace the current relationships, effectively detaching all previous relationships and attaching new ones, you can pass an array to sync():

```
$user->contacts()->sync([1, 2, 3]);
$user->contacts()->sync([
    1 => ['status' => 'donor'],
    2,
    3,
]);
```

Polymorphic

Remember, our polymorphic relationship is where we have multiple Eloquent classes corresponding to the same relationship. We're going to use Stars (like favorites) right now. A user can star both Contacts and Events, and that's where the name *polymorphic* comes from: there's a single interface to objects of multiple types.

So, we'll need three tables, and three models: Star, Contact, and Event (four of each, technically, because we'll need users and User, but we'll get there in a second). The contacts and events tables will just be as they normally are, and the stars table will contain id, starrable_id, and starrable_type fields. For each Star, we'll be defining which "type" (e.g., Contact or Event) and which ID of that type (e.g., 1) it is.

Let's create our models, as seen in Example 5-54.

Example 5-54. Creating the models for a polymorphic starring system

```
class Star extends Model
{
    public function starrable()
    {
        return $this->morphTo();
    }
}

class Contact extends Model
{
    public function stars()
    {
```

```
        return $this->morphMany(Star::class, 'starrable');
    }
}

class Event extends Model
{
    public function stars()
    {
        return $this->morphMany(Star::class, 'starrable');
    }
}
```

So, how do we create a Star?

```
$contact = Contact::first();
$contact->stars()->create();
```

It's that easy. The Contact is now starred.

In order to find all of the Stars on a given Contact, we call the stars() method like in Example 5-55.

Example 5-55. Retrieving the instances of a polymorphic relationship

```
$contact = Contact::first();

$contact->stars->each(function ($star) {
    // Do stuff
});
```

If we have an instance of Star, we can get its target by calling the method we used to define its morphTo relationship, which in this context is starrable(). Take a look at Example 5-56.

Example 5-56. Retrieving the target of a polymorphic instance

```
$stars = Star::all();

$stars->each(function ($star) {
    var_dump($star->starrable); // An instance of Contact or Event
});
```

Finally, you might be wondering, "What if I want to know who starred this contact?" That's a great question. It's as simple as adding user_id to your stars table, and then setting up that a User *has many* Stars and a Star *belongs to* one User—a one-to-many relationship (Example 5-57). The stars table becomes almost a pivot table between your User and your Contacts and Events.

Example 5-57. Extending a polymorphic system to differentiate by user

```
class Star extends Model
{
    public function starrable()
    {
        return $this->morphsTo;
    }

    public function user()
    {
        return $this->belongsTo(User::class);
    }
}

class User extends Model
{
    public function stars()
    {
        return $this->hasMany(Star::class);
    }
}
```

That's it! You can now run `$star->user` or `$user->stars` to find a list of a `User`'s `Stars` or to find the starring `User` from a `Star`. Also, when you create a new `Star`, you'll now want to pass the `User`:

```
$user = User::first();
$event = Event::first();
$event->stars()->create(['user_id' => $user->id]);
```

Many to many polymorphic

The most complex and least common of the relationship types, many-to-many polymorphic relationships are like polymorphic relationships, except instead of being one to many, they're many to many.

The most common example for this relationship type is the tag, so I'll keep it safe and use that as our example. Let's imagine you want to be able to tag `Contacts` and `Events`. The uniqueness of many-to-many polymorphism is that it's many to many: each tag may be applied to multiple items, and each tagged item might have multiple tags. And to add to that, it's polymorphic: tags can be related to items of several different types. For the database, we'll start with the normal structure of the polymorphic relationship but also add a pivot table.

This means we'll need a `contacts` table, an `events` table, and a `tags` table, all shaped like normal with an ID and whatever properties you want, *and* a new `taggables` table, which will have `tag_id`, `taggable_id`, and `taggable_type` fields. Each entry into the `taggables` table will relate a tag with one of the taggable content types.

Now let's define this relationship on our models, as seen in Example 5-58.

Example 5-58. Defining a polymorphic many-to-many relationship

```
class Contact extends Model
{
    public function tags()
    {
        return $this->morphToMany(Tag::class, 'taggable');
    }
}

class Event extends Model
{
    public function tags()
    {
        return $this->morphToMany(Tag::class, 'taggable');
    }
}

class Tag extends Model
{
    public function contacts()
    {
        return $this->morphedByMany(Contact::class, 'taggable');
    }

    public function events()
    {
        return $this->morphedByMany(Event::class, 'taggable');
    }
}
```

Here's how to create your first tag:

```
$tag = Tag::firstOrCreate(['name' => 'likes-cheese']);
$contact = Contact::first();
$contact->tags()->attach($tag->id);
```

We get the results of this relationship like normal, as seen in Example 5-59.

Example 5-59. Accessing the related items from both sides of a many-to-many polymorphic relationship

```
$contact = Contact::first();

$contact->tags->each(function ($tag) {
    // Do stuff
});

$tag = Tag::first();
```

```
$tag->contacts->each(function ($contact) {
    // Do stuff
});
```

Child Records Updating Parent Record Timestamps

Remember, any Eloquent models by default will have `created_at` and `updated_at` timestamps. Eloquent will set the `updated_at` timestamp automatically any time you make any changes to a record.

When a related item has a `belongsTo` or `belongsToMany` relationship with another item, it might be valuable to mark the other item as updated any time the related item is updated. For example, if a `PhoneNumber` is updated, maybe the `Contact` it's connected to should be marked as having been updated as well.

We can accomplish this by adding the method name for that relationship to a `$touches` array property on the child class, as in Example 5-60.

Example 5-60. Updating a parent record any time the child record is updated

```
class PhoneNumber extends Model
{
    protected $touches = ['contact'];

    public function contact()
    {
        return $this->belongsTo(Contact::class);
    }
}
```

Eager loading

By default, Eloquent loads relationships using "lazy loading." This means when you first load a model instance, its related models will not be loaded along with it. Rather, they'll only be loaded once you access them on the model; they're "lazy" and don't do any work until called upon.

This can become a problem if you're iterating over a list of model instances and each has a related item (or items) that you're working on. The problem with lazy loading is that it can introduce significant database load (often the $N+1$ problem, if you're familiar with the term; if not, just ignore this parenthetical remark). For instance, every time the loop in Example 5-61 runs, it executes a new database query to look up the phone numbers for that `Contact`.

Example 5-61. Retrieving one related item for each item in a list (N+1)

```
$contacts = Contact::all();

foreach ($contacts as $contact) {
    foreach ($contact->phone_numbers as $phone_number) {
        echo $phone_number->number;
    }
}
```

If you are loading a model instance, and you know you'll be working with its relationships, you can instead choose to "eager-load" one or many of its sets of related items:

```
$contacts = Contact::with('phoneNumbers')->get();
```

Using the `with()` method with a retrieval gets all of the items related to the pulled item(s); as you can see in this example, you pass it the name of the method the relationship is defined by.

When we use eager loading, instead of pulling the related items one at a time when they're requested (e.g., selecting one contact's phone numbers each time a `foreach` loop runs), we have a single query to pull the initial items (selecting all contacts) and a second query to pull all their related items (selecting all phone numbers owned by the contacts we just pulled).

You can eager-load multiple relationships by passing multiple parameters to the `with()` call:

```
$contacts = Contact::with('phoneNumbers', 'addresses')->get();
```

And you can nest eager loading to eager-load the relationships of relationships:

```
$authors = Author::with('posts.comments')->get();
```

Constraining eager loads. If you want to eager-load a relationship, but not all of the items, you can pass a closure to `with()` to define exactly which related items to eager-load:

```
$contacts = Contact::with(['addresses' => function ($query) {
    $query->where('mailable', true);
}])->get();
```

Lazy eager loading. I know it sounds crazy, because we just defined eager loading as sort of the opposite of lazy loading, but sometimes you don't know you want to perform an eager-load query until after the initial instances have been pulled. In this context, you're still able to make a single query to look up all of the related items, avoiding N+1 cost. We call this "lazy eager loading":

```
$contacts = Contact::all();
```

```
if ($showPhoneNumbers) {
    $contacts->load('phoneNumbers');
}
```

To load a relationship only when it has not already been loaded, use the
loadMissing() method (available only since Laravel 5.5):

```
$contacts = Contact::all();

if ($showPhoneNumbers) {
    $contacts->loadMissing('phoneNumbers');
}
```

Eager loading only the count

If you want to eager-load relationships but only so you can have access to the count of
items in each relationship, you can try withCount():

```
$authors = Author::withCount('posts')->get();

// Adds a "posts_count" integer to each Author with a count of that
// author's related posts
```

Eloquent Events

Eloquent models fire events out into the void of your application every time certain
actions happen, regardless of whether you're listening. If you're familiar with pub/
sub, it's this same model (you'll learn more about Laravel's entire event system in
Chapter 16).

Here's a quick rundown of binding a listener to when a new Contact is created. We're
going to bind it in the boot() method of AppServiceProvider, and let's imagine
we're notifying a third-party service every time we create a new Contact.

Example 5-62. Binding a listener to an Eloquent event

```
class AppServiceProvider extends ServiceProvider
{
    public function boot()
    {
        $thirdPartyService = new SomeThirdPartyService;

        Contact::creating(function ($contact) use ($thirdPartyService) {
            try {
                $thirdPartyService->addContact($contact);
            } catch (Exception $e) {
                Log::error('Failed adding contact to ThirdPartyService; canceled.');

                return false; // Cancels Eloquent create()
            }
```

```
        });
    }
```

We can see a few things in Example 5-62. First, we use *Modelname::eventName()* as the method, and pass it a closure. The closure gets access to the model instance that is being operated on. Second, we're going to need to define this listener in a service provider somewhere. And third, if we return `false`, the operation will cancel and the `save()` or `update()` will be canceled.

Here are the events that every Eloquent model fires:

- `creating`
- `created`
- `updating`
- `updated`
- `saving`
- `saved`
- `deleting`
- `deleted`
- `restoring`
- `restored`
- `retrieved`

Most of these should be pretty clear, except possibly `restoring` and `restored`, which fire when you're restoring a soft-deleted row. Also, `saving` is fired for both `creating` and `updating` and `saved` is fired for both `created` and `updated`.

 `retrieved` (available in Laravel 5.5 and later) is fired when an existing model is retrieved from the database.

Testing

Laravel's entire application testing framework makes it easy to test your database—not by writing unit tests against Eloquent, but by just being willing to test your entire application.

Take this scenario. You want to test to ensure that a particular page shows one contact but not another. Some of that logic has to do with the interplay between the URL and the controller and the database, so the best way to test it is an application test. You might be thinking about mocking Eloquent calls and trying to avoid the system hitting the database. *Don't do it.* Try Example 5-63 instead.

Example 5-63. Testing database interactions with simple application tests

```
public function test_active_page_shows_active_and_not_inactive_contacts()
{
    $activeContact = factory(Contact::class)->create();
    $inactiveContact = factory(Contact::class)->states('inactive')->create();

    $this->get('active-contacts')
        ->assertSee($activeContact->name)
        ->assertDontSee($inactiveContact->name);
}
```

As you can see, model factories and Laravel's application testing features are great for testing database calls.

Alternatively, you can look for that record directly in the database, as in Example 5-64.

Example 5-64. Using assertDatabaseHas() to check for certain records in the database

```
public function test_contact_creation_works()
{
    $this->post('contacts', [
        'email' => 'jim@bo.com'
    ]);

    $this->assertDatabaseHas('contacts', [
        'email' => 'jim@bo.com'
    ]);
}
```

Eloquent and Laravel's database framework are tested extensively. *You don't need to test them.* You don't need to mock them. If you really want to avoid hitting the database, you can use a repository and then return unsaved instances of your Eloquent models. But the most important message is, test the way your application uses your database logic.

If you have custom accessors, mutators, scopes, or whatever else, you can also test them directly, as in Example 5-65.

Example 5-65. Testing accessors, mutators, and scopes

```
public function test_full_name_accessor_works()
{
    $contact = factory(Contact::class)->make([
        'first_name' => 'Alphonse',
        'last_name' => 'Cumberbund'
    ]);
```

```
        $this->assertEquals('Alphonse Cumberbund', $contact->fullName);
}

public function test_vip_scope_filters_out_non_vips()
{
        $vip = factory(Contact::class)->states('vip')->create();
        $nonVip = factory(Contact::class)->create();

        $vips = Contact::vips()->get();

        $this->assertTrue($vips->contains('id', $vip->id));
        $this->assertFalse($vips->contains('id', $nonVip->id));
}
```

Just avoid writing tests that leave you creating complex "Demeter chains" to assert that a particular fluent stack was called on some database mock. If your testing starts to get overwhelming and complex around the database layer, it's because you're allowing preconceived notions to force you into unnecessarily complex systems. Keep it simple.

Different Names for Testing Methods Prior to Laravel 5.4

In projects running versions of Laravel prior to 5.4, assertDatabaseHas() should be replaced by seeInDatabase(), get() should be replaced by visit(), assertSee() should be replaced by see(), and assertDontSee() should be replaced by dontSee().

TL;DR

Laravel comes with a suite of powerful database tools, including migrations, seeding, an elegant query builder, and Eloquent, a powerful ActiveRecord ORM. Laravel's database tools don't require you to use Eloquent at all—you can access and manipulate the database with a thin layer of convenience without having to write SQL directly. But adding an ORM, whether it's Eloquent or Doctrine or whatever else, is easy and can work neatly with Laravel's core database tools.

Eloquent follows the Active Record pattern, which makes it simple to define a class of database-backed objects, including which table they're stored in and the shape of their columns, accessors, and mutators. Eloquent can handle every sort of normal SQL action and also complex relationships, up to and including polymorphic many-to-many relationships.

Laravel also has a robust system for testing databases, including model factories.

## CHAPTER 6

Frontend Components

Laravel is primarily a PHP framework, but it also has a series of components focused on generating frontend code. Some of these, like pagination and message bags, are PHP helpers that target the frontend, but Laravel also provides a Webpack-based build system called Mix and some conventions around non-PHP assets.

Laravel's Build Tools Before and After Laravel 5.4

Prior to Laravel 5.4, Laravel's frontend build tool was named Elixer, and it was based on Gulp. In 5.4 and later, the new build tool is named Mix, and it's based on Webpack.

Since Mix is at the core of the non-PHP frontend components, let's start there.

Laravel Mix

Mix is a build tool that provides a simple user interface and a series of conventions on top of Webpack (*https://webpack.js.org/*). Mix's core value proposition is simplifying the most common build and compilation Webpack tasks by means of a cleaner API and a series of naming and application structure conventions.

A Quick Introduction to Webpack

Webpack is a JavaScript tool designed for compiling static assets; the Webpack team describes its purpose as bundling "modules with dependencies" together and producing "static assets."

Webpack is similar to Gulp or Grunt in that, like Webpack, those tools are often used for processing and bundling dependencies for websites. This will commonly include

---

running a CSS preprocessor like Sass or Less or PostCSS, copying files, and concatenating and minifying JavaScript.

Unlike the others, Webpack is *specifically* focused on bundling together modules with dependencies and producing static assets as a result. Gulp and Grunt are task runners, which, like Make and Rake before them, can be used to automate any activities that are programmable and repeatable. They all *can* be used to bundle assets, but that's not their core focus, and as a result they can be limited in some of the more complex needs for asset bundling—for example, identifying which of the generated assets won't be used and discarding them from the final output.

At its core, Mix is just a tool in your Webpack toolbox. The "Mix file" you'll use to set your configurations is simply a Webpack configuration file which lives at the root of your project, named *webpack.mix.js*. However, the configuration you have to set there is a lot simpler than most Webpack configuration is out of the box, and you'll have to do a lot less work to get most common asset compilation tasks working.

Let's look at a common example: running Sass to preprocess your CSS styles. In a normal Webpack environment, that might look a little bit like Example 6-1.

Example 6-1. Compiling a Sass file in Webpack, before Mix

```
var path = require('path');
var MiniCssExtractPlugin = require("mini-css-extract-plugin");

module.exports = {
    entry: './src/sass/app.scss',
    module: {
        rules: [
            {
                test: /\.s[ac]ss$/,
                use: [
                    MiniCssExtractPlugin.loader,
                    "css-loader",
                    "sass-loader"
                ]
            }
        ]
    },
    plugins: [
        new MiniCssExtractPlugin({
            path: path.resolve(__dirname, './dist'),
            filename: 'app.css'
        })
    ]
}
```

Now, I've seen worse. There aren't an unimaginable number of configuration properties, and it's relatively clear what's going on. But this is the sort of code that you copy from project to project, not code you feel comfortable writing yourself or even modifying to any significant degree. Working like this can get confusing and repetitive.

Let's try that same task in Mix (Example 6-2).

Example 6-2. Compiling a Sass file in Mix

```
let mix = require('laravel-mix');

mix.sass('resources/sass/app.scss', 'public/css');
```

That's it. And not only is it infinitely simpler, it also covers file watching, browser syncing, notifications, prescribed folder structures, autoprefixing, URL processing, and much more.

Mix Folder Structure

Much of Mix's simplicity comes from the assumed directory structure. Why decide for every new application where the source and compiled assets will live? Just stick with Mix's conventions, and you won't have to think about it ever again.

Every new Laravel app comes with a *resources* folder, which is where Mix will expect your frontend assets to live. Your Sass will live in *resources/sass*, or your Less in *resources/less*, or your source CSS in *resources/css*, and your JavaScript will live in *resources/js*. These will export to *public/css* and *public/js*.

The Assets Subdirectory Prior to Laravel 5.7

In versions of Laravel prior to 5.7, the *sass*, *less*, and *js* directories were nested under the *resources/assets* directory instead of directly underneath the *resources* directory.

Running Mix

Since Mix runs on Webpack, you'll need to set up a few tools before using it:

1. First, you'll need Node.js installed. Visit the Node website (*http://nodejs.org/*) to learn how to get it running.

   Once Node (and NPM with it) is installed once, you will not have to do this again for each project. Now you're ready to install this project's dependencies.

2. Open the project root in your terminal, and run `npm install` to install the required packages (Laravel ships with a Mix-ready *package.json* file to direct NPM).

You're now set up! You can run `npm run dev` to run Webpack/Mix once, `npm run watch` to listen for relevant file changes and run in response, or `npm run prod` to run Mix once with production settings (such as minifying the output). You can also run `npm run watch-poll` if `npm run watch` doesn't work in your environment, or `npm run hot` for Hot Module Replacement (HMR; discussed in the next section).

What Does Mix Provide?

I've already mentioned that Mix can preprocess your CSS using Sass, Less, and/or PostCSS. It can also concatenate any sort of files, minify them, rename them, and copy them, and it can copy entire directories or individual files.

Additionally, Mix can process all flavors of modern JavaScript and provide autoprefixing, concatenation, and minification specifically as a part of the JavaScript build stack. It makes it easy to set up Browsersync, HMR, and versioning, and there are plug-ins available for many other common build scenarios.

The Mix documentation (*http://bit.ly/2OqiyIL*) covers all of these options and more, but we'll discuss a few specific use cases in the following sections.

Source maps

If you're not familiar with source maps, they work with any sort of preprocessor to teach your browser's web inspector which files generated the compiled source you're inspecting.

By default, Mix will not generate source maps for your files. But you can enable them by chaining the `sourceMaps()` method after your Mix calls, as you can see in Example 6-3.

Example 6-3. Enabling source maps in Mix

```
let mix = require('laravel-mix');

mix.js('resources/js/app.js', 'public/js')
   .sourceMaps();
```

Once you configure Mix this way, you'll see the source maps appear as a *.{filename}.map* file next to each generated file.

Without source maps, if you use your browser's development tools to inspect a particular CSS rule or JavaScript action, you'll just see a big mess of compiled code. With source maps, your browser can pinpoint the exact line of the source file, whether it be Sass or JavaScript or whatever else, that generated the rule you're inspecting.

Pre- and post-processors

We've already covered Sass and Less, but Mix can also handle Stylus (Example 6-4), and you can chain PostCSS onto any other style calls (Example 6-5).

Example 6-4. Preprocessing CSS with Stylus

```
mix.stylus('resources/stylus/app.styl', 'public/css');
```

Example 6-5. Post-processing CSS with PostCSS

```
mix.sass('resources/sass/app.scss', 'public/css')
    .options({
        postCss: [
            require('postcss-css-variables')()
        ]
    });
```

Preprocessorless CSS

If you don't want to deal with a preprocessor, there's a command for that—it will grab all of your CSS files, concatenate them, and output them to the *public/css* directory, just as if they had been run through a preprocessor. There are a few options, which you can see in Example 6-6.

Example 6-6. Combining stylesheets with Mix

```
// Combines all files from resources/css
mix.styles('resources/css', 'public/css/all.css');

// Combines files from resources/css
mix.styles([
    'resources/css/normalize.css',
    'resources/css/app.css'
], 'public/css/all.css');
```

Concatenating JavaScript

The options available for working with normal JavaScript files are very similar to those available for normal CSS files. Take a look at Example 6-7.

Example 6-7. Combining JavaScript files with Mix

```
let mix = require('laravel-mix');
```

```
// Combines all files from resources/js
mix.scripts('resources/js', 'public/js/all.js');

// Combines files from resources/js
mix.scripts([
    'resources/js/normalize.js',
    'resources/js/app.js'
], 'public/js/all.js');
```

Processing JavaScript

If you want to process your JavaScript—for example, to compile your ES6 code into plain JavaScript—Mix makes it easy to use Webpack for this purpose (see Example 6-8).

Example 6-8. Processing JavaScript files in Mix with Webpack

```
let mix = require('laravel-mix');

mix.js('resources/js/app.js', 'public/js');
```

These scripts look for the provided filename in *resources/js* and output to *public/js/app.js*.

You can use more complicated aspects of Webpack's feature set by creating a *webpack.config.js* file in your project root.

Copying files or directories

To move either a single file or an entire directory, use the copy() method or the copy Directory() method:

```
    mix.copy('node_modules/pkgname/dist/style.css', 'public/css/pkgname.css');
    mix.copyDirectory('source/images', 'public/images');
```

Versioning

Most of the tips from Steve Souders's *Even Faster Web Sites* (O'Reilly) have made their way into our everyday development practices. We move scripts to the footer, reduce the number of HTTP requests, and more, often without even realizing where those ideas originated.

One of Steve's tips is still very rarely implemented, though, and that is setting a very long cache life on assets (scripts, styles, and images). Doing this means there will be fewer requests to your server to get the latest version of your assets. But it also means that users are extremely likely to have a cached version of your assets, which will make things get outdated, and therefore break, quickly.

The solution to this is *versioning*. Append a unique hash to each asset's filename *every time you run your build script*, and then that unique file will be cached indefinitely—or at least until the next build.

What's the problem? Well, first you need to get the unique hashes generated and appended to your filenames. But you also will need to update your views on every build to reference the new filenames.

As you can probably guess, Mix handles that for you, and it's incredibly simple. There are two components: the versioning task in Mix, and the `mix()` PHP helper. First, you can version your assets by running `mix.version()` like in Example 6-9.

Example 6-9. mix.version

```
let mix = require('laravel-mix');

mix.sass('resources/sass/app.scss', 'public/css')
    .version();
```

The version of the file that's generated is no different—it's just named *app.css* and lives in *public/css*.

Versioning Assets Using Query Parameters

The way versioning is handled in Laravel is a little different from traditional versioning, in that the versioning is appended with a query parameter instead of by modifying filenames. It still functions the same way, because browsers read it as a "new" file, but it handles a few edge cases with caches and load balancers.

Next, use the PHP `mix()` helper in your views to refer to that file like in Example 6-10.

Example 6-10. Using the mix() helper in views

```
<link rel="stylesheet" href="{{ mix("css/app.css") }}">

// Will output something like:

<link rel="stylesheet" href="/css/app.css?id=5ee7141a759a5fb7377a">
```

Vue and React

Mix can handle building both Vue (with single-file components) and React components. Mix's default `js()` call handles Vue, and you can replace it with a `react()` call if you want to build React components:

```
mix.react('resources/js/app.js', 'public/js');
```

If you take a look at the default Laravel sample *app.js* and the components it imports (Example 6-11), you'll see that you don't have to do anything special to work with Vue components. A simple `mix.js()` call makes this possible in your *app.js*.

Example 6-11. App.js configured to work with Vue

```
window.Vue = require('vue');

Vue.component('example-component', require('./components/ExampleComponent.vue'));

const app = new Vue({
    el: '#app'
});
```

And if you switch to `react()`, this is all you need to run in your file for your first component:

```
require('./components/Example');
```

Both presets also bring in Axios, Lodash, and Popper.js, so you don't have to spend any time getting your Vue or React ecosystems set up.

Hot Module Replacement

 When you're writing single components with Vue or React, you're likely used to either refreshing the page every time your build tool recompiles your components or, if you're using something like Mix, relying on Browsersync to reload it for you.

That's great, but if you're working with single-page apps (SPAs), that means you're booted back to the beginning of the app; that refresh wipes any state you had built up as you navigated through the app.

Hot Module Replacement (HMR, sometimes called *hot reloading*) solves this problem. It's not always easy to set up, but Mix comes with it enabled out of the box. HMR works essentially as if you'd taught Browsersync to not reload the entire file that was recompiled, but instead to just reload the bits of code you changed. That means you can get the updated code injected into your browser, but still retain the state you had built up as you got your SPA into just the right spot for testing.

To use HMR, you'll want to run npm run hot instead of npm run watch. In order for it to work correctly, all of your <script> references have to be pulling the right versions of your JavaScript files. Essentially, Mix is booting up a small Node server at localhost:8080, so if your <script> tag points to a different version of the script, HMR won't work.

The easiest way to achieve this is to just use the mix() helper to reference your scripts. This helper will handle prepending either localhost:8080 if in HMR mode or your domain if you're in a normal development mode. Here's what it looks like inline:

```
<body>
    <div id="app"></div>

    <script src="{{ mix('js/app.js') }}"></script>
</body>
```

If you develop your applications on an HTTPS connection—for example, if you run valet secure—all your assets must also be served via an HTTPS connection. This is a little bit trickier, so it's best to consult the HMR docs (*http://bit.ly/2U2xvGb*).

Vendor extraction

The most common frontend bundling pattern, which Mix also encourages, ends up generating a single CSS file and a single JavaScript file that encompasses both the app-specific code for your project and the code for all its dependencies.

However, this means that vendor file updates require the entire file to be rebuilt and recached, which might introduce an undesirable load time.

Mix makes it easy to extract all of the JavaScript from your app's dependencies into a separate *vendor.js* file. Simply supply a list of the vendor's library names to the extract() method, chained after your js() call. Take a look at Example 6-12 to see how it looks.

Example 6-12. Extracting a vendor library into a separate file

```
mix.js('resources/js/app.js', 'public/js')
    .extract(['vue'])
```

This outputs your existing *app.js* and then two new files: *manifest.js*, which gives instructions to your browser about how to load the dependencies and app code, and *vendor.js*, which contains the vendor-specific code.

It's important to load these files in the correct order in your frontend code—first *manifest.js*, then *vendor.js*, and finally *app.js*:

Extracting All Dependencies Using extract() in Mix 4.0+

If your project is using Laravel Mix 4.0 or greater, you can call the extract() method with no arguments. This will extract the entire dependency list for your application.

```
<script src="{{ mix('js/manifest.js') }}"></script>
<script src="{{ mix('js/vendor.js') }}"></script>
<script src="{{ mix('js/app.js') }}"></script>
```

Environment variables in Mix

As Example 6-13 shows, if you prefix an environment variable (in your *.env* file) with MIX_, it will become available in your Mix-compiled files with the naming convention process.env.*ENV_VAR_NAME*.

Example 6-13. Using .env variables in Mix-compiled JavaScript

```
# In your .env file
MIX_BUGSNAG_KEY=lj12389g08bq1234
MIX_APP_NAME="Your Best App Now"

// In Mix-compiled files
process.env.MIX_BUGSNAG_KEY

// For example, this code:
console.log("Welcome to " + process.env.MIX_APP_NAME);

// Will compile down to this:
console.log("Welcome to " + "Your Best App Now");
```

You can also access those variables in your Webpack configuration files using Node's *dotenv* package, as shown in Example 6-14.

Example 6-14. Using .env variables in Webpack configuration files

```
// webpack.mix.js
let mix = require('laravel-mix');
require('dotenv').config();

let isProduction = process.env.MIX_ENV === "production";
```

Frontend Presets and Auth Scaffolding

As a full-stack framework, Laravel has more connections to and opinions about frontend tooling than your average backend framework. Out of the box it provides an entire build system, which we've already covered, but it also builds and has components for Vue and includes Bootstrap, Axios, and Lodash.

Frontend Presets

You can get a sense of the frontend tools that come along with each new Laravel install by taking a look at *package.json*, *webpack.mix.js* (or *gulpfile.js* in older versions of Laravel), and the views, JavaScript files, and CSS files in the *resources* directory. This default set of components and files is called the *Vue preset*, and every new Laravel project comes stocked with it.

 But what if you'd rather work in React? What if you want Bootstrap but not all that JavaScript? And what if you want to just rip it all out? Enter *frontend presets*, introduced in Laravel 5.5: these are pre-baked scripts that modify or remove part or all of the Vue- and Bootstrap-loaded default presets. You can use the presets that are provided out of the box, or you can pull in third-party presets from GitHub.

To use a built-in preset, simply run php artisan present *preset_name*:

```
php artisan preset react
php artisan preset bootstrap
php artisan preset none
```

There's also a vue preset, which is what each new application has applied on a fresh install.

Third-party frontend presets

If you're interested in creating your own preset, or using one created by another community member, that's also possible with the frontend preset system. There's a GitHub organization (*http://bit.ly/2OraXt6*) designed to make it easy to find great third-party frontend presets, and they're easy to install. For most, the steps are as follows:

1. Install the package (e.g., composer require laravel-frontend-presets/tail windcss).

2. Install the preset (e.g., php artisan preset tailwindcss).

3. Just like with the built-in presets, run npm install and npm run dev.

If you want to create a preset of your own, the same organization has a skeleton repository (*http://bit.ly/2U4ZLrH*) you can fork to make it easier.

Auth Scaffolding

Although they're technically not a part of the frontend presets, Laravel has a series of routes and views called the *auth scaffold* that are, essentially, frontend presets. If you run php artisan make:auth, you'll get a login page, a signup page, a new master template for the "app" view of your app, routes to serve these pages, and more. Take a look at Chapter 9 to learn more.

Pagination

For something that is so common across web applications, pagination still can be wildly complicated to implement. Thankfully, Laravel has a built-in concept of pagination, and it's also hooked into Eloquent results *and* the router by default.

Paginating Database Results

The most common place you'll see pagination is when you are displaying the results of a database query and there are too many results for a single page. Eloquent and the query builder both read the page query parameter from the current page request and use it to provide a paginate() method on any result sets; the single parameter you should pass paginate() is how many results you want per page. Take a look at Example 6-15 to see how this works.

Example 6-15. Paginating a query builder response

```
// PostsController
public function index()
{
    return view('posts.index', ['posts' => DB::table('posts')->paginate(20)]);
}
```

Example 6-15 specifies that this route should return 20 posts per page, and will define which "page" of results the current user is on based on the URL's page query parameter, if it has one. Eloquent models all have the same paginate() method.

When you display the results in your view, your collection will now have a links() method on it (or render() for Laravel 5.1) that will output the pagination controls, with class names from the Bootstrap component library assigned to them by default (see Example 6-16).

Example 6-16. Rendering pagination links in a template

```php
// posts/index.blade.php
<table>
@foreach ($posts as $post)
    <tr><td>{{ $post->title }}</td></tr>
@endforeach
</table>

{{ $posts->links() }}

// By default, $posts->links() will output something like this:
<ul class="pagination">
    <li class="page-item disabled"><span>&laquo;</span></li>
    <li class="page-item active"><span>1</span></li>
    <li class="page-item">
        <a class="page-link" href="http://myapp.com/posts?page=2">2</a>
    </li>
    <li class="page-item">
        <a class="page-link" href="http://myapp.com/posts?page=3">3</a>
    </li>
    <li class="page-item">
        <a class="page-link" href="http://myapp.com/posts?page=2" rel="next">
            &raquo;
        </a>
    </li>
</ul>
```

Customizing the Number of Pagination Links in Laravel 5.7 and Later

If you'd like to control how many links show on either side of the current page, projects running Laravel 5.7 and later can customize this number easily with the onEachSide() method:

```php
DB::table('posts')->paginate(10)->onEachSide(3);

// Outputs:
// 5 6 7 [8] 9 10 11
```

Manually Creating Paginators

If you're not working with Eloquent or the query builder, or if you're working with a complex query (e.g., one using groupBy), you might find yourself needing to create a paginator manually. Thankfully, you can do that with the Illuminate\Pagination \Paginator or Illuminate\Pagination\LengthAwarePaginator classes.

The difference between the two classes is that `Paginator` will only provide previous and next buttons, but no links to each page; `LengthAwarePaginator` needs to know the length of the full result so that it can generate links for each individual page. You may find yourself wanting to use `Paginator` on large result sets, so your paginator doesn't have to be aware of a massive count of results that might be costly to run.

Both `Paginator` and `LengthAwarePaginator` require you to manually extract the subset of content that you want to pass to the view. Take a look at Example 6-17 for an example.

Example 6-17. Manually creating a paginator

```
use Illuminate\Http\Request;
use Illuminate\Pagination\Paginator;

Route::get('people', function (Request $request) {
    $people = [...]; // huge list of people

    $perPage = 15;
    $offsetPages = $request->input('page', 1) - 1;

    // The Paginator will not slice your array for you
    $people = array_slice(
        $people,
        $offsetPages * $perPage,
        $perPage
    );

    return new Paginator(
        $people,
        $perPage
    );
});
```

> The `Paginator` syntax has changed over the last few versions of Laravel, so if you're using 5.1, take a look at the docs (*http://bit.ly/2U6M37I*) to find the correct syntax.

Message Bags

Another common but painful feature in web applications is passing messages between various components of the app, when the end goal is to share them with the user. Your controller, for example, might want to send a validation message: "The `email` field must be a valid email address." However, that particular message doesn't just need to make it to the view layer; it actually needs to survive a redirect and then end up in the view layer of a different page. How do you structure this messaging logic?

Illuminate\Support\MessageBag is a class tasked with storing, categorizing, and returning messages that are intended for the end user. It groups all messages by key, where the keys are likely to be something like errors and messages, and it provides convenience methods for getting all its stored messages or only those for a particular key and outputting these messages in various formats.

You can spin up a new instance of MessageBag manually like in Example 6-18. To be honest though, you likely won't ever do this manually—this is just a thought exercise to show how it works.

Example 6-18. Manually creating and using a message bag

```
$messages = [
    'errors' => [
        'Something went wrong with edit 1!',
    ],
    'messages' => [
        'Edit 2 was successful.',
    ],
];
$messagebag = new \Illuminate\Support\MessageBag($messages);

// Check for errors; if there are any, decorate and echo
if ($messagebag->has('errors')) {
    echo '<ul id="errors">';
    foreach ($messagebag->get('errors', '<li><b>:message</b></li>') as $error) {
        echo $error;
    }
    echo '</ul>';
}
```

Message bags are also closely connected to Laravel's validators (you'll learn more about these in "Validation" on page 189): when validators return errors, they actually return an instance of MessageBag, which you can then pass to your view or attach to a redirect using redirect('route')->withErrors($messagebag).

Laravel passes an empty instance of MessageBag to every view, assigned to the variable $errors; if you've flashed a message bag using withErrors() on a redirect, it will get assigned to that $errors variable instead. That means every view can always assume it has an $errors MessageBag it can check wherever it handles validation, which leads to Example 6-19 as a common snippet developers place on every page.

Example 6-19. Error bag snippet

```
// partials/errors.blade.php
@if ($errors->any())
    <div class="alert alert-danger">
```

```
        <ul>
        @foreach ($errors as $error)
            <li>{{ $error }}</li>
        @endforeach
        </ul>
    </div>
@endif
```

 Missing $errors Variable

If you have any routes that aren't under the web middleware group,
they won't have the session middleware, which means they won't
have this $errors variable available.

Named Error Bags

Sometimes you need to differentiate message bags not just by key (notices versus
errors) but also by component. Maybe you have a login form and a signup form on
the same page; how do you differentiate them?

When you send errors along with a redirect using withErrors(), the second parameter is the name of the bag: redirect('dashboard')->withErrors($validator,
'login'). Then, on the dashboard, you can use $errors->login to call all of the
methods you saw before: any(), count(), and more.

String Helpers, Pluralization, and Localization

As developers, we tend to look at blocks of text as big placeholder divs, waiting for
the client to put real content into them. Seldom are we involved in any logic inside
these blocks.

But there are a few circumstances where you'll be grateful for the tools Laravel provides for string manipulation.

The String Helpers and Pluralization

Laravel has a series of helpers for manipulating strings. They're available as methods
on the Str class (e.g., Str::plural()), but most also have a global helper function
(e.g., str_plural()).

The Laravel documentation (*http://bit.ly/2HQKaFC*) covers all of them in detail, but
here are a few of the most commonly used string helpers:

e()
    A shortcut for html_entities(); encodes all HTML entities for safety.

`starts_with()`, `ends_with()`, `str_contains()`
> Check a string (first parameter) to see if it starts with, ends with, or contains another string (second parameter).

`str_is()`
> Checks whether a string (second parameter) matches a particular pattern (first parameter)—for example, `foo*` will match `foobar` and `foobaz`.

`str_slug()`
> Converts a string to a URL-type slug with hyphens.

`str_plural(`*word*`, `*count*`)`, `str_singular()`
> Pluralizes a word or singularizes it; English-only (e.g., `str_plural('dog')` returns `dogs`; `str_plural('dog', 1'))` returns `dog`).

`camel_case()`, `kebab_case()`, `snake_case()`, `studly_case()`, `title_case()`
> Convert a provided string to a different capitalization "case".

`str_after()`, `str_before()`, `str_limit()`
> Trim a string and provide a substring. `str_after()` returns everything after a given string and `str_before()` everything before the given string (both accept the full string as the first parameter and the string you're using to cut as the second). `str_limit()` truncates a string (first parameter) to a given number of characters (second parameter).

Localization

Localization allows you to define multiple languages and mark any strings as targets for translation. You can set a fallback language, and even handle pluralization variations.

In Laravel, you'll need to set an "application locale" at some point during the page load so the localization helpers know which bucket of translations to pull from. Each "locale" is usually connected to a translation, and will often look like "en" (for English). You'll do this with `App::setLocale($localeName)`, and you'll likely put it in a service provider. For now you can just put it in the `boot()` method of `AppServiceProvider`, but you may want to create a `LocaleServiceProvider` if you end up with more than just this one locale-related binding.

Setting the Locale for Each Request

It can be confusing at first to work out how Laravel "knows" the user's locale, or provides translations. Most of that work is down to you as the developer. Let's look at a likely scenario.

You'll probably have some functionality allowing the user to choose a locale, or possibly attempting to automatically detect it. Either way, your application will determine the locale, and then you'll store that in a URL parameter or a session cookie. Then your service provider—something like a `LocaleServiceProvider`, maybe—will grab that key and set it as a part of Laravel's bootstrap.

So maybe your user is at *http://myapp.com/es/contacts*. Your `LocaleServiceProvider` will grab that `es` string and then run `App::setLocale('es')`. Going forward, every time you ask for a translation of a string, Laravel will look for the Spanish (`es` means Español) version of that string, which you will need to have defined somewhere.

You can define your fallback locale in *config/app.php*, where you should find a `fallback_locale` key. This allows you to define a default language for your application, which Laravel will use if it can't find a translation for the requested locale.

Basic localization

So, how do we call for a translated string? There's a helper function, `__($key)`, that will pull the string for the current locale for the passed key or, if it doesn't exist, grab it from the default locale. In Blade you can also use the `@lang()` directive. Example 6-20 demonstrates how a basic translation works. We'll use the example of a "back to the dashboard" link at the top of a detail page.

Example 6-20. Basic use of __()

```
// Normal PHP
<?php echo __('navigation.back'); ?>

// Blade
{{ __('navigation.back') }}

// Blade directive
@lang('navigation.back')
```

Let's assume we are using the `es` locale right now. Laravel will look for a file in *resources/lang/es/navigation.php*, which it will expect to return an array. It'll look for a `back` key on that array, and if it exists, it'll return its value. Take a look at Example 6-21 for a sample.

Example 6-21. Using a translation

```
// resources/lang/es/navigation.php
return [
    'back' => 'Volver al panel',
];
```

```
// routes/web.php
Route::get('/es/contacts/show/{id}', function () {
    // Setting it manually, for this example, instead of in a service provider
    App::setLocale('es');
    return view('contacts.show');
});

// resources/views/contacts/show.blade.php
<a href="/contacts">{{ __('navigation.back') }}</a>
```

The Translation Helper Prior to Laravel 5.4

In projects running versions of Laravel prior to 5.4, the __() helper isn't available. You will instead have to use the trans() helper, which accesses an older translation system that works similarly to what we're describing here, but can't access the JSON translation system.

Parameters in localization

The preceding example was relatively simple. Let's dig into some that are more complex. What if we want to define *which* dashboard we're returning to? Take a look at Example 6-22.

Example 6-22. Parameters in translations

```
// resources/lang/en/navigation.php
return [
    'back' => 'Back to :section dashboard',
];

// resources/views/contacts/show.blade.php
{{ __('navigation.back', ['section' => 'contacts']) }}
```

As you can see, prepending a word with a colon (:section) marks it as a placeholder that can be replaced. The second, optional, parameter of __() is an array of values to replace the placeholders with.

Pluralization in localization

We already covered pluralization, so now just imagine you're defining your own pluralization rules. There are two ways to do it; we'll start with the simplest, as shown in Example 6-23.

Example 6-23. Defining a simple translation with an option for pluralization

```
// resources/lang/en/messages.php
return [
```

```
        'task-deletion' => 'You have deleted a task|You have successfully deleted tasks',
];

// resources/views/dashboard.blade.php
@if ($numTasksDeleted > 0)
    {{ trans_choice('messages.task-deletion', $numTasksDeleted) }}
@endif
```

As you can see, we have a `trans_choice()` method, which takes the count of items affected as its second parameter; from this it will determine which string to use.

You can also use any translation definitions that are compatible with Symfony's much more complex `Translation` component; see Example 6-24 for an example.

Example 6-24. Using the Symfony's Translation component

```
// resources/lang/es/messages.php
return [
    'task-deletion' => "{0} You didn't manage to delete any tasks.|" .
        "[1,4] You deleted a few tasks.|" .
        "[5,Inf] You deleted a whole ton of tasks.",
];
```

Storing the default string as the key with JSON

One common difficulty with localization is that it's hard to ensure there's a good system for defining key namespacing—for example, remembering a key nested three or four levels deep or being unsure which key a phrase used twice in the site should use.

An alternative to the slug key/string value pair system is to store your translations using your primary language string as the key, instead of a made-up slug. You can indicate to Laravel that you're working this way by storing your translation files as JSON in the *resources/lang* directory, with the filename reflecting the locale (Example 6-25).

Example 6-25. Using JSON translations and the __() helper

```
// In Blade
{{ __('View friends list') }}

// resources/lang/es.json
{
  'View friends list': 'Ver lista de amigos'
}
```

This is taking advantage of the fact that the __() translation helper, if it can't find a matching key for the current language, will just display the key. If your key is the string in your app's default language, that's a much more reasonable fallback than, for example, `widgets.friends.title`.

 JSON Translations Unavailable Prior to Laravel 5.4

The JSON string translation format is only available in Laravel 5.4 and later.

Testing

In this chapter we focused primarily on Laravel's frontend components. These are less likely the objects of unit tests, but they may at times be used in your integration tests.

Testing Message and Error Bags

There are two primary ways of testing messages passed along with message and error bags. First, you can perform a behavior in your application tests that sets a message that will eventually be displayed somewhere, then redirect to that page and assert that the appropriate message is shown.

Second, for errors (which is the most common use case), you can assert the session has errors with `$this->assertSessionHasErrors($bindings = [])`. Take a look at Example 6-26 to see what this might look like.

Example 6-26. Asserting the session has errors

```
public function test_missing_email_field_errors()
{
    $this->post('person/create', ['name' => 'Japheth']);
    $this->assertSessionHasErrors(['email']);
}
```

In order for Example 6-26 to pass, you'll need to add input validation to that route. We'll cover this in Chapter 7.

Translation and Localization

The simplest way to test localization is with application tests. Set the appropriate context (whether by URL or session), "visit" the page with `get()`, and assert that you see the appropriate content.

TL;DR

As a full-stack framework, Laravel provides tools and components for the frontend as well as the backend.

Mix is a layer in front of Webpack that makes common tasks and configurations much simpler. Mix makes it easy to use popular CSS pre- and post-processors, common JavaScript processing steps, and much more.

Laravel also offers other internal tools that target the frontend, including tools for implementing pagination, message and error bags, and localization.

## CHAPTER 7

Collecting and Handling User Data

Websites that benefit from a framework like Laravel often don't just serve static content. Many deal with complex and mixed data sources, and one of the most common (and most complex) of these sources is user input in its myriad forms: URL paths, query parameters, POST data, and file uploads.

Laravel provides a collection of tools for gathering, validating, normalizing, and filtering user-provided data. We'll look at those here.

Injecting a Request Object

The most common tool for accessing user data in Laravel is injecting an instance of the Illuminate\Http\Request object. It offers easy access to all of the ways users can provide input to your site: POSTed form data or JSON, GET requests (query parameters), and URL segments.

Other Options for Accessing Request Data

There's also a request() global helper and a Request facade, both of which expose the same methods. Each of these options exposes the entire Illuminate Request object, but for now we're only going to cover the methods that specifically relate to user data.

Since we're planning on injecting a Request object, let's take a quick look at how to get the $request object we'll be calling all these methods on:

```
Route::post('form', function (Illuminate\Http\Request $request) {
    // $request->etc()
});
```

$request->all()

Just like the name suggests, `$request->all()` gives you an array containing all of the input the user has provided, from every source. Let's say, for some reason, you decided to have a form POST to a URL with a query parameter—for example, sending a POST to *http://myapp.com/signup?utm=12345*. Take a look at Example 7-1 to see what you'd get from `$request->all()`. (Note that `$request->all()` also contains information about any files that were uploaded, but we'll cover that later in the chapter.)

Example 7-1. $request->all()

```
<!-- GET route form view at /get-route -->
<form method="post" action="/signup?utm=12345">
    @csrf
    <input type="text" name="first_name">
    <input type="submit">
</form>
// routes/web.php
Route::post('signup', function (Request $request) {
    var_dump($request->all());
});

// Outputs:
/**
 * [
 *     '_token' => 'CSRF token here',
 *     'first_name' => 'value',
 *     'utm' => 12345,
 * ]
 */
```

$request->except() and $request->only()

`$request->except()` provides the same output as `$request->all()`, but you can choose one or more fields to exclude—for example, _token. You can pass it either a string or an array of strings.

Example 7-2 shows what it looks like when we use `$request->except()` on the same form as in Example 7-1.

Example 7-2. $request->except()

```
Route::post('post-route', function (Request $request) {
    var_dump($request->except('_token'));
});

// Outputs:
/**
```

```
 * [
 *     'firstName' => 'value',
 *     'utm' => 12345
 * ]
 */
```

`$request->only()` is the inverse of `$request->except()`, as you can see in Example 7-3.

Example 7-3. $request->only()

```
Route::post('post-route', function (Request $request) {
    var_dump($request->only(['firstName', 'utm']));
});

// Outputs:
/**
 * [
 *     'firstName' => 'value',
 *     'utm' => 12345
 * ]
 */
```

$request->has()

With `$request->has()` you can detect whether a particular piece of user input is available to you. Check out Example 7-4 for an analytics example with our `utm` query string parameter from the previous examples.

Example 7-4. $request->has()

```
// POST route at /post-route
if ($request->has('utm')) {
    // Do some analytics work
}
```

$request->input()

Whereas `$request->all()`, `$request->except()`, and `$request->only()` operate on the full array of input provided by the user, `$request->input()` allows you to get the value of just a single field. Example 7-5 provides an example. Note that the second parameter is the default value, so if the user hasn't passed in a value, you can have a sensible (and nonbreaking) fallback.

Example 7-5. $request->input()

```
Route::post('post-route', function (Request $request) {
    $userName = $request->input('name', 'Matt');
});
```

$request->method() and ->isMethod()

$request->method() returns the HTTP verb for the request, and $request->isMethod() checks whether it matches the specified verb. Example 7-6 illustrates their use.

Example 7-6. $request->method() and $request->isMethod()

```
$method = $request->method();

if ($request->isMethod('patch')) {
    // Do something if request method is PATCH
}
```

Array Input

Laravel also provides convenience helpers for accessing data from array input. Just use the "dot" notation to indicate the steps of digging into the array structure, like in Example 7-7.

Example 7-7. Dot notation to access array values in user data

```
<!-- GET route form view at /employees/create -->
<form method="post" action="/employees/">
    @csrf
    <input type="text" name="employees[0][firstName]">
    <input type="text" name="employees[0][lastName]">
    <input type="text" name="employees[1][firstName]">
    <input type="text" name="employees[1][lastName]">
    <input type="submit">
</form>

// POST route at /employees
Route::post('employees', function (Request $request) {
    $employeeZeroFirstName = $request->input('employees.0.firstName');
    $allLastNames = $request->input('employees.*.lastName');
    $employeeOne = $request->input('employees.1');
    var_dump($employeeZeroFirstname, $allLastNames, $employeeOne);
});

// If forms filled out as "Jim" "Smith" "Bob" "Jones":
// $employeeZeroFirstName = 'Jim';
```

```
// $allLastNames = ['Smith', 'Jones'];
// $employeeOne = ['firstName' => 'Bob', 'lastName' => 'Jones'];
```

JSON Input (and $request->json())

So far we've covered input from query strings (GET) and form submissions (POST). But there's another form of user input that's becoming more common with the advent of JavaScript SPAs: the JSON request. It's essentially just a POST request with the body set to JSON instead of a traditional form POST.

Let's take a look at what it might look like to submit some JSON to a Laravel route, and how to use $request->input() to pull out that data (Example 7-8).

Example 7-8. Getting data from JSON with $request->input()

```
POST /post-route HTTP/1.1
Content-Type: application/json

{
    "firstName": "Joe",
    "lastName": "Schmoe",
    "spouse": {
        "firstName": "Jill",
        "lastName":"Schmoe"
    }
}

// Post-route
Route::post('post-route', function (Request $request) {
    $firstName = $request->input('firstName');
    $spouseFirstname = $request->input('spouse.firstName');
});
```

Since $request->input() is smart enough to pull user data from GET, POST, or JSON, you may wonder why Laravel even offers $request->json(). There are two reasons you might prefer $request->json(). First, you might want to just be more explicit to other programmers working on your project about where you're expecting the data to come from. And second, if the POST doesn't have the correct application/json headers, $request->input() won't pick it up as JSON, but $request->json() will.

Facade Namespaces, the request() Global Helper, and Injecting $request

Any time you're using facades inside of namespaced classes (e.g., controllers), you'll have to add the full facade path to the import block at the top of your file (e.g., use Illuminate\Support\Facades\Request).

Because of this, several of the facades also have a companion global helper function. If these helper functions are run with no parameters, they expose the same syntax as the facade (e.g., `request()->has()` is the same as `Request::has()`). They also have a default behavior for when you pass them a parameter (e.g., `request('firstName')` is a shortcut to `request()->input('firstName')`).

With `Request`, we've been covering injecting an instance of the `Request` object, but you could also use the `Request` facade or the `request()` global helper. Take a look at Chapter 10 to learn more.

Route Data

It might not be the first thing you think of when you imagine "user data," but the URL is just as much user data as anything else in this chapter.

There are two primary ways you'll get data from the URL: via `Request` objects and via route parameters.

From Request

Injected `Request` objects (and the `Request` facade and the `request()` helper) have several methods available to represent the state of the current page's URL, but right now let's focus on at getting information about the URL segments.

If you're not familiar with the idea, each group of characters after the domain in a URL is called a *segment*. So, *http://www.myapp.com/users/15/* has two segments: *users* and *15*.

As you can probably guess, we have two methods available to us: `$request->segments()` returns an array of all segments, and `$request->segment($segmentId)` allows us to get the value of a single segment. Note that segments are returned on a 1-based index, so in the preceding example, `$request->segment(1)` would return *users*.

`Request` objects, the `Request` facade, and the `request()` global helper provide quite a few more methods to help us get data out of the URL. To learn more, check out Chapter 10.

From Route Parameters

The other primary way we get data about the URL is from route parameters, which are injected into the controller method or closure that is serving a current route, as shown in Example 7-9.

Example 7-9. Getting URL details from route parameters

```php
// routes/web.php
Route::get('users/{id}', function ($id) {
    // If the user visits myapp.com/users/15/, $id will equal 15
});
```

To learn more about routes and route binding, check out Chapter 3.

Uploaded Files

We've talked about different ways to interact with users' text input, but there's also the matter of file uploads to consider. *Request* objects provide access to any uploaded files using the `$request->file()` method, which takes the file's input name as a parameter and returns an instance of `Symfony\Component\HttpFoundation\File\Uploaded File`. Let's walk through an example. First, our form, in Example 7-10.

Example 7-10. A form to upload files

```html
<form method="post" enctype="multipart/form-data">
    @csrf
    <input type="text" name="name">
    <input type="file" name="profile_picture">
    <input type="submit">
</form>
```

Now let's take a look at what we get from running `$request->all()`, as shown in Example 7-11. Note that `$request->input('profile_picture')` will return null; we need to use `$request->file('profile_picture')` instead.

Example 7-11. The output from submitting the form in Example 7-10

```php
Route::post('form', function (Request $request) {
    var_dump($request->all());
});

// Output:
// [
//     "_token" => "token here",
//     "name" => "asdf",
//     "profile_picture" => UploadedFile {},
// ]

Route::post('form', function (Request $request) {
    if ($request->hasFile('profile_picture')) {
        var_dump($request->file('profile_picture'));
    }
});
```

```
// Output:
// UploadedFile (details)
```

Validating a File Upload

As you can see in Example 7-11, we have access to `$request->hasFile()` to see whether the user uploaded a file. We can also check whether the file upload was successful by using `isValid()` on the file itself:

```
if ($request->file('profile_picture')->isValid()) {
    //
}
```

Because `isValid()` is called on the file itself, it will error if the user didn't upload a file. So, to check for both, you'd need to check for the file's existence first:

```
if ($request->hasFile('profile_picture') &&
    $request->file('profile_picture')->isValid()) {
    //
}
```

Symfony's `UploadedFile` class extends PHP's native `SplFileInfo` with methods allowing you to easily inspect and manipulate the file. This list isn't exhaustive, but it gives you a taste of what you can do:

- `guessExtension()`
- `getMimeType()`
- `store($path, $storageDisk = default disk)`
- `storeAs($path, $newName, $storageDisk = default disk)`
- `storePublicly($path, $storageDisk = default disk)`
- `storePubliclyAs($path, $newName, $storageDisk = default disk)`
- `move($directory, $newName = null)`
- `getClientOriginalName()`
- `getClientOriginalExtension()`
- `getClientMimeType()`
- `guessClientExtension()`
- `getClientSize()`
- `getError()`
- `isValid()`

As you can see, most of the methods have to do with getting information about the uploaded file, but there's one that you'll likely use more than all the others: `store()` (available since Laravel 5.3), which takes the file that was uploaded with the request and stores it in a specified directory on your server. Its first parameter is the destination directory, and the optional second parameter will be the storage disk (`s3`, `local`, etc.) to use to store the file. You can see a common workflow in Example 7-12.

Example 7-12. Common file upload workflow

```
if ($request->hasFile('profile_picture')) {
    $path = $request->profile_picture->store('profiles', 's3');
    auth()->user()->profile_picture = $path;
    auth()->user()->save();
}
```

If you need to specify the filename, you can use `storeAs()` instead of `store()`. The first parameter is still the path; the second is the filename, and the optional third parameter is the storage disk to use.

> **Proper Form Encoding for File Uploads**
>
> If you get `null` when you try to get the contents of a file from your request, you might've forgotten to set the encoding type on your form. Make sure to add the attribute `enctype="multipart/form-data"` on your form:
>
> ```
> <form method="post" enctype="multipart/form-data">
> ```

Validation

Laravel has quite a few ways you can validate incoming data. We'll cover form requests in the next section, so that leaves us with two primary options: validating manually or using the `validate()` method on the `Request` object. Let's start with the simpler, and more common, `validate()`.

validate() on the Request Object

The `Request` object has a `validate()` method that provides a convenient shortcut for the most common validation workflow. Take a look at Example 7-13.

Example 7-13. Basic usage of request validation

```
// routes/web.php
Route::get('recipes/create', 'RecipesController@create');
Route::post('recipes', 'RecipesController@store');
```

```
// app/Http/Controllers/RecipesController.php
class RecipesController extends Controller
{
    public function create()
    {
        return view('recipes.create');
    }

    public function store(Request $request)
    {
        $request->validate([
            'title' => 'required|unique:recipes|max:125',
            'body' => 'required'
        ]);

        // Recipe is valid; proceed to save it
    }
}
```

We only have four lines of code running our validation here, but they're doing a lot.

First, we explicitly define the fields we expect and apply rules (here separated by the pipe character, |) to each individually.

Next, the `validate()` method checks the incoming data from the `$request` and determines whether or not it is valid.

If the data is valid, the `validate()` method ends and we can move on with the controller method, saving the data or whatever else.

But if the data isn't valid, it throws a `ValidationException`. This contains instructions to the router about how to handle this exception. If the request is from Java-Script (or if it's requesting JSON as a response), the exception will create a JSON response containing the validation errors. If not, the exception will return a redirect to the previous page, together with all of the user input and the validation errors—perfect for repopulating a failed form and showing some errors.

 Calling the validate() Method on the Controller Prior to Laravel 5.5

In projects running versions of Laravel prior to 5.5, this validation shortcut is called on the controller (running `$this->validate()`) instead of on the request.

More on Laravel's Validation Rules

In our examples here (like in the docs) we're using the "pipe" syntax: `'fieldname':` `'rule|otherRule|anotherRule'`. But you can also use the array syntax to do the same thing: `'fieldname': ['rule', 'otherRule', 'anotherRule']`.

Additionally, you can validate nested properties. This matters if you use HTML's array syntax, which allows you to, for example, have multiple "users" on an HTML form, each with an associated name. Here's how you validate that:

```
$request->validate([
    'user.name' => 'required',
    'user.email' => 'required|email',
]);
```

We don't have enough space to cover every possible validation rule here, but here are a few of the most common rules and their functions:

Require the field
  `required`; `required_if:anotherField,equalToThisValue`;
  `required_unless:anotherField,equalToThisValue`

Field must contain certain types of character
  `alpha`; `alpha_dash`; `alpha_num`; `numeric`; `integer`

Field must contain certain patterns
  `email`; `active_url`; `ip`

Dates
  `after:date`; `before:date` (*date* can be any valid string that `strtotime()` can handle)

Numbers
  `between:min,max`; `min:num`; `max:num`; `size:num` (`size` tests against length for strings, value for integers, `count` for arrays, or size in KB for files)

Image dimensions
  `dimensions:min_width=XXX`; can also use and/or combine with `max_width`, `min_height`, `max_height`, `width`, `height`, and `ratio`

Databases
  `exists:tableName`; `unique:tableName` (expects to look in the same table column as the field name; see the docs (*http://bit.ly/2eMLZDl*) for how to customize)

Manual Validation

If you are not working in a controller, or if for some other reason the previously described flow is not a good fit, you can manually create a `Validator` instance using the `Validator` facade and check for success or failure like in Example 7-14.

Example 7-14. Manual validation

```
Route::get('recipes/create', function () {
    return view('recipes.create');
});

Route::post('recipes', function (Illuminate\Http\Request $request) {
    $validator = Validator::make($request->all(), [
        'title' => 'required|unique:recipes|max:125',
        'body' => 'required'
    ]);

    if ($validator->fails()) {
        return redirect('recipes/create')
            ->withErrors($validator)
            ->withInput();
    }

    // Recipe is valid; proceed to save it
});
```

As you can see, we create an instance of a validator by passing it our input as the first parameter and the validation rules as the second parameter. The validator exposes a `fails()` method that we can check against and can be passed into the `withErrors()` method of the redirect.

Custom Rule Objects

If the validation rule you need doesn't exist in Laravel, you can create your own. To create a custom rule, run `php artisan make:rule` *RuleName* and then edit that file in *app/Rules/{RuleName}.php*.

You'll get two methods in your rule out of the box: `passes()` and `message()`. `passes()` should accept an attribute name as the first parameter and the user-provided value as the second, and then return a Boolean indicating whether or not this input passes this validation rule. `message()` should return the validation error message; you can use `:attribute` as a placeholder in your message for the attribute name.

Take a look at Example 7-15 as an example.

Example 7-15. A sample custom rule

```
class WhitelistedEmailDomain implements Rule
{
    public function passes($attribute, $value)
    {
        return in_array(str_after($value, '@'), ['tighten.co']);
    }

    public function message()
    {
        return 'The :attribute field is not from a whitelisted email provider.';
    }
}
```

To use this rule, just pass an instance of the rule object to your validator:

```
$request->validate([
    'email' => new WhitelistedEmailDomain,
]);
```

 In projects running versions of Laravel prior to 5.5, custom val‐
idation rules have to be written using Validator::extend().
You can learn more about this in the docs (*http://bit.ly/2Wl87J1*).

Displaying Validation Error Messages

We've already covered much of this in Chapter 6, but here's a quick refresher on how
to display errors from validation.

The validate() method on requests (and the withErrors() method on redirects
that it relies on) flashes any errors to the session. These errors are made available to
the view you're being redirected to in the $errors variable. And remember that as a
part of Laravel's magic, that $errors variable will be available every time you load the
view, even if it's just empty, so you don't have to check if it exists with isset().

That means you can do something like Example 7-16 on every page.

Example 7-16. Echo validation errors

```
@if ($errors->any())
    <ul id="errors">
        @foreach ($errors->all() as $error)
            <li>{{ $error }}</li>
        @endforeach
    </ul>
@endif
```

Form Requests

As you build out your applications, you might start noticing some patterns in your controller methods. There are certain patterns that are repeated—for example, input validation, user authentication and authorization, and possible redirects. If you find yourself wanting a structure to normalize and extract these common behaviors out of your controller methods, you may be interested in Laravel's form requests.

A form request is a custom request class that is intended to map to the submission of a form, and the request takes the responsibility for validating the request, authorizing the user, and optionally redirecting the user upon a failed validation. Each form request will usually, but not always, explicitly map to a single HTTP request—for example, "Create Comment."

Creating a Form Request

You can create a new form request from the command line:

```
php artisan make:request CreateCommentRequest
```

You now have a form request object available at *app/Http/Requests/ CreateCommentRequest.php*.

Every form request class provides either one or two public methods. The first is `rules()`, which needs to return an array of validation rules for this request. The second (optional) method is `authorize()`; if this returns `true`, the user is authorized to perform this request, and if `false`, the user is rejected. Take a look at Example 7-17 to see a sample form request.

Example 7-17. Sample form request

```php
<?php

namespace App\Http\Requests;

use App\BlogPost;
use Illuminate\Foundation\Http\FormRequest;

class CreateCommentRequest extends FormRequest
{
    public function authorize()
    {
        $blogPostId = $this->route('blogPost');

        return auth()->check() && BlogPost::where('id', $blogPostId)
            ->where('user_id', auth()->id())->exists();
    }
```

```
    public function rules()
    {
        return [
            'body' => 'required|max:1000',
        ];
    }
}
```

The `rules()` section of Example 7-17 is pretty self-explanatory, but let's look at `authorize()` briefly.

We're grabbing the segment from the route named `blogPost`. That's implying the route definition for this route probably looks a bit like this: `Route::post('blog Posts/`*blogPost*`', function () // Do stuff)`. As you can see, we named the route parameter `blogPost`, which makes it accessible in our `Request` using `$this->route('blogPost')`.

We then look at whether the user is logged in and, if so, whether any blog posts exist with that identifier that are owned by the currently logged-in user. You've already learned some easier ways to check ownership in Chapter 5, but we'll keep it more explicit here to keep it clean. We'll cover what implications this has shortly, but the important thing to know is that returning `true` means the user is authorized to perform the specified action (in this case, creating a comment), and `false` means the user is not authorized.

Requests Extend Userland Request Prior to Laravel 5.3

In projects running versions of Laravel prior to 5.3, form requests extended `App\Http\Requests\Request` instead of `Illuminate\Foundation\Http\FormRequest`.

Using a Form Request

Now that we've created a form request object, how do we use it? It's a little bit of Laravel magic. Any route (closure or controller method) that typehints a form request as one of its parameters will benefit from the definition of that form request.

Let's try it out, in Example 7-18.

Example 7-18. Using a form request

```
Route::post('comments', function (App\Http\Requests\CreateCommentRequest $request) {
    // Store comment
});
```

You might be wondering where we call the form request, but Laravel does it for us. It validates the user input and authorizes the request. If the input is invalid, it'll act just like the `Request` object's `validate()` method, redirecting the user to the previous page with their input preserved and with the appropriate error messages passed along. And if the user is not authorized, Laravel will return a 403 Forbidden error and not execute the route code.

Eloquent Model Mass Assignment

Until now, we've been looking at validating at the controller level, which is absolutely the best place to start. But you can also filter the incoming data at the model level.

It's a common (but not recommended) pattern to pass the entirety of a form's input directly to a database model. In Laravel, that might look like Example 7-19.

Example 7-19. Passing the entirety of a form to an Eloquent model

```
Route::post('posts', function (Request $request) {
    $newPost = Post::create($request->all());
});
```

We're assuming here that the end user is kind and not malicious, and has kept only the fields we want them to edit—maybe the post `title` or `body`.

But what if our end user can guess, or discern, that we have an `author_id` field on that `posts` table? What if they used their browser tools to add an `author_id` field and set the ID to be someone else's ID, and impersonated the other person by creating fake blog posts attributed to them?

Eloquent has a concept called "mass assignment" that allows you to either whitelist fields that should be fillable (using the model's `$fillable` property) or blacklist fields that shouldn't be fillable (using the model's `$guarded` property) by passing them in an array to `create()` or `update()`. See "Mass assignment" on page 124 for more information.

In our example, we might want to fill out the model like in Example 7-20 to keep our app safe.

Example 7-20. Guarding an Eloquent model from mischievous mass assignment

```
<?php

namespace App;

use Illuminate\Database\Eloquent\Model;
```

```
class Post extends Model
{
    // Disable mass assignment on the author_id field
    protected $guarded = ['author_id'];
}
```

By setting `author_id` to guarded, we ensure that malicious users will no longer be able to override the value of this field by manually adding it to the contents of a form that they're sending to our app.

> **Double Protection Using $request->only()**
>
> While it's important to do a good job of protecting our models from mass assignment, it's also worth being careful on the assigning end. Rather than using $request->all(), consider using $request->only() so you can specify which fields you'd like to pass into your model:
>
> ```
> Route::post('posts', function (Request $request) {
>     $newPost = Post::create($request->only([
>         'title',
>         'body',
>     ]));
> });
> ```

{{ Versus {!!

Any time you display content on a web page that was created by a user, you need to guard against malicious input, such as script injection.

Let's say you allow your users to write blog posts on your site. You probably don't want them to be able to inject malicious JavaScript that will run in your unsuspecting visitors' browsers, right? So, you'll want to escape any user input that you show on the page to avoid this.

Thankfully, this is almost entirely covered for you. If you use Laravel's Blade templating engine, the default "echo" syntax ({{ *$stuffToEcho* }}) runs the output through `htmlentities()` (PHP's best way of making user content safe to echo) automatically. You actually have to do *extra* work to avoid escaping the output, by using the {!! *$stuffToEcho* !!} syntax.

Testing

If you're interested in testing your interactions with user input, you're probably most interested in simulating valid and invalid user input and ensuring that if the input is invalid the user is redirected, and if the input is valid it ends up in the proper place (e.g., the database).

Laravel's end-to-end application testing makes this simple.

Requiring BrowserKit After Laravel 5.4

If you want to work with test specific user interactions on the page and with your forms, and you're working in a project running Laravel 5.4 or later, you'll want to pull in Laravel's BrowserKit testing package. Simply require the package:

```
composer require laravel/browser-kit-testing --dev
```

and modify your application's base `TestCase` class to extend `Laravel\BrowserKitTesting\TestCase` instead of `Illuminate\Foundation\Testing\TestCase`.

Let's start with an invalid route that we expect to be rejected, as in Example 7-21.

Example 7-21. Testing that invalid input is rejected

```
public function test_input_missing_a_title_is_rejected()
{
    $response = $this->post('posts', ['body' => 'This is the body of my post']);
    $response->assertRedirect();
    $response->assertSessionHasErrors();
}
```

Here we assert that after invalid input the user is redirected, with errors attached. You can see we're using a few custom PHPUnit assertions that Laravel adds here.

Different Names for Testing Methods Prior to Laravel 5.4

Prior to Laravel 5.4, the `assertRedirect()` assertion was named `assertRedirectedTo()`.

So, how do we test our route's success? Check out Example 7-22.

Example 7-22. Testing that valid input is processed

```
public function test_valid_input_should_create_a_post_in_the_database()
{
    $this->post('posts', ['title' => 'Post Title', 'body' => 'This is the body']);
    $this->assertDatabaseHas('posts', ['title' => 'Post Title']);
}
```

Note that if you're testing something using the database, you'll need to learn more about database migrations and transactions. More on that in Chapter 12.

Different Names for Testing Methods Prior to Laravel 5.4

In projects that are running versions of Laravel prior to 5.4, assertDatabaseHas() should be replaced by seeInDatabase().

TL;DR

There are a lot of ways to get the same data: using the Request facade, using the request() global helper, and injecting an instance of Illuminate\Http\Request. Each exposes the ability to get all input, some input, or specific pieces of data, and there can be some special considerations for files and JSON input.

URI path segments are also a possible source of user input, and they're also accessible via the request tools.

Validation can be performed manually with Validator::make(), or automatically using the validate() request method or form requests. Each automatic tool, upon failed validation, redirects the user to the previous page with all old input stored and errors passed along.

Views and Eloquent models also need to be protected from nefarious user input. Protect Blade views using the double curly brace syntax ({{ }}), which escapes user input, and protect models by only passing specific fields into bulk methods using $request->only() and by defining the mass assignment rules on the model itself.

## CHAPTER 8

Artisan and Tinker

From installation onward, modern PHP frameworks expect many interactions to take place on the command line. Laravel provides three primary tools for command-line interaction: Artisan, a suite of built-in command-line actions with the ability to add more; Tinker, a REPL or interactive shell for your application; and the installer, which we've already covered in Chapter 2.

An Introduction to Artisan

If you've been reading through this book chapter by chapter, you've already learned how to use Artisan commands. They look something like this:

```
php artisan make:controller PostsController
```

If you look in the root folder of your application, you'll see that *artisan* is actually just a PHP file. That's why you're starting your call with `php artisan`; you're passing that file into PHP to be parsed. Everything after that is just passed into Artisan as arguments.

Symfony Console Syntax

Artisan is actually a layer on top of the Symfony Console component (*http://bit.ly/2fVqOT8*); so, if you're familiar with writing Symfony Console commands, you should feel right at home.

Since the list of Artisan commands for an application can be changed by a package or by the specific code of the application, it's worth checking every new application you encounter to see what commands are available.

To get a list of all available Artisan commands, you can run `php artisan list` from the project root (although if you just run `php artisan` with no parameters, it will do the same thing).

Basic Artisan Commands

There's not enough space here to cover all of the Artisan commands, but we'll cover many of them. Let's get started with the basic commands:

`clear-compiled`
Removes Laravel's compiled class file, which is like an internal Laravel cache; run this as a first resort when things are going wrong and you don't know why

`down, up`
Puts your application in "maintenance mode" in order for you to fix an error, run migrations, or whatever else and restore an application from maintenance mode, respectively

`dump-server` *(5.7+)*
Starts the dump server (see "Laravel Dump Server" on page 218) to collect and output dumped variables

`env`
Displays which environment Laravel is running in at the moment; it's the equivalent of echoing `app()->environment()` in-app

`help`
Provides help for a command; for example, `php artisan help` *commandName*

`migrate`
Runs all database migrations

`optimize`
Clears and refreshes the configuration and route files

`preset`
Changes out the frontend scaffolding for another

`serve`
Pins up a PHP server at `localhost:8000` (you can customize the host and/or port with `--host` and `--port`)

`tinker`
Brings up the Tinker REPL, which we'll cover later in this chapter

Changes to the Artisan Commands List Over time

The list of Artisan commands and their names have changed in small ways over the lifetime of Laravel. I'll try to note any time they've changed, but everything here is current for Laravel 5.8. If you're not working in 5.8, the best way to see what's available to you is to run `php artisan` from your application.

Options

Before we cover the rest of the commands, let's look at a few notable options you can pass any time you run an Artisan command:

`-q`
  Suppresses all output

`-v`, `-vv`, *and* `-vvv`
  Specify the level of output verbosity (normal, verbose, and debug)

`--no-interaction`
  Suppresses interactive questions, so the command won't interrupt automated processes running it

`--env`
  Allows you to define which environment the Artisan command should operate in (`local`, `production`, etc.).

`--version`
  Shows you which version of Laravel your application is running on.

You've probably guessed from looking at these options that Artisan commands are intended to be used much like basic shell commands: you might run them manually, but they can also function as a part of some automated process at some point.

For example, there are many automated deploy processes that might benefit from certain Artisan commands. You might want to run `php artisan config:cache` every time you deploy an application. Flags like `-q` and `--no-interaction` ensure that your deploy scripts, not attended by a human being, can keep running smoothly.

The Grouped Commands

The rest of the commands available out of the box are grouped by context. We won't cover them all here, but we'll cover each context broadly:

app

This just contains `app:name`, which allows you to replace every instance of the default top-level App\ namespace with a namespace of your choosing; for example, `php artisan app:name MyApplication`. I recommend avoiding this feature and keeping your app's root namespace as App.

auth

All we have here is `auth:clear-resets`, which flushes all of the expired password reset tokens from the database.

cache

`cache:clear` clears the cache, `cache:forget` removes an individual item from the cache, and `cache:table` creates a database migration if you plan to use the database cache driver.

config

`config:cache` caches your configuration settings for faster lookup; to clear the cache, use `config:clear`.

db

`db:seed` seeds your database, if you have configured database seeders.

event

`event:generate` builds missing event and event listener files based on the definitions in `EventServiceProvider`. You'll learn more about events in Chapter 16.

key

`key:generate` creates a random application encryption key in your *.env* file.

Rerunning artisan key:generate Means Losing Some Encrypted Data

If you run `php artisan key:generate` more than once on your application, every currently logged-in user will be logged out. Additionally, any data you have manually encrypted will no longer be decryptable. To learn more, check out the article "APP_KEY and You" (*http://bit.ly/2U972qd*) by fellow Tightenite Jake Bathman.

make

`make:auth` scaffolds out the views and corresponding routes for a landing page, a user dashboard, and login and register pages.

All the rest of the make: actions create a single item, and have parameters that vary accordingly. To learn more about any individual command's parameters, use help to read its documentation.

For example, you could run php artisan help make:migration and learn that you can pass --create=*tableNameHere* to create a migration that already has the create table syntax in the file, as shown here: php artisan make:migration create_posts_table --create=posts.

migrate

The migrate command used to run all migrations was mentioned earlier, but there are several other migration-related commands. You can create the migra tions table (to keep track of the migrations that are executed) with migrate:install, reset your migrations and start from scratch with migrate:reset, reset your migrations and run them all again with migrate:refresh, roll back just one migration with migrate:rollback, drop all tables and rerun all the migrations with migrate:fresh, or check the status of your migrations with migrate:status.

notifications

notifications:table generates a migration that creates the table for database notifications.

package

 In versions of Laravel prior to 5.5, including a new Laravel-specific package in your app requires registering it manually in *config/app.php*. However, in 5.5 it's possible for Laravel to "autodiscover" those packages so you don't have to man-ually register them. package:discover rebuilds Laravel's "discovered" manifest of the service providers from your external packages.

queue

We'll cover Laravel's queues in Chapter 16, but the basic idea is that you can push jobs up into remote queues to be executed one after another by a worker. This command group provides all the tools you need to interact with your queues, like queue:listen to start listening to a queue, queue:table to create a migration for database-backed queues, and queue:flush to flush all failed queue jobs. There are quite a few more, which you'll learn about in Chapter 16.

route

If you run route:list, you'll see the definitions of every route defined in the application, including each route's verb(s), path, name, controller/closure action, and middleware. You can cache the route definitions for faster lookups with route:cache and clear your cache with route:clear.

schedule
: We'll cover Laravel's cron-like scheduler in Chapter 16, but in order for it to work, you need to set the system cron to run `schedule:run` once a minute:

```
* * * * * php /home/myapp.com/artisan schedule:run >> /dev/null 2>&1
```

As you can see, this Artisan command is intended to be run regularly in order to power a core Laravel service.

session
: `session:table` creates a migration for applications using database-backed sessions.

storage
: `storage:link` creates a symbolic link from *public/storage* to *storage/app/public*. This is a common convention in Laravel apps, to make it easy to put user uploads (or other files that commonly end up in *storage/app*) somewhere where they'll be accessible at a public URL.

vendor
: Some Laravel-specific packages need to "publish" some of their assets, either so that they can be served from your *public* directory or so that you can modify them. Either way, these packages register these "publishable assets" with Laravel, and when you run `vendor:publish`, it publishes them to their specified locations.

view
: Laravel's view rendering engine automatically caches your views. It usually does a good job of handling its own cache invalidation, but if you ever notice it's gotten stuck, run `view:clear` to clear the cache.

Writing Custom Artisan Commands

Now that we've covered the Artisan commands that come with Laravel out of the box, let's talk about writing your own.

First, you should know: there's an Artisan command for that! Running `php artisan make:command` *YourCommandName* generates a new Artisan command in *app/Console/Commands/{YourCommandName}.php*.

php artisan make:command

The command signature for make:command has changed a few times. It was originally command:make, but for a while in 5.2 it was console:make and then make:console.

Finally, in 5.3, it was settled: all of the generators are under the make: namespace, and the command to generate new Artisan commands is now make:command.

Your first argument should be the class name of the command, and you can optionally pass a --command parameter to define what the terminal command will be (e.g., appname:action). So, let's do it:

```
php artisan make:command WelcomeNewUsers --command=email:newusers
```

Take a look at Example 8-1 to see what you'll get.

Example 8-1. The default skeleton of an Artisan command

```php
<?php

namespace App\Console\Commands;

use Illuminate\Console\Command;

class WelcomeNewUsers extends Command
{
    /**
     * The name and signature of the console command
     *
     * @var string
     */
    protected $signature = 'email:newusers';

    /**
     * The console command description
     *
     * @var string
     */
    protected $description = 'Command description';

    /**
     * Create a new command instance
     *
     * @return void
     */
    public function __construct()
    {
        parent::__construct();
    }
```

```
    /**
     * Execute the console command
     *
     * @return mixed
     */
    public function handle()
    {
        //
    }
}
```

As you can see, it's very easy to define the command signature, the help text it shows in command lists, and the command's behavior on instantiation (__construct()) and on execution (handle()).

Manually Binding Commands Prior to Laravel 5.5

In projects running versions of Laravel prior to 5.5, commands had to be manually bound into *app\Console\Kernel.php*. If your app is running an older version of Laravel, just add the fully qualified class name for your command to the $commands array in that file and it'll be registered:

```
protected $commands = [
    \App\Console\Commands\WelcomeNewUsers::class,
];
```

A Sample Command

We haven't covered mail or Eloquent yet in this chapter (see Chapter 15 for mail and Chapter 5 for Eloquent), but the sample handle() method in Example 8-2 should read pretty clearly.

Example 8-2. A sample Artisan command handle() method

```
...
class WelcomeNewUsers extends Command
{
    public function handle()
    {
        User::signedUpThisWeek()->each(function ($user) {
            Mail::to($user)->send(new WelcomeEmail);
        });
    }
```

Now every time you run php artisan email:newusers, this command will grab every user that signed up this week and send them the welcome email.

If you would prefer injecting your mail and user dependencies instead of using facades, you can typehint them in the command constructor, and Laravel's container will inject them for you when the command is instantiated.

Take a look at Example 8-3 to see what Example 8-2 might look like using dependency injection and extracting its behavior out to a service class.

Example 8-3. The same command, refactored

```
...
class WelcomeNewUsers extends Command
{
    public function __construct(UserMailer $userMailer)
    {
        parent::__construct();

        $this->userMailer = $userMailer
    }

    public function handle()
    {
        $this->userMailer->welcomeNewUsers();
    }
}
```

Keep It Simple

It is possible to call Artisan commands from the rest of your code, so you can use them to encapsulate chunks of application logic.

However, the Laravel docs recommend instead packaging the application logic into a service class and injecting that service into your command. Console commands are seen as being similar to controllers: they're not domain classes; they're traffic cops that just route incoming requests to the correct behavior.

Arguments and Options

The `$signature` property of the new command looks like it might just contain the command name. But this property is also where you'll define any arguments and options for the command. There's a specific, simple syntax you can use to add arguments and options to your Artisan commands.

Before we dig into that syntax, take a look at an example for some context:

```
protected $signature = 'password:reset {userId} {--sendEmail}';
```

Arguments—required, optional, and/or with defaults

To define a required argument, surround it with braces:

```
password:reset {userId}
```

To make the argument optional, add a question mark:

```
password:reset {userId?}
```

To make it optional and provide a default, use:

```
password:reset {userId=1}
```

Options—required values, value defaults, and shortcuts

Options are similar to arguments, but they're prefixed with -- and can be used with no value. To add a basic option, surround it with braces:

```
password:reset {userId} {--sendEmail}
```

If your option requires a value, add an = to its signature:

```
password:reset {userId} {--password=}
```

And if you want to pass a default value, add it after the =:

```
password:reset {userId} {--queue=default}
```

Array arguments and array options

Both for arguments and for options, if you want to accept an array as input, use the
* character:

```
password:reset {userIds*}
```

```
password:reset {--ids=*}
```

Using array arguments and parameters looks a bit like Example 8-4.

Example 8-4. Using array syntax with Artisan commands

```
// Argument
php artisan password:reset 1 2 3

// Option
php artisan password:reset --ids=1 --ids=2 --ids=3
```

Array Arguments Must Be the Last Argument

Since an array argument captures every parameter after its definition and adds them as array items, an array argument has to be the
last argument within an Artisan command's signature.

Input descriptions

Remember how the built-in Artisan commands can give us more information about their parameters if we use `artisan help`? We can provide that same information about our custom commands. Just add a colon and the description text within the curly braces, like in Example 8-5.

Example 8-5. Defining description text for Artisan arguments and options

```
protected $signature = 'password:reset
                        {userId : The ID of the user}
                        {--sendEmail : Whether to send user an email}';
```

Using Input

Now that we've prompted for this input, how do we use it in our command's `handle()` method? We have two sets of methods for retrieving the values of arguments and options.

argument() and arguments()

`$this->arguments()` returns an array of all arguments (the first array item will be the command name). `$this->argument()` called with no parameters returns the same response; the plural method, which I prefer, is just available for better readability, and is only available after Laravel 5.3.

To get just the value of a single argument, pass the argument name as a parameter to `$this->argument()`, as shown in Example 8-6.

Example 8-6. Using $this->arguments() in an Artisan command

```
// With definition "password:reset {userId}"
php artisan password:reset 5

// $this->arguments() returns this array
[
    "command": "password:reset",
    "userId": "5",
]

// $this->argument('userId') returns this string
"5"
```

option() and options()

`$this->options()` returns an array of all options, including some that will by default be `false` or `null`. `$this->option()` called with no parameters returns the same response; again, the plural method, which I prefer, is just available for better readability and is only available after Laravel 5.3.

To get just the value of a single option, pass the argument name as a parameter to $this->option(), as shown in Example 8-7.

Example 8-7. Using $this->options() in an Artisan command

```
// With definition "password:reset {--userId=}"
php artisan password:reset --userId=5

// $this->options() returns this array
[
    "userId" => "5",
    "help" => false,
    "quiet" => false,
    "verbose" => false,
    "version" => false,
    "ansi" => false,
    "no-ansi" => false,
    "no-interaction" => false,
    "env" => null,
]

// $this->option('userId') returns this string
"5"
```

Example 8-8 shows an Artisan command using argument() and option() in its handle() method.

Example 8-8. Getting input from an Artisan command

```
public function handle()
{
    // All arguments, including the command name
    $arguments = $this->arguments();

    // Just the 'userId' argument
    $userid = $this->argument('userId');

    // All options, including some defaults like 'no-interaction' and 'env'
    $options = $this->options();

    // Just the 'sendEmail' option
    $sendEmail = $this->option('sendEmail');
}
```

Prompts

There are a few more ways to get user input from within your `handle()` code, and they all involve prompting the user to enter information during the execution of your command:

`ask()`

   Prompts the user to enter freeform text:

```
$email = $this->ask('What is your email address?');
```

`secret()`

   Prompts the user to enter freeform text, but hides the typing with asterisks:

```
$password = $this->secret('What is the DB password?');
```

`confirm()`

   Prompts the user for a yes/no answer, and returns a Boolean:

```
if ($this->confirm('Do you want to truncate the tables?')) {
    //
}
```

   All answers except y or Y will be treated as a "no."

`anticipate()`

   Prompts the user to enter freeform text, and provides autocomplete suggestions. Still allows the user to type whatever they want:

```
$album = $this->anticipate('What is the best album ever?', [
    "The Joshua Tree", "Pet Sounds", "What's Going On"
]);
```

`choice()`

   Prompts the user to choose one of the provided options. The last parameter is the default if the user doesn't choose:

```
$winner = $this->choice(
    'Who is the best football team?',
    ['Gators', 'Wolverines'],
    0
);
```

   Note that the final parameter, the default, should be the array key. Since we passed a nonassociative array, the key for Gators is 0. You could also key your array, if you'd prefer:

```
$winner = $this->choice(
    'Who is the best football team?',
    ['gators' => 'Gators', 'wolverines' => 'Wolverines'],
```

```
        'gators'
    );
```

Output

During the execution of your command, you might want to write messages to the user. The most basic way to do this is to use `$this->info()` to output basic green text:

```
$this->info('Your command has run successfully.');
```

You also have available the `comment()` (orange), `question()` (highlighted teal), `error()` (highlighted red), and `line()` (uncolored) methods to echo to the command line.

Please note that the exact colors may vary from machine to machine, but they try to be in line with the local machine's standards for communicating to the end user.

Table output

The `table()` method makes it simple to create ASCII tables full of your data. Take a look at Example 8-9.

Example 8-9. Outputting tables with Artisan commands

```
$headers = ['Name', 'Email'];

$data = [
    ['Dhriti', 'dhriti@amrit.com'],
    ['Moses', 'moses@gutierez.com'],
];

// Or, you could get similar data from the database:
$data = App\User::all(['name', 'email'])->toArray();

$this->table($headers, $data);
```

Note that Example 8-9 has two sets of data: the headers, and the data itself. Both contain two "cells" per "row"; the first cell in each row is the name, and the second is the email. That way the data from the Eloquent call (which is constrained to pull only name and email) matches up with the headers.

Take a look at Example 8-10 to see what the table output looks like.

Example 8-10. Sample output of an Artisan table

```
+---------+--------------------+
| Name    | Email              |
+---------+--------------------+
| Dhriti  | dhriti@amrit.com   |
| Moses   | moses@gutierez.com |
+---------+--------------------+
```

Progress bars

If you've ever run `npm install`, you've seen a command-line progress bar before. Let's build one in Example 8-11.

Example 8-11. Sample Artisan progress bar

```php
$totalUnits = 10;
$this->output->progressStart($totalUnits);

for ($i = 0; $i < $totalUnits; $i++) {
    sleep(1);

    $this->output->progressAdvance();
}

$this->output->progressFinish();
```

What did we do here? First, we informed the system how many "units" we needed to work through. Maybe a unit is a user, and you have 350 users. The bar will then divide the entire width it has available on your screen by 350, and increment it by 1/350th every time you run `progressAdvance()`. Once you're done, run `progressFinish()` so that it knows it's done displaying the progress bar.

Writing Closure-Based Commands

If you'd prefer to keep your command definition process simpler, you can write commands as closures instead of classes by defining them in *routes/console.php*. Everything we discuss in this chapter will apply the same way, but you will define and register the commands in a single step in that file, as shown in Example 8-12.

Example 8-12. Defining an Artisan command using a closure

```php
// routes/console.php
Artisan::command(
    'password:reset {userId} {--sendEmail}',
    function ($userId, $sendEmail) {
        $userId = $this->argument('userId');
        // Do something...
```

```
    }
);
```

Calling Artisan Commands in Normal Code

While Artisan commands are designed to be run from the command line, you can also call them from other code.

The easiest way is to use the Artisan facade. You can either call a command using Artisan::call() (which will return the command's exit code) or queue a command using Artisan::queue().

Both take two parameters: first, the terminal command (password:reset); and second, an array of parameters to pass it. Take a look at Example 8-13 to see how it works with arguments and options.

Example 8-13. Calling Artisan commands from other code

```
Route::get('test-artisan', function () {
    $exitCode = Artisan::call('password:reset', [
        'userId' => 15,
        '--sendEmail' => true,
    ]);
});
```

As you can see, arguments are passed by keying to the argument name, and options with no value can be passed true or false.

> In Laravel 5.8+, you can call Artisan commands much more naturally from your code. Just pass the same string you'd call from the command line into Artisan::call():
>
> ```
> Artisan::call('password:reset 15 --sendEmail')
> ```

You can also call Artisan commands from other commands using $this->call(), (which is the same as Artisan::call()) or $this->callSilent(), which is the same but suppresses all output. See Example 8-14 for an example.

Example 8-14. Calling Artisan commands from other Artisan commands

```
public function handle()
{
    $this->callSilent('password:reset', [
        'userId' => 15,
    ]);
}
```

Finally, you can inject an instance of the `Illuminate\Contracts\Console\Kernel` contract, and use its `call()` method.

Tinker

Tinker is a REPL, or read–eval–print loop. If you've ever used IRB in Ruby, you'll be familiar with how a REPL works.

REPLs give you a prompt, similar to the command-line prompt, that mimics a "waiting" state of your application. You type your commands into the REPL, hit Return, and then expect what you typed to be evaluated and the response printed out.

Example 8-15 provides a quick sample to give you a sense of how it works and how it might be useful. We start the REPL with `php artisan tinker` and are then presented with a blank prompt (>>>); every response to our commands is printed on a line prefaced with =>.

Example 8-15. Using Tinker

```
$ php artisan tinker

>>> $user = new App\User;
=> App\User: {}
>>> $user->email = 'matt@mattstauffer.com';
=> "matt@mattstauffer.com"
>>> $user->password = bcrypt('superSecret');
=> "$2y$10$TWPGBC7e8d1bvJ1q5kv.VDUGfYDnE9gANl4mleuB3htIY2dxcQfQ5"
>>> $user->save();
=> true
```

As you can see, we created a new user, set some data (hashing the password with `bcrypt()` for security), and saved it to the database. And this is real. If this were a production application, we would've just created a brand new user in our system.

This makes Tinker a great tool for simple database interactions, for trying out new ideas, and for running snippets of code when it'd be a pain to find a place to put them in the application source files.

Tinker is powered by Psy Shell (*http://psysh.org/*), so check that out to see what else you can do with Tinker.

Laravel Dump Server

One common method of debugging the state of your data during development is to use Laravel's dump() helper, which runs a decorated var_dump() on anything you pass to it. This is fine, but it can often run into view issues.

In projects running Laravel 5.7 and later, you can now enable the Laravel dump server, which catches those dump() statements and displays them in your console instead of rendering them to the page.

To run the dump server in your local console, navigate to your project's root directory and run php artisan dump-server:

```
$ php artisan dump-server

Laravel Var Dump Server
=======================

 [OK] Server listening on tcp://127.0.0.1:9912

 // Quit the server with CONTROL-C.
```

Now, try using the dump() helper function in your code somewhere. To test it out, try this code in your *routes/web.php* file:

```
Route::get('/', function () {
    dump('Dumped Value');

    return 'Hello World';
});
```

Without the dump server, you'd see both the dump and your "Hello World." But with the dump server running, you'll only see "Hello World" in the browser. In your console, you'll see that the dump server caught that dump(), and you can inspect it there:

```
GET http://myapp.test/
-------------------


 ----------- --------------------------------
  date        Tue, 18 Sep 2018 22:43:10 +0000
  controller  "Closure"
  source      web.php on line 20
  file        routes/web.php
 ----------- --------------------------------

"Dumped Value"
```

Testing

Since you know how to call Artisan commands from code, it's easy to do that in a test and ensure that whatever behavior you expected to be performed has been performed correctly, as in Example 8-16. In our tests, we use `$this->artisan()` instead of `Artisan::call()` because it has the same syntax but adds a few testing-related assertions.

Example 8-16. Calling Artisan commands from a test

```
public function test_empty_log_command_empties_logs_table()
{
    DB::table('logs')->insert(['message' => 'Did something']);
    $this->assertCount(1, DB::table('logs')->get());

    $this->artisan('logs:empty'); // Same as Artisan::call('logs:empty');
    $this->assertCount(0, DB::table('logs')->get());
}
```

In projects running Laravel 5.7 and later, you can chain on a few new assertions to your `$this->artisan()` calls that make it even easier to test Artisan commands—not just the impact they have on the rest of your app, but also how they actually operate. Take a look at Example 8-17 to see an example of this syntax.

Example 8-17. Making assertions against the input and output of Artisan commands

```
public function testItCreatesANewUser()
{
    $this->artisan('myapp:create-user')
        ->expectsQuestion("What's the name of the new user?", "Wilbur Powery")
        ->expectsQuestion("What's the email of the new user?", "wilbur@thisbook.co")
        ->expectsQuestion("What's the password of the new user?", "secret")
        ->expectsOutput("User Wilbur Powery created!");

    $this->assertDatabaseHas('users', [
        'email' => 'wilbur@thisbook.co'
    ]);
}
```

TL;DR

Artisan commands are Laravel's command-line tools. Laravel comes with quite a few out of the box, but it's also easy to create your own Artisan commands and call them from the command line or your own code.

Tinker is a REPL that makes it simple to get into your application environment and interact with real code and real data, and the dump server lets you debug your code without stopping the code's execution.

## CHAPTER 9

User Authentication and Authorization

Setting up a basic user authentication system—including registration, login, sessions, password resets, and access permissions—can often be one of the more time-consuming pieces of creating the foundation of an application. It's a prime candidate for extracting functionality out to a library, and there are quite a few such libraries.

But because of how much authentication needs vary across projects, most authentication systems grow bulky and unusable quickly. Thankfully, Laravel has found a way to make an authentication system that's easy to use and understand, but flexible enough to fit in a variety of settings.

Every new install of Laravel has a `create_users_table` migration and a `User` model built in out of the box. Laravel offers an Artisan `make:auth` command that seeds a collection of authentication-related views and routes. And every install comes with a `RegisterController`, a `LoginController`, a `ForgotPasswordController`, and a `ResetPasswordController`. The APIs are clean and clear, and the conventions all work together to provide a simple—and seamless—authentication and authorization system.

Differences in Auth Structure in Laravel Before 5.3

Note that in Laravel 5.1 and 5.2, most of this functionality lived in the `AuthController`; in 5.3 and higher, this functionality has been split out into multiple controllers. Many of the specifics we'll cover here about how to customize redirect routes, auth guards, and such are different in 5.1 and 5.2 (though all the core functionality is the same). So, if you're on 5.1 or 5.2 and want to change some of the default authentication behaviors, you'll likely need to dig a bit into your `AuthController` to see how exactly you should customize it.

The User Model and Migration

When you create a new Laravel application, the first migration and model you'll see are the `create_users_table` migration and the `App\User` model. Example 9-1 shows, straight from the migration, the fields you'll get in your `users` table.

Example 9-1. Laravel's default user migration

```
Schema::create('users', function (Blueprint $table) {
    $table->bigIncrements('id');
    $table->string('name');
    $table->string('email')->unique();
    $table->string('password');
    $table->rememberToken();
    $table->timestamps();
});
```

We have an autoincrementing primary key ID, a name, a unique email, a password, a "remember me" token, and created and modified timestamps. This covers everything you need to handle basic user authentication in most apps.

The Difference Between Authentication and Authorization

Authentication means verifying who someone is, and allowing them to act as that person in your system. This includes the login and logout processes, and any tools that allow the users to identify themselves during their time using the application.

Authorization means determining whether the authenticated user is *allowed* (authorized) to perform a specific behavior. For example, an authorization system allows you to forbid any non-administrators from viewing the site's earnings.

The `User` model is a bit more complex, as you can see in Example 9-2. The `App\User` class itself is simple, but it extends the `Illuminate\Foundation\Auth\User` class, which pulls in several traits.

Example 9-2. Laravel's default User model

```
<?php
// App\User

namespace App;

use Illuminate\Notifications\Notifiable;
use Illuminate\Contracts\Auth\MustVerifyEmail;
use Illuminate\Foundation\Auth\User as Authenticatable;
```

```php
class User extends Authenticatable
{
    use Notifiable;

    /**
     * The attributes that are mass assignable.
     *
     * @var array
     */
    protected $fillable = [
        'name', 'email', 'password',
    ];

    /**
     * The attributes that should be hidden for arrays.
     *
     * @var array
     */
    protected $hidden = [
        'password', 'remember_token',
    ];

    /**
     * The attributes that should be cast to native types.
     *
     * @var array
     */
    protected $casts = [
        'email_verified_at' => 'datetime',
    ];
}
<?php
// Illuminate\Foundation\Auth\User

namespace Illuminate\Foundation\Auth;

use Illuminate\Auth\Authenticatable;
use Illuminate\Auth\MustVerifyEmail;
use Illuminate\Database\Eloquent\Model;
use Illuminate\Auth\Passwords\CanResetPassword;
use Illuminate\Foundation\Auth\Access\Authorizable;
use Illuminate\Contracts\Auth\Authenticatable as AuthenticatableContract;
use Illuminate\Contracts\Auth\Access\Authorizable as AuthorizableContract;
use Illuminate\Contracts\Auth\CanResetPassword as CanResetPasswordContract;

class User extends Model implements
    AuthenticatableContract,
    AuthorizableContract,
    CanResetPasswordContract
{
```

```
        use Authenticatable, Authorizable, CanResetPassword, MustVerifyEmail;
}
```

 Eloquent Model Refresher

If this is entirely unfamiliar, consider reading Chapter 5 before continuing to learn how Eloquent models work.

So, what can we learn from this model? First, users live in the `users` table; Laravel will infer this from the class name. We are able to fill out the `name`, `email`, and `password` properties when creating a new user, and the `password` and `remember_token` properties are excluded when outputting the user as JSON. Looking good so far.

We also can see from the contracts and the traits in the `Illuminate\Foundation\Auth` version of `User` that there are some features in the framework (the ability to authenticate, to authorize, and to reset passwords) that theoretically could be applied to other models, not just the `User` model, and that could be applied individually or together.

Contracts and Interfaces

You may have noticed that sometimes I write the word "contract" and sometimes "interface," and that almost all of the interfaces in Laravel are under the `Contracts` namespace.

A PHP interface is essentially an agreement between two classes that one of the classes will "behave" a certain way. It's a bit like a contract between them, and thinking about it as a contract gives a little more inherent meaning to the name than calling it an interface does.

In the end, though, they're the same thing: an agreement that a class will provide certain methods with a certain signature.

On a related note, the `Illuminate\Contracts` namespace contains a group of interfaces that Laravel components implement and typehint. This makes it easy to develop similar components that implement the same interfaces and swap them into your application in place of the stock `Illuminate` components. When the Laravel core and components typehint a mailer, for example, they don't typehint the `Mailer` class. Instead, they typehint the `Mailer` contract (interface), making it easy to provide your own mailer. To learn more about how to do this, take a look at Chapter 11.

The `Authenticatable` contract requires methods (e.g., `getAuthIdentifier()`) that allow the framework to authenticate instances of this model to the auth system; the

---

`Authenticatable` trait includes the methods necessary to satisfy that contract with an average Eloquent model.

The `Authorizable` contract requires a method (`can()`) that allows the framework to authorize instances of this model for their access permissions in different contexts. Unsurprisingly, the `Authorizable` trait provides methods that will satisfy the `Authorizable` contract for an average Eloquent model.

Finally, the `CanResetPassword` contract requires methods (`getEmail ForPasswordReset()`, `sendPasswordResetNotification()`) that allow the framework to—you guessed it—reset the password of any entity that satisfies this contract. The `CanResetPassword` trait provides methods to satisfy that contract for an average Eloquent model.

At this point, we have the ability to easily represent an individual user in the database (with the migration), and to pull them out with a model instance that can be authenticated (logged in and out), authorized (checked for access permissions to a particular resource), and sent a password reset email.

Using the auth() Global Helper and the Auth Facade

The `auth()` global helper is the easiest way to interact with the status of the authenticated user throughout your app. You can also inject an instance of `Illuminate\Auth \AuthManager` and get the same functionality, or use the `Auth` facade.

The most common usages are to check whether a user is logged in (`auth()->check()` returns `true` if the current user is logged in; `auth()->guest()` returns `true` if the user is not logged in) and to get the currently logged-in user (use `auth()->user()`, or `auth()->id()` for just the ID; both return `null` if no user is logged in).

Take a look at Example 9-3 for a sample usage of the global helper in a controller.

Example 9-3. Sample usage of the auth() global helper in a controller

```
public function dashboard()
{
    if (auth()->guest()) {
        return redirect('sign-up');
    }

    return view('dashboard')
        ->with('user', auth()->user());
}
```

The next section explores how the auth system works behind the scenes. It's useful information but not *vital*, so if you want to skip it for now, check out the following section, "The Auth Scaffold" on page 231.

The Auth Controllers

So, how do we actually log users in? And how do we trigger those password resets?

It all happens in the `Auth`-namespaced controllers: `RegisterController`, `Login Controller`, `ResetPasswordController`, and `ForgotPasswordController`.

RegisterController

The `RegisterController`, in combination with the `RegistersUsers` trait, contains sensible defaults for how to show new users a registration form, how to validate their input, how to create new users once their input is validated, and where to redirect them afterward.

The controller itself just contains a few hooks that the traits will call at given points. That makes it easy to customize a few common behaviors without having to dig deeply into the code that makes it all work.

The `$redirectTo` property defines where users will be redirected after registration. The `validator()` method defines how to validate registrations. And the `create()` method defines how to create a new user based on an incoming registration. Take a look at Example 9-4 to see the default `RegisterController`.

Example 9-4. Laravel's default RegisterController

```
...
class RegisterController extends Controller
{
    use RegistersUsers;

    protected $redirectTo = '/home';

    ...

    protected function validator(array $data)
    {
        return Validator::make($data, [
            'name' => 'required|string|max:255',
            'email' => 'required|string|email|max:255|unique:users',
            'password' => 'required|string|min:6|confirmed',
        ]);
    }

    protected function create(array $data)
```

```
    {
        return User::create([
            'name' => $data['name'],
            'email' => $data['email'],
            'password' => Hash::make($data['password']),
        ]);
    }
}
```

RegistersUsers trait

The `RegistersUsers` trait, which the `RegisterController` imports, handles a few primary functions for the registration process. First, it shows users the registration form view, with the `showRegistrationForm()` method. If you want new users to register with a view other than `auth.register` you can override the `showRegistrationForm()` method in your `RegisterController`.

Next, it handles the `POST` of the registration form with the `register()` method. This method passes the user's registration input to the validator from the `validator()` method of your `RegisterController`, and then on to the `create()` method.

And finally, the `redirectPath()` method (pulled in via the `RedirectsUsers` trait) defines where users should be redirected after a successful registration. You can define this URI with the `$redirectTo` property on your controller, or you can override the `redirectPath()` method and return whatever you want.

If you want this trait to use a different auth guard than the default (you'll learn more about guards in "Guards" on page 236), you can override the `guard()` method and have it return whichever guard you'd like.

LoginController

The `LoginController`, unsurprisingly, allows the user to log in. It brings in the `AuthenticatesUsers` trait, which brings in the `RedirectsUsers` and `ThrottlesLogins` traits.

Like the `RegistrationController`, the `LoginController` has a `$redirectTo` property that allows you to customize the path the user will be redirected to after a successful login. Everything else lives behind the `AuthenticatesUsers` trait.

AuthenticatesUsers trait

The `AuthenticatesUsers` trait is responsible for showing users the login form, validating their logins, throttling failed logins, handling logouts, and redirecting users after a successful login.

The `showLoginForm()` method defaults to showing the user the `auth.login` view, but you can override it if you'd like it to use a different view.

The `login()` method accepts the POST from the login form. It validates the request using the `validateLogin()` method, which you can override if you'd like to customize the validation. It then hooks into the functionality of the `ThrottlesLogins` trait, which we'll cover shortly, to reject users with too many failed logins. And finally, it redirects the user to either their intended path (if the user was redirected to the login page when attempting to visit a page within the app) or the path defined by the `redirectPath()` method, which returns your `$redirectTo` property.

The trait calls the empty `authenticated()` method after a successful login, so if you'd like to perform any sort of behavior in response to a successful login, just override this method in your `LoginController`.

There's a `username()` method that defines which of your `users` columns is the "username"; this defaults to `email`, but you can change that by overwriting the `username()` method in your controller to return the name of your username column.

And, like in the `RegistersUsers` trait, you can override the `guard()` method to define which auth guard (more on that in "Guards" on page 236) this controller should use.

ThrottlesLogins trait

The `ThrottlesLogins` trait is an interface to Laravel's `Illuminate\Cache\RateLimiter` class, which is a utility to rate-limit any event using the cache. This trait applies rate limiting to user logins, limiting users from using the login form if they've had too many failed logins within a certain amount of time. This functionality does not exist in Laravel 5.1.

If you import the `ThrottlesLogins` trait, all of its methods are protected, which means they can't actually be accessed as routes. Instead, the `AuthenticatesUsers` trait looks to see whether you've imported the `ThrottlesLogins` trait, and if so, it'll attach its functionality to your logins without any work on your part. Since the default `LoginController` imports both, you'll get this functionality for free if you use the auth scaffold (discussed in "The Auth Scaffold" on page 231).

`ThrottlesLogins` limits any given combination of username and IP address to 5 attempts per 60 seconds. Using the cache, it increments the "failed login" count of a given username/IP address combination, and if any user reaches 5 failed login attempts within 60 seconds, it redirects that user back to the login page with an appropriate error until the 60 seconds is over.

ResetPasswordController

The `ResetPasswordController` simply pulls in the `ResetsPasswords` trait. This trait provides validation and access to basic password reset views, and then uses an instance of Laravel's `PasswordBroker` class (or anything else implementing the `PasswordBroker` interface, if you choose to write your own) to handle sending password reset emails and actually resetting the passwords.

Just like the other traits we've covered, it handles showing the reset password view (`showResetForm()` shows the `auth.passwords.reset` view) and the POST request that is sent from that view (`reset()` validates and sends the appropriate response). The `resetPassword()` method actually resets the password, and you can customize the broker with `broker()` and the auth guard with `guard()`.

If you're interested in customizing any of this behavior, just override the specific method you want to customize in your controller.

ForgotPasswordController

The `ForgotPasswordController` simply pulls in the `SendsPasswordResetEmails` trait. It shows the `auth.passwords.email` form with the `showLinkRequestForm()` method and handles the POST of that form with the `sendResetLinkEmail()` method. You can customize the broker with the `broker()` method.

VerificationController

The `VerificationController` pulls in the `VerifiesEmails` trait, which handles verifying the email addresses of newly signed-up users. You can customize the path to send users to after validation.

Auth::routes()

Now that we have the auth controllers providing some methods for a series of predefined routes, we'll want our users to actually be able to *hit* those routes. We could add all the routes manually to *routes/web.php*, but there's already a convenience tool for that, called `Auth::routes()`:

```
// routes/web.php
Auth::routes();
```

As you can probably guess, `Auth::routes()` brings a bundle of predefined routes into your routes file. In Example 9-5 you can see the routes that are actually being defined there.

Example 9-5. The routes provided by Auth::routes()

```
// Authentication routes
$this->get('login', 'Auth\LoginController@showLoginForm')->name('login');
$this->post('login', 'Auth\LoginController@login');
$this->post('logout', 'Auth\LoginController@logout')->name('logout');

// Registration routes
$this->get('register', 'Auth\RegisterController@showRegistrationForm')
    ->name('register');
$this->post('register', 'Auth\RegisterController@register');

// Password reset routes
$this->get('password/reset', 'Auth\ForgotPasswordController@showLinkRequestForm')
    ->name('password.request');
$this->post('password/email', 'Auth\ForgotPasswordController@sendResetLinkEmail')
    ->name('password.email');
$this->get('password/reset/{token}', 'Auth\ResetPasswordController@showResetForm')
    ->name('password.reset');
$this->post('password/reset', 'Auth\ResetPasswordController@reset');

// If email verification is enabled
$this->get('email/verify', 'Auth\VerificationController@show')
    ->name('verification.notice');
$this->get('email/verify/{id}', 'Auth\VerificationController@verify')
    ->name('verification.verify');
$this->get('email/resend', 'Auth\VerificationController@resend')
    ->name('verification.resend');
```

Basically, `Auth::routes()` includes the routes for authentication, registration, and password resets. As you can see, there are also optional routes for email verification, a feature introduced in Laravel 5.7.

 To enable Laravel's email verification service, which requires new users to verify they have access to the email address they signed up with, update your `Auth::routes()` call to enable it, as shown here:

```
Auth::routes(['verify' => true]);
```

We'll discuss this further in "Email Verification" on page 235.

 In applications running Laravel 5.7+, you can use `Auth::routes()` but disable the registration and/or password reset links by adding "register" and "reset" keys to the array you're passing to `Auth::routes()`:

```
Auth::routes(['register' => false, 'reset' => false]);
```

The Auth Scaffold

At this point you have a migration, a model, controllers, and routes for your authentication system. But what about your views?

Laravel handles these by providing an *auth scaffold* (available since 5.2) that's intended to be run on a new application and provide you with even more skeleton code to get your auth system running quickly.

The auth scaffold takes care of adding `Auth::routes()` to your routes file, adds a view for each route, and creates a `HomeController` to serve as the landing page for logged-in users; it also routes to the `index()` method of `HomeController` at the `/home` URI.

Just run `php artisan make:auth`, and the following files will be made available to you:

```
app/Http/Controllers/HomeController.php
resources/views/auth/login.blade.php
resources/views/auth/register.blade.php
resources/views/auth/verify.blade.php
resources/views/auth/passwords/email.blade.php
resources/views/auth/passwords/reset.blade.php
resources/views/layouts/app.blade.php
resources/views/home.blade.php
```

At this point, you have / returning the `welcome` view, /home returning the `home` view, and a series of auth routes for login, logout, registration, and password reset pointing to the auth controllers. Each of the seeded views has Bootstrap-based layouts and form fields for all necessary fields for login, registration, and password reset, and they already point to the correct routes.

You now have all of the pieces in place for every step of the normal user registration and authentication flow. You can tweak all you want, but you're entirely ready to register and authenticate users.

Let's review quickly the steps from new site to full authentication system:

```
laravel new MyApp
cd MyApp

# Edit your .env file to specify the correct database connection details

php artisan make:auth
php artisan migrate
```

That's it. Run those commands, and you will have a landing page and a Bootstrap-based user registration, login, logout, and password reset system, with a basic landing page for all authenticated users.

"Remember Me"

The auth scaffold has this implemented out of the box, but it's still worth learning how it works and how to use it on your own. If you want to implement a "remember me"–style long-lived access token, make sure you have a remember_token column on your users table (which you will if you used the default migration).

When you're normally logging in a user (and this is how the LoginController does it, with the AuthenticatesUsers trait), you'll "attempt" an authentication with the user-provided information, like in Example 9-6.

Example 9-6. Attempting a user authentication

```
if (auth()->attempt([
    'email' => request()->input('email'),
    'password' => request()->input('password'),
])) {
    // Handle the successful login
}
```

This provides you with a user login that lasts as long as the user's session. If you want Laravel to extend the login indefinitely using cookies (as long as the user is on the same computer and doesn't log out), you can pass a Boolean true as the second parameter of the auth()->attempt() method. Take a look at Example 9-7 to see what that request looks like.

Example 9-7. Attempting a user authentication with a "remember me" checkbox check

```
if (auth()->attempt([
    'email' => request()->input('email'),
    'password' => request()->input('password'),
]), request()->filled('remember')) {
    // Handle the successful login
}
```

You can see that we checked whether the input has a nonempty ("filled") remember property, which will return a Boolean. This allows our users to decide if they want to be remembered with a checkbox in the login form.

And later, if you need to manually check whether the current user was authenticated by a remember token, there's a method for that: auth()->viaRemember() returns a Boolean indicating whether or not the current user authenticated via a remember token. This will allow you to prevent certain higher-sensitivity features from being accessible by remember token; instead, you can require users to reenter their passwords.

Manually Authenticating Users

The most common case for user authentication is that you'll allow the user to provide their credentials, and then use `auth()->attempt()` to see whether the provided credentials match any real users. If so, you log them in.

But sometimes there are contexts where it's valuable for you to be able to choose to log a user in on your own. For example, you may want to allow admin users to switch users.

There are four methods that make this possible. First, you can just pass a user ID:

```
auth()->loginUsingId(5);
```

Second, you can pass a `User` object (or any other object that implements the `Illuminate\Contracts\Auth\Authenticatable` contract):

```
auth()->login($user);
```

And third and fourth, you can choose to authenticate the given user for only the current request, which won't impact your session or cookies at all, using `once()` or `onceUsingId()`:

```
auth()->once(['username' => 'mattstauffer']);
// or
auth()->onceUsingId(5);
```

Note that the array you pass to the `once()` method can contain any key/value pairs to uniquely identify the user you'd like to authenticate as. You can even pass multiple keys and values, if it's what is appropriate for your project. For example:

```
auth()->once([
    'last_name' => 'Stauffer',
    'zip_code' => 90210,
])
```

Manually Logging Out a User

If you ever need to log out a user manually, just call `logout()`:

```
auth()->logout();
```

Invalidating Sessions on Other Devices

 If you'd like to log out not just a user's current session, but also those on any other devices, you'll need to prompt the user for their password and pass it to the `logoutOtherDevices()` method (available in Laravel 5.6 and later). In order to do this, you'll have to add the (commented-out-by-default) `AuthenticateSession` middleware to your web group in *app\Http\Kernel.php*:

```
'web' => [
    // ...
    \Illuminate\Session\Middleware\AuthenticateSession::class,
],
```

Then you can use it inline anywhere you need:

```
auth()->logoutOtherDevices($password);
```

Auth Middleware

In Example 9-3, you saw how to check whether visitors are logged in and redirect them if not. You could perform these sorts of checks on every route in your application, but it would very quickly get tedious. It turns out that route middleware (see Chapter 10 to learn more about how they work) are a perfect fit for restricting certain routes to guests or to authenticated users.

Once again, Laravel comes with the middleware we need out of the box. You can see which route middleware you have defined in `App\Http\Kernel`:

```
protected $routeMiddleware = [
    'auth' => \Illuminate\Auth\Middleware\Authenticate::class,
    'auth.basic' => \Illuminate\Auth\Middleware\AuthenticateWithBasicAuth::class,
    'bindings' => \Illuminate\Routing\Middleware\SubstituteBindings::class,
    'cache.headers' => \Illuminate\Http\Middleware\SetCacheHeaders::class,
    'can' => \Illuminate\Auth\Middleware\Authorize::class,
    'guest' => \App\Http\Middleware\RedirectIfAuthenticated::class,
    'signed' => \Illuminate\Routing\Middleware\ValidateSignature::class,
    'throttle' => \Illuminate\Routing\Middleware\ThrottleRequests::class,
    'verified' => \Illuminate\Auth\Middleware\EnsureEmailIsVerified::class,
];
```

Four of the default route middleware are authentication-related:

auth
:   restricts route access to authenticated users.

auth.basic
:   restricts access to authenticated users using HTTP Basic Authentication.

guest
:   restricts access to unauthenticated users.

can
:   used for authorizing user access to given routes.

It's most common to use `auth` for your authenticated-user-only sections and `guest` for any routes you don't want authenticated users to see (like the login form). `auth.basic` is a much less commonly used middleware for authenticating via request headers.

Example 9-8 shows an example of a few routes protected by the `auth` middleware.

Example 9-8. Sample routes protected by auth middleware

```
Route::middleware('auth')->group(function () {
    Route::get('account', 'AccountController@dashboard');
});

Route::get('login', 'Auth\LoginController@getLogin')->middleware('guest');
```

Email Verification

 Laravel 5.7 introduced a new feature that makes it possible to require a user to verify that they have access to the email address they registered with.

In order to enable email verification, update your `App\User` class and make it implement the `Illuminate\Contracts\Auth\MustVerifyEmail` contract, as shown in Example 9-9.

Example 9-9. Adding the MustVerifyEmail trait to an Authenticatable model

```
class User extends Authenticatable implements MustVerifyEmail
{
    use Notifiable;

    // ...
}
```

The users table must also contain a nullable timestamp column named `email_verified_at`, which the new default `CreateUsersTable` migration will have already provided for you in apps created in 5.7 or later.

Finally, you'll need to enable the email verification routes in your controller. The easiest method is to use `Auth::routes()` in your routes file with the `verify` parameter set to `true`:

```
Auth::routes(['verify' => true]);
```

Now, you can protect any routes you'd like from being accessed by any users who haven't verified their email address:

```
Route::get('posts/create', function () {
    // Only verified users may enter...
})->middleware('verified');
```

You can customize the route where users are redirected after verifying in your `Verification Controller`:

```
protected $redirectTo = '/profile';
```

Blade Authentication Directives

If you want to check whether a user is authenticated, not at the route level but in your views, you can, with @auth and @guest (see Example 9-10).

Example 9-10. Checking a user's authentification status in templates

```
@auth
    // The user is authenticated
@endauth

@guest
    // The user is not authenticated
@endguest
```

You can also specify which guard you'd like to use with both methods by passing the guard name as a parameter, as shown in Example 9-11.

Example 9-11. Checking a specific auth guard's authentification in templates

```
@auth('trainees')
    // The user is authenticated
@endauth

@guest('trainees')
    // The user is not authenticated
@endguest
```

Guards

Every aspect of Laravel's authentication system is routed through something called a *guard*. Each guard is a combination of two pieces: a *driver* that defines how it persists and retrieves the authentication state (for example, session), and a *provider* that allows you to get a user by certain criteria (for example, users).

Out of the box, Laravel has two guards: web and api. web is the more traditional authentication style, using the session driver and the basic user provider. api uses the same user provider, but it uses the token driver instead of session to authenticate each request.

You'd change drivers if you wanted to handle the identification and persistence of a user's identity differently (for example, changing from a long-running session to a provided-every-page-load token), and you'd change providers if you wanted to change the storage type or retrieval methods for your users (for example, moving to storing your users in Mongo instead of MySQL).

Changing the Default Guard

The guards are defined in *config/auth.php*, and you can change them, add new guards, and also define which guard will be the default there. For what it's worth, this is a relatively uncommon configuration; most Laravel apps just use one guard.

The "default" guard is the one that will be used any time you use any auth features without specifying a guard. For example, `auth()->user()` will pull the currently authenticated user using the default guard. You can change this guard by changing the `auth.defaults.guard` setting in *config/auth.php*:

```
'defaults' => [
    'guard' => 'web', // Change the default here
    'passwords' => 'users',
],
```

If you're using Laravel 5.1, you'll notice that the structure of the authentication information is a little different from this. Don't worry—the features all still work the same; they're just structured differently.

Configuration Conventions

You may have noticed that I refer to configuration sections with references like `auth.defaults.guard`. What that translates to is: in *config/auth.php*, in the array section keyed `defaults`, there should be a property keyed `guard`.

Using Other Guards Without Changing the Default

If you want to use another guard but *not* change the default, you can start your `auth()` calls with `guard()`:

```
$apiUser = auth()->guard('api')->user();
```

This will, just for this call, get the current user using the `api` guard.

Adding a New Guard

You can add a new guard at any time in *config/auth.php*, in the `auth.guards` setting:

```
'guards' => [
    'trainees' => [
        'driver' => 'session',
        'provider' => 'trainees',
    ],
],
```

Here, we've created a new guard (in addition to `web` and `api`) named `trainees`. Let's imagine, for the rest of this section, that we're building an app where our users are physical trainers and they each have their *own* users—trainees—who can log in to their subdomains. So, we need a separate guard for them.

The only two options for `driver` are `token` and `session`. Out of the box, the only option for `provider` is `users`, which supports authentication against your default `users` table, but you can create your own provider easily.

Closure Request Guards

If you want to define a custom guard, and your guard conditions (how to look up a given user against the request) can be described simply enough in response to any given HTTP request, you might just want to throw the user lookup code into a closure and not deal with creating a new custom guard class.

The `viaRequest()` auth method makes it possible to define a guard (named in the first parameter) using just a closure (defined in the second parameter) that takes the HTTP request and returns the appropriate user. To register a closure request guard, call `viaRequest()` in the `boot()` method of your `AuthServiceProvider`, as shown in Example 9-12.

Example 9-12. Defining a closure request guard

```
public function boot()
{
    $this->registerPolicies();

    Auth::viaRequest('token-hash', function ($request) {
        return User::where('token-hash', $request->token)->first();
    });
}
```

Creating a Custom User Provider

Just below where guards are defined in *config/auth.php*, there's an `auth.providers` section that defines the available providers. Let's create a new provider named `train ees`:

```
'providers' => [
    'users' => [
        'driver' => 'eloquent',
        'model' => App\User::class,
    ],

    'trainees' => [
        'driver' => 'eloquent',
        'model' => App\Trainee::class,
    ],
],
```

The two options for `driver` are `eloquent` and `database`. If you use `eloquent`, you'll need a `model` property that contains an Eloquent class name (the model to use for your User class); and if you use `database`, you'll need a `table` property to define which table it should authenticate against.

In our example, you can see that this application has a `User` and a `Trainee`, and they need to be authenticated separately. This way, the code can differentiate between `auth()->guard('users')` and `auth()->guard('trainees')`.

One last note: the `auth` route middleware can take a parameter that is the guard name. So, you can guard certain routes with a specific guard:

```
Route::middleware('auth:trainees')->group(function () {
    // Trainee-only routes here
});
```

Custom User Providers for Nonrelational Databases

The user provider creation flow just described still relies on the same `UserProvider` class, which means it's expecting to pull the identifying information out of a relational database. But if you're using Mongo or Riak or something similar, you'll actually need to create your own class.

To do this, create a new class that implements the `Illuminate\Contracts\Auth\UserProvider` interface, and then bind it in `AuthServiceProvider@boot`:

```
auth()->provider('riak', function ($app, array $config) {
    // Return an instance of Illuminate\Contracts\Auth\UserProvider...
    return new RiakUserProvider($app['riak.connection']);
});
```

Auth Events

We'll talk more about events in Chapter 16, but Laravel's event system is a basic pub/sub framework. There are system- and user-generated events that are broadcast, and the user has the ability to create event listeners that do certain things in response to certain events.

So, what if you wanted to send a ping to a particular security service every time a user was locked out after too many failed login attempts? Maybe this service watches out for a certain number of failed logins from certain geographic regions, or something else. You could, of course, inject a call in the appropriate controller. But with events, you can just create an event listener that listens to the "user locked out" event, and register that.

Take a look at Example 9-13 to see all of the events that the authentication system emits.

Example 9-13. Authentication events generated by the framework

```
protected $listen = [
    'Illuminate\Auth\Events\Registered' => [],
    'Illuminate\Auth\Events\Attempting' => [],
    'Illuminate\Auth\Events\Authenticated' => [],
    'Illuminate\Auth\Events\Login' => [],
    'Illuminate\Auth\Events\Failed' => [],
    'Illuminate\Auth\Events\Logout' => [],
    'Illuminate\Auth\Events\Lockout' => [],
    'Illuminate\Auth\Events\PasswordReset' => [],
];
```

As you can see, there are listeners for "user registered," "user attempting login," "user authenticated," "successful login," "failed login," "logout," "lockout," and "password reset." To learn more about how to build event listeners for these events, check out Chapter 16.

Authorization (ACL) and Roles

Finally, let's cover Laravel's authorization system. It enables you to determine whether a user is *authorized* to do a particular thing, which you'll check using a few primary verbs: can, cannot, allows, and denies. The access control list (ACL) system was introduced in Laravel 5.2.

Most of this authorization control will be performed using the Gate facade, but there are also convenience helpers available in your controllers, on the User model, as middleware, and as Blade directives. Take a look at Example 9-14 to get a taste of what we'll be able to do.

Example 9-14. Basic usage of the Gate facade

```
if (Gate::denies('edit-contact', $contact)) {
    abort(403);
}

if (! Gate::allows('create-contact', Contact::class)) {
    abort(403);
}
```

Defining Authorization Rules

The default location for defining authorization rules is in the boot() method of the AuthServiceProvider, where you'll be calling methods on the Auth facade.

An authorization rule is called an *ability* and is comprised of two things: a string key (e.g., update-contact) and a closure that returns a Boolean. Example 9-15 shows an ability for updating a contact.

Example 9-15. Sample ability for updating a contact

```
class AuthServiceProvider extends ServiceProvider
{
    public function boot()
    {
        $this->registerPolicies();

        Gate::define('update-contact', function ($user, $contact) {
            return $user->id == $contact->user_id;
        });
    }
}
```

Let's walk through the steps for defining an ability.

First, you want to define a key. In naming this key, you should consider what string makes sense in your code's flow to refer to the ability you're providing to the user. You can see the code sample uses the convention {*verb*}-{*modelName*}: create-contact, update-contact, etc.

Second, you define the closure. The first parameter will be the currently authenticated user, and all parameters after that will be the object(s) you're checking for access to—in this instance, the contact.

So, given those two objects, we can check whether the user is authorized to update this contact. You can write this logic however you want, but in the app we're looking at the moment, authorization depends on being the creator of the contact row. The closure will return true (authorized) if the current user created the contact, and false (unauthorized) if not.

Just like with route definitions, you could also use a class and method instead of a closure to resolve this definition:

```
$gate->define('update-contact', 'ContactACLChecker@updateContact');
```

The Gate Facade (and Injecting Gate)

Now that you've defined an ability, it's time to test against it. The simplest way is to use the Gate facade, as in Example 9-16 (or you can inject an instance of Illuminate \Contracts\Auth\Access\Gate).

Example 9-16. Basic Gate facade usage

```
if (Gate::allows('update-contact', $contact)) {
    // Update contact
}

// or
if (Gate::denies('update-contact', $contact)) {
    abort(403);
}
```

You might also define an ability with multiple parameters—maybe a contact can be in groups, and you want to authorize whether the user has access to add a contact to a group. Example 9-17 shows how to do this.

Example 9-17. Abilities with multiple parameters

```
// Definition
Gate::define('add-contact-to-group', function ($user, $contact, $group) {
    return $user->id == $contact->user_id && $user->id == $group->user_id;
});

// Usage
if (Gate::denies('add-contact-to-group', [$contact, $group])) {
    abort(403);
}
```

And if you need to check authorization for a user other than the currently authenticated user, try `forUser()`, like in Example 9-18.

Example 9-18. Specifying the user for Gate

```
if (Gate::forUser($user)->denies('create-contact')) {
    abort(403);
}
```

Resource Gates

The most common use for ACLs is to define access to individual "resources" (think an Eloquent model, or something you're allowing users to administer from their admin panel).

The `resource()` method makes it possible to apply the four most common gates, `view`, `create`, `update`, and `delete`, to a single resource at once:

```
Gate::resource('photos', 'App\Policies\PhotoPolicy');
```

This is equivalent to defining the following:

```
Gate::define('photos.view', 'App\Policies\PhotoPolicy@view');
Gate::define('photos.create', 'App\Policies\PhotoPolicy@create');
Gate::define('photos.update', 'App\Policies\PhotoPolicy@update');
Gate::define('photos.delete', 'App\Policies\PhotoPolicy@delete');
```

The Authorize Middleware

If you want to authorize entire routes, you can use the `Authorize` middleware (which has a shortcut of `can`), like in Example 9-19.

Example 9-19. Using the Authorize middleware

```
Route::get('people/create', function () {
    // Create a person
})->middleware('can:create-person');

Route::get('people/{person}/edit', function () {
    // Edit person
})->middleware('can:edit,person');
```

Here, the `{person}` parameter (whether it's defined as a string or as a bound route model) will be passed to the ability method as an additional parameter.

The first check in Example 9-19 is a normal ability, but the second is a policy, which we'll talk about in "Policies" on page 247.

If you need to check for an action that doesn't require a model instance (for example, `create`, unlike `edit`, doesn't get passed an actual route model–bound instance), you can just pass the class name:

```
Route::post('people', function () {
    // Create a person
})->middleware('can:create,App\Person');
```

Controller Authorization

The parent `App\Http\Controllers\Controller` class in Laravel imports the `AuthorizesRequests` trait, which provides three methods for authorization: `authorize()`, `authorizeForUser()`, and `authorizeResource()`.

`authorize()` takes an ability key and an object (or array of objects) as parameters, and if the authorization fails, it'll quit the application with a 403 (Unauthorized) status code. That means this feature can turn three lines of authorization code into just one, as you can see in Example 9-20.

Example 9-20. Simplifying controller authorization with authorize()

```
// From this:
public function edit(Contact $contact)
{
    if (Gate::cannot('update-contact', $contact)) {
        abort(403);
    }

    return view('contacts.edit', ['contact' => $contact]);
}

// To this:
public function edit(Contact $contact)
{
    $this->authorize('update-contact', $contact);

    return view('contacts.edit', ['contact' => $contact]);
}
```

authorizeForUser() is the same, but allows you to pass in a User object instead of defaulting to the currently authenticated user:

```
$this->authorizeForUser($user, 'update-contact', $contact);
```

authorizeResource(), called once in the controller constructor, maps a predefined set of authorization rules to each of the RESTful controller methods in that controller —something like Example 9-21.

Example 9-21. The authorization-to-method mappings of authorizeResource()

```
...
class ContactsController extends Controller
{
    public function __construct()
    {
        // This call does everything you see in the methods below.
        // If you put this here, you can remove all authorize()
        // calls in the individual resource methods here.
        $this->authorizeResource(Contact::class);
    }

    public function index()
    {
        $this->authorize('view', Contact::class);
    }

    public function create()
    {
        $this->authorize('create', Contact::class);
    }
```

```
    public function store(Request $request)
    {
        $this->authorize('create', Contact::class);
    }

    public function show(Contact $contact)
    {
        $this->authorize('view', $contact);
    }

    public function edit(Contact $contact)
    {
        $this->authorize('update', $contact);
    }

    public function update(Request $request, Contact $contact)
    {
        $this->authorize('update', $contact);
    }

    public function destroy(Contact $contact)
    {
        $this->authorize('delete', $contact);
    }
}
```

Checking on the User Instance

If you're not in a controller, you're more likely to be checking the capabilities of a specific user than the currently authenticated user. That's already possible with the Gate facade using the forUser() method, but sometimes the syntax can feel a little off.

Thankfully, the Authorizable trait on the User class provides three methods to make a more readable authorization feature: $user->can(), $user->cant(), and $user->cannot(). As you can probably guess, cant() and cannot() do the same thing, and can() is their exact inverse.

That means you can do something like Example 9-22.

Example 9-22. Checking authorization on a User instance

```
$user = User::find(1);

if ($user->can('create-contact')) {
    // Do something
}
```

Behind the scenes, these methods are just passing your params to `Gate`; in the preceding example, `Gate::forUser($user)->check('create-contact')`.

Blade Checks

Blade also has a little convenience helper: the @can directive. Example 9-23 illustrates its usage.

Example 9-23. Using Blade's @can directive

```
<nav>
    <a href="/">Home</a>
    @can('edit-contact', $contact)
        <a href="{{ route('contacts.edit', [$contact->id]) }}">Edit This Contact</a>
    @endcan
</nav>
```

You can also use @else in between @can and @endcan, and you can use @cannot and @endcannot as in Example 9-24.

Example 9-24. Using Blade's @cannot directive

```
<h1>{{ $contact->name }}</h1>
@cannot('edit-contact', $contact)
    LOCKED
@endcannot
```

Intercepting Checks

If you've ever built an app with an admin user class, you've probably looked at all of the simple authorization closures so far in this chapter and thought about how you could add a superuser class that overrides these checks in every case. Thankfully, there's already a tool for that.

In `AuthServiceProvider`, where you're already defining your abilities, you can also add a `before()` check that runs before all the others and can optionally override them, like in Example 9-25.

Example 9-25. Overriding Gate checks with before()

```
Gate::before(function ($user, $ability) {
    if ($user->isOwner()) {
        return true;
    }
});
```

Note that the string name for the ability is also passed in, so you can differentiate your `before()` hooks based on your ability naming scheme.

Policies

Up until this point, all of the access controls have required you to manually associate Eloquent models with the ability names. You could have created an ability named something like `visit-dashboard` that's not related to a specific Eloquent model, but you'll probably have noticed that most of our examples have had to do with *doing something to something*—and in most of these cases, the *something* that's the recipient of the action is an Eloquent model.

Authorization policies are organizational structures that help you group your authorization logic based on the resource you're controlling access to. They make it easy to manage defining authorization rules for behavior toward a particular Eloquent model (or other PHP class), all together in a single location.

Generating policies

Policies are PHP classes, which can be generated with an Artisan command:

```
php artisan make:policy ContactPolicy
```

Once they're generated, they need to be registered. The `AuthServiceProvider` has a `$policies` property, which is an array. The key of each item is the class name of the protected resource (almost always an Eloquent class), and the value is the policy class name. Example 9-26 shows what this will look like.

Example 9-26. Registering policies in AuthServiceProvider

```
class AuthServiceProvider extends ServiceProvider
{
    protected $policies = [
        Contact::class => ContactPolicy::class,
    ];
```

A policy class that's generated by Artisan doesn't have any special properties or methods. But every method that you add is now mapped as an ability key for this object.

Policy Auto-Discovery

In applications running Laravel 5.8+, Laravel tries to "guess" the links between your policies and their corresponding models. For example, it'll apply the `PostPolicy` to your `Post` model automatically.

If you need to customize the logic Laravel uses to guess this mapping, check out the Policy docs (*http://bit.ly/2HJ4itY*).

Let's define an `update()` method to take a look at how it works (Example 9-27).

Example 9-27. A sample update() policy method

```php
<?php

namespace App\Policies;

class ContactPolicy
{
    public function update($user, $contact)
    {
        return $user->id == $contact->user_id;
    }
}
```

Notice that the contents of this method look exactly like they would in a `Gate` definition.

Policy Methods That Don't Take an Instance

What if you want to define a policy method that relates to the class but not a specific instance—for example, "can this user create contacts at all?" rather than just "can this user view this specific contact?" In Laravel 5.3, you can treat this just like a normal method. In Laravel 5.2, when you create that method, you'll need to add "Any" at the end of its name:

```php
...
class ContactPolicy
{
    public function createAny($user)
    {
        return $user->canCreateContacts();
    }
}
```

Checking policies

If there's a policy defined for a resource type, the `Gate` facade will use the first parameter to figure out which method to check on the policy. If you run `Gate::allows('update', $contact)`, it will check the `ContactPolicy@update` method for authorization.

This also works for the `Authorize` middleware and for `User` model checking and Blade checking, as seen in Example 9-28.

Example 9-28. Checking authorization against a policy

```
// Gate
if (Gate::denies('update', $contact)) {
    abort(403);
}

// Gate if you don't have an explicit instance
if (! Gate::check('create', Contact::class)) {
    abort(403);
}

// User
if ($user->can('update', $contact)) {
    // Do stuff
}

// Blade
@can('update', $contact)
    // Show stuff
@endcan
```

Additionally, there's a `policy()` helper that allows you to retrieve a policy class and run its methods:

```
if (policy($contact)->update($user, $contact)) {
    // Do stuff
}
```

Overriding policies

Just like with normal ability definitions, policies can define a `before()` method that allows you to override any call before it's even processed (see Example 9-29).

Example 9-29. Overriding policies with the before() method

```
public function before($user, $ability)
{
    if ($user->isAdmin()) {
        return true;
    }
}
```

Testing

Application tests often need to perform a particular behavior on behalf of a particular user. We therefore need to be able to authenticate as a user in application tests, and we need to test authorization rules and authentication routes.

Of course, it's possible to write an application test that manually visits the login page and then fills out the form and submits it, but that's not necessary. Instead, the simplest option is to use the `->be()` method to simulate being logged in as a user. Take a look at Example 9-30.

Example 9-30. Authenticating as a user in application tests

```php
public function test_it_creates_a_new_contact()
{
    $user = factory(User::class)->create();
    $this->be($user);

    $this->post('contacts', [
        'email' => 'my@email.com',
    ]);

    $this->assertDatabaseHas('contacts', [
        'email' => 'my@email.com',
        'user_id' => $user->id,
    ]);
}
```

You can also use, and chain, the `actingAs()` method instead of `be()`, if you prefer how it reads:

```php
public function test_it_creates_a_new_contact()
{
    $user = factory(User::class)->create();

    $this->actingAs($user)->post('contacts', [
        'email' => 'my@email.com',
    ]);

    $this->assertDatabaseHas('contacts', [
        'email' => 'my@email.com',
        'user_id' => $user->id,
    ]);
}
```

We can also test authorization like in Example 9-31.

Example 9-31. Testing authorization rules

```php
public function test_non_admins_cant_create_users()
{
    $user = factory(User::class)->create([
        'admin' => false,
    ]);
    $this->be($user);
```

```
$this->post('users', ['email' => 'my@email.com']);

    $this->assertDatabaseMissing('users', [
        'email' => 'my@email.com',
    ]);
}
```

Or we can test for a 403 response like in Example 9-32.

Example 9-32. Testing authorization rules by checking status code

```
public function test_non_admins_cant_create_users()
{
    $user = factory(User::class)->create([
        'admin' => false,
    ]);
    $this->be($user);

    $response = $this->post('users', ['email' => 'my@email.com']);

    $response->assertStatus(403);
}
```

We need to test that our authentication (signup and sign-in) routes work too, as illustrated in Example 9-33.

Example 9-33. Testing authentication routes

```
public function test_users_can_register()
{
    $this->post('register', [
        'name' => 'Sal Leibowitz',
        'email' => 'sal@leibs.net',
        'password' => 'abcdefg123',
        'password_confirmation' => 'abcdefg123',
    ]);

    $this->assertDatabaseHas('users', [
        'name' => 'Sal Leibowitz',
        'email' => 'sal@leibs.net',
    ]);
}

public function test_users_can_log_in()
{
    $user = factory(User::class)->create([
        'password' => Hash::make('abcdefg123')
    ]);

    $this->post('login', [
```

```
                'email' => $user->email,
                'password' => 'abcdefg123',
        ]);

        $this->assertTrue(auth()->check());
        $this->assertTrue($user->is(auth()->user()));
}
```

We can also use the integration test features to direct the test to "click" our authentication fields and "submit" the fields to test the entire flow. We'll talk about that more in Chapter 12.

Different Names for Testing Methods Prior to Laravel 5.4

In projects running versions of Laravel prior to 5.4, `assertDatabaseHas()` should be replaced by `seeInDatabase()`, `assertDatabaseMissing()` should likewise be replaced by `dontSeeInDatabase()`, `assertDatabaseHas()` should be replaced by `seeInDatabase()`, and `assertStatus()` should be called on `$this` instead of `$response`.

TL;DR

Between the default `User` model, the `create_users_table` migration, the auth controllers, and the auth scaffold, Laravel provides a full user authentication system out of the box. The `RegisterController` handles user registration, the `LoginController` handles user authentication, and the `ResetPasswordController` and the `ForgotPasswordController` handle password resets. Each has certain properties and methods that can be used to override some of the default behavior.

The `Auth` facade and the `auth()` global helper provide access to the current user (`auth()->user()`) and make it easy to check whether a user is logged in (`auth()->check()` and `auth()->guest()`).

Laravel also has an authorization system built in that allows you to define specific abilities (`create-contact`, `visit-secret-page`) or define policies for user interaction with entire models.

You can check for authorization with the `Gate` facade, the `can()` and `cannot()` methods on the `User` class, the `@can` and `@cannot` directives in Blade, the `authorize()` methods on the controller, or the `can` middleware.

## CHAPTER 10

Requests, Responses, and Middleware

We've already talked a bit about the Illuminate `Request` object. In Chapter 3, for example, you saw how you can typehint it in constructors to get an instance or use the `request()` helper to retrieve it, and in Chapter 7 we looked at how you can use it to get information about the user's input.

In this chapter, you'll learn more about what the `Request` object is, how it's generated and what it represents, and what part it plays in your application's lifecycle. We'll also talk about the `Response` object and Laravel's implementation of the middleware pattern.

Laravel's Request Lifecycle

Every request coming into a Laravel application, whether generated by an HTTP request or a command-line interaction, is immediately converted into an Illuminate `Request` object, which then crosses many layers and ends up being parsed by the application itself. The application then generates an Illuminate `Response` object, which is sent back out across those layers and finally returned to the end user.

This request/response lifecycle is illustrated in Figure 10-1. Let's take a look at what it takes to make each of these steps happen, from the first line of code to the last.

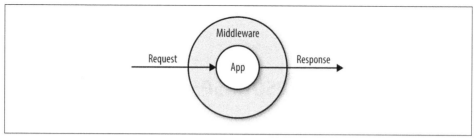

Figure 10-1. Request/response lifecycle

Bootstrapping the Application

Every Laravel application has some form of configuration set up at the web server level, in an Apache *.htaccess* file or an Nginx configuration setting or something similar, that captures every web request regardless of URL and routes it to *public/index.php* in the Laravel application directory (*app*).

index.php doesn't actually have that much code in it. It has three primary functions.

First, it loads Composer's autoload file, which registers all of the Composer-loaded dependencies.

Composer and Laravel

Laravel's core functionality is separated into a series of components under the Illuminate namespace, which are all pulled into each Laravel app using Composer. Laravel also pulls in quite a few packages from Symfony and several other community-developed packages. In this way, Laravel is just as much an opinionated collection of components as it is a framework.

Next, it kicks off Laravel's bootstrap, creating the application container (you'll learn more about the container in Chapter 11) and registering a few core services (including the kernel, which we'll talk about in just a bit).

Finally, it creates an instance of the kernel, creates a request representing the current user's web request, and passes the request to the kernel to handle. The kernel responds with an Illuminate `Response` object, which *index.php* returns to the end user. Then, the kernel terminates the page request.

Laravel's kernel

The kernel is the core router of every Laravel application, responsible for taking in a user request, processing it through middleware, handling exceptions and passing it to the page router, and then returning the final response. Actually, there are two kernels, but only one is used for each page request. One of the routers handles web requests (the HTTP kernel) and the other handles console, cron, and Artisan requests (the console kernel). Each has a `handle()` method that's responsible for taking in an Illuminate `Request` object and returning an Illuminate `Response` object.

The kernel runs all of the bootstraps that need to run before every request, including determining which environment the current request is running in (staging, local, production, etc.) and running all of the service providers. The HTTP kernel additionally defines the list of middleware that will wrap each request, including the core middleware responsible for sessions and CSRF protection.

Service Providers

While there's a bit of procedural code in these bootstraps, almost all of Laravel's bootstrap code is separated into something Laravel calls *service providers*. A service provider is a class that encapsulates logic that various parts of your application need to run in order to bootstrap their core functionality.

For example, there's an `AuthServiceProvider` that bootstraps all of the registrations necessary for Laravel's authentication system and a `RouteServiceProvider` that bootstraps the routing system.

The concept of service providers can be a little hard to understand at first, so think about it this way: many components of your application have bootstrap code that needs to run when the application initializes. Service providers are a tool for grouping that bootstrap code into related classes. If you have any code that needs to run *in preparation* for your application code to work, it's a strong candidate for a service provider.

For example, if you ever find that the feature you're working on requires some classes registered in the container (you'll learn more about this in Chapter 11), you would create a service provider just for that piece of functionality. You might have a `GitHubServiceProvider` or a `MailerServiceProvider`.

boot(), register(), and deferring on service providers

Service providers have two important methods: `boot()` and `register()`. There's also a `DeferrableProvider` interface (5.8+) or a `$defer` property (5.7 and earlier) that you might choose to use. Here's how they work.

First, all of the service providers' `register()` methods are called. This is where you'll want to bind classes and aliases to the container. You don't want to do anything in `register()` that relies on the entire application being bootstrapped.

Second, all of the service providers' boot() methods are called. You can now do any other bootstrapping here, like binding event listeners or defining routes—anything that may rely on the entire Laravel application having been bootstrapped.

If your service provider is only going to register bindings in the container (i.e., teach the container how to resolve a given class or interface), but not perform any other bootstrapping, you can "defer" its registrations, which means they won't run unless one of their bindings is explicitly requested from the container. This can speed up your application's average time to bootstrap.

If you want to defer your service provider's registrations, in 5.8+, first implement the Illuminate\Contracts\Support\DeferrableProvider interface; or, in 5.7 and earlier, first give it a protected $defer property and set it to true; and then, in all versions, give the service provider a provides() method that returns a list of bindings the provider provides, as shown in Example 10-1.

Example 10-1. Deferring the registration of a service provider

```
...
use Illuminate\Contracts\Support\DeferrableProvider;

class GitHubServiceProvider extends ServiceProvider implements DeferrableProvider
{
    public function provides()
    {
        return [
            GitHubClient::class,
        ];
    }
}
```

More Uses for Service Providers

Service providers also have a suite of methods and configuration options that can provide advanced functionality to the end user when the provider is published as part of a Composer package. Take a look at the service provider definition in the Laravel source (*http://bit.ly/2HEEC1t*) to learn more about how this can work.

Now that we've covered the application bootstrap, let's take a look at the Request object, the most important output of the bootstrap.

The Request Object

The `Illuminate\Http\Request` class is a Laravel-specific extension of Symfony's `HttpFoundation\Request` class.

Symfony HttpFoundation

If you're not familiar with it, Symfony's `HttpFoundation` suite of classes powers almost every PHP framework in existence at this point; this is the most popular and powerful set of abstractions available in PHP for representing HTTP requests, responses, headers, cookies, and more.

The `Request` object is intended to represent every relevant piece of information you might care to know about a user's HTTP request.

In native PHP code, you might find yourself looking to `$_SERVER`, `$_GET`, `$_POST`, and other combinations of globals and processing logic to get information about the current user's request. What files has the user uploaded? What's their IP address? What fields did they post? All of this is sprinkled around the language—and your code—in a way that's hard to understand and harder to mock.

Symfony's `Request` object instead collects all of the information necessary to represent a single HTTP request into a single object, and then tacks on convenience methods to make it easy to get useful information from it. The Illuminate `Request` object adds even more convenience methods to get information about the request it's representing.

Capturing a Request

You'll very likely never need to do this in a Laravel app, but if you ever need to capture your own Illuminate `Request` object directly from PHP's globals, you can use the `capture()` method:

```
$request = Illuminate\Http\Request::capture();
```

Getting a Request Object in Laravel

Laravel creates an internal `Request` object for each request, and there are a few ways you can get access to it.

First—and again, we'll cover this more in Chapter 11—you can typehint the class in any constructor or method that's resolved by the container. That means you can typehint it in a controller method or a service provider, as seen in Example 10-2.

Example 10-2. Typehinting in a container-resolved method to receive a Request object

```
...
use Illuminate\Http\Request;

class PeopleController extends Controller
{
    public function index(Request $request)
    {
        $allInput = $request->all();
    }
}
```

Alternatively, you can use the `request()` global helper, which allows you to call methods on it (e.g., `request()->input()`) and also allows you to call it on its own to get an instance of `$request`:

```
$request = request();
$allInput = $request->all();
// or
$allInput = request()->all();
```

Finally, you can use the `app()` global method to get an instance of `Request`. You can pass either the fully qualified class name or the shortcut `request`:

```
$request = app(Illuminate\Http\Request::class);
$request = app('request');
```

Getting Basic Information About a Request

Now that you know how to get an instance of `Request`, what can you do with it? The primary purpose of the `Request` object is to represent the current HTTP request, so the primary functionality the `Request` class offers is to make it easy to get useful information about the current request.

I've categorized the methods described here, but note that there's certainly overlap between the categories, and the categories are a bit arbitrary—for example, query parameters could just as easily be in "User and request state" as they are in "Basic user input." Hopefully these categories will make it easy for you to learn what's available, and then you can throw away the categories.

Also, be aware that there are many more methods available on the `Request` object; these are just the most commonly used methods.

Basic user input

The basic user input methods make it simple to get information that the users themselves explicitly provide—likely through submitting a form or an Ajax component. When I reference "user-provided input" here, I'm talking about input from query strings (GET), form submissions (POST), or JSON. The basic user input methods include the following:

`all()`
> Returns an array of all user-provided input.

`input(fieldName)`
> Returns the value of a single user-provided input field.

`only(fieldName|[array,of,field,names])`
> Returns an array of all user-provided input for the specified field name(s).

`except(fieldName|[array,of,field,names])`
> Returns an array of all user-provided input except for the specified field name(s).

`exists(fieldName)`
> Returns a Boolean indicating whether the field exists in the input. `has()` is an alias.

`filled(fieldName)`
> Returns a Boolean indicating whether the field exists in the input and is not empty (that is, has a value).

`json()`
> Returns a `ParameterBag` if the page had JSON sent to it.

`json(keyName)`
> Returns the value of the given key from the JSON sent to the page.

ParameterBag

Sometimes in Laravel you'll run into a `ParameterBag` object. This class is sort of like an associative array. You can get a particular key using `get()`:

```
echo $bag->get('name');
```

You can also use `has()` to check for the existence of a key, `all()` to get an array of all keys and values, `count()` to count the number of items, and `keys()` to get an array of just the keys.

Example 10-3 gives a few quick examples of how to use the user-provided information methods from a request.

Example 10-3. Getting basic user-provided information from the request

```
// form
<form method="POST" action="/form">
    @csrf
    <input name="name"> Name<br>
    <input type="submit">
</form>

// Route receiving the form
Route::post('form', function (Request $request) {
    echo 'name is ' . $request->input('name') . '<br>';
    echo 'all input is ' . print_r($request->all()) . '<br>';
    echo 'user provided email address: ' . $request->has('email') ? 'true' : 'false';
});
```

User and request state

The user and request state methods include input that wasn't explicitly provided by the user through a form:

method()
:   Returns the method (GET, POST, PATCH, etc.) used to access this route.

path()
:   Returns the path (without the domain) used to access this page; for example, *http://www.myapp.com/abc/def* would return abc/def.

url()
:   Returns the URL (with the domain) used to access this page; for example, *http://www.myapp.com/abc* would return http://www.myapp.com/abc.

is()
:   Returns a Boolean indicating whether or not the current page request fuzzy-matches a provided string (e.g., /a/b/c would be matched by $request->is('*b*'), where * stands for any characters); uses a custom regex parser found in Str::is().

ip()
:   Returns the user's IP address.

header()
:   Returns an array of headers (e.g., ['accept-language' => ['en-US,en;q=0.8']]), or, if passed a header name as a parameter, returns just that header.

`server()`
> Returns an array of the variables traditionally stored in $_SERVER (e.g., REMOTE_ADDR), or, if passed a $_SERVER variable name, returns just that value.

`secure()`
> Returns a Boolean indicating whether this page was loaded using HTTPS.

`pjax()`
> Returns a Boolean indicating whether this page request was loaded using Pjax.

`wantsJson()`
> Returns a Boolean indicating whether this request has any /json content types in its Accept headers.

`isJson()`
> Returns a Boolean indicating whether this page request has any /json content types in its Content-Type header.

`accepts()`
> Returns a Boolean indicating whether this page request accepts a given content type.

Files

So far, all of the input we've covered is either explicit (retrieved by methods like all(), input(), etc.) or defined by the browser or referring site (retrieved by methods like pjax()). File inputs are similar to explicit user input, but they're handled much differently:

`file()`
> Returns an array of all uploaded files, or, if a key is passed (the file upload field name), returns just the one file.

`allFiles()`
> Returns an array of all uploaded files; useful as opposed to file() because of clearer naming.

`hasFile()`
> Returns a Boolean indicating whether a file was uploaded at the specified key.

Every file that's uploaded will be an instance of Symfony\Component\HttpFoundation\File\UploadedFile, which provides a suite of tools for validating, processing, and storing uploaded files.

Take a look at Chapter 14 for more examples of how to handle uploaded files.

Persistence

The request can also provide functionality for interacting with the session. Most session functionality lives elsewhere, but there are a few methods that are particularly relevant to the current page request:

`flash()`
> Flashes the current request's user input to the session to be retrieved later, which means it's saved to the session but disappears after the next request.

`flashOnly()`
> Flashes the current request's user input for any keys in the provided array.

`flashExcept()`
> Flashes the current request's user input, except for any keys in the provided array.

`old()`
> Returns an array of all previously flashed user input, or, if passed a key, returns the value for that key if it was previously flashed.

`flush()`
> Wipes all previously flashed user input.

`cookie()`
> Retrieves all cookies from the request, or, if a key is provided, retrieves just that cookie.

`hasCookie()`
> Returns a Boolean indicating whether the request has a cookie for the given key.

The `flash*()` and `old()` methods are used for storing user input and retrieving it later, often after the input is validated and rejected.

The Response Object

Similar to the `Request` object, there's an Illuminate `Response` object that represents the response your application is sending to the end user, complete with headers, cookies, content, and anything else used for sending the end user's browser instructions on rendering a page.

Just like `Request`, the `Illuminate\Http\Response` class extends a Symfony class: `Symfony\Component\HttpFoundation\Response`. This is a base class with a series of properties and methods that make it possible to represent and render a response; Illuminate's `Response` class decorates it with a few helpful shortcuts.

Using and Creating Response Objects in Controllers

Before we talk about how you can customize your `Response` objects, let's step back and see how we most commonly work with `Response` objects.

In the end, any `Response` object returned from a route definition will be converted into an HTTP response. It may define specific headers or specific content, set cookies, or whatever else, but eventually it will be converted into a response your users' browsers can parse.

Let's take a look at the simplest possible response, in Example 10-4.

Example 10-4. Simplest possible HTTP response

```
Route::get('route', function () {
    return new Illuminate\Http\Response('Hello!');
});

// Same, using global function:
Route::get('route', function () {
    return response('Hello!');
});
```

We create a response, give it some core data, and then return it. We can also customize the HTTP status, headers, cookies, and more, like in Example 10-5.

Example 10-5. Simple HTTP response with customized status and headers

```
Route::get('route', function () {
    return response('Error!', 400)
        ->header('X-Header-Name', 'header-value')
        ->cookie('cookie-name', 'cookie-value');
});
```

Setting headers

We define a header on a response by using the `header()` fluent method, like in Example 10-5. The first parameter is the header name, and the second is the header value.

Adding cookies

We can also set cookies directly on the `Response` object if we'd like. We'll cover Laravel's cookie handling a bit more in Chapter 14, but take a look at Example 10-6 for a simple use case for attaching cookies to a response.

Example 10-6. Attaching a cookie to a response

```
return response($content)
    ->cookie('signup_dismissed', true);
```

Specialized Response Types

There are also a few special response types for views, downloads, files, and JSON. Each is a predefined macro that makes it easy to reuse particular templates for headers or content structure.

View responses

In Chapter 4, I used the global `view()` helper to show how to return a template—for example, `view('view.name.here')` or something similar. But if you need to customize the headers, HTTP status, or anything else when returning a view, you can use the `view()` response type as shown in Example 10-7.

Example 10-7. Using the view() response type

```
Route::get('/', function (XmlGetterService $xml) {
    $data = $xml->get();
    return response()
        ->view('xml-structure', $data)
        ->header('Content-Type', 'text/xml');
});
```

Download responses

Sometimes you want your application to force the user's browser to download a file, whether you're creating the file in Laravel or serving it from a database or a protected location. The `download()` response type makes this simple.

The required first parameter is the path for the file you want the browser to download. If it's a generated file, you'll need to save it somewhere temporarily.

The optional second parameter is the filename for the downloaded file (e.g., *export.csv*). If you don't pass a string here, it will be generated automatically. The optional third parameter allows you to pass an array of headers. Example 10-8 illustrates the use of the `download()` response type.

Example 10-8. Using the download() response type

```
public function export()
{
    return response()
        ->download('file.csv', 'export.csv', ['header' => 'value']);
}
```

```
public function otherExport()
{
    return response()->download('file.pdf');
}
```

If you wish to delete the original file from the disk after returning a download response, you can chain the deleteFileAfterSend() method after the download() method:

```
public function export()
{
    return response()
        ->download('file.csv', 'export.csv')
        ->deleteFileAfterSend();
}
```

File responses

The file response is similar to the download response, except it allows the browser to display the file instead of forcing a download. This is most common with images and PDFs.

The required first parameter is the filename, and the optional second parameter can be an array of headers (see Example 10-9).

Example 10-9. Using the file() response type

```
public function invoice($id)
{
    return response()->file("./invoices/{$id}.pdf", ['header' => 'value']);
}
```

JSON responses

JSON responses are so common that, even though they're not really particularly complex to program, there's a custom response for them as well.

JSON responses convert the passed data to JSON (with json_encode()) and set the Content-Type to application/json. You can also optionally use the setCallback() method to create a JSONP response instead of JSON, as seen in Example 10-10.

Example 10-10. Using the json() response type

```
public function contacts()
{
    return response()->json(Contact::all());
}
```

```
public function jsonpContacts(Request $request)
{
    return response()
        ->json(Contact::all())
        ->setCallback($request->input('callback'));
}

public function nonEloquentContacts()
{
    return response()->json(['Tom', 'Jerry']);
}
```

Redirect responses

Redirects aren't commonly called on the `response()` helper, so they're a bit different from the other custom response types we've discussed already, but they're still just a different sort of response. Redirects, returned from a Laravel route, send the user a redirect (often a 301) to another page or back to the previous page.

You technically *can* call a redirect from `response()`, as in `return response()->redirectTo('/')`. But more commonly, you'll use the redirect-specific global helpers.

There is a global `redirect()` function that can be used to create redirect responses, and a global `back()` function that is a shortcut to `redirect()->back()`.

Just like most global helpers, the `redirect()` global function can either be passed parameters or be used to get an instance of its class that you then chain method calls onto. If you don't chain, but just pass parameters, `redirect()` performs the same as `redirect()->to()`; it takes a string and redirects to that string URL. Example 10-11 shows some examples of its use.

Example 10-11. Examples of using the redirect() global helper

```
return redirect('account/payment');
return redirect()->to('account/payment');
return redirect()->route('account.payment');
return redirect()->action('AccountController@showPayment');

// If redirecting to an external domain
return redirect()->away('https://tighten.co');

// If named route or controller needs parameters
return redirect()->route('contacts.edit', ['id' => 15]);
return redirect()->action('ContactsController@edit', ['id' => 15]);
```

You can also redirect "back" to the previous page, which is especially useful when handling and validating user input. Example 10-12 shows a common pattern in validation contexts.

Example 10-12. Redirect back with input

```
public function store()
{
    // If validation fails...
    return back()->withInput();
}
```

Finally, you can redirect and flash data to the session at the same time. This is common with error and success messages, like in Example 10-13.

Example 10-13. Redirect with flashed data

```
Route::post('contacts', function () {
    // Store the contact

    return redirect('dashboard')->with('message', 'Contact created!');
});

Route::get('dashboard', function () {
    // Get the flashed data from session--usually handled in Blade template
    echo session('message');
});
```

Custom response macros

You can also create your own custom response types using *macros*. This allows you to define a series of modifications to make to the response and its provided content.

Let's recreate the json() custom response type, just to see how it works. As always, you should probably create a custom service provider for these sorts of bindings, but for now we'll just put it in AppServiceProvider, as seen in Example 10-14.

Example 10-14. Creating a custom response macro

```
...
class AppServiceProvider
{
    public function boot()
    {
        Response::macro('myJson', function ($content) {
            return response(json_encode($content))
                ->withHeaders(['Content-Type' => 'application/json']);
        });
    }
```

Then, we can use it just like we would use the predefined json() macro:

```
return response()->myJson(['name' => 'Sangeetha']);
```

This will return a response with the body of that array encoded for JSON, with the JSON-appropriate `Content-Type` header.

The Responsable interface

If you'd like to customize how you're sending responses and a macro doesn't offer enough space or enough organization, or if you want any of your objects to be capable of being returned as a "response" with their own logic of how to be displayed, the Responsable interface (introduced in Laravel 5.5) is for you.

The `Responsable` interface, `Illuminate\Contracts\Support\Responsable`, dictates its implementors must have a `toResponse()` method. This needs to return an Illuminate Response object. Example 10-15 illustrates how to create a `Responsable` object.

Example 10-15. Creating a simple Responsable object

```
...
use Illuminate\Contracts\Support\Responsable;

class MyJson implements Responsable
{
    public function __construct($content)
    {
        $this->content = $content;
    }

    public function toResponse()
    {
        return response(json_encode($this->content))
            ->withHeaders(['Content-Type' => 'application/json']);
    }
}
```

Then, we can use it just like our custom macro:

```
return new MyJson(['name' => 'Sangeetha']);
```

This probably looks like a lot of work relative to the response macros we covered earlier. But the `Responsable` interface really shines when you're working with more complicated controller manipulations. One common example is to use it to create view models (or view objects), like in Example 10-16.

Example 10-16. Using Responsable to create a view object

```
...
use Illuminate\Contracts\Support\Responsable;

class GroupDonationDashboard implements Responsable
{
    public function __construct($group)
```

```
    {
        $this->group = $group;
    }

    public function budgetThisYear()
    {
        // ...
    }

    public function giftsThisYear()
    {
        // ...
    }

    public function toResponse()
    {
        return view('groups.dashboard')
            ->with('annual_budget', $this->budgetThisYear())
            ->with('annual_gifts_received', $this->giftsThisYear());
    }
```

It starts to make a little bit more sense in this context—move your complex view preparation into a dedicated, *testable* object, and keep your controllers clean. Here's a controller that uses that `Responsable` object:

```
...
class GroupController
{
    public function index(Group $group)
    {
        return new GroupDonationsDashboard($group);
    }
```

Laravel and Middleware

Take a look back at Figure 10-1, at the start of this chapter.

We've covered the requests and responses, but we haven't actually looked into what middleware is. You may already be familiar with middleware; it's not unique to Laravel, but rather a widely used architecture pattern.

An Introduction to Middleware

The idea of middleware is that there is a series of layers wrapping around your application, like a multilayer cake or an onion.[1] Just as shown in Figure 10-1, every request passes through every middleware layer on its way into the application, and then the

---

1 Or an ogre (*https://en.wikipedia.org/wiki/Shrek*).

resulting response passes back through the middleware layers on its way out to the end user.

Middleware are most often considered separate from your application logic, and usually are constructed in a way that should theoretically be applicable to any application, not just the one you're working on at the moment.

A middleware can inspect a request and decorate it, or reject it, based on what it finds. That means middleware is great for something like rate limiting: it can inspect the IP address, check how many times it's accessed this resource in the last minute, and send back a 429 (Too Many Requests) status if a threshold is passed.

Because middleware also gets access to the response on its way out of the application, it's great for decorating responses. For example, Laravel uses a middleware to add all of the queued cookies from a given request/response cycle to the response right before it is sent to the end user.

But some of the most powerful uses of middleware come from the fact that it can be nearly the *first* and the *last* thing to interact with the request/response cycle. That makes it perfect for something like enabling sessions—PHP needs you to open the session very early and close it very late, and middleware is also great for this.

Creating Custom Middleware

Let's imagine we want to have a middleware that rejects every request that uses the DELETE HTTP method, and also sends a cookie back for every request.

There's an Artisan command to create custom middleware. Let's try it out:

```
php artisan make:middleware BanDeleteMethod
```

You can now open up the file at *app/Http/Middleware/BanDeleteMethod.php*. The default contents are shown in Example 10-17.

Example 10-17. Default middleware contents

```
...
class BanDeleteMethod
{
    public function handle($request, Closure $next)
    {
        return $next($request);
    }
}
```

How this handle() method represents the processing of both the incoming request *and* the outgoing response is the most difficult thing to understand about middleware, so let's walk through it.

Understanding middleware's handle() method

First, remember that middleware are layered one on top of another, and then finally on top of the app. The first middleware that's registered gets *first* access to a request when it comes in, then that request is passed to every other middleware in turn, then to the app; then the resulting response is passed outward through the middleware, and finally this first middleware gets *last* access to the response when it goes out.

Let's imagine we've registered BanDeleteMethod as the first middleware to run. That means the $request coming into it is the raw request, unadulterated by any other middleware. Now what?

Passing that request to $next() means handing it off to the rest of the middleware. The $next() closure just takes that $request and passes it to the handle() method of the next middleware in the stack. It then gets passed on down the line until there are no more middleware to hand it to, and it finally ends up at the application.

Next, how does the response come out? This is where it might be hard to follow. The application returns a response, which is passed back up the chain of middleware—because each middleware returns its response. So, within that same handle() method, the middleware can decorate a $request and pass it to the $next() closure, and can then choose to do something with the output it receives before finally returning that output to the end user. Let's look at some pseudocode to make this clearer (Example 10-18).

Example 10-18. Pseudocode explaining the middleware call process

```
...
class BanDeleteMethod
{
    public function handle($request, Closure $next)
    {
        // At this point, $request is the raw request from the user.
        // Let's do something with it, just for fun.
        if ($request->ip() === '192.168.1.1') {
            return response('BANNED IP ADDRESS!', 403);
        }

        // Now we've decided to accept it. Let's pass it on to the next
        // middleware in the stack. We pass it to $next(), and what is
        // returned is the response after the $request has been passed
        // down the stack of middleware to the application and the
        // application's response has been passed back up the stack.
        $response = $next($request);

        // At this point, we can once again interact with the response
        // just before it is returned to the user
        $response->cookie('visited-our-site', true);
```

```
        // Finally, we can release this response to the end user
        return $response;
    }
}
```

Finally, let's make the middleware do what we actually promised (Example 10-19).

Example 10-19. Sample middleware banning the delete method

```
...
class BanDeleteMethod
{
    public function handle($request, Closure $next)
    {
        // Test for the DELETE method
        if ($request->method() === 'DELETE') {
            return response(
                "Get out of here with that delete method",
                405
            );
        }

        $response = $next($request);

        // Assign cookie
        $response->cookie('visited-our-site', true);

        // Return response
        return $response;
    }
}
```

Binding Middleware

We're not quite done yet. We need to register this middleware in one of two ways: globally or for specific routes.

Global middleware are applied to every route; route middleware are applied on a route-by-route basis.

Binding global middleware

Both bindings happen in *app/Http/Kernel.php*. To add a middleware as global, add its class name to the $middleware property, as in Example 10-20.

Example 10-20. Binding global middleware

```
// app/Http/Kernel.php
protected $middleware = [
    \Illuminate\Foundation\Http\Middleware\CheckForMaintenanceMode::class,
    \App\Http\Middleware\BanDeleteMethod::class,
];
```

Binding route middleware

Middleware intended for specific routes can be added as a route middleware or as part of a middleware group. Let's start with the former.

Route middleware are added to the $routeMiddleware array in *app/Http/Kernel.php*. It's similar to adding them to $middleware, except we have to give one a key that will be used when applying this middleware to a particular route, as seen in Example 10-21.

Example 10-21. Binding route middleware

```
// app/Http/Kernel.php
protected $routeMiddleware = [
    'auth' => \App\Http\Middleware\Authenticate::class,
    ...
    'ban-delete' => \App\Http\Middleware\BanDeleteMethod::class,
];
```

We can now use this middleware in our route definitions, like in Example 10-22.

Example 10-22. Applying route middleware in route definitions

```
// Doesn't make much sense for our current example...
Route::get('contacts', 'ContactsController@index')->middleware('ban-delete');

// Makes more sense for our current example...
Route::prefix('api')->middleware('ban-delete')->group(function () {
    // All routes related to an API
});
```

Using middleware groups

Laravel 5.2 introduced the concept of middleware groups. They're essentially pre-packaged bundles of middleware that make sense to be together in specific contexts.

Middleware Groups in 5.2 and 5.3

The default routes file in earlier releases of 5.2, *routes.php*, had three distinct sections: the root route (/) wasn't under any middleware group, and then there was a web middleware group and an api middleware group. It was a bit confusing for new users, and it meant the root route didn't have access to the session or anything else that's kicked off in the middleware.

In later releases of 5.2 everything's simplified: every route in *routes.php* is in the web middleware group. In 5.3 and later, you get a *routes/web.php* file for web routes and a *routes/api.php* file for API routes. If you want to add routes in other groups, read on.

Out of the box there are two groups: web and api. web has all the middleware that will be useful on almost every Laravel page request, including middleware for cookies, sessions, and CSRF protection. api has none of those—it has a throttling middleware and a route model binding middleware, and that's it. These are all defined in *app/Http/Kernel.php*.

You can apply middleware groups to routes just like you apply route middleware to routes, with the middleware() fluent method:

```
Route::get('/', 'HomeController@index')->middleware('web');
```

You can also create your own middleware groups and add and remove route middleware to and from preexisting middleware groups. It works just like adding route middleware normally, but you're instead adding them to keyed groups in the $middlewareGroups array.

You might be wondering how these middleware groups match up with the two default routes files. Unsurprisingly, the *routes/web.php* file is wrapped with the web middleware group, and the *routes/api.php* file is wrapped with the api middleware group.

The *routes/** files are loaded in the RouteServiceProvider. Take a look at the map() method there (Example 10-23) and you'll find a mapWebRoutes() method and a mapApiRoutes() method, each of which loads its respective files already wrapped in the appropriate middleware group.

Example 10-23. Default route service provider in Laravel 5.3+

```
// App\Providers\RouteServiceProvider
public function map()
{
    $this->mapApiRoutes();
    $this->mapWebRoutes();
}
```

```
protected function mapApiRoutes()
{
    Route::prefix('api')
        ->middleware('api')
        ->namespace($this->namespace)
        ->group(base_path('routes/api.php'));
}

protected function mapWebRoutes()
{
    Route::middleware('web')
        ->namespace($this->namespace)
        ->group(base_path('routes/web.php'));
}
```

As you can see in Example 10-23, we're using the router to load a route group under the default namespace (App\Http\Controllers) and with the web middleware group, and another under the api middleware group.

Passing Parameters to Middleware

It's not common, but there are times when you need to pass parameters to a route middleware. For example, you might have an authentication middleware that will act differently depending on whether you're guarding for the member user type or the owner user type:

```
Route::get('company', function () {
    return view('company.admin');
})->middleware('auth:owner');
```

To make this work, you'll need to add one or more parameters to the middleware's handle() method and update that method's logic accordingly, as shown in Example 10-24.

Example 10-24. Defining a route middleware that accepts parameters

```
public function handle($request, $next, $role)
{
    if (auth()->check() && auth()->user()->hasRole($role)) {
        return $next($request);
    }

    return redirect('login');
}
```

Note that you can also add more than one parameter to the handle() method, and pass multiple parameters to the route definition by separating them with commas:

```
Route::get('company', function () {
    return view('company.admin');
})->middleware('auth:owner,view');
```

Form Request Objects

In this chapter we covered how to inject an Illuminate `Request` object, which is the base—and most common—request object.

However, you can also extend the `Request` object and inject that instead. You'll learn more about how to bind and inject custom classes in Chapter 11, but there's one special type, called the form request, that has its own set of behaviors.

See "Form Requests" on page 194 to learn more about creating and using form requests.

Trusted Proxies

If you use any Laravel tools to generate URLs within the app, you'll notice that Laravel detects whether the current request was via HTTP or HTTPS and will generate any links using the appropriate protocol.

However, this doesn't always work when you have a proxy (e.g., a load balancer or other web-based proxy) in front of your app. Many proxies send nonstandard headers like `X_FORWARDED_PORT` and `X_FORWARDED_PROTO` to your app, and expect your app to "trust" those, interpret them, and use them as a part of the process of interpreting the HTTP request. In order to make Laravel correctly treat proxied HTTPS calls like secure calls, and in order for Laravel to process other headers from proxied requests, you need to define how it should do so.

You likely don't just want to allow *any* proxy to send traffic to your app; rather, you want to lock your app to only trust certain proxies, and even from those proxies you may only want to trust certain forwarded headers.

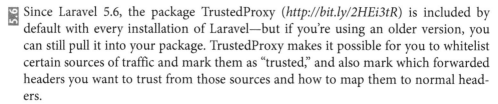 Since Laravel 5.6, the package TrustedProxy (*http://bit.ly/2HEi3tR*) is included by default with every installation of Laravel—but if you're using an older version, you can still pull it into your package. TrustedProxy makes it possible for you to whitelist certain sources of traffic and mark them as "trusted," and also mark which forwarded headers you want to trust from those sources and how to map them to normal headers.

To configure which proxies your app will trust, you can edit the `App\Http\Middleware\TrustProxies` middleware and add the IP address for your load balancer or proxy to the `$proxies` array, as shown in Example 10-25.

Example 10-25. Configuring the TrustProxies middleware

```
/**
 * The trusted proxies for this application
 *
 * @var array
 */
protected $proxies = [
    '192.168.1.1',
    '192.168.1.2',
];

/**
 * The headers that should be used to detect proxies
 *
 * @var string
 */
protected $headers = Request::HEADER_X_FORWARDED_ALL;
```

As you can see, the $headers array defaults to trusting all forwarded headers from the trusted proxies; if you want to customize this list, take a look at the Symfony docs on trusting proxies (*http://bit.ly/2UY7Pri*).

Testing

Outside of the context of you as a developer using requests, responses, and middleware in your own testing, Laravel itself actually uses each quite a bit.

When you're doing application testing with calls like $this->get('/'), you're instructing Laravel's application testing framework to generate request objects that represent the interactions that you're describing. Then those request objects are passed to your application as these were actual visits. That's why the application tests are so accurate: your application doesn't actually "know" that it's not a real user that's interacting with it.

In this context, many of the assertions you're making—say, assertResponseOk()— are assertions against the response object generated by the application testing framework. The assertResponseOk() method just looks at the response object and asserts that its isOk() method returns true—which is just checking that its status code is 200. In the end, *everything* in application testing is acting as if this were a real page request.

Find yourself in a context where you need a request to work with in your tests? You can always pull one from the container with $request = request(). Or you could create your own—the constructor parameters for the Request class, all optional, are as follows:

```
$request = new Illuminate\Http\Request(
    $query,      // GET array
    $request,    // POST array
    $attributes, // "attributes" array; empty is fine
    $cookies,    // Cookies array
    $files,      // Files array
    $server,     // Servers array
    $content     // Raw body data
);
```

If you're really interested in an example, check out the method Symfony uses to create a new Request from the globals PHP provides: Symfony\Component\HttpFoundation\Request@createFromGlobals().

Response objects are even simpler to create manually, if you need to. Here are the (optional) parameters:

```
$response = new Illuminate\Http\Response(
    $content, // response content
    $status,  // HTTP status, default 200
    $headers  // array headers array
);
```

Finally, if you need to disable your middleware during an application test, import the WithoutMiddleware trait into that test. You can also use the $this->withoutMiddleware() method to disable middleware just for a single test method.

TL;DR

Every request coming into a Laravel application is converted into an Illuminate Request object, which then passes through all the middleware and is processed by the application. The application generates a Response object, which is then passed back through all of the middleware (in reverse order) and returned to the end user.

Request and Response objects are responsible for encapsulating and representing every relevant piece of information about the incoming user request and the outgoing server response.

Service providers collect together related behavior for binding and registering classes for use by the application.

Middleware wrap the application and can reject or decorate any request and response.

## CHAPTER 11

The Container

Laravel's service container, or dependency injection container, sits at the core of almost every other feature. The container is a simple tool you can use to bind and resolve concrete instances of classes and interfaces, and at the same time it's a powerful and nuanced manager of a network of interrelated dependencies. In this chapter, you'll learn more about what it is, how it works, and how you can use it.

Naming and the Container

You'll notice in this book, in the documentation, and in other educational sources that there are quite a few names folks use for the container. These include:

- Application container
- IoC (inversion of control) container
- Service container
- DI (dependency injection) container

All are useful and valid, but just know they're all talking about the same thing. They're all referring to the service container.

A Quick Introduction to Dependency Injection

Dependency injection means that, rather than being instantiated ("newed up") within a class, each class's dependencies will be *injected* in from the outside. This most commonly occurs with *constructor injection*, which means an object's dependencies are injected when it's created. But there's also *setter injection*, where the class exposes a method specifically for injecting a given dependency, and *method injection*, where one or more methods expect their dependencies to be injected when they're called.

Take a look at Example 11-1 for a quick example of constructor injection, the most common type of dependency injection.

Example 11-1. Basic dependency injection

```php
<?php

class UserMailer
{
    protected $mailer;

    public function __construct(Mailer $mailer)
    {
        $this->mailer = $mailer;
    }

    public function welcome($user)
    {
        return $this->mailer->mail($user->email, 'Welcome!');
    }
}
```

As you can see, this `UserMailer` class expects an object of type `Mailer` to be injected when it's instantiated, and its methods then refer to that instance.

The primary benefits of dependency injection are that it gives us the freedom to change what we're injecting, to mock dependencies for testing, and to instantiate shared dependencies just once for shared use.

Inversion of Control

You may have heard the phrase "inversion of control" used in conjunction with "dependency injection," and sometimes Laravel's container is called the IoC container.

The two concepts are very similar. Inversion of control references the idea that, in traditional programming, the lowest-level code—specific classes, instances, and procedural code—"controls" which instance of a particular pattern or interface to use. For example, if you're instantiating your mailer in each class that needs it, each class gets to decide whether to use Mailgun or Mandrill or Sendgrid.

The idea of inversion of control refers to flipping that "control" the opposite end of your application. Now the definition of which mailer to use lives at the highest, most abstract level of the application, often in configuration. Every instance, every piece of low-level code, looks up to the high-level configuration to essentially "ask": "Can you give me a mailer?" They don't "know" which mailer they're getting, just that they're getting one.

> Dependency injection and especially DI containers provide a great opportunity for inversion of control because, for example, you can define once which concrete instance of the `Mailer` interface to provide when injecting mailers into any class that needs them.

Dependency Injection and Laravel

As you saw in Example 11-1, the most common pattern for dependency injection is constructor injection, or injecting the dependencies of an object when it's instantiated ("constructed").

Let's take our `UserMailer` class from Example 11-1. Example 11-2 shows what it might look like to create and use an instance of it.

Example 11-2. Simple manual dependency injection

```
$mailer = new MailgunMailer($mailgunKey, $mailgunSecret, $mailgunOptions);
$userMailer = new UserMailer($mailer);

$userMailer->welcome($user);
```

Now let's imagine we want our `UserMailer` class to be able to log messages, as well as sending a notification to a Slack channel every time it sends a message. Example 11-3 shows what this would look like. As you can see, it would start to get pretty unwieldy if we had to do all this work every time we wanted to create a new instance—especially when you consider that we'll have to get all these parameters from somewhere.

Example 11-3. More complex manual dependency injection

```
$mailer = new MailgunMailer($mailgunKey, $mailgunSecret, $mailgunOptions);
$logger = new Logger($logPath, $minimumLogLevel);
$slack = new Slack($slackKey, $slackSecret, $channelName, $channelIcon);
$userMailer = new UserMailer($mailer, $logger, $slack);

$userMailer->welcome($user);
```

Imagine having to write that code every time you wanted a `UserMailer`. Dependency injection is great, but this is a mess.

The app() Global Helper

Before we go too far into how the container actually works, let's take a quick look at the simplest way to get an object out of the container: the `app()` helper.

Pass any string to that helper, whether it's a fully qualified class name (FQCN, like *App \ThingDoer*) or a Laravel shortcut (we'll talk about those more in a second), and it'll return an instance of that class:

```
$logger = app(Logger::class);
```

This is the absolute simplest way to interact with the container. It creates an instance of this class and returns it for you, nice and easy. It's like new Logger but, as you'll see shortly, much better.

Different Syntaxes for Making a Concrete Instance

The simplest way to "make" a concrete instance of any class or interface is to use the global helper and pass the class or interface name directly to the helper, using app('*FQCN*').

However, if you have an instance of the container—whether it was injected somewhere, or if you're in a service provider and using $this->app, or (a lesser-known trick) if you get one by just running $container = app()—there are a few ways to make an instance from there.

The most common way is to run the make() method. $app->make('*FQCN*') works well. However, you may also see other developers and the documentation use this syntax sometimes: $app['*FQCN*']. Don't worry. That's doing the same thing; it's just a different way of writing it.

Creating the Logger instance as shown here seems simple enough, but you might've noticed that our $logger class in Example 11-3 has two parameters: $logPath and $minimumLogLevel. How does the container know what to pass here?

Short answer: it doesn't. You can use the app() global helper to create an instance of a class that has no parameters in its constructor, but at that point you could've just run new Logger yourself. The container shines when there's some complexity in the constructor, and that's when we need to look at how exactly the container can figure out how to construct classes with constructor parameters.

How the Container Is Wired

Before we dig further into the Logger class, take a look at Example 11-4.

Example 11-4. Laravel autowiring

```
class Bar
{
    public function __construct() {}
```

```
}

class Baz
{
    public function __construct() {}
}

class Foo
{
    public function __construct(Bar $bar, Baz $baz) {}
}

$foo = app(Foo::class);
```

This looks similar to our mailer example in Example 11-3. What's different is that these dependencies (Bar and Baz) are both so simple that the container can resolve them without any further information. The container reads the typehints in the Foo constructor, resolves an instance of both Bar and Baz, and then injects them into the new Foo instance when it's creating it. This is called *autowiring*: resolving instances based on typehints without the developer needing to explicitly bind those classes in the container.

Autowiring means that, if a class has not been explicitly bound to the container (like Foo, Bar, or Baz in this context) but the container can figure out how to resolve it anyway, the container will resolve it. This means any class with no constructor dependencies (like Bar and Baz) and any class with constructor dependencies that the container can resolve (like Foo) can be resolved out of the container.

That leaves us only needing to bind classes that have unresolvable constructor parameters—for example, our $logger class in Example 11-3, which has parameters related to our log path and log level.

For those, we'll need to learn how to explicitly bind something to the container.

Binding Classes to the Container

Binding a class to Laravel's container is essentially telling the container, "If a developer asks for an instance of Logger, here's the code to run in order to instantiate one with the correct parameters and dependencies and then return it correctly."

We're teaching the container that, when someone asks for this particular string (which is usually the FQCN of a class), it should resolve it this way.

Binding to a Closure

So, let's look at how to bind to the container. Note that the appropriate place to bind to the container is in a service provider's register() method (see Example 11-5).

Example 11-5. Basic container binding

```
// In any service provider (maybe LoggerServiceProvider)
public function register()
{
    $this->app->bind(Logger::class, function ($app) {
        return new Logger('\log\path\here', 'error');
    });
}
```

There are a few important things to note in this example. First, we're running `$this->app->bind()`. `$this->app` is an instance of the container that's always available on every service provider. The container's `bind()` method is what we use to bind to the container.

The first parameter of `bind()` is the "key" we're binding to. Here we've used the FQCN of the class. The second parameter differs depending on what you're doing, but essentially it should be *something* that shows the container what to do to resolve an instance of that bound key.

So, in this example, we're passing a closure. And now, any time someone runs `app(Logger::class)`, they'll get the result of this closure. The closure is passed an instance of the container itself (`$app`), so if the class you're resolving has a dependency you want resolved out of the container, you can use it in your definition as seen in Example 11-6.

Example 11-6. Using the passed $app instance in a container binding

```
// Note that this binding is not doing anything technically useful, since this
// could all be provided by the container's auto-wiring already.
$this->app->bind(UserMailer::class, function ($app) {
    return new UserMailer(
        $app->make(Mailer::class),
        $app->make(Logger::class),
        $app->make(Slack::class)
    );
});
```

Note that every time you ask for a new instance of your class, this closure will be run again and the new output returned.

Binding to Singletons, Aliases, and Instances

If you want the output of the binding closure to be cached so that this closure isn't re-run every time you ask for an instance, that's the Singleton pattern, and you can run `$this->app->singleton()` to do that. Example 11-7 shows what this looks like.

Example 11-7. Binding a singleton to the container

```
public function register()
{
    $this->app->singleton(Logger::class, function () {
        return new Logger('\log\path\here', 'error');
    });
}
```

You can also get similar behavior if you already have an instance of the object you want the singleton to return, as seen in Example 11-8.

Example 11-8. Binding an existing class instance to the container

```
public function register()
{
    $logger = new Logger('\log\path\here', 'error');
    $this->app->instance(Logger::class, $logger);
}
```

Finally, if you want to alias one class to another, bind a class to a shortcut, or bind a shortcut to a class, you can just pass two strings, as shown in Example 11-9.

Example 11-9. Aliasing classes and strings

```
// Asked for Logger, give FirstLogger
$this->app->bind(Logger::class, FirstLogger::class);

// Asked for log, give FirstLogger
$this->app->bind('log', FirstLogger::class);

// Asked for log, give FirstLogger
$this->app->alias(FirstLogger::class, 'log');
```

Note that these shortcuts are common in Laravel's core; it provides a system of shortcuts to classes that provide core functionality, using easy-to-remember keys like log.

Binding a Concrete Instance to an Interface

Just like we can bind a class to another class, or a class to a shortcut, we can also bind to an interface. This is extremely powerful, because we can now typehint interfaces instead of class names, like in Example 11-10.

Example 11-10. Typehinting and binding to an interface

```
...
use Interfaces\Mailer as MailerInterface;
```

```
class UserMailer
{
    protected $mailer;

    public function __construct(MailerInterface $mailer)
    {
        $this->mailer = $mailer;
    }
}

// Service provider
public function register()
{
    $this->app->bind(\Interfaces\Mailer::class, function () {
        return new MailgunMailer(...);
    });
}
```

You can now typehint `Mailer` or `Logger` interfaces all across your code, and then choose once in a service provider which specific mailer or logger you want to use everywhere. That's inversion of control.

One of the key benefits you get from using this pattern is that later, if you choose to use a different mail provider than Mailgun, as long as you have a mailer class for that new provider that implements the `Mailer` interface, you can swap it once in your service provider and everything in the rest of your code will just work.

Contextual Binding

Sometimes you need to change how to resolve an interface depending on the context. You might want to log events from one place to a local syslog and from others out to an external service. So, let's tell the container to differentiate—check out Example 11-11.

Example 11-11. Contextual binding

```
// In a service provider
public function register()
{
    $this->app->when(FileWrangler::class)
        ->needs(Interfaces\Logger::class)
        ->give(Loggers\Syslog::class);

    $this->app->when(Jobs\SendWelcomeEmail::class)
        ->needs(Interfaces\Logger::class)
        ->give(Loggers\PaperTrail::class);
}
```

Constructor Injection in Laravel Framework Files

We've covered the concept of constructor injection, and we've looked at how the container makes it easy to resolve instances of a class or interface out of the container. You saw how easy it is to use the `app()` helper to make instances, and also how the container will resolve the constructor dependencies of a class when it's creating it.

What we haven't covered yet is how the container is also responsible for resolving many of the core operating classes of your application. For example, every controller is instantiated by the container. That means if you want an instance of a logger in your controller, you can simply typehint the logger class in your controller's constructor, and when Laravel creates the controller, it will resolve it out of the container and that logger instance will be available to your controller. Take a look at Example 11-12.

Example 11-12. Injecting dependencies into a controller

```
...
class MyController extends Controller
{
    protected $logger;

    public function __construct(Logger $logger)
    {
        $this->logger = $logger;
    }

    public function index()
    {
        // Do something
        $this->logger->error('Something happened');
    }
}
```

The container is responsible for resolving controllers, middleware, queue jobs, event listeners, and any other classes that are automatically generated by Laravel in the process of your application's lifecycle—so any of those classes can typehint dependencies in their constructors and expect them to be automatically injected.

Method Injection

There are a few places in your application where Laravel doesn't just read the constructor signature: it also reads the *method* signature and will inject dependencies for you there as well.

The most common place to use method injection is in controller methods. If you have a dependency you only want to use for a single controller method, you can inject it into just that method like in Example 11-13.

Example 11-13. Injecting dependencies into a controller method

```
...
class MyController extends Controller
{
    // Method dependencies can come after or before route parameters.
    public function show(Logger $logger, $id)
    {
        // Do something
        $logger->error('Something happened');
    }
}
```

Passing Unresolvable Constructor Parameters Using makeWith()

All of the primary tools for resolving a concrete instance of a class
—app(), $container->make(), etc.—assume that all of the class's
dependencies can be resolved without passing anything in. But
what if your class accepts a value in its constructor, instead of a
dependency the container can resolve for you? Use the makeWith()
method:

```
class Foo
{
    public function __construct($bar)
    {
        // ...
    }
}

$foo = $this->app->makeWith(
    Foo::class,
    ['bar' => 'value']
);
```

This is a bit of an edge case. Most classes that you'll be resolving
out of the container should *only* have dependencies injected into
their constructors.

You can do the same in the boot() method of service providers, and you can also
arbitrarily call a method on any class using the container, which will allow for method
injection there (see Example 11-14).

Example 11-14. Manually calling a class method using the container's call() method

```
class Foo
{
    public function bar($parameter1) {}
}
```

```
// Calls the 'bar' method on 'Foo' with a first parameter of 'value'
app()->call('Foo@bar', ['parameter1' => 'value']);
```

Facades and the Container

We've covered facades quite a bit so far in the book, but we haven't actually talked about how they work.

Laravel's facades are classes that provide simple access to core pieces of Laravel's functionality. There are two trademark features of facades: first, they're all available in the global namespace (\Log is an alias to \Illuminate\Support\Facades\Log); and second, they use static methods to access nonstatic resources.

Let's take a look at the Log facade, since we've been looking at logging already in this chapter. In your controller or views, you could use this call:

```
Log::alert('Something has gone wrong!');
```

Here's what it would look like to make that same call without the facade:

```
$logger = app('log');
$logger->alert('Something has gone wrong!');
```

As you can see, facades translate static calls (any method call that you make on a class itself, using ::, instead of on an instance) to normal method calls on instances.

Importing Facade Namespaces

If you're in a namespaced class, you'll want to be sure to import the facade at the top:

```
...
use Illuminate\Support\Facades\Log;

class Controller extends Controller
{
    public function index()
    {
        // ...
        Log::error('Something went wrong!');
    }
}
```

How Facades Work

Let's take a look at the Cache facade and see how it actually works.

First, open up the class Illuminate\Support\Facades\Cache. You'll see something like Example 11-15.

Example 11-15. The Cache facade class

```php
<?php

namespace Illuminate\Support\Facades;

class Cache extends Facade
{
    protected static function getFacadeAccessor()
    {
        return 'cache';
    }
}
```

Every facade has a single method: `getFacadeAccessor()`. This defines the key that Laravel should use to look up this facade's backing instance from the container.

In this instance, we can see that every call to the `Cache` facade is proxied to be a call to an instance of the `cache` shortcut from the container. Of course, that's not a real class or interface name, so we know it's one of those shortcuts I mentioned earlier.

So, here's what's really happening:

```php
Cache::get('key');

// Is the same as...

app('cache')->get('key');
```

There are a few ways to look up exactly what class each facade accessor points to, but checking the documentation is the easiest. There's a table on the facades documentation page (*http://bit.ly/2WpJdIu*) that shows you, for each facade, which container binding (shortcut, like `cache`) it's connected to, and which class that returns. It looks like this:

Facade	Class	Service container binding
App	Illuminate\Foundation\Application	app
...	...	...
Cache	Illuminate\Cache\CacheManager	cache
...	...	...

Now that you have this reference, you can do three things.

First, you can figure out what methods are available on a facade. Just find its backing class and look at the definition of that class, and you'll know that any of its public methods are callable on the facade.

Second, you can figure out how to inject a facade's backing class using dependency injection. If you ever want the functionality of a facade but prefer to use dependency injection, just typehint the facade's backing class or get an instance of it with `app()` and call the same methods you would've called on the facade.

Third, you can see how to create your own facades. Create a class for the facade that extends `Illuminate\Support\Facades\Facade`, and give it a `getFacadeAccessor()` method, which returns a string. Make that string something that can be used to resolve your backing class out of the container—maybe just the FQCN of the class. Finally, you have to register the facade by adding it to the `aliases` array in *config/ app.php*. Done! You just made your own facade.

Real-Time Facades

Laravel 5.4 introduced a new concept called *real-time facades*. Rather than creating a new class to make your class's instance methods available as static methods, you can simply prefix your class's FQCN with `Facades\` and use it *as if it were a facade*. Example 11-16 illustrates how this works.

Example 11-16. Using real-time facades

```
namespace App;

class Charts
{
    public function burndown()
    {
        // ...
    }
}
<h2>Burndown Chart</h2>
{{ Facades\App\Charts::burndown() }}
```

As you can see here, the nonstatic method `burndown()` becomes accessible as a static method on the real-time facade, which we create by prepending the class's full name with `Facades\`.

Service Providers

We covered the basics of service providers in the previous chapter (see "Service Providers" on page 255). What's most important with regard to the container is that you remember to register your bindings in the `register()` method of some service provider somewhere.

You can just dump loose bindings into App\Providers\AppServiceProvider, which is a bit of a catchall, but it's generally better practice to create a unique service provider for each group of functionality you're developing and bind its classes in its unique register() method.

Testing

The ability to use inversion of control and dependency injection makes testing in Laravel extremely versatile. You can bind a different logger, for instance, depending on whether the app is live or under testing. Or you can change the transactional email service from Mailgun to a local email logger for easy inspection. Both of these swaps are actually so common that it's even easier to make them using Laravel's *.env* configuration files, but you can make similar swaps with any interfaces or classes you'd like.

The easiest way to do this is to explicitly rebind classes and interfaces when you need them rebound, directly in the test. Example 11-17 shows how.

Example 11-17. Overriding a binding in tests

```
public function test_it_does_something()
{
    app()->bind(Interfaces\Logger, function () {
        return new DevNullLogger;
    });

    // Do stuff
}
```

If you need certain classes or interfaces rebound globally for your tests (which is not a particularly common occurrence), you can do this either in the test class's setUp() method or in Laravel's TestCase base test's setUp() method, as shown in Example 11-18.

Example 11-18. Overriding a binding for all tests

```
class TestCase extends \Illuminate\Foundation\Testing\TestCase
{
    public function setUp()
    {
        parent::setUp();

        app()->bind('whatever', 'whatever else');
    }
}
```

When using something like Mockery, it's common to create a mock or spy or stub of a class and then to rebind that to the container in place of its referent.

TL;DR

Laravel's service container has many names, but regardless of what you call it, in the end its goal is to make it easy to define how to resolve certain string names as concrete instances. These string names are going to be the fully qualified class names of classes or interfaces, or shortcuts like `log`.

Each binding teaches the application, given a string key (e.g., `app('log')`), how to resolve a concrete instance.

The container is smart enough to do recursive dependency resolution, so if you try to resolve an instance of something that has constructor dependencies, the container will try to resolve those dependencies based on their typehints, then pass them into your class, and finally return an instance.

There are a few ways to bind to the container, but in the end they all define what to return, given a particular string.

Facades are simple shortcuts that make it easy to use static calls on a root namespace–aliased class to call nonstatic methods on classes resolved out of the container. Real-time facades allow you to treat any class like a facade by prepending its fully qualified class name with `Facades\`.

## CHAPTER 12

Testing

Most developers know that testing your code is A Good Thing. We're supposed to do it. We likely have an idea of why it's good, and we might've even read some tutorials about how it's supposed to work.

But the gap between knowing *why* you should test and knowing *how* to test is wide. Thankfully, tools like PHPUnit, Mockery, and PHPSpec provide an incredible number of options for testing in PHP—but it can still be pretty overwhelming to get everything set up.

Out of the box, Laravel comes with baked-in integrations to PHPUnit (unit testing), Mockery (mocking), and Faker (creating fake data for seeding and testing). It also provides its own simple and powerful suite of application testing tools, which allow you to "crawl" your site's URIs, submit forms, check HTTP status codes, and validate and assert against JSON. It also provides a robust frontend testing framework called Dusk that can even interact with your JavaScript applications and test against them. In case this hasn't made it clear, we're going to cover a lot of ground in this chapter.

To make it easy for you to get started, Laravel's testing setup comes with sample application test that can run successfully the moment you create a new app. That means you don't have to spend any time configuring your testing environment, and that's one less barrier to writing your tests.

Testing Basics

 Tests in Laravel live in the *tests* folder. There are two files in the root: *TestCase.php*, which is the base root test which all of your tests will extend, and *CreatesApplication.php*, a trait (imported by *TestCase.php*) which allows any class to boot a sample Laravel application for testing.

There are also two subfolders: *Features*, for tests that cover the interaction between multiple units, and *Unit*, for tests that are intended to cover just one unit of your code (class, module, function, etc.). Each of these folders contains an *ExampleTest.php* file, each of which has a single sample test inside it, ready to run.

Differences in Testing Prior to Laravel 5.4

In projects running versions of Laravel prior to 5.4, there will be only two files in the *tests* directory: *ExampleTest.php*, your sample test, and *TestCase.php*, your base test.

Additionally, if your app is pre-5.4, the syntax in all of the examples in this chapter will not be quite right. All the ideas are the same, but the syntax is a bit different across the board. You can learn more in the Laravel 5.3 testing docs (*http://bit.ly/2YnwDev*). Here are the four biggest changes:

1. In 5.3 and before, you're not creating response objects; instead, you're just calling methods on $this, and the test class stores the responses. So, $response = $this->get('people') in 5.4+ would look like $this->get('people') in 5.3 and earlier.

2. Many of the assertions have been renamed in small ways in 5.4+ to make them look more like PHPUnit's normal assertion names; for example, assertSee() instead of see().

3. Some of the "crawling" methods that in 5.4+ have been extracted out to browser-kit-testing were built into the core in previous versions.

4. Dusk didn't exist prior to 5.4.

Because testing prior to 5.4 was so different, I've made the testing chapter for the first edition of this book available as a free PDF. If you're working with 5.3 or earlier, I'd recommend skipping this chapter in the book and using this PDF of the testing chapter from the first edition (*http://bit.ly/2CNFCN1*) instead.

The ExampleTest in your *Unit* directory contains one simple assertion: $this->assertTrue(true). Anything in your unit tests is likely to be relatively simple PHPUnit syntax (asserting that values are equal or different, looking for entries in arrays, checking Booleans, etc.), so there's not much to learn there.

The Basics of PHPUnit Assertions

If you're not yet familiar with PHPUnit, most of our assertions will be run on the $this object with this syntax:

```
$this->assertWHATEVER($expected, $real);
```

So, for example, if we're asserting that two variables should be equal, we'll pass it first our expected result, and second the actual outcome of the object or system we're testing:

```
$multiplicationResult = $myCalculator->multiply(5, 3);
$this->assertEqual(15, $multiplicationResult);
```

As you can see in Example 12-1, the `ExampleTest` in the *Feature* directory makes a simulated HTTP request to the page at the root path of your application and checks that its HTTP status is 200 (successful). If it is, it'll pass; if not, it'll fail. Unlike your average PHPUnit test, we're running these assertions on the `TestResponse` object that's returned when we make test HTTP calls.

Example 12-1. tests/Feature/ExampleTest.php

```php
<?php

namespace Tests\Feature;

use Tests\TestCase;
use Illuminate\Foundation\Testing\RefreshDatabase;

class ExampleTest extends TestCase
{
    /**
     * A basic test example
     *
     * @return void
     */
    public function testBasicTest()
    {
        $response = $this->get('/');

        $response->assertStatus(200);
    }
}
```

To run the tests, run `./vendor/bin/phpunit` on the command line from the root folder of your application. You should see something like the output in Example 12-2.

Example 12-2. Sample ExampleTest output

```
PHPUnit 7.3.5 by Sebastian Bergmann and contributors.

..                                                                2 / 2 (100%)

Time: 139 ms, Memory: 12.00MB

OK (2 test, 2 assertions)
```

You just ran your first Laravel application test! Those two dots indicate that you have two passing tests. As you can see, you're set up out of the box not only with a functioning PHPUnit instance, but also a full-fledged application testing suite that can make mock HTTP calls and test your application's responses. Further, you'll soon learn that you have easy access to a fully featured DOM crawler ("A Quick Introduc-

---

tion to BrowserKit Testing" on page 324) and a regression testing tool with full Java-Script support ("Testing with Dusk" on page 324).

In case you're not familiar with PHPUnit, let's take a look at what it's like to have a test fail. Instead of modifying the previous test, we'll make our own. Run `php artisan make:test FailingTest`. This will create the file *tests/Feature/FailingTest.php*; you can modify its `testExample()` method to look like Example 12-3.

Example 12-3. tests/Feature/FailingTest.php, edited to fail

```
public function testExample()
{
    $response = $this->get('/');

    $response->assertStatus(301);
}
```

As you can see, it's the same as the test we ran previously, but we're now testing against the wrong status. Let's run PHPUnit again.

Generating Unit Tests

If you want your test to be generated in the Unit directory instead of the Feature directory, pass the --unit flag:

```
php artisan make:test SubscriptionTest --unit
```

Whoops! This time the output will probably look a bit like Example 12-4.

Example 12-4. Sample failing test output

```
PHPUnit 7.3.5 by Sebastian Bergmann and contributors.

.F.                                                     3 / 3 (100%)

Time: 237 ms, Memory: 12.00MB

There was 1 failure:

1) Tests\Feature\FailingTest::testExample
Expected status code 301 but received 200.
Failed asserting that false is true.

/path-to-your-app/vendor/.../Foundation/Testing/TestResponse.php:124
/path-to-your-app/tests/Feature/FailingTest.php:20

FAILURES!
Tests: 3, Assertions: 3, Failures: 1.
```

Let's break this down. Last time there were only two dots, representing the two passing tests, but this time there's an F between them indicating that one of the three tests run here has failed.

Then, for each error, we see the test name (here, `FailingTest::testExample`), the error message (`Expected status code...`), *and* a full stack trace, so we can see what was called. Since this was an application test, the stack trace just shows us that it was called via the `TestResponse` class, but if this were a unit or feature test, we'd see the entire call stack of the test.

Now that we've run both a passing test and a failing test, it's time for you to learn more about Laravel's testing environment.

Naming Tests

By default, Laravel's testing system will run any files in the *tests* directory whose names end with the word *Test*. That's why *tests/ExampleTest.php* was run by default.

If you're not familiar with PHPUnit, you might not know that only the methods in your tests with names that start with the word `test` will be run—or methods with a `@test` documentation block, or docblock. See Example 12-5 for which methods will and won't run.

Example 12-5. Naming PHPUnit methods

```
class NamingTest
{
    public function test_it_names_things_well()
    {
        // Runs as "It names things well"
    }

    public function testItNamesThingsWell()
    {
        // Runs as "It names things well"
    }

    /** @test */
    public function it_names_things_well()
    {
        // Runs as "It names things well"
    }

    public function it_names_things_well()
    {
        // Doesn't run
    }
}
```

The Testing Environment

Any time a Laravel application is running, it has a current "environment" name that represents the environment it's running in. This name may be set to local, staging, production, or anything else you want. You can retrieve this by running app()->environment(), or you can run if (app()->environment('local')) or something similar to test whether the current environment matches the passed name.

When you run tests, Laravel automatically sets the environment to testing. This means you can test for if (app()->environment('testing')) to enable or disable certain behaviors in the testing environment.

Additionally, Laravel doesn't load the normal environment variables from *.env* for testing. If you want to set any environment variables for your tests, edit *phpunit.xml* and, in the <php> section, add a new <env> for each environment variable you want to pass in—for example, <env name="DB_CONNECTION" value="sqlite"/>.

> ## Using .env.testing to Exclude Testing Environment Variables from Version Control
>
> If you want to set environment variables for your tests, you can do so in *phpunit.xml* as just described. But what if you have environment variables for your tests that you want to be different for each testing environment? Or what if you want them to be excluded from source control?
>
> Thankfully, handling these conditions is pretty easy. First, create an *.env.testing.example* file, just like Laravel's *.env.example* file. Next, add the variables you'd like to be environment-specific to *.env.testing.example*, just like they're set in *.env.example*. Then, make a copy of *.env.testing.example* and name it *.env.testing*. Finally, add *.env.testing* to your *.gitignore* file just below *.env* and set any values you want in *.env.testing*.
>
> In most versions of Laravel, the framework will automatically load this file for you. In Laravel prior to 5.2, or in some of the earlier minor releases prior to 5.5, you might not have this at the framework level; I've written a blog post (*http://bit.ly/2YwnyQG*) showing you how to add it when the framework doesn't have it.

The Testing Traits

Before we get into the methods you can use for testing, you need to know about the four testing traits you can pull into any test class.

RefreshDatabase

 `Illuminate\Foundation\Testing\RefreshDatabase` is imported at the top of every newly generated test file, and it's the most commonly used database migration trait. This trait was introduced in Laravel 5.5 and is only available in projects running on that version or later.

The point of this, and the other database traits, is to ensure your database tables are correctly migrated at the start of each test.

`RefreshDatabase` takes two steps to do this. First, it runs your migrations on your test database *once* at the beginning of each test run (when you run `phpunit`, not for each individual test method). And second, it wraps each individual test method in a database transaction and rolls back the transaction at the end of the test.

That means you have your database migrated for your tests and cleared out fresh after each test runs, without having to run your migrations again before every test—making this the fastest possible option. When in doubt, stick with this.

WithoutMiddleware

If you import `Illuminate\Foundation\Testing\WithoutMiddleware` into your test class, it will disable all middleware for any test in that class. This means you won't have to worry about the authentication middleware, or CSRF protection, or anything else that might be useful in the real application but distracting in a test.

If you'd like to disable middleware for just a single method instead of the entire test class, call `$this->withoutMiddleware()` at the top of the method for that test.

DatabaseMigrations

If you import the `Illuminate\Foundation\Testing\DatabaseMigrations` trait instead of the `RefreshDatabase` trait, it will run your entire set of database migrations fresh before each test. Laravel makes this happen by running `php artisan migrate:fresh` in the `setUp()` method before every test runs.

DatabaseTransactions

`Illuminate\Foundation\Testing\DatabaseTransactions`, on the other hand, expects your database to be properly migrated before your tests start. It wraps every test in a database transaction, which it rolls back at the end of each test. This means that, at the end of each test, your database will be returned to the exact same state it was in prior to the test.

Simple Unit Tests

With simple unit tests, you almost don't need any of these traits. You *may* reach for database access or inject something out of the container, but it's very likely that unit tests in your applications won't rely on the framework very much. Take a look at Example 12-6 for an example of what a simple test might look like.

Example 12-6. A simple unit test

```
class GeometryTest extends TestCase
{
    public function test_it_calculates_area()
    {
        $square = new Square;
        $square->sideLength = 4;

        $calculator = new GeometryCalculator;

        $this->assertEquals(16, $calculator->area($square));
    }
}
```

Obviously, this is a bit of a contrived example. But you can see here that we're testing a single class (`GeometryCalculator`) and its single method (`area()`), and we're doing so without worrying about the entire Laravel application.

Some unit tests might be testing something that technically is connected to the framework—for example, Eloquent models—but you can still test them without worrying about the framework. For example, in Example 12-7, we'll use `Package::make()` instead of `Package::create()` so the object is created and evaluated in memory without ever hitting the database.

Example 12-7. A more complicated unit test

```
class PopularityTest extends TestCase
{
    use RefreshDatabase;

    public function test_votes_matter_more_than_views()
    {
        $package1 = Package::make(['votes' => 1, 'views' => 0]);
        $package2 = Package::make(['votes' => 0, 'views' => 1]);

        $this->assertTrue($package1->popularity > $package2->popularity);
    }
}
```

Some people may call this an integration or feature test, since this "unit" will likely touch the database in actual usage and it's connected to the entire Eloquent codebase.

The most important point is that you can have simple tests that test a single class or method, even when the objects under test are framework-connected.

All of this said, it's still going to be more likely that your tests—especially as you first get started—are broader and more at the "application" level. Accordingly, for the rest of the chapter we're going to dig deeper into application testing.

Application Testing: How It Works

In "Testing Basics" on page 296 we saw that, with a few lines of code, we can "request" URIs in our application and actually check the status of the response. But how can PHPUnit request pages as if it were a browser?

TestCase

Any application tests should extend the `TestCase` class (*tests/TestCase.php*) that's included with Laravel by default. Your application's `TestCase` class will extend the abstract `Illuminate\Foundation\Testing\TestCase` class, which brings in quite a few goodies.

The first thing the two `TestCase` classes (yours and its abstract parent) do is handle booting the Illuminate application instance for you, so you have a fully bootstrapped application available. They also "refresh" the application between each test, which means they're not *entirely* recreating the application between tests, but rather making sure you don't have any data lingering.

The parent `TestCase` also sets up a system of hooks that allow callbacks to be run before and after the application is created, and imports a series of traits that provide you with methods for interacting with every aspect of your application. These traits include `InteractsWithContainer`, `MakesHttpRequests`, and `InteractsWithConsole`, and they bring in a broad variety of custom assertions and testing methods.

As a result, your application tests have access to a fully bootstrapped application instance and application-test-minded custom assertions, with a series of simple and powerful wrappers around each to make them easy to use.

That means you can write `$this->get('/')->assertStatus(200)` and know that your application is actually behaving as if it were responding to a normal HTTP request, and that the response is being fully generated and then checked as a browser would check it. It's pretty powerful stuff, considering how little work you had to do to get it running.

HTTP Tests

Let's take a look at our options for writing HTTP-based tests. You've already seen `$this->get('/')`, but let's dive deeper into how you can use that call, how you can assert against its results, and what other HTTP calls you can make.

Testing Basic Pages with $this->get() and Other HTTP Calls

At the very basic level, Laravel's HTTP testing allows you to make simple HTTP requests (`GET`, `POST`, etc.) and then make simple assertions about their impact or response.

There are more tools we'll cover later (in "A Quick Introduction to BrowserKit Testing" on page 324 and "Testing with Dusk" on page 324) that allow for more complex page interactions and assertions, but let's start at the base level. Here are the calls you can make:

- `$this->get($uri, $headers = [])`
- `$this->post($uri, $data = [], $headers = [])`
- `$this->put($uri, $data = [], $headers = [])`
- `$this->patch($uri, $data = [], $headers = [])`
- `$this->delete($uri, $data = [], $headers = [])`

These methods are the basis of the HTTP testing framework. Each takes at least a URI (usually relative) and headers, and all but `get()` also allow for passing data along with the request.

And, importantly, each returns a `$response` object that represents the HTTP response. This response object is almost exactly the same as an Illuminate `Response` object, the same thing we return out of our controllers. However, it's actually an instance of `Illuminate\Foundation\Testing\TestResponse`, which wraps a normal `Response` with some assertions for testing.

Take a look at Example 12-8 to see a common usage of `post()` and a common response assertion.

Example 12-8. A simple use of post() in testing

```
public function test_it_stores_new_packages()
{
    $response = $this->post(route('packages.store'), [
        'name' => 'The greatest package',
    ]);
```

```
    $response->assertOk();
}
```

In most examples like Example 12-8, you'll also test that the record exists in the data-base and shows up on the index page, and maybe that it doesn't test successfully unless you define the package author and are logged in. But don't worry, we'll get to all of that. For now, you can make calls to your application routes with many different verbs and make assertions against both the response and the state of your application afterward. Great!

Testing JSON APIs with $this->getJson() and Other JSON HTTP Calls

You can also do all of the same sorts of HTTP tests with your JSON APIs. There are convenience methods for that, too:

- `$this->getJson($uri, $headers = [])`
- `$this->postJson($uri, $data = [], $headers = [])`
- `$this->putJson($uri, $data = [], $headers = [])`
- `$this->patchJson($uri, $data = [], $headers = [])`
- `$this->deleteJson($uri, $data = [], $headers = [])`

These methods work just the same as the normal HTTP call methods, except they also add JSON-specific `Accept`, `CONTENT_LENGTH`, and `CONTENT_TYPE` headers. Take a look at Example 12-9 to see an example.

Example 12-9. A simple use of postJSON() in testing

```
public function test_the_api_route_stores_new_packages()
{
    $response = $this->postJSON(route('api.packages.store'), [
        'name' => 'The greatest package',
    ], ['X-API-Version' => '17']);

    $response->assertOk();
}
```

Assertions Against $response

There are 40 assertions available on the `$response` object in Laravel 5.8, so I'll refer you to the testing docs (*http://bit.ly/2HUQJqz*) for details on all of them. Let's look at a few of the most important and most common ones:

`$response->assertOk()`
    Asserts that the response's status code is 200:

```
$response = $this->get('terms');
$response->assertOk();
```

`$response->assertStatus($status)`

Asserts that the response's status code is equal to the provided *$status*:

```
$response = $this->get('admin');
$response->assertStatus(401); // Unauthorized
```

`$response->assertSee($text)` *and* `$response->assertDontSee($text)`

Asserts that the response contains (or doesn't contain) the provided *$text*:

```
$package = factory(Package::class)->create();
$response = $this->get(route('packages.index'));
$response->assertSee($package->name);
```

`$response->assertJson(_array $json)`

Asserts that the passed array is represented (in JSON format) in the returned JSON:

```
$this->postJson(route('packages.store'), ['name' => 'GreatPackage2000']);
$response = $this->getJson(route('packages.index'));
$response->assertJson(['name' => 'GreatPackage2000']);
```

`$response->assertViewHas($key, $value = null)`

Asserts that the view on the visited page had a piece of data available at *$key*, and optionally checks that the value of that variable was *$value*:

```
$package = factory(Package::class)->create();
$response = $this->get(route('packages.show'));
$response->assertViewHas('name', $package->name);
```

`$response->assertSessionHas($key, $value = null)`

Asserts that the session has data set at *$key*, and optionally checks that the value of that data is *$value*:

```
$response = $this->get('beta/enable');
$response->assertSessionHas('beta-enabled', true);
```

`$response->assertSessionHasErrors()`

With no parameters, asserts that there's at least one error set in Laravel's special errors session container. Its first parameter can be an array of key/value pairs that define the errors that should be set and its second parameter can be the string format that the checked errors should be formatted against, as demonstrated here:

```
// Assuming the "/form" route requires an email field, and we're
// posting an empty submission to it to trigger the error
$response = $this->post('form', []);
```

```
$response->assertSessionHasErrors();
$response->assertSessionHasErrors([
    'email' => 'The email field is required.',
]);
$response->assertSessionHasErrors(
    ['email' => '<p>The email field is required.</p>'],
    '<p>:message</p>'
);
```

If you're working with named error bags, you can pass the error bag name as the third parameter.

$response->assertCookie($name, $value = null)

Asserts that the response contains a cookie with name $name, and optionally checks that its value is $value:

```
$response = $this->post('settings', ['dismiss-warning']);
$response->assertCookie('warning-dismiss', true);
```

$response->assertCookieExpired($name)

Asserts that the response contains a cookie with name $name and that it is expired:

```
$response->assertCookieExpired('warning-dismiss');
```

$response->assertCookieNotExpired($name)

Asserts that the response contains a cookie with name $name and that it is not expired:

```
$response->assertCookieNotExpired('warning-dismiss');
```

$response->assertRedirect($uri)

Asserts that the requested route returns a redirect to the given URI:

```
$response = $this->post(route('packages.store'), [
    'email' => 'invalid'
]);

$response->assertRedirect(route('packages.create'));
```

For each of these assertions, you can assume that there are many related assertions I haven't listed here. For example, in addition to assertSessionHasErrors() there are also assertSessionHasNoErrors() and assertSessionHasErrorsIn() assertions; as well as assertJson(), there are also assertJsonCount(), assertJsonFragment(), assertJsonMissing(), assertJsonMissingExact(), assertJsonStructure(), and assertJsonValidationErrors() assertions. Again, take a look at the docs and make yourself familiar with the whole list.

Authenticating Responses

One piece of your application it's common to test with application tests is authentication and authorization. Most of the time your needs will be met with the `actingAs()` chainable method, which takes a user (or other `Authenticatable` object, depending on how your system is set up), as you can see in Example 12-10.

Example 12-10. Basic auth in testing

```
public function test_guests_cant_view_dashboard()
{
    $user = factory(User::class)->states('guest')->create();
    $response = $this->actingAs($user)->get('dashboard');
    $response->assertStatus(401); // Unauthorized
}

public function test_members_can_view_dashboard()
{
    $user = factory(User::class)->states('member')->create();
    $response = $this->actingAs($user)->get('dashboard');
    $response->assertOk();
}

public function test_members_and_guests_cant_view_statistics()
{
    $guest = factory(User::class)->states('guest')->create();
    $response = $this->actingAs($guest)->get('statistics');
    $response->assertStatus(401); // Unauthorized

    $member = factory(User::class)->states('member')->create();
    $response = $this->actingAs($member)->get('statistics');
    $response->assertStatus(401); // Unauthorized
}

public function test_admins_can_view_statistics()
{
    $user = factory(User::class)->states('admin')->create();
    $response = $this->actingAs($user)->get('statistics');
    $response->assertOk();
}
```

Using Factory States for Authorization

It's common to use model factories (discussed in "Model Factories" on page 99) in testing, and model factory states make tasks like creating users with different access levels simple.

A Few Other Customizations to Your HTTP Tests

If you'd like to set session variables on your requests, you can also chain withSession():

```
$response = $this->withSession([
    'alert-dismissed' => true,
]) ->get('dashboard');
```

If you'd prefer to set your request headers fluently, you can chain withHeaders():

```
$response = $this->withHeaders([
    'X-THE-ANSWER' => '42',
]) ->get('the-restaurant-at-the-end-of-the-universe');
```

Handling Exceptions in Application Tests

Usually, an exception that's thrown inside your application when you're making HTTP calls will be captured by Laravel's exception handler and processed as it would be in normal application. So, the test and route in Example 12-11 would still pass, since the exception would never bubble up the whole way to our test.

Example 12-11. An exception that will be captured by Laravel's exception handler and result in a passing test

```
// routes/web.php
Route::get('has-exceptions', function () {
    throw new Exception('Stop!');
});

// tests/Feature/ExceptionsTest.php
public function test_exception_in_route()
{
    $this->get('/has-exceptions');

    $this->assertTrue(true);
}
```

In a lot of cases, this might make sense; maybe you're expecting a validation exception and you want it to be caught like it would normally be by the framework.

But if you want to temporarily disable the exception handler, that's an option; just run $this->withoutExceptionHandling(), as shown in Example 12-12.

Example 12-12. Temporarily disabling exception handling in a single test

```
// tests/Feature/ExceptionsTest.php
public function test_exception_in_route()
{
    // Now throws an error
```

```
$this->withoutExceptionHandling();

$this->get('/has-exceptions');

$this->assertTrue(true);
}
```

And if for some reason you need to turn it back on (maybe you turned it off in setUp() but want it back on for just one test), you can run $this->withException Handling().

Database Tests

Often, the effect we want to test for after our tests have run is in the database. Imagine you want to test that the "create package" page works correctly. What's the best way? Make an HTTP call to the "store package" endpoint and then assert that that package exists in the database. It's easier and safer than inspecting the resulting "list packages" page.

We have two primary assertions for the database: $this->assertDatabaseHas() and $this->assertDatabaseMissing(). For both, pass the table name as the first parameter, the data you're looking for as the second, and, optionally, the specific database connection you want to test as the third.

Take a look at Example 12-13 to see how you might use them.

Example 12-13. Sample database tests

```
public function test_create_package_page_stores_package()
{
    $this->post(route('packages.store'), [
        'name' => 'Package-a-tron',
    ]);

    $this->assertDatabaseHas('packages', ['name' => 'Package-a-tron']);
}
```

As you can see, the second (data) parameter of assertDatabaseHas() is structured like a SQL WHERE statement—you pass a key and a value (or multiple keys and values), and then Laravel looks for any records in the specified database table that match your key(s) and value(s).

As always, assertDatabaseMissing() is the inverse.

Using Model Factories in Tests

Model factories are amazing tools that make it easy to seed randomized, well-structured database data for testing (or other purposes). You've already seen them in use in several examples in this chapter.

We've already covered them in depth, so check out "Model Factories" on page 99 to learn more.

Seeding in Tests

If you use seeds in your application, you can run the equivalent of php artisan db:seed by running $this->seed() in your test.

You can also pass a seeder class name to just seed that one class:

```
$this->seed(); // Seeds all
$this->seed(UserSeeder::class); // Seeds users
```

Testing Other Laravel Systems

When testing Laravel systems, you'll often want to pause their true function for the duration of the testing and instead write tests against what has happened to those systems. You can do this by "faking" different facades, such as Event, Mail, and Notification. We'll talk more about what fakes are in "Mocking" on page 318, but first, let's look at some examples. All of the following features in Laravel have their own set of assertions you can make after faking them, but you can also just choose to fake them to restrict their effects.

Event Fakes

Let's use event fakes as our first example of how Laravel makes it possible to mock its internal systems. There are likely going to be times when you want to fake events just for the sake of suppressing their actions. For example, suppose your app pushes notifications to Slack every time a new user signs up. You have a "user signed up" event that's dispatched when this happens, and it has a listener that notifies a Slack channel that a user has signed up. You don't want those notifications to go to Slack every time you run your tests, but you might want to assert that the event was sent, or the listener was triggered, or something else. This is one reason for faking certain aspects of Laravel in our tests: to pause the default behavior and instead make assertions against the system we're testing.

Let's take a look at how to suppress these events by calling the fake() method on Illuminate\Support\Facades\Event, as shown in Example 12-14.

Example 12-14. Suppressing events without adding assertions

```
public function test_controller_does_some_thing()
{
    Event::fake();

    // Call controller and assert it does whatever you want without
    // worrying about it pinging Slack
}
```

Once we've run the `fake()` method, we can also call special assertions on the `Event` facade: namely, `assertDispatched()` and `assertNotDispatched()`. Take a look at Example 12-15 to see them in use.

Example 12-15. Making assertions against events

```
public function test_signing_up_users_notifies_slack()
{
    Event::fake();

    // Sign user up

    Event::assertDispatched(UserJoined::class, function ($event) use ($user) {
        return $event->user->id === $user->id;
    });

    // Or sign multiple users up and assert it was dispatched twice

    Event::assertDispatched(UserJoined::class, 2);

    // Or sign up with validation failures and assert it wasn't dispatched

    Event::assertNotDispatched(UserJoined::class);
}
```

Note that the (optional) closure we're passing to `assertDispatched()` makes it so we're not just asserting that the event was dispatched, but also that the dispatched event contains certain data.

Event::fake() Disables Eloquent Model Events

`Event::fake()` also disables Eloquent model events. So if you have any important code, for example, in a model's `creating` event, make sure to create your models (through your factories or however else) *before* calling `Event::fake()`.

Bus and Queue Fakes

The Bus facade, which represents how Laravel dispatches jobs, works just like Event. You can run fake() on it to disable the impact of your jobs, and after faking it you can run assertDispatched() or assertNotDispatched().

The Queue facade represents how Laravel dispatches jobs when they're pushed up to queues. Its available methods are assertedPushed(), assertPushedOn(), and assertNotPushed().

Take a look at Example 12-16 to see how to use both.

Example 12-16. Faking jobs and queued jobs

```php
public function test_popularity_is_calculated()
{
    Bus::fake();

    // Synchronize package data...

    // Assert a job was dispatched
    Bus::assertDispatched(
        CalculatePopularity::class,
        function ($job) use ($package) {
            return $job->package->id === $package->id;
        }
    );

    // Assert a job was not dispatched
    Bus::assertNotDispatched(DestroyPopularityMaybe::class);
}

public function test_popularity_calculation_is_queued()
{
    Queue::fake();

    // Synchronize package data...

    // Assert a job was pushed to any queue
    Queue::assertPushed(CalculatePopularity::class, function ($job) use ($package) {
        return $job->package->id === $package->id;
    });

    // Assert a job was pushed to a given queue named "popularity"
    Queue::assertPushedOn('popularity', CalculatePopularity::class);

    // Assert a job was pushed twice
    Queue::assertPushed(CalculatePopularity::class, 2);

    // Assert a job was not pushed
```

```
    Queue::assertNotPushed(DestroyPopularityMaybe::class);
}
```

Mail Fakes

The Mail facade, when faked, offers four methods: assertSent(), assertNotSent(), assertQueued(), and assertNotQueued(). Use the Queued methods when your mail is queued and the Sent methods when it's not.

Just like with assertDispatched(), the first parameter will be the name of the mailable and the second parameter can be empty, the number of times the mailable has been sent, or a closure testing that the mailable has the right data in it. Take a look at Example 12-17 to see a few of these methods in action.

Example 12-17. Making assertions against mail

```
public function test_package_authors_receive_launch_emails()
{
    Mail::fake();

    // Make a package public for the first time...

    // Assert a message was sent to a given email address
    Mail::assertSent(PackageLaunched::class, function ($mail) use ($package) {
        return $mail->package->id === $package->id;
    });

    // Assert a message was sent to given email addresses
    Mail::assertSent(PackageLaunched::class, function ($mail) use ($package) {
        return $mail->hasTo($package->author->email) &&
               $mail->hasCc($package->collaborators) &&
               $mail->hasBcc('admin@novapackages.com');
    });

    // Or, launch two packages...

    // Assert a mailable was sent twice
    Mail::assertSent(PackageLaunched::class, 2);

    // Assert a mailable was not sent
    Mail::assertNotSent(PackageLaunchFailed::class);
}
```

All of the messages checking for recipients (hasTo(), hasCc(), and hasBcc()) can take either a single email address or an array or collection of addresses.

Notification Fakes

The `Notification` facade, when faked, offers two methods: `assertSentTo()` and `assertNothingSent()`.

Unlike with the `Mail` facade, you're not going to test who the notification was sent to manually in a closure. Rather, the assertion itself requires the first parameter be either a single notifiable object or an array or collection of them. Only after you've passed in the desired notification target can you test anything about the notification itself.

The second parameter is the class name for the notification, and the (optional) third parameter can be a closure defining more expectations about the notification. Take a look at Example 12-18 to learn more.

Example 12-18. Notification fakes

```
public function test_users_are_notified_of_new_package_ratings()
{
    Notification::fake();

    // Perform package rating...

    // Assert author was notified
    Notification::assertSentTo(
        $package->author,
        PackageRatingReceived::class,
        function ($notification, $channels) use ($package) {
            return $notification->package->id === $package->id;
        }
    );

    // Assert a notification was sent to the given users
    Notification::assertSentTo(
        [$package->collaborators], PackageRatingReceived::class
    );

    // Or, perform a duplicate package rating...

    // Assert a notification was not sent
    Notification::assertNotSentTo(
        [$package->author], PackageRatingReceived::class
    );
}
```

You may also find yourself wanting to assert that your channel selection is working—that notifications are sent via the right channels. You can test that as well, as you can see in Example 12-19.

Example 12-19. Testing notification channels

```
public function test_users_are_notified_by_their_preferred_channel()
{
    Notification::fake();

    $user = factory(User::class)->create(['slack_preferred' => true]);

    // Perform package rating...

    // Assert author was notified via Slack
    Notification::assertSentTo(
        $user,
        PackageRatingReceived::class,
        function ($notification, $channels) use ($package) {
            return $notification->package->id === $package->id
                && in_array('slack', $channels);
        }
    );
```

Storage Fakes

Testing files can be extraordinarily complex. Many traditional methods require you to actually move files around in your test directories, and formatting the form input and output can be very complicated.

Thankfully, if you use Laravel's Storage facade, it's infinitely simpler to test file uploads and other storage-related items. Example 12-20 demonstrates.

Example 12-20. Testing storage and file uploads with storage fakes

```
public function test_package_screenshot_upload()
{
    Storage::fake('screenshots');

    // Upload a fake image
    $response = $this->postJson('screenshots', [
        'screenshot' => UploadedFile::fake()->image('screenshot.jpg'),
    ]);

    // Assert the file was stored
    Storage::disk('screenshots')->assertExists('screenshot.jpg');

    // Or, assert a file does not exist
    Storage::disk('screenshots')->assertMissing('missing.jpg');
}
```

Mocking

Mocks (and their brethren, spies and stubs and dummies and fakes and any number of other tools) are common in testing. We saw some examples of fakes in the previous section. I won't go into too much detail here, but it's unlikely you can thoroughly test an application of any size without mocking at least one thing or another.

So, lets take a quick look at mocking in Laravel and how to use Mockery, the mocking library.

A Quick Introduction to Mocking

Essentially, mocks and other similar tools make it possible to create an object that in some way mimics a real class, but for testing purposes isn't the real class. Sometimes this is done because the real class is too difficult to instantiate just to inject it into a test, or maybe because the real class communicates with an external service.

As you can probably tell from the examples that follow, Laravel encourages working with the real application as much as possible—which means avoiding too great of a dependence on mocks. But they have their place, which is why Laravel includes Mockery, a mocking library, out of the box, and is why many of its core services offer faking utilities.

A Quick Introduction to Mockery

Mockery allows you to quickly and easily create mocks from any PHP class in your application. Imagine you have a class that depends on a Slack client, but you don't want the calls to actually go out to Slack. Mockery makes it simple to create a fake Slack client to use in your tests, like you can see in Example 12-21.

Example 12-21. Using Mockery in Laravel

```
// app/SlackClient.php
class SlackClient
{
    // ...

    public function send($message, $channel)
    {
        // Actually sends a message to Slack
    }
}

// app/Notifier.php
class Notifier
{
    private $slack;
```

```
    public function __construct(SlackClient $slack)
    {
        $this->slack = $slack;
    }

    public function notifyAdmins($message)
    {
        $this->slack->send($message, 'admins');
    }
}

// tests/Unit/NotifierTest.php
public function test_notifier_notifies_admins()
{
    $slackMock = Mockery::mock(SlackClient::class)->shouldIgnoreMissing();

    $notifier = new Notifier($slackMock);
    $notifier->notifyAdmins('Test message');
}
```

There are a lot of elements at work here, but if you look at them one by one, they make sense. We have a class named `Notifier` that we're testing. It has a dependency named `SlackClient` that does something that we don't want it to do when we're running our tests: it sends actual Slack notifications. So we're going to mock it.

We use Mockery to get a mock of our `SlackClient` class. If we don't care about what happens to that class—if it should simply exist to keep our tests from throwing errors —we can just use `shouldIgnoreMissing()`:

```
    $slackMock = Mockery::mock(SlackClient::class)-shouldIgnoreMissing();
```

No matter what `Notifier` calls on `$slackMock`, it'll just accept it and return `null`.

But take a look at `test_notifier_notifies_admins()`. At this point, it doesn't actually *test* anything.

We could just keep `shouldIgnoreMissing()` and then write some assertions below it. That's usually what we do with `shouldIgnoreMissing()`, which makes this object a "fake" or a "stub."

But what if we want to actually assert that a call was made to the `send()` method of `SlackClient`? That's when we drop `shouldIgnoreMissing()` and reach for the other `should*` methods (Example 12-22).

Example 12-22. Using the shouldReceive() method on a Mockery mock

```
public function test_notifier_notifies_admins()
{
    $slackMock = Mockery::mock(SlackClient::class);
```

```
$slackMock->shouldReceive('send')->once();

$notifier = new Notifier($slackMock);
$notifier->notifyAdmins('Test message');
}
```

shouldReceive('send')->once() is the same as saying "assert that $slackMock will have its send() method called once and only once." So, we're now asserting that Notifier, when we call notifyAdmins(), makes a single call to the send() method on SlackClient.

We could also use something like shouldReceive('send')->times(3) or shouldReceive('send')->never(). We can define what parameter we expect to be passed along with that send() call using with(), and we can define what to return with andReturn():

```
$slackMock->shouldReceive('send')->with('Hello, world!')->andReturn(true);
```

What if we wanted to use the IoC container to resolve our instance of the Notifier? This might be useful if Notifier had several other dependencies that we didn't need to mock.

We can do that! We just use the instance() method on the container, as in Example 12-23, to tell Laravel to provide an instance of our mock to any classes that request it (which, in this example, will be Notifier).

Example 12-23. Binding a Mockery instance to the container

```
public function test_notifier_notifies_admins()
{
    $slackMock = Mockery::mock(SlackClient::class);
    $slackMock->shouldReceive('send')->once();

    app()->instance(SlackClient::class, $slackMock);

    $notifier = app(Notifier::class);
    $notifier->notifyAdmins('Test message');
}
```

In Laravel 5.8+, there's also a convenient shortcut to creating and binding a Mockery instance to the container:

Example 12-24. Binding Mockery instances to the container more easily in Laravel 5.8+

```
$this->mock(SlackClient::class, function ($mock) {
    $mock->shouldReceive('send')->once();
});
```

There's a lot more you can do with Mockery: you can use spies, and partial spies, and much more. Going deeper into how to use Mockery is out of the scope of this book, but I encourage you to learn more about the library and how it works by reading the Mockery docs (*http://bit.ly/2Op4yyN*).

Faking Other Facades

There's one other clever thing you can do with Mockery: you can use Mockery methods (e.g., shouldReceive()) on any facades in your app.

Imagine we have a controller method that uses a facade that's not one of the fakeable systems we've already covered; we want to test that controller method and assert that a certain facade call was made.

Thankfully, it's simple: we can run our Mockery-style methods on the facade, as you can see in Example 12-25.

Example 12-25. Mocking a facade

```
// PeopleController
public function index()
{
    return Cache::remember('people', function () {
        return Person::all();
    });
}

// PeopleTest
public function test_all_people_route_should_be_cached()
{
    $person = factory(Person::class)->create();

    Cache::shouldReceive('remember')
        ->once()
        ->andReturn(collect([$person]));

    $this->get('people')->assertJsonFragment(['name' => $person->name]);
}
```

As you can see, you can use methods like shouldReceive() on the facades, just like you do on a Mockery object.

You can also use your facades as spies, which means you can set your assertions at the end and use shouldHaveReceived() instead of shouldReceive(). Example 12-26 illustrates this.

Example 12-26. Facade spies

```
public function test_package_should_be_cached_after_visit()
{
    Cache::spy();

    $package = factory(Package::class)->create();

    $this->get(route('packages.show', [$package->id]));

    Cache::shouldHaveReceived('put')
        ->once()
        ->with('packages.' . $package->id, $package->toArray());
}
```

Testing Artisan Commands

We've covered a lot in this chapter, but we're almost done! We have just two more pieces of Laravel's testing arsenal to cover: Artisan and the browser.

 If you're working in Laravel prior to 5.7, the best way to test Artisan commands is to call them with $this->artisan($commandName, $parameters) and then test their impact, like in Example 12-27.

Example 12-27. Simple Artisan tests

```
public function test_promote_console_command_promotes_user()
{
    $user = factory(User::class)->create();

    $this->artisan('user:promote', ['userId' => $user->id]);

    $this->assertTrue($user->isPromoted());
}
```

You can also make assertions against the response code you get from Artisan, as you can see in Example 12-28.

Example 12-28. Manually asserting Artisan exit codes

```
$code = $this->artisan('do:thing', ['--flagOfSomeSort' => true]);
$this->assertEquals(0, $code); // 0 means "no errors were returned"
```

Asserting Against Artisan Command Syntax

If you're working with Laravel 5.7 and later, you can also chain three new methods onto your $this->artisan() call: expectsQuestion(), expectsOutput(), and assertExitCode(). The expects* methods will work on any of the interactive

---

prompts, including confirm(), and anticipate(), and the assertExitCode() method is a shortcut to what we saw in Example 12-28.

Take a look at Example 12-29 to see how it works.

Example 12-29. Basic Artisan "expects" tests

```php
// routes/console.php
Artisan::command('make:post {--expanded}', function () {
    $title = $this->ask('What is the post title?');
    $this->comment('Creating at ' . str_slug($title) . '.md');

    $category = $this->choice('What category?', ['technology', 'construction'], 0);

    // Create post here

    $this->comment('Post created');
});

// Test file
public function test_make_post_console_commands_performs_as_expected()
{
    $this->artisan('make:post', ['--expanded' => true])
        ->expectsQuestion('What is the post title?', 'My Best Post Now')
        ->expectsOutput('Creating at my-best-post-now.md')
        ->expectsQuestion('What category?', 'construction')
        ->expectsOutput('Post created')
        ->assertExitCode(0);
}
```

As you can see, the first parameter of expectsQuestion() is the text we're expecting to see from the question, and the second parameter is the text we're answering with. expectsOutput() just tests that the passed string is returned.

Browser Tests

We've made it to browser tests! These allow you to actually interact with the DOM of your pages: in browser tests you can click buttons, fill out and submit forms, and, with Dusk, even interact with JavaScript.

Laravel actually has two separate browser testing tools: BrowserKit Testing and Dusk. Only Dusk is actively maintained; BrowserKit Testing seems to have become a bit of a second-class citizen, but it's still available on GitHub and still works at the time of this writing.

Choosing a Tool

For browser testing, I suggest you use the core application testing tools whenever possible (those we've covered up to this point). If your app is not JavaScript-based and you need to test actual DOM manipulation or form UI elements, use BrowserKit. If you're developing a JavaScript-heavy app, you'll likely want to use Dusk, which we'll cover next.

However, there will also be many instances where you'll want to use a JavaScript-based test stack (which is out of scope for this book) based on something like Jest and `vue-test-utils`. This toolset can be very useful for Vue component testing, and Jest's snapshot functionality simplifies the process of keeping API and frontend test data in sync. To learn more, check out Caleb Porzio's "Getting Started" blog post (*http://bit.ly/2OucHSI*) and Samantha Geitz's 2018 Laracon talk (*http://bit.ly/2UY8nNS*).

If you're working with a JavaScript framework other than Vue, there are no currently preferred frontend testing solutions in the Laravel world. However, the broad React world seems to have settled on Jest and Enzyme.

A Quick Introduction to BrowserKit Testing

The BrowserKit Testing package is the code from Laravel pre-5.4 application testing pulled out into a separate package. BrowserKit is a component that parses the DOM and allows you to "select" DOM elements and interact with them. This is great for simple page interactions like clicking links and filling out forms, but it doesn't work for JavaScript.

BrowserKit Testing hasn't been abandoned, but it's also not ever mentioned in the docs, and it definitely has the feel of deprecated legacy code. For this reason, and because of the robustness of the built-in application testing suite, I'm going to skip covering it here. However, the first edition of this book covered it extensively, so if you are interested in working with Browserkit Testing, check out the free PDF of the first edition's testing chapter (*http://bit.ly/2CNFCN1*).

Testing with Dusk

Dusk is a Laravel tool (installable as a Composer package) that makes it easy to write Selenium-style directions for a ChromeDriver-based browser to interact with your app. Unlike most other Selenium-based tools, Dusk's API is simple and it's easy to write code to interact with it by hand. Take a look:

```
$this->browse(function ($browser) {
    $browser->visit('/register')
        ->type('email', 'test@example.com')
        ->type('password', 'secret')
```

```
        ->press('Sign Up')
        ->assertPathIs('/dashboard');
});
```

With Dusk, there's an actual browser spinning up your entire application and interacting with it. That means you can have complex interactions with your JavaScript and get screenshots of failure states—but it also means everything's a bit slower and it's more prone to failure than Laravel's base application testing suite.

Personally, I've found that Dusk is most useful as a regression testing suite, and it works better than something like Selenium. Rather than using it for any sort of test-driven development, I use it to assert that the user experience hasn't broken ("regressed") as the app continues to develop. Think of this more like writing tests about your user interface after the interface is built.

The Dusk docs (*http://bit.ly/2JF0POY*) are robust, so I'm not going to go into great depth here, but I want to show you the basics of working with Dusk.

Installing Dusk

To install Dusk, run these two commands:

```
composer require --dev laravel/dusk
php artisan dusk:install
```

Then edit your *.env* file to set your APP_URL variable to the same URL you use to view your site in your local browser; something like `http://mysite.test`.

To run your Dusk tests, just run `php artisan dusk`. You can pass in all the same parameters you're used to from PHPUnit (for example, `php artisan dusk --filter=my_best_test`).

Writing Dusk tests

To generate a new Dusk test, use a command like the following:

```
php artisan dusk:make RatingTest
```

This test will be placed in *tests/Browser/RatingTest.php*.

 Customizing Dusk Environment Variables

You can customize the environment variables for Dusk by creating a new file named *.env.dusk.local* (and you can replace *.local* if you're working in a different environment, like "staging").

To write your Dusk tests, imagine that you're directing one or more web browsers to visit your application and take certain actions. That's what the syntax will look like, as you can see in Example 12-30.

Example 12-30. A simple Dusk test

```
public function testBasicExample()
{
    $user = factory(User::class)->create();

    $this->browse(function ($browser) use ($user) {
        $browser->visit('login')
            ->type('email', $user->email)
            ->type('password', 'secret')
            ->press('Login')
            ->assertPathIs('/home');
    });
}
```

`$this->browse()` creates a browser, which you pass into a closure; then, within the closure you instruct the browser which actions to take.

It's important to note that—unlike Laravel's other application testing tools, which mimic the behavior of your forms—Dusk is actually spinning up a browser, sending events to the browser to type those words, and then sending an event to the browser to press that button. This is a real browser and Dusk is fully driving it.

You can also "ask" for more than one browser by adding parameters to the closure, which allows you to test how multiple users might interact with the website (for example, with a chat system). Take a look at Example 12-31, from the docs.

Example 12-31. Multiple Dusk browsers

```
$this->browse(function ($first, $second) {
    $first->loginAs(User::find(1))
        ->visit('home')
        ->waitForText('Message');

    $second->loginAs(User::find(2))
        ->visit('home')
        ->waitForText('Message')
        ->type('message', 'Hey Taylor')
        ->press('Send');

    $first->waitForText('Hey Taylor')
        ->assertSee('Jeffrey Way');
});
```

There's a huge suite of actions and assertions available that we won't cover here (check the docs), but let's look at a few of the other tools Dusk provides.

Authentication and databases

As you can see in Example 12-31, the syntax for authentication is a little different from the rest of the Laravel application testing: `$browser->loginAs($user)`.

> **Avoid the RefreshDatabase Trait with Dusk**
>
> Don't use the `RefreshDatabase` trait with Dusk! Use the `Database Migrations` trait instead; transactions, which `RefreshDatabase` uses, don't last across requests.

Interactions with the page

If you've ever written jQuery, interacting with the page using Dusk will come naturally. Take a look at Example 12-32 to see the common patterns for selecting items with Dusk.

Example 12-32. Selecting items with Dusk

```
<-- Template -->
<div class="search"><input><button id="search-button"></button></div>
<button dusk="expand-nav"></button>

// Dusk tests
// Option 1: jQuery-style syntax
$browser->click('.search button');
$browser->click('#search-button');

// Option 2: dusk="selector-here" syntax; recommended
$browser->click('@expand-nav');
```

As you can see, adding the dusk attribute to your page elements allows you to reference them directly in a way that won't change when the display or layout of the page changes later; when any method asks for a selector, pass in the @ sign and then the content of your dusk attribute.

Let's take a look at a few of the methods you can call on `$browser`.

To work with text and attribute values, use these methods:

`value($selector, $value = null)`
:   Returns the value of any text input if only one parameter is passed; sets the value of an input if a second parameter is passed.

`text($selector)`
:   Gets the text content of a nonfillable item like a `<div>` or a `<span>`.

`attribute($selector, $attributeName)`
:   Returns the value of a particular attribute on the element matching `$selector`.

Methods for working with forms and files include the following:

type(*$selector*, *$valueToType*)
> Similar to value(), but actually types the characters rather than directly setting the value.

Dusk's Selector Matching Order

With methods like type() that target inputs, Dusk will start by trying to match a Dusk or CSS selector, and then will look for an input with the provided name, and finally will try to find a <textarea> with the provided name.

select(*$selector*, *$optionValue*)
> Selects the option with the value of *$optionValue* in a drop-down selectable by *$selector*.

check(*$selector*) *and* uncheck(*$selector*)
> Checks or unchecks a checkbox selectable by *$selector*.

radio(*$selector*, *$optionValue*)
> Selects the option with the value of *$optionValue* in a radio group selectable by *$selector*.

attach(*$selector*, *$filePath*)
> Attaches a file at *$filePath* to the file input selectable by *$selector*.

The methods for keyboard and mouse input are:

clickLink(*$selector*)
> Follows a text link to its target.

click(*$selector*) *and* mouseover(*$selector*)
> Triggers a mouse click or a mouseover event on *$selector*.

drag(*$selectorToDrag*, *$selectorToDragTo*)
> Drags an item to another item.

dragLeft(), dragRight(), dragUp(), dragDown()
> Given a first parameter of a selector and a second parameter of a number of pixels, drags the selected item that many pixels in the given direction.

keys(*$selector*, *$instructions*)
> Sends keypress events within the context of *$selector* according to the instructions in *$instructions*. You can even combine modifiers with your typing:

```
$browser->keys('selector', 'this is ', ['{shift}', 'great']);
```

This would type "this is GREAT". As you can see, adding an array to the list of items to type allows you to combine modifiers (wrapped with {}) with typing. You can see a full list of the possible modifiers in the Facebook WebDriver source (*http://bit.ly/2uB5APj*).

If you'd like to just send your key sequence to the page (for example, to trigger a keyboard shortcut), you can target the top level of your app or page as your selector. For example, if it's a Vue app and the top level is a <div> with an ID of app:

```
$browser->keys('#app', ['{command}', '/']);
```

Waiting

Because Dusk interacts with JavaScript and is directing an actual browser, the concept of time and timeouts and "waiting" needs to be addressed. Dusk offers a few methods you can use to ensure your tests handle timing issues correctly. Some of these methods are useful for interacting with intentionally slow or delayed elements of the page, but some of them are also just useful for getting around initialization times on your components. The available methods include the following:

pause(*$milliseconds*)
: Pauses the execution of Dusk tests for the given number of milliseconds. This is the simplest "wait" option; it makes any future commands you send to the browser wait that amount of time before operating.

    You can use this and other waiting methods in the midst of an assertion chain, as shown here:

    ```
    $browser->click('chat')
        ->pause(500)
        ->assertSee('How can we help?');
    ```

waitFor(*$selector, $maxSeconds = null*) *and* waitForMissing(*$selector, $maxSeconds = null*)
: Waits until the given element exists on the page (waitFor()) or disappears from the page (waitForMissing()) or times out after the optional second parameter's second count:

    ```
    $browser->waitFor('@chat', 5);
    $browser->waitUntilMissing('@loading', 5);
    ```

whenAvailable(*$selector, $callback*)
: Similar to waitFor(), but accepts a closure as the second parameter which will define what action to take when the specified element becomes available:

    ```
    $browser->whenAvailable('@chat', function ($chat) {
        $chat->assertSee('How can we help you?');
    });
    ```

waitForText(*$text, $maxSeconds = null*)

Waits for text to show up on the page, or times out after the optional second parameter's second count:

```
$browser->waitForText('Your purchase has been completed.', 5);
```

waitForLink(*$linkText, $maxSeconds = null*)

Waits for a link to exist with the given link text, or times out after the optional second parameter's second count:

```
$browser->waitForLink('Clear these results', 2);
```

waitForLocation(*$path*)

Waits until the page URL matches the provided path:

```
$browser->waitForLocation('auth/login');
```

waitForRoute(*$routeName*)

Waits until the page URL matches the URL for the provided route:

```
$browser->waitForRoute('packages.show', [$package->id]);
```

waitForReload()

Waits until the page reloads.

waitUntil(*$expression*)

Waits until the provided JavaScript expression evaluates as true:

```
$browser->waitUntil('App.packages.length > 0', 7);
```

Other assertions

As I've mentioned, there's a huge list of assertions you can make against your app with Dusk. Here are a few that I use most commonly—you can see the full list in the Dusk docs (*https://laravel.com/docs/dusk*):

- assertTitleContains(*$text*)
- assertQueryStringHas(*$keyName*)
- assertHasCookie(*$cookieName*)
- assertSourceHas(*$htmlSourceCode*)
- assertChecked(*$selector*)
- assertSelectHasOption(*$selectorForSelect, $optionValue*)
- assertVisible(*$selector*)
- assertFocused()
- assertVue(*$dataLocation, $dataValue, $selector*)

Other organizational structures

So far, everything we've covered makes it possible to test individual elements on our pages. But we'll often use Dusk to test more complex applications and single-page apps, which means we're going to need organizational structures around our assertions.

The first organizational structures we have encountered have been the dusk attribute (e.g., `<div dusk="abc">`, creating a selector named `@abc` we can refer to later) and the closures we can use to wrap certain portions of our code (e.g., with `whenAvailable()`).

Dusk offers two more organizational tools: pages and components. Let's start with pages.

Pages.   A page is a class that you'll generate which contains two pieces of functionality: first, a URL and assertions to define which page in your app should be attached to this Dusk page; and second, shorthand like we used inline (the `@abc` selector generated by the `dusk="abc"` attribute in our HTML) but just for this page, and without needing to edit our HTML.

Let's imagine our app has a "create package" page. We can generate a Dusk page for it as follows:

```
php artisan dusk:page CreatePackage
```

Take a look at Example 12-33 to see what our generated class will look like.

Example 12-33. The generated Dusk page

```php
<?php

namespace Tests\Browser\Pages;

use Laravel\Dusk\Browser;

class CreatePackage extends Page
{
    /**
     * Get the URL for the page
     *
     * @return string
     */
    public function url()
    {
        return '/';
    }

    /**
```

```
 * Assert that the browser is on the page
 *
 * @param  Browser  $browser
 * @return void
 */
public function assert(Browser $browser)
{
    $browser->assertPathIs($this->url());
}

/**
 * Get the element shortcuts for the page
 *
 * @return array
 */
public function elements()
{
    return [
        '@element' => '#selector',
    ];
}
}
```

The url() method defines the location where Dusk should expect this page to be; assert() lets you run additional assertions to verify you're on the right page, and elements() provides shortcuts for @dusk-style selectors.

Let's make a few quick modifications to our "create package" page, to make it look like Example 12-34.

Example 12-34. A simple "create package" Dusk page

```
class CreatePackage extends Page
{
    public function url()
    {
        return '/packages/create';
    }

    public function assert(Browser $browser)
    {
        $browser->assertTitleContains('Create Package');
        $browser->assertPathIs($this->url());
    }

    public function elements()
    {
        return [
            '@title' => 'input[name=title]',
            '@instructions' => 'textarea[name=instructions]',
        ];
```

```
    }
}
```

Now that we have a functional page, we can navigate to it and access its defined elements:

```
// In a test
$browser->visit(new Tests\Browser\Pages\CreatePackage)
    ->type('@title', 'My package title');
```

One common use for pages is to define a common action you want to take in your tests; consider these almost like macros for Dusk. You can define a method on your page and then call it from your code, as you can see in Example 12-35.

Example 12-35. Defining and using a custom page method

```
class CreatePackage extends Page
{
    // ... url(), assert(), elements()

    public function fillBasicFields(Browser $browser, $packageTitle = 'Best package')
    {
        $browser->type('@title', $packageTitle)
            ->type('@instructions', 'Do this stuff and then that stuff');
    }
}
$browser->visit(new CreatePackage)
    ->fillBasicFields('Greatest Package Ever')
    ->press('Create Package')
    ->assertSee('Greatest Package Ever');
```

Components. If you want the same functionality as Dusk pages offer, but without it being constrained to a specific URL, you'll likely want to reach for Dusk *components*. These classes are shaped very similarly to pages, but instead of being bound to a URL, they're each bound to a selector.

In NovaPackages.com, we have a little Vue component for rating packages and displaying ratings. Let's make a Dusk component for it:

```
php artisan dusk:component RatingWidget
```

Take a look at Example 12-36 to see what that will generate.

Example 12-36. The default source of a generated Dusk component

```
<?php

namespace Tests\Browser\Components;
```

```
use Laravel\Dusk\Browser;
use Laravel\Dusk\Component as BaseComponent;

class RatingWidget extends BaseComponent
{
    /**
     * Get the root selector for the component
     *
     * @return string
     */
    public function selector()
    {
        return '#selector';
    }

    /**
     * Assert that the browser page contains the component
     *
     * @param  Browser  $browser
     * @return void
     */
    public function assert(Browser $browser)
    {
        $browser->assertVisible($this->selector());
    }

    /**
     * Get the element shortcuts for the component
     *
     * @return array
     */
    public function elements()
    {
        return [
            '@element' => '#selector',
        ];
    }
}
```

As you can see, this is basically the same as a Dusk page, but we're encapsulating our work to an HTML element instead of a URL. Everything else is basically the same. Take a look at Example 12-37 to see our rating widget example in Dusk component form.

Example 12-37. A Dusk component for the rating widget

```
class RatingWidget extends BaseComponent
{
    public function selector()
    {
        return '.rating-widget';
```

```
    }

    public function assert(Browser $browser)
    {
        $browser->assertVisible($this->selector());
    }

    public function elements()
    {
        return [
            '@5-star' => '.five-star-rating',
            '@4-star' => '.four-star-rating',
            '@3-star' => '.three-star-rating',
            '@2-star' => '.two-star-rating',
            '@1-star' => '.one-star-rating',
            '@average' => '.average-rating',
            '@mine' => '.current-user-rating',
        ];
    }

    public function ratePackage(Browser $browser, $rating)
    {
        $browser->click("@{$rating}-star")
            ->assertSeeIn('@mine', $rating);
    }
}
```

Using components works just like using pages, as you can see in Example 12-38.

Example 12-38. Using Dusk components

```
$browser->visit('/packages/tightenco/nova-stock-picker')
    ->within(new RatingWidget, function ($browser) {
        $browser->ratePackage(2);
        $browser->assertSeeIn('@average', 2);
    });
```

That's a good, brief overview of what Dusk can do. There's a lot more—more assertions, more edge cases, more gotchas, more examples—in the Dusk docs (*http://bit.ly/2JF0POY*), so I'd recommend a read through there if you plan to work with Dusk.

TL;DR

Laravel can work with any modern PHP testing framework, but it's optimized for PHPUnit (especially if your tests extend Laravel's TestCase). Laravel's application testing framework makes it simple to send fake HTTP and console requests through your application and inspect the results.

Tests in Laravel can easily and powerfully interact with and assert against the database, cache, session, filesystem, mail, and many other systems. Quite a few of these systems have fakes built in to make them even easier to test. You can test DOM and browser-like interactions with BrowserKit Testing or Dusk.

Laravel brings in Mockery in case you need mocks, stubs, spies, dummies, or anything else, but the testing philosophy of Laravel is to use real collaborators as much as possible. Don't fake it unless you have to.

## CHAPTER 13

Writing APIs

One of the most common tasks Laravel developers are given is to create an API, usually JSON and REST or REST-like, that allows third parties to interact with the Laravel application's data.

Laravel makes it incredibly easy to work with JSON, and its resource controllers are already structured around REST verbs and patterns. In this chapter you'll learn about some basic API-writing concepts, the tools Laravel provides for writing APIs, and some external tools and organizational systems you'll want to consider when writing your first Laravel API.

The Basics of REST-Like JSON APIs

Representational State Transfer (REST) is an architectural style for building APIs. Technically, REST is either a broad definition that could apply to almost the entirety of the internet or something so specific that *no one* actually uses it, so don't let yourself get overwhelmed by the definition or caught in an argument with a pedant. When we talk about RESTful or REST-like APIs in the Laravel world, we're generally talking about APIs with a few common characteristics:

- They're structured around "resources" that can be uniquely represented by URIs, like /cats for all cats, /cats/15 for a single cat with the ID of 15, etc.
- Interactions with resources primarily take place using HTTP verbs (GET /cats/15 versus DELETE /cats/15).
- They're stateless, meaning there's no persistent session authentication between requests; each request must uniquely authenticate itself.

- They're cacheable and consistent, meaning each request (except for a few authenticated user–specific requests) should return the same result regardless of who the requester is.
- They return JSON.

The most common API pattern is to have a unique URL structure for each of your Eloquent models that's exposed as an API resource, and allow for users to interact with that resource with specific verbs and get JSON back. Example 13-1 shows a few possible examples.

Example 13-1. Common REST API endpoint structures

```
GET /api/cats
[
    {
        id: 1,
        name: 'Fluffy'
    },
    {
        id: 2,
        name: 'Killer'
    }
]

GET /api/cats/2
{
    id: 2,
    name: 'Killer'
}

DELETE /api/cats/2
(deletes cat)

POST /api/cats with body:
{
    name: 'Mr Bigglesworth'
}
(creates new cat)

PATCH /api/cats/3 with body:
{
    name: 'Mr. Bigglesworth'
}
(updates cat)
```

This gives you the idea of the basic set of interactions we are likely to have with our APIs. Let's dig into how to make them happen with Laravel.

Controller Organization and JSON Returns

Laravel's API resource controllers are like normal resource controllers (see "Resource Controllers" on page 47) but modified to align with RESTful API routes. For example, they exclude the `create()` and `edit()` methods, both of which are irrelevant in an API. Let's get started there. First we'll create a new controller for our resource, which we'll route at `/api/dogs`:

```
php artisan make:controller Api\DogsController --api
```

> **Escaping Slashes in Artisan Commands Prior to Laravel 5.3**
>
> In versions of Laravel prior to 5.3, you need to escape the \ in namespace separators with a forward slash in Artisan commands, like this:
>
> ```
> php artisan make:controller Api/\DogsController --api
> ```

Note that in projects running versions of Laravel prior to 5.5, the concepts of API resource controllers and API resource routes don't exist. You can still just use regular resource controllers and resource routes instead; they're almost exactly the same but have a few view-related routes that aren't used in APIs. Example 13-2 shows what our API resource controller will look like.

Example 13-2. A generated API resource controller

```php
<?php

namespace App\Http\Controllers\Api;

use Illuminate\Http\Request;
use App\Http\Controllers\Controller;

class DogsController extends Controller
{
    /**
     * Display a listing of the resource
     *
     * @return \Illuminate\Http\Response
     */
    public function index()
    {
        //
    }

    /**
     * Store a newly created resource in storage
     *
     * @param  \Illuminate\Http\Request  $request
```

```php
     * @return \Illuminate\Http\Response
     */
    public function store(Request $request)
    {
        //
    }

    /**
     * Display the specified resource
     *
     * @param  int  $id
     * @return \Illuminate\Http\Response
     */
    public function show($id)
    {
        //
    }

    /**
     * Update the specified resource in storage
     *
     * @param  \Illuminate\Http\Request  $request
     * @param  int  $id
     * @return \Illuminate\Http\Response
     */
    public function update(Request $request, $id)
    {
        //
    }

    /**
     * Remove the specified resource from storage
     *
     * @param  int  $id
     * @return \Illuminate\Http\Response
     */
    public function destroy($id)
    {
        //
    }
}
```

The docblocks pretty much tell the story. index() lists all of the dogs, show() lists a single dog, store() stores a new dog, update() updates a dog, and destroy() removes a dog.

Let's quickly make a model and a migration so we can work with it:

```
php artisan make:model Dog --migration
php artisan migrate
```

Great! Now we can fill out our controller methods.

Database Requirements for These Code Samples to Work

If you want the code we're writing here to actually work, you'll want to add a string() column to the migration named name and another named breed, and either add those columns to the Eloquent model's fillable property or just set the guarded property of that model equal to an empty array ([]).

We can take advantage of a great feature of Eloquent here: if you echo an Eloquent results collection, it'll automatically convert itself to JSON (using the __toString() magic method, if you're curious). That means if you return a collection of results from a route, you'll in effect be returning JSON. So, as Example 13-3 demonstrates, this will be some of the simplest code you'll ever write.

Example 13-3. A sample API resource controller for the Dog entity

```
...
class DogsController extends Controller
{
    public function index()
    {
        return Dog::all();
    }

    public function store(Request $request)
    {
        return Dog::create($request->only(['name', 'breed']));
    }

    public function show($id)
    {
        return Dog::findOrFail($id);
    }

    public function update(Request $request, $id)
    {
        $dog = Dog::findOrFail($id);
        $dog->update($request->only(['name', 'breed']));
        return $dog;
    }

    public function destroy($id)
    {
        Dog::findOrFail($id)->delete();
    }
}
```

Example 13-4 shows how we can link this up in our routes file. As you can see, we can use `Route::apiResource()` to automatically map all of these default methods to their appropriate routes and HTTP verbs.

Example 13-4. Binding the routes for a resource controller

```
// routes/api.php
Route::namespace('Api')->group(function () {
    Route::apiResource('dogs', 'DogsController');
});
```

There you have it! Your first RESTful API in Laravel. Of course, you'll need much more nuance: pagination, sorting, authentication, more defined response headers. But this is the foundation of everything else.

Reading and Sending Headers

REST APIs often read, and send, non-content information using headers. For example, any request to GitHub's API will return headers detailing the current user's rate limiting status:

```
X-RateLimit-Limit: 5000
X-RateLimit-Remaining: 4987
X-RateLimit-Reset: 1350085394
```

X-* Headers

You might be wondering why the GitHub rate limiting headers are prefixed with X-, especially if you see them in the context of other headers returned with the same request:

```
HTTP/1.1 200 OK
Server: nginx
Date: Fri, 12 Oct 2012 23:33:14 GMT
Content-Type: application/json; charset=utf-8
Connection: keep-alive
Status: 200 OK
ETag: "a00049ba79152d03380c34652f2cb612"
X-GitHub-Media-Type: github.v3
X-RateLimit-Limit: 5000
X-RateLimit-Remaining: 4987
X-RateLimit-Reset: 1350085394
Content-Length: 5
Cache-Control: max-age=0, private, must-revalidate
X-Content-Type-Options: nosniff
```

Any header whose name starts with X- is a header that's not in the HTTP spec. It might be entirely made up (e.g., X-How-Much-Matt-Loves-This-Page), or part of a common convention that hasn't made it into the spec yet (e.g., X-Requested-With).

Similarly, many APIs allow developers to customize their requests using request headers. For example, GitHub's API makes it easy to define which version of the API you'd like to use with the Accept header:

```
Accept: application/vnd.github.v3+json
```

If you were to change v3 to v2, GitHub would pass your request to version 2 of its API instead.

Let's learn quickly how to do both in Laravel.

Sending Response Headers in Laravel

We already covered this topic quite a bit in Chapter 10, but here's a quick refresher. Once you have a response object, you can add a header using header(*$headerName*, *$headerValue*), as seen in Example 13-5.

Example 13-5. Adding a response header in Laravel

```
Route::get('dogs', function () {
    return response(Dog::all())
        ->header('X-Greatness-Index', 12);
});
```

Nice and easy.

Reading Request Headers in Laravel

If you have an incoming request, it's also simple to read any given header. Example 13-6 illustrates this.

Example 13-6. Reading a request header in Laravel

```
Route::get('dogs', function (Request $request) {
    var_dump($request->header('Accept'));
});
```

Now that you can read incoming request headers and set headers on your API responses, let's take a look at how you might want to customize your API.

Eloquent Pagination

Pagination is one of the first places where most APIs need to consider special instructions. Eloquent comes out of the box with a pagination system that hooks directly into the query parameters of any page request. We already covered the paginator component a bit in Chapter 6, but here's a quick refresher.

Any Eloquent call provides a `paginate()` method, to which you can pass the number of items you'd like to return per page. Eloquent then checks the URL for a page query parameter and, if it's set, treats that as an indicator of how many pages the user is into a paginated list.

To make your API route ready for automated Laravel pagination, use `paginate()` instead of `all()` or `get()` to call your Eloquent queries in your route; something like Example 13-7.

Example 13-7. A paginated API route

```
Route::get('dogs', function () {
    return Dog::paginate(20);
});
```

We've defined that Eloquent should get 20 results from the database. Depending on what the `page` query parameter is set to, Laravel will know exactly *which* 20 results to pull for us:

```
GET /dogs        - Return results 1-20
GET /dogs?page=1 - Return results 1-20
GET /dogs?page=2 - Return results 21-40
```

Note that the `paginate()` method is also available on query builder calls, as seen in Example 13-8.

Example 13-8. Using the paginate() method on a query builder call

```
Route::get('dogs', function () {
    return DB::table('dogs')->paginate(20);
});
```

Here's something interesting, though: this isn't just going to return 20 results when you convert it to JSON. Instead, it's going to build a response object that automatically passes some useful pagination-related details to the end user, *along with* the paginated data. Example 13-9 shows a possible response from our call, truncated to only three records to save space.

Example 13-9. Sample output from a paginated database call

```json
{
    "current_page": 1,
    "data": [
        {
            'name': 'Fido'
        },
        {
            'name': 'Pickles'
        },
        {
            'name': 'Spot'
        }
    ]
    "first_page_url": "http://myapp.com/api/dogs?page=1",
    "from": 1,
    "last_page": 2,
    "last_page_url": "http://myapp.com/api/dogs?page=2",
    "next_page_url": "http://myapp.com/api/dogs?page=2",
    "path": "http://myapp.com/api/dogs",
    "per_page": 2,
    "prev_page_url": null,
    "to": 2,
    "total": 4
}
```

Sorting and Filtering

While there is a convention and some built-in tooling for pagination in Laravel, there isn't any for sorting, so you have to figure that out on your own. I'll give a quick code sample here, and I'll style the query parameters similarly to the JSON API spec (described in the following sidebar).

The JSON API Spec

The JSON API (*http://jsonapi.org/*) is a standard for how to handle many of the most common tasks in building JSON-based APIs: filtering, sorting, pagination, authentication, embedding, links, metadata, and more.

Laravel's default pagination doesn't work *exactly* according to the JSON API spec, but it gets you started in the right direction. The majority of the rest of the JSON API spec is something you'll just have to choose (or not) to implement manually.

For example, here's a piece of the JSON API spec that helpfully handles how to structure data versus error returns:

A document MUST contain at least one of the following top-level members:

- data: the document's "primary data"
- errors: an array of error objects
- meta: a meta object that contains non-standard meta-information.

The members data and errors MUST NOT coexist in the same document.

Be warned, however: it's wonderful to have the JSON API as a spec, but it also takes quite a bit of groundwork to get running with it. We won't use it entirely in these examples, but I'll use its general ideas as inspiration.

Sorting Your API Results

First, let's set up the ability to sort our results. We start in Example 13-10 with the ability to sort by only a single column, and in only a single direction.

Example 13-10. Simplest API sorting

```
// Handles /dogs?sort=name
Route::get('dogs', function (Request $request) {
    // Get the sort query parameter (or fall back to default sort "name")
    $sortColumn = $request->input('sort', 'name');
    return Dog::orderBy($sortColumn)->paginate(20);
});
```

We add the ability to invert it (e.g., ?sort=-weight) in Example 13-11.

Example 13-11. Single-column API sorting, with direction control

```
// Handles /dogs?sort=name and /dogs?sort=-name
Route::get('dogs', function (Request $request) {
    // Get the sort query parameter (or fall back to default sort "name")
    $sortColumn = $request->input('sort', 'name');

    // Set the sort direction based on whether the key starts with -
    // using Laravel's starts_with() helper function
    $sortDirection = starts_with($sortColumn, '-') ? 'desc' : 'asc';
    $sortColumn = ltrim($sortColumn, '-');

    return Dog::orderBy($sortColumn, $sortDirection)
        ->paginate(20);
});
```

Finally, we do the same for multiple columns (e.g., ?sort=name,-weight) in Example 13-12.

Example 13-12. JSON API–style sorting

```
// Handles ?sort=name,-weight
Route::get('dogs', function (Request $request) {
    // Grab the query parameter and turn it into an array exploded by ,
    $sorts = explode(',', $request->input('sort', ''));

    // Create a query
    $query = Dog::query();

    // Add the sorts one by one
    foreach ($sorts as $sortColumn) {
        $sortDirection = starts_with($sortColumn, '-') ? 'desc' : 'asc';
        $sortColumn = ltrim($sortColumn, '-');

        $query->orderBy($sortColumn, $sortDirection);
    }

    // Return
    return $query->paginate(20);
});
```

As you can see, it's not the simplest process ever, and you'll likely want to build some helper tooling around the repetitive processes, but we're building up the customizability of our API piece by piece using logical and simple features.

Filtering Your API Results

Another common task in building APIs is filtering out all but a certain subset of data. For example, the client might ask for a list of the dogs that are chihuahuas.

The JSON API doesn't give us any great ideas for syntax here, other than that we should use the `filter` query parameter. Let's think along the lines of the sort syntax, where we're putting everything into a single key—maybe `?filter=breed:chihuahua`. You can see how to do this in Example 13-13.

Example 13-13. Single filter on API results

```
Route::get('dogs', function () {
    $query = Dog::query();

    $query->when(request()->filled('filter'), function ($query) {
        [$criteria, $value] = explode(':', request('filter'));
        return $query->where($criteria, $value);
    });

    return $query->paginate(20);
});
```

Note that in Example 13-13 we're using the `request()` helper instead of injecting an instance of `$request`. Both work the same, but sometimes the `request()` helper can be easier when you're working inside of a closure so you don't have to pass variables in manually.

 Conditional Query Modifications Prior to Laravel 5.2

In projects running versions of Laravel prior to 5.2, you'll have to replace use of `$query->when()` with a regular PHP `if` statement.

And, just for kicks, in Example 13-14 we allow for multiple filters, like `?filter=breed:chihuahua,color:brown`.

Example 13-14. Multiple filters on API results

```
Route::get('dogs', function (Request $request) {
    $query = Dog::query();

    $query->when(request()->filled('filter'), function ($query) {
        $filters = explode(',', request('filter'));

        foreach ($filters as $filter) {
            [$criteria, $value] = explode(':', $filter);
            $query->where($criteria, $value);
        }

        return $query;
    });

    return $query->paginate(20);
});
```

Transforming Results

We've covered how to sort and filter our result sets. But right now, we're relying on Eloquent's JSON serialization, which means we return every field on every model.

Eloquent provides a few convenience tools for defining which fields to show when you're serializing an array. You can read more in Chapter 5, but the gist is that if you set a `$hidden` array property on your Eloquent class, any field listed in that array will not be shown in the serialized model output. You can alternatively set a `$visible` array that defines the fields that are allowed to be shown. You could also either overwrite or mimic the `toArray()` function on your model, crafting a custom output format.

Another common pattern is to create a transformer for each data type. Transformers are helpful because they give you more control, isolate API-specific logic away from the model itself, and allow you to provide a more consistent API even when the models and their relationships change down the road.

There's a fantastic but complicated package for this, Fractal (*http://bit.ly/2fEt8Nr*), that sets up a series of convenience structures and classes for transforming your data.

Laravel 5.5 introduced a concept called API resources that cover the needs of the majority of APIs for transforming and collecting results, so if you're working with 5.5 or later, skip the next section and move on to "API Resources" on page 352. If you're working with 5.4 or earlier, read on.

Writing Your Own Transformer

The general concept of a transformer is that we are going to run every instance of our model through another class that *transforms* its data to a different state. It might add fields, rename fields, delete fields, manipulate fields, add nested children, or whatever else. Let's start with a simple example (Example 13-15).

Example 13-15. A simple transformer

```
Route::get('users/{id}', function ($userId) {
    return (new UserTransformer(User::findOrFail($userId)));
});

class UserTransformer
{
    protected $user;

    public function __construct($user)
    {
        $this->user = $user;
    }

    public function toArray()
    {
        return [
            'id' => $this->user->id,
            'name' => sprintf(
                "%s %s",
                $this->user->first_name,
                $this->user->last_name
            ),
            'friendsCount' => $this->user->friends->count(),
        ];
    }

    public function toJson()
```

```
    {
        return json_encode($this->toArray());
    }

    public function __toString()
    {
        return $this->toJson();
    }
}
```

Classic Transformers

A more classic transformer would probably offer a `transform()` method that takes a `$user` parameter. This would likely spit out an array or JSON directly.

However, I've been using this pattern, which we sometimes call "API objects," for a few years and really love how much more power and flexibility it provides.

As you can see in Example 13-15, transformers accept the model they're transforming as a parameter and then manipulate that model—and its relationships—to create the final output that you want to send to the API.

Nesting and Relationships with Custom Transformers

Whether, and how, to nest relationships in APIs is an issue of much debate. Thankfully, people more experienced than me have written on this at length; I'd recommend reading Phil Sturgeon's *Build APIs You Won't Hate* (*https://apisyouwonthate.com/*) (Leanpub) to learn more about this and about REST APIs in general.

There are a few primary ways to approach nesting relationships. These examples will assume your primary resource is a `user` and your related resource is a `friend`:

- Include related resources directly in the primary resource (e.g., the `users/5` resource has its friends nested in it).

- Include just the foreign keys in the primary resource (e.g., the `users/5` resource has an array of friend IDs nested in it).

- Allow the user to query the related resource filtered by the originating resource (e.g., `/friends?user=5`, or "give me all friends who are related to user #5").

- Create a subresource (e.g., `/users/5/friends`).

- Allow optional including (e.g., `/users/5` does not include, but `/users/5?include=friends` does include; so does `/users/5?include=friends,dogs`).

Let's assume for a minute that we want to (optionally) include related items. How would we do that? Our transformer example in Example 13-15 gives us a great head start. Let's adjust it, as seen in Example 13-16, to add optional subresource including.

Example 13-16. Allowing for optional including of a subresource in a transformer

```
// e.g. myapp.com/api/users/15?include=friends,bookmarks
Route::get('users/{id}', function ($userId, Request $request) {
    // Get the include query parameter and split by commas
    $includes = explode(',', $request->input('include', ''));
    // Pass both user and includes to the user transformer
    return (new UserTransformer(User::findOrFail($userId), $includes));
});

class UserTransformer
{
    protected $user;
    protected $includes;

    public function __construct($user, $includes = [])
    {
        $this->user = $user;
        $this->includes = $includes;
    }

    public function toArray()
    {
        $append = [];

        if (in_array('friends', $this->includes)) {
            // If you have more than one include, you'll want to generalize this
            $append['friends'] = $this->user->friends->map(function ($friend) {
                return (new FriendTransformer($friend))->toArray();
            });
        }

        return array_merge([
            'id' => $this->user->id,
            'name' => sprintf(
                "%s %s",
                $this->user->first_name,
                $this->user->last_name
            )
        ], $append);
    }
...
```

You learn more about the map() functionality when we look at collections in Chapter 17, but everything else in here should be pretty familiar.

In the route, we're splitting the `include` query parameter by commas and passing it into our transformer. Currently our transformer can just handle the `friends` include, but it could be abstracted to handle others. If the user has requested the `friends` include, the transformer maps over each `friend` (using the `hasMany` friends relationship on the `user` model), passes that `friend` to the `FriendTransformer()`, and includes the array of all transformed `friends` in the user response.

API Resources

If you're working with Laravel prior to 5.5, you can skip this section and move on to "API Authentication with Laravel Passport" on page 357.

In the past, one of the first challenges we'd run into when developing APIs in Laravel was how to transform our data. The simplest APIs can just return Eloquent objects as JSON, but very quickly the needs of most APIs outgrow that structure. How should we convert our Eloquent results into the right format? What if we want to embed other resources, or do so but only optionally, or add a computed field, or hide some fields from APIs but not other JSON output? An API-specific transformer is the solution.

In Laravel 5.5 and later we have access to a feature called Eloquent API resources, which are structures that define how to transform an Eloquent object (or a collection of Eloquent objects) of a given class to API results. For example, your `Dog` Eloquent model now has a `Dog` resource whose responsibility it is to translate each instance of `Dog` to the appropriate `Dog`-shaped API response object.

Creating a Resource Class

Let's walk through this `Dog` example to see what it looks like to transform our API output. First, use the Artisan command `make:resource` to create your first resource:

```
php artisan make:resource Dog
```

This will create a new class in *app/Http/Resources/Dog.php*, which contains one method: `toArray()`. You can see what the file looks like in Example 13-17.

Example 13-17. Generated API resource

```
<?php

namespace App\Http\Resources;

use Illuminate\Http\Resources\Json\JsonResource;

class Dog extends JsonResource
{
```

```
/**
 * Transform the resource into an array
 *
 * @param \Illuminate\Http\Request $request
 * @return array
 */
public function toArray($request)
{
    return parent::toArray($request);
}
}
```

The toArray() method we're working with here has access to two important pieces of data. First, it has access to the Illuminate Request object, so we can customize our response based on query parameters and headers and anything else important. And second, it has access to the entire Eloquent object being transformed by calling its properties and methods on $this, as you can see in Example 13-18.

Example 13-18. Simple API resource for the Dog model

```
class Dog extends JsonResource
{
    public function toArray($request)
    {
        return [
            'id' => $this->id,
            'name' => $this->name,
            'breed' => $this->breed,
        ];
    }
}
```

To use this new resource, you'd want to update any API endpoint that returns a single Dog to wrap the response in your new resource, like in Example 13-19.

Example 13-19. Using the simple Dog resource

```
use App\Dog;
use App\Http\Resources\Dog as DogResource;

Route::get('dogs/{dogId}', function ($dogId) {
    return new DogResource(Dog::find($dogId));
});
```

Resource Collections

Now, let's talk about what happens if you have more than one of your entity returning from a given API endpoint. This is possible using an API resource's `collection()` method, as you can see in Example 13-20.

Example 13-20. Using the default API resource collection method

```
use App\Dog;
use App\Http\Resources\Dog as DogResource;

Route::get('dogs', function () {
    return DogResource::collection(Dog::all());
});
```

This method iterates over every entry that's passed to it, transforms it with the `DogResource` API resource, and then returns the collection.

This will likely be enough for many APIs, but if you need to customize any of the structure or add metadata to your collection responses, you'll want to instead create a custom API resource collection.

In order to do so, let's reach for the `make:resource` Artisan command again. This time we'll name it `DogCollection`, which signals to Laravel this is an API resource collection, not just an API resource:

```
php artisan make:resource DogCollection
```

This will generate a new file very similar to the API resource file, living at *app/Http/Resources/DogCollection.php*, which again contains one method: `toArray()`. You can see what the file looks like in Example 13-21.

Example 13-21. Generated API resource collection

```php
<?php

namespace App\Http\Resources;

use Illuminate\Http\Resources\Json\ResourceCollection;

class DogCollection extends ResourceCollection
{
    /**
     * Transform the resource collection into an array
     *
     * @param  \Illuminate\Http\Request  $request
     * @return array
     */
    public function toArray($request)
```

```
    {
        return parent::toArray($request);
    }
}
```

Just like with the API resource, we have access to the request and the underlying data. But unlike with the API resource, we're dealing with a collection of items instead of just one, so we will access that (already transformed) collection as $this->collection. Take a look at Example 13-22 for an example.

Example 13-22. A simple API resource collection for the Dog model

```
class DogCollection extends ResourceCollection
{
    public function toArray($request)
    {
        return [
            'data' => $this->collection,
            'links' => [
                'self' => route('dogs.index'),
            ],
        ];
    }
}
```

Nesting Relationships

One of the more complicated aspects of any API is how relationships are nested. The simplest way with API resources is to add a key to your returned array that's set to an API resource collection, like in Example 13-23.

Example 13-23. A simple included API relationship

```
public function toArray()
{
    return [
        'name' => $this->name,
        'breed' => $this->breed,
        'friends' => DogResource::collection($this->friends),
    ];
}
```

You may also want this to be a conditional property; you can choose to only nest it if it's asked for in the request, or only if it's already been eager-loaded on the Eloquent object that's passed in. Take a look at Example 13-24.

Example 13-24. Conditionally loading API relationship

```php
public function toArray()
{
    return [
        'name' => $this->name,
        'breed' => $this->breed,
        // Only load this relationship if it's been eager-loaded
        'bones' => BoneResource::collection($this->whenLoaded('bones')),
        // Or only load this relationship if the URL asks for it
        'bones' => $this->when(
            $request->get('include') == 'bones',
            BoneResource::collection($this->bones)
        ),
    ];
}
```

Using Pagination with API Resources

Just like you can pass a collection of Eloquent models to a resource, you can also pass a paginator instance. Take a look at Example 13-25.

Example 13-25. Passing a paginator instance to an API resource collection

```php
Route::get('dogs', function () {
    return new DogCollection(Dog::paginate(20));
});
```

If you pass a paginator instance, the transformed result will have additional links containing pagination information (`first` page, `last` page, `prev` page, and `next` page) and meta-information about the entire collection.

You can take a look at Example 13-26 to see what this information looks like. In this example, I've set the items-per-page count to 2 by calling `Dog::paginate(2)` so you can more easily see how the links work.

Example 13-26. A sample paginated resource response with pagination links

```json
{
    "data": [
        {
            "name": "Pickles",
            "breed": "Chorkie",
        },
        {
            "name": "Gandalf",
            "breed": "Golden Retriever Mix",
        }
    ],
```

```
    "links": {
        "first": "http://gooddogbrant.com/api/dogs?page=1",
        "last": "http://gooddogbrant.com/api/dogs?page=3",
        "prev": null,
        "next": "http://gooddogbrant.com/api/dogs?page=2"
    },
    "meta": {
        "current_page": 1,
        "from": 1,
        "last_page": 3,
        "path": "http://gooddogbrant.com/api/dogs",
        "per_page": 2,
        "to": 2,
        "total": 5
    }
}
```

Conditionally Applying Attributes

You can also specify that certain attributes in your response should only be applied when a particular test is satisfied, as illustrated in Example 13-27.

Example 13-27. Conditionally applying attributes

```
public function toArray($request)
{
    return [
        'name' => $this->name,
        'breed' => $this->breed,
        'rating' => $this->when(Auth::user()->canSeeRatings(), 12),
    ];
}
```

More Customizations for API Resources

The default shape of how the data property is wrapped might not be how you like it, or you may find yourself needing to add or customize metadata for the responses. Take a look at the docs (*http://bit.ly/2HP8xTU*) for details on how to customize every aspect of your API responses.

API Authentication with Laravel Passport

Most APIs require some form of authentication to access some or all of the data. Laravel 5.2 introduced a simple "token" authentication scheme, which we'll cover shortly, but in Laravel 5.3 and later we got a new tool called Passport (by way of a separate package, brought in via Composer) that makes it easy to set up a full-featured OAuth 2.0 server in your application, complete with an API and UI components for managing clients and tokens.

A Brief Introduction to OAuth 2.0

OAuth is by far the most common auth system used in RESTful APIs. Unfortunately, it's far too complex a topic for us to cover here in depth. For further reading, Matt Frost has written a great book on OAuth and PHP titled *Integrating Web Services with OAuth and PHP* (php[architect]).

Here's the simplest concept behind OAuth: because APIs are stateless, we can't rely on the same session-based authentication that we do in normal browser-based viewing sessions, where the user logs in and their authenticated state is saved to the session for subsequent views. Instead, the API client needs to make a single call to an authentication endpoint and perform some form of handshake to prove itself. It then gets back a token which it must send along with every future request (via the `Authorization` header, usually) to prove its identity.

There are a few different types of OAuth "grant," which basically means that there are several different scenarios and types of interaction that can define that authentication handshake. Different projects and different sorts of end consumer will necessitate different grants.

If you're working with Laravel 5.1 or 5.2, there's a package called OAuth 2.0 Server for Laravel (*http://bit.ly/2e2lFYi*) that makes it relatively easy to add a basic OAuth 2.0 authentication server to your Laravel application. It's a Laravel convenience bridge to a PHP package called PHP OAuth 2.0 Server (*http://bit.ly/2f1dUyP*).

 However, if you're on Laravel 5.3 or higher, Passport gives you everything provided by that package and much more, with a simpler and more powerful API and interface.

Installing Passport

Passport is a separate package, so your first step is to install it. I'll sum up the steps here, but you can get more in-depth installation instructions in the docs (*http://bit.ly/2fEBjtk*).

First, bring it in with Composer:

```
composer require laravel/passport
```

If you're working with a version of Laravel below 5.5, add `Laravel\Passport\PassportServiceProvider::class` to the `providers` array of *config/app.php*.

Passport imports a series of migrations, so run those with `php artisan migrate` to create the tables necessary for OAuth clients, scopes, and tokens.

Next, run the installer with `php artisan passport:install`. This will create encryption keys for the OAuth server (*storage/oauth-private.key* and *storage/oauth-*

---

public.key) and insert OAuth clients into the database for our personal and password grant type tokens (which we'll cover later).

You'll need to import the `Laravel\Passport\HasApiTokens` trait into your `User` model; this will add OAuth client- and token-related relationships to each `User`, as well as a few token-related helper methods. Next, add a call to `Laravel\Passport` `\Passport::routes()` in the `boot()` method of the `AuthServiceProvider`. This will add the following routes:

- `oauth/authorize`
- `oauth/clients`
- `oauth/clients/client_id`
- `oauth/personal-access-tokens`
- `oauth/personal-access-tokens/token_id`
- `oauth/scopes`
- `oauth/token`
- `oauth/token/refresh`
- `oauth/tokens`
- `oauth/tokens/token_id`

Finally, look for the `api` guard in *config/auth.php*. By default this guard will use the token driver (which we'll cover shortly), but we'll change that to be the `passport` driver instead.

You now have a fully functional OAuth 2.0 server! You can create new clients with `php artisan passport:client`, and you have an API for managing your clients and tokens available under the `/oauth` route prefix.

To protect a route behind your Passport auth system, add the `auth:api` middleware to the route or route group, as shown in Example 13-28.

Example 13-28. Protecting an API route with the Passport auth middleware

```
// routes/api.php
Route::get('/user', function (Request $request) {
    return $request->user();
})->middleware('auth:api');
```

In order to authenticate to these protected routes, your client apps will need to pass a token (we'll cover how to get one shortly) as a `Bearer` token in the `Authorization` header. Example 13-29 shows what this would look like if you were making a request using the Guzzle HTTP library.

Example 13-29. Making a sample API request with a Bearer token

```
$http = new GuzzleHttp\Client;
$response = $http->request('GET', 'http://tweeter.test/api/user', [
    'headers' => [
        'Accept' => 'application/json',
        'Authorization' => 'Bearer ' . $accessToken,
    ],
]);
```

Now, let's take a closer look at how it all works.

Passport's API

Passport exposes an API in your application under the /oauth route prefix. The API provides two primary functions: first, to authorize users with OAuth 2.0 authorization flows (/oauth/authorize and /oauth/token), and second, to allow users to manage their clients and tokens (the rest of the routes).

This is an important distinction, especially if you're unfamiliar with OAuth. Every OAuth server needs to expose the ability for consumers to authenticate with your server; that's the entire point of the service. But Passport *also* exposes an API for managing the state of your OAuth server's clients and tokens. This means you can easily build a frontend to let your users manage their information in your OAuth application, and Passport actually comes with Vue-based manager components that you can either use or use for inspiration.

We'll cover the API routes that allow you to manage clients and tokens, and the Vue components that Passport ships with to make it easy, but first let's dig into the various ways your users can authenticate with your Passport-protected API.

Passport's Available Grant Types

Passport makes it possible for you to authenticate users in four different ways. Two are traditional OAuth 2.0 grants (the password grant and authorization code grant) and two are convenience methods that are unique to Passport (the personal token and synchronizer token).

Password grant

The password grant, while less common than the authorization code grant, is much simpler. If you want users to be able to authenticate directly with your API using their username and password—for example, if you have a mobile app for your company consuming your own API—you can use the password grant.

Creating a Password Grant Client

In order to use the password grant flow, you need a password grant client in your database. This is because every request to an OAuth server needs to be made by a client. Usually, the client identifies which app or site the user is authenticating against—for example, if you used Facebook to log in to a third-party website, that website would be the client.

With the password grant flow, however, there is no client coming along with the request, so you have to make one—and that's the password grant client. One will have been added when you ran php artisan passport:install, but if you ever need to generate a new password grant client for any reason, you can do so as follows:

```
$php artisan passport:client --password

What should we name the password grant client?
  [My Application Password Grant Client]:
 > Client_name

Password grant client created successfully.
Client ID: 3
Client Secret: Pg1EEzt18JAnFoUIM9n38Nqewg1aekB4rvFk2Pma
```

With the password grant type, there is just one step to getting a token: sending the user's credentials to the /oauth/token route, like in Example 13-30.

Example 13-30. Making a request with the password grant type

```php
// Routes/web.php in the *consuming application*
Route::get('tweeter/password-grant-auth', function () {
    $http = new GuzzleHttp\Client;

    // Make call to "Tweeter," our Passport-powered OAuth server
    $response = $http->post('http://tweeter.test/oauth/token', [
        'form_params' => [
            'grant_type' => 'password',
            'client_id' => config('tweeter.id'),
            'client_secret' => config('tweeter.secret'),
            'username' => 'matt@mattstauffer.co',
            'password' => 'my-tweeter-password',
            'scope' => '',
        ],
    ]);

    $thisUsersTokens = json_decode((string) $response->getBody(), true);
```

```
    // Do stuff with the tokens
});
```

This route will return an `access_token` and a `refresh_token`. You can now save those tokens to use to authenticate with the API (access token) and to request more tokens later (refresh token).

Note that the ID and secret we'd use for the password grant type would be those in the `oauth_clients` database table of our Passport app in the row whose name matches that of our Passport grant client. You'll also see entries in this table for the two clients that are generated by default when you run `passport:install`: "Laravel Personal Access Client" and "Laravel Password Grant Client."

Authorization code grant

The most common OAuth 2.0 auth workflow is also the most complex one Passport supports. Let's imagine we're developing an application that's like Twitter but for sound clips; we'll call it Tweeter. And we'll imagine another website, a social network for science fiction fans, called SpaceBook. SpaceBook's developer wants to let people embed their Tweeter data into their SpaceBook newsfeeds. We're going to install Passport in our Tweeter app so that other apps—SpaceBook, for example—can allow their users to authenticate with their Tweeter information.

In the authorization code grant type, each consuming website—SpaceBook, in this example—needs to create a client in our Passport-enabled app. In most scenarios, the other sites' admins will have user accounts at Tweeter, and we'll build tools for them to create clients there. But for starters, we can just manually create a client for the SpaceBook admins:

```
$php artisan passport:client
Which user ID should the client be assigned to?:
 > 1 ❶

What should we name the client?:
 > SpaceBook
Where should we redirect the request after authorization?
   [http://tweeter.test/auth/callback]:
 > http://spacebook.test/tweeter/callback

New client created successfully.
Client ID: 4
Client secret: 5rzqKpeCjIgz3MXpi3tjQ37HBnLLykrgWgmc18uH
```

❶   Every client needs to be assigned to a user in your app. Imagine user #1 is writing SpaceBook; they'll be the "owner" of this client we're creating.

Now we have the ID and secret for the SpaceBook client. At this point, SpaceBook can use this ID and secret to build tooling allowing an individual SpaceBook user (who is also a Tweeter user) to get an auth token from Tweeter for use when Space-Book wants to make API calls to Tweeter on that user's behalf. Example 13-31 illustrates this. (This and the following examples assume SpaceBook is a Laravel app, too; they also assume the Spacebook's developer created a file at *config/tweeter.php* that returns the ID and secret we just created.)

Example 13-31. A consumer app redirecting a user to our OAuth server

```
// In SpaceBook's routes/web.php:
Route::get('tweeter/redirect', function () {
    $query = http_build_query([
        'client_id' => config('tweeter.id'),
        'redirect_uri' => url('tweeter/callback'),
        'response_type' => 'code',
        'scope' => '',
    ]);

    // Builds a string like:
    // client_id={$client_id}&redirect_uri={$redirect_uri}&response_type=code

    return redirect('http://tweeter.test/oauth/authorize?' . $query);
});
```

When users hit that route in SpaceBook, they'll now be redirected to the /oauth/authorize Passport route in our Tweeter app. At this point they'll see a confirmation page—you can use the default Passport confirmation page by running this command:

```
php artisan vendor:publish --tag=passport-views
```

This will publish the view to *resources/views/vendor/passport/authorize.blade.php*, and your users will see the page shown in Figure 13-1.

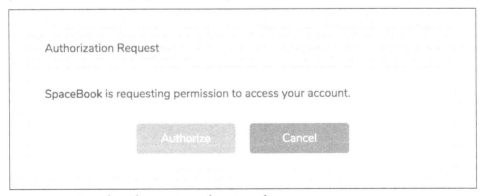

Figure 13-1. OAuth authorization code approval page

Once a user chooses to accept or reject the authorization, Passport will redirect that user back to the provided redirect_uri. In Example 13-31 we set a redirect_uri of url('tweeter/callback'), so the user will be redirected back to *http://space-book.test/tweeter/callback*.

An approval request will contain a code that our consumer app's callback route can now use to get a token back from our Passport-enabled app, Tweeter. A rejection request will contain an error. SpaceBook's callback route might look something like Example 13-32.

Example 13-32. The authorization callback route in the sample consuming app

```
// In SpaceBook's routes/web.php:
Route::get('tweeter/callback', function (Request $request) {
    if ($request->has('error')) {
        // Handle error condition
    }

    $http = new GuzzleHttp\Client;

    $response = $http->post('http://tweeter.test/oauth/token', [
        'form_params' => [
            'grant_type' => 'authorization_code',
            'client_id' => config('tweeter.id'),
            'client_secret' => config('tweeter.secret'),
            'redirect_uri' => url('tweeter/callback'),
            'code' => $request->code,
        ],
    ]);

    $thisUsersTokens = json_decode((string) $response->getBody(), true);
    // Do stuff with the tokens
});
```

What the SpaceBook developer has done here is build a Guzzle HTTP request to the /oauth/token Passport route on Tweeter. They then send a POST request containing the authorization code they received when the user approved access, and Tweeter will return a JSON response containing a few keys:

access_token
    the token SpaceBook will want to save for this user. This token is what the user will use to authenticate in future requests to Tweeter (using the Authorization header).

refresh_token
    a token SpaceBook will need *if* you decide to set your tokens to expire. By default, Passport's access tokens last for one year.

expires_in
    the number of seconds until an access_token expires (needs to be refreshed).

token_type

the type of token you're getting back, which will be `Bearer`; this means you pass a header with all future requests with the name of `Authorization` and the value of `Bearer` *YOURTOKENHERE*.

Using Refresh Tokens

If you'd like to force users to reauthenticate more often, you need to set a shorter refresh time on the tokens, and then you can use the `refresh_token` to request a new `access_token` when needed—most likely whenever you receive a 401 (Unauthorized) response from an API call.

Example 13-33 illustrates how to set a shorter refresh time.

Example 13-33. Defining token refresh times

```
// AuthServiceProvider's boot() method
public function boot()
{
    $this->registerPolicies();

    Passport::routes();

    // How long a token lasts before needing refreshing
    Passport::tokensExpireIn(
        now()->addDays(15)
    );

    // How long a refresh token will last before re-auth
    Passport::refreshTokensExpireIn(
        now()->addDays(30)
    );
}
```

To request a new token using a refresh token, the consuming application will need to have first saved the `refresh_token` from the initial auth response in Example 13-32. Once it's time to refresh, it will make a call similar to that example, but modified slightly as shown in Example 13-34.

Example 13-34. Requesting a new token using a refresh token

```
// In SpaceBook's routes/web.php:
Route::get('tweeter/request-refresh', function (Request $request) {
    $http = new GuzzleHttp\Client;

    $params = [
        'grant_type' => 'refresh_token',
        'client_id' => config('tweeter.id'),
        'client_secret' => config('tweeter.secret'),
        'redirect_uri' => url('tweeter/callback'),
```

```
            'refresh_token' => $theTokenYouSavedEarlier,
            'scope' => '',
    ];

    $response = $http->post(
        'http://tweeter.test/oauth/token',
        ['form_params' => $params]
    );

    $thisUsersTokens = json_decode(
        (string) $response->getBody(),
        true
    );

     // Do stuff with the tokens
});
```

In the response, the consuming app will receive a fresh set of tokens to save to its user.

You now have all the tools you need to perform basic authorization code flows. We'll cover how to build an admin panel for your clients and tokens later, but first, let's take a quick look at the other grant types.

Personal access tokens

The authorization code grant is great for your users' apps and the password code grant is great for your own apps, but what if your users want to create tokens for themselves to test out your API or to use when they're developing their apps? That's what personal tokens are for.

Creating a Personal Access Client

In order to create personal tokens, you need a personal access client in your database. Running `php artisan passport:install` will have added one already, but if you ever need to generate a new personal access client for any reason, you can run `php artisan passport:client --personal`:

```
$php artisan passport:client --personal

What should we name the personal access client?
   [My Application Personal Access Client]:
 > My Application Personal Access Client

Personal access client created successfully.
```

Personal access tokens are not quite a "grant" type; there's no OAuth-prescribed flow here. Rather, they're a convenience method that Passport adds to make it easy to have a single client registered in your system that exists solely to facilitate the creation of convenience tokens for your users who are developers.

For example, maybe you have a user who's developing a competitor to SpaceBook named RaceBook (it's for marathon runners), and they want to toy around with the Tweeter API a bit to figure out how it works *before* starting to code. Does this developer have the facility to create tokens using the authorization code flow? Not yet—they haven't even written any code yet! That's what personal access tokens are for.

You can create personal access tokens through the JSON API, which we'll cover shortly, but you can also create one for your user directly in code:

```
// Creating a token without scopes
$token = $user->createToken('Token Name')->accessToken;

// Creating a token with scopes
$token = $user->createToken('My Token', ['place-orders'])->accessToken;
```

Your users can use these tokens just as if they were tokens created with the authorization code grant flow. We'll talk more about scopes in "Passport Scopes" on page 371.

Tokens from Laravel session authentication (synchronizer tokens)

There's one final way for your users to get tokens to access your API, and it's another convenience method that Passport adds but normal OAuth servers don't provide. This method is for when your users are already authenticated because they've logged in to your Laravel app like normal, and you want your app's JavaScript to be able to access the API. It'd be a pain to have to reauthenticate the users with the authorization code or password grant flow, so Laravel provides a helper for that.

If you add the `Laravel\Passport\Http\Middleware\CreateFreshApiToken` middleware to your web middleware group (in *app/Http/Kernel.php*), every response Laravel sends to your authenticated users will have a cookie named `laravel_token` attached to it. This cookie is a JSON Web Token (JWT) that contains encoded information about the CSRF token. Now, if you send the normal CSRF token with your JavaScript requests in the `X-CSRF-TOKEN` header and also send the `X-Requested-With` header with any API requests you make, the API will compare your CSRF token with this cookie and this will authenticate your users to the API just like any other token.

JSON Web Tokens (JWT)

JWT is a relatively new format for "representing claims securely between two parties" that has gained prominence over the last few years. A JSON Web Token is a JSON object containing all of the information necessary to determine a user's authentication

---

state and access permissions. This JSON object is digitally signed using a keyed-hash message authentication code (HMAC) or RSA, which is what makes it trustworthy.

The token is usually encoded and then delivered via URL or POST request, or in a header. Once a user authenticates with the system somehow, every HTTP request after that will contain the token, describing the user's identity and authorization.

JSON Web Tokens consist of three Base64-encoded strings separated by dots (.); something like *xxx.yyy.zzz*. The first section is a Base64-encoded JSON object containing information about which hashing algorithm is being used; the second section is a series of "claims" about the user's authorization and identity; and the third is the signature, or the first and second sections encrypted and signed using the algorithm specified in the first section.

To learn more about JWT, check out JWT.IO (*https://jwt.io/*) or the jwt-auth Laravel package (*http://bit.ly/2U6Uxf4*).

The default JavaScript bootstrap setup that Laravel comes bundled with sets up this header for you, but if you're using a different framework, you'll need to set it up manually. Example 13-35 shows how to do it with jQuery.

Example 13-35. Setting jQuery to pass Laravel's CSRF tokens and the X-Requested-With header with all Ajax requests

```
$.ajaxSetup({
    headers: {
        'X-CSRF-TOKEN': "{{ csrf_token() }}",
        'X-Requested-With': 'XMLHttpRequest'
    }
});
```

If you add the CreateFreshApiToken middleware to your web middleware group and pass those headers with every JavaScript request, your JavaScript requests will be able to hit your Passport-protected API routes without worrying about any of the complexity of the authorization code or password grants.

Managing Clients and Tokens with the Passport API and Vue Components

Now that we've covered how to manually create clients and tokens and how to authorize as a consumer, let's take a look at the aspects of the Passport API that make it possible to build user interface elements allowing your users to manage their clients and tokens.

The routes

The easiest way to dig into the API routes is by looking at how the sample provided Vue components work and which routes they rely on, so I'll just give a brief overview:

```
/oauth/clients (GET, POST)
/oauth/clients/{id} (DELETE, PUT)
/oauth/personal-access-tokens (GET, POST)
/oauth/personal-access-tokens/{id} (DELETE)
/oauth/scopes (GET)
/oauth/tokens (GET)
/oauth/tokens/{id} (DELETE)
```

As you can see, we have a few entities here (clients, personal access tokens, scopes, and tokens). We can list all of them; we can create some (you can't create scopes, since they're defined in code, and you can't create tokens, because they're created in the authorization flow); and we can delete and update (PUT) some.

The Vue components

Passport comes with a set of Vue components out of the box that make it easy to allow your users to administer their clients (those they've created), authorized clients (those they've allowed access to their account), and personal access tokens (for their own testing purposes).

To publish these components into your application, run this command:

```
php artisan vendor:publish --tag=passport-components
```

You'll now have three new Vue components in *resources/js/components/passport*. To add them to your Vue bootstrap so they're accessible in your templates, register them in your *resources/js/app.js* file, as shown in Example 13-36.

Example 13-36. Importing Passport's Vue components into app.js

```
require('./bootstrap');

Vue.component(
    'passport-clients',
    require('./components/passport/Clients.vue')
);

Vue.component(
    'passport-authorized-clients',
    require('./components/passport/AuthorizedClients.vue')
);

Vue.component(
    'passport-personal-access-tokens',
    require('./components/passport/PersonalAccessTokens.vue')
);
```

```
const app = new Vue({
    el: '#app'
});
```

You now get three components that you can use anywhere in your application:

```
<passport-clients></passport-clients>
<passport-authorized-clients></passport-authorized-clients>
<passport-personal-access-tokens></passport-personal-access-tokens>
```

`<passport-clients>` shows your users all of the clients they've created. This means SpaceBook's creator will see the SpaceBook client listed here when they log in to Tweeter.

`<passport-authorized-clients>` shows your users all of the clients they've authorized to have access to their accounts. This means any users of both SpaceBook and Tweeter who have given SpaceBook access to their Tweeter account will see Space-Book listed here.

`<passport-personal-access-tokens>` shows your users any personal access tokens they've created. For example, the creator of RaceBook, SpaceBook's competitor, will see the personal access token they've been using to test out the Tweeter API.

If you are on a fresh install of Laravel and want to test these out, there are a few steps to take to get it working:

1. Follow the instructions given earlier in this chapter to get Passport installed.

2. In your terminal, run the following commands:

```
php artisan vendor:publish --tag=passport-components
npm install
npm run dev
php artisan make:auth
```

3. Open *resources/views/home.blade.php* and add the Vue component references (e.g., `<passport-clients></passport-clients>`) just below the `<div class="card-body">`.

If you'd like, you can just use those components as they are. But you can also use them as reference points to understand how to use the API and create your own frontend components in whatever format you'd like.

Compiling Passport's Frontend Components Using Laravel Elixer

A few of these commands and directions will look different if you're using Laravel Elixir. Check the Passport (*http://bit.ly/2CFjF2y*) and Elixir (*http://bit.ly/2upTDf2*) docs to learn more.

Passport Scopes

If you're familiar with OAuth, you've probably noticed we haven't talked much about scopes yet. Everything we've covered so far can be customized by scope—but before we get into that, let's first quickly cover what scopes are.

In OAuth, scopes are defined sets of privileges that are something other than "can do everything." If you've ever gotten a GitHub API token before, for example, you might've noticed that some apps want access just to your name and email address, some want access to all of your repos, and some want access to your gists. Each of these is a "scope," which allows both the user and the consumer app to define what access the consumer app needs to perform its job.

As shown in Example 13-37, you can define the scopes for your application in the boot() method of your AuthServiceProvider.

Example 13-37. Defining Passport scopes

```
// AuthServiceProvider
use Laravel\Passport\Passport;
...
    public function boot()
    {
        ...

        Passport::tokensCan([
            'list-clips' => 'List sound clips',
            'add-delete-clips' => 'Add new and delete old sound clips',
            'admin-account' => 'Administer account details',
        ]);
    }
```

Once you have your scopes defined, the consumer app can define which scopes it's asking for access to. Just add a space-separated list of tokens in the scope field in the initial redirect, as shown in Example 13-38.

Example 13-38. Requesting authorization to access specific scopes

```
// In SpaceBook's routes/web.php:
Route::get('tweeter/redirect', function () {
    $query = http_build_query([
        'client_id' => config('tweeter.id'),
        'redirect_uri' => url('tweeter/callback'),
        'response_type' => 'code',
        'scope' => 'list-clips add-delete-clips',
    ]);
```

```
        return redirect('http://tweeter.test/oauth/authorize?' . $query);
});
```

When the user tries to authorize with this app, it'll present the list of requested scopes. This way, the user will know whether "SpaceBook is requesting to see your email address" or "SpaceBook is requesting access to post as you and delete your posts and message your friends."

You can check for scope using middleware or on the User instance. Example 13-39 shows how to check on the User.

Example 13-39. Checking whether the token a user authenticated with can perform a given action

```
Route::get('/events', function () {
    if (auth()->user()->tokenCan('add-delete-clips')) {
        //
    }
});
```

There are two middleware you can use for this too, scope and scopes. To use these in your app, add them to $routeMiddleware in your *app/Http/Kernel.php* file:

```
'scopes' => \Laravel\Passport\Http\Middleware\CheckScopes::class,
'scope' => \Laravel\Passport\Http\Middleware\CheckForAnyScope::class,
```

You can now use the middleware as illustrated in Example 13-40. scopes requires *all* of the defined scopes to be on the user's token in order for the user to access the route, while scope requires *at least one* of the defined scopes to be on the user's token.

Example 13-40. Using middleware to restrict access based on token scopes

```
// routes/api.php
Route::get('clips', function () {
    // Access token has both the "list-clips" and "add-delete-clips" scopes
})->middleware('scopes:list-clips,add-delete-clips');

// or

Route::get('clips', function () {
    // Access token has at least one of the listed scopes
})->middleware('scope:list-clips,add-delete-clips')
```

If you haven't defined any scopes, the app will just work as if they don't exist. The moment you use scopes, however, your consumer apps will have to explicitly define which scopes they're requesting access with. The one exception to this rule is that if you're using the password grant type, your consumer app can request the * scope, which gives the token access to everything.

Deploying Passport

The first time you deploy your Passport-powered app, the Passport API won't function until you generate keys for the app. This can be accomplished by running `php artisan passport:keys` on your production server, which will generate the encryption keys Passport uses to generate tokens.

API Token Authentication

 Laravel offers a simple API token authentication mechanism. It's not much different from a username and password: there's a single token assigned to each user that clients can pass along with a request to authenticate that request for that user.

This API token mechanism is not nearly as secure as OAuth 2.0, so make sure you know it's the right fit for your application before deciding to use it. Because there's just a single token, it's almost like a password—if someone gets that token, they have access to your whole system. It's more secure, though, because you can force the tokens to be less guessable, and you can wipe and reset tokens at the slightest hint of a breach, which you can't do with passwords.

So, token API authentication might not be the best fit for your app; but if it is, it couldn't be much simpler to implement.

First, add a 60-character unique `api_token` column to your `users` table:

```
$table->string('api_token', 60)->unique();
```

Next, update whatever method creates your new users and ensure it sets a value for this field for each new user. Laravel has a helper for generating random strings, so if you want to use that, just set the field to `str_random(60)` for each. You'll also need to do this for preexisting users if you're adding this to a live application.

To wrap any routes with this authentication method, use the `auth:api` route middleware, as in Example 13-41.

Example 13-41. Applying the API auth middleware to a route group

```
Route::prefix('api')->middleware('auth:api')->group(function () {
    //
});
```

Note that, since you're using an authentication guard other than the standard guard, you'll need to specify that guard any time you use any `auth()` methods:

```
$user = auth()->guard('api')->user();
```

Customizing 404 Responses

 Laravel offers customizable error message pages for normal HTML views, but you can also customize the default 404 fallback response for calls with a JSON content type. To do so, add a `Route::fallback()` call to your API, as shown in Example 13-42.

Example 13-42. Defining a fallback route

```
// routes/api.php
Route::fallback(function () {
    return response()->json(['message' => 'Route Not Found'], 404);
})->name('api.fallback.404');
```

Triggering the Fallback Route

 If you want to customize which route is returned when Laravel catches "not found" exceptions, you can update the exception handler using the `respondWithRoute()` method, as illustrated in Example 13-43.

Example 13-43. Calling the fallback route when "not found" exceptions are caught

```
// App\Exceptions\Handler
public function render($request, Exception $exception)
{
    if ($exception instanceof ModelNotFoundException && $request->isJson()) {
        return Route::respondWithRoute('api.fallback.404');
    }

    return parent::render($request, $exception);
}
```

Testing

Fortunately, testing APIs is actually simpler than testing almost anything else in Laravel.

We cover this in more depth in Chapter 12, but there are a series of methods for making assertions against JSON. Combine that capability with the simplicity of full-stack application tests and you can put together your API tests quickly and easily. Take a look at the common API testing pattern in Example 13-44.

Example 13-44. A common API testing pattern

```
...
class DogsApiTest extends TestCase
```

```
{
    use WithoutMiddleware, RefreshDatabase;

    public function test_it_gets_all_dogs()
    {
        $dog1 = factory(Dog::class)->create();
        $dog2 = factory(Dog::class)->create();

        $response = $this->getJson('api/dogs');

        $response->assertJsonFragment(['name' => $dog1->name]);
        $response->assertJsonFragment(['name' => $dog2->name]);
    }
}
```

Note that we're using `WithoutMiddleware` to avoid worrying about authentication. You'll want to test that separately, if at all (for more on authentication, see Chapter 9).

In this test we insert two `Dogs` into the database, then visit the API route for listing all `Dogs` and make sure both are present in the output.

You can cover all of your API routes simply and easily here, including modifying actions like `POST` and `PATCH`.

Testing Passport

You can use the `actingAs()` method on the `Passport` facade to test your scopes. Take a look at Example 13-45 to see a common pattern for testing scopes in Passport.

Example 13-45. Testing scoped access

```
public function test_it_lists_all_clips_for_those_with_list_clips_scope()
{
    Passport::actingAs(
        factory(User::class)->create(),
        ['list-clips']
    );

    $response = $this->getJson('api/clips');
    $response->assertStatus(200);
}
```

TL;DR

Laravel is geared toward building APIs and makes it simple to work with JSON and RESTful APIs. There are some conventions, like for pagination, but much of the definition of exactly how your API will be sorted, or authenticated, or whatever else is up to you.

Laravel provides tools for authentication and testing, easy manipulation and reading of headers, and working with JSON, even automatically encoding all Eloquent results to JSON if they're returned directly from a route.

Laravel Passport is a separate package that makes it simple to create and manage an OAuth server in your Laravel apps.

## CHAPTER 14

Storage and Retrieval

We looked at how to store data in relational databases in Chapter 5, but there's a lot more that can be stored, both locally and remotely. In this chapter we'll cover filesystem and in-memory storage, file uploads and manipulation, nonrelational data stores, sessions, the cache, logging, cookies, and full-text search.

Local and Cloud File Managers

Laravel provides a series of file manipulation tools through the `Storage` facade, and a few helper functions.

Laravel's filesystem access tools can connect to the local filesystem as well as S3, Rackspace, and FTP. The S3 and Rackspace file drivers are provided by Flysystem (*http://bit.ly/2upKDXr*), and it's simple to add additional Flysystem providers to your Laravel app—for example, Dropbox or WebDAV.

Configuring File Access

The definitions for Laravel's file manager live in *config/filesystems.php*. Each connection is called a "disk," and Example 14-1 lists the disks that are available out of the box.

Example 14-1. Default available storage disks

```
...
'disks' => [
    'local' => [
        'driver' => 'local',
        'root' => storage_path('app'),
    ],
```

```
'public' => [
    'driver' => 'local',
    'root' => storage_path('app/public'),
    'url' => env('APP_URL').'/storage',
    'visibility' => 'public',
],

's3' => [
    'driver' => 's3',
    'key' => env('AWS_ACCESS_KEY_ID'),
    'secret' => env('AWS_SECRET_ACCESS_KEY'),
    'region' => env('AWS_DEFAULT_REGION'),
    'bucket' => env('AWS_BUCKET'),
    'url' => env('AWS_URL'),
],
],
```

The storage_path() Helper

The `storage_path()` helper used in Example 14-1 links to Laravel's configured storage directory, *storage/*. Anything you pass to it is added to the end of the directory name, so `storage_path('public')` will return the string `storage/public`.

The `local` disk connects to your local storage system and presumes it will be interacting with the *app* directory of the storage path, which is *storage/app*.

The `public` disk is also a local disk (although you can change it if you'd like), which is intended for use with any files you intend to be served by your application. It defaults to the *storage/app/public* directory, and if you want to use this directory to serve files to the public, you'll need to add a symbolic link (symlink) to somewhere within the *public/* directory. Thankfully, there's an Artisan command that maps *public/storage* to serve the files from *storage/app/public*:

```
php artisan storage:link
```

The `s3` disk shows how Laravel connects to cloud-based file storage systems. If you've ever connected to S3 or any other cloud storage provider, this will be familiar; pass it your key and secret and some information defining the "folder" you're working with, which in S3 is the region and the bucket.

Using the Storage Facade

In *config/filesystem.php* you can set the default disk, which is what will be used any time you call the `Storage` facade without specifying a disk. To specify a disk, call `disk('diskname')` on the facade:

```
Storage::disk('s3')->get('file.jpg');
```

The filesystems each provide the following methods:

get('*file.jpg*')
> Retrieves the file at *file.jpg*

put('*file.jpg*', *$contentsOrStream*)
> Puts the given file contents to *file.jpg*

putFile('*myDir*', *$file*)
> Puts the contents of a provided file (in the form of an instance of either Illuminate\Http\File or Illuminate\Http\UploadedFile) to the *myDir* directory, but with Laravel managing the entire streaming process and naming the file

exists('*file.jpg*')
> Returns a Boolean indicating whether *file.jpg* exists

getVisibility('*myPath*')
> Gets the visibility for the given path ("public" or "private")

setVisibility('*myPath*')
> Sets the visibility for the given path ("public" or "private")

copy('*file.jpg*', '*newfile.jpg*')
> Copies *file.jpg* to *newfile.jpg*

move('*file.jpg*', '*newfile.jpg*')
> Moves *file.jpg* to *newfile.jpg*

prepend('*my.log*', '*log text*')
> Adds content at the beginning of *my.log*

append('*my.log*', '*log text*')
> Adds content to the end of *my.log*

delete('*file.jpg*')
> Deletes *file.jpg*

size('*file.jpg*')
> Returns the size in bytes of *file.jpg*

lastModified('*file.jpg*')
> Returns the Unix timestamp when *file.jpg* was last modified

files('*myDir*')
> Returns an array of filenames in the directory *myDir*

allFiles('*myDir*')
> Returns an array of filenames in the directory *myDir* and all subdirectories

```
directories('myDir')
```
Returns an array of directory names in the directory *myDir*

```
allDirectories('myDir')
```
Returns an array of directory names in the directory *myDir* and all subdirectories

```
makeDirectory('myDir')
```
Creates a new directory

```
deleteDirectory('myDir')
```
Deletes *myDir*

Injecting an Instance

If you'd prefer injecting an instance instead of using the `File` facade, typehint or inject `Illuminate\Filesystem\Filesystem` and you'll have all the same methods available to you.

Adding Additional Flysystem Providers

If you want to add an additional Flysystem provider, you'll need to "extend" Laravel's native storage system. In a service provider somewhere—it could be the `boot()` method of `AppServiceProvider`, but it'd be more appropriate to create a unique service provider for each new binding—use the `Storage` facade to add new storage systems, as seen in Example 14-2.

Example 14-2. Adding additional Flysystem providers

```
// Some service provider
public function boot()
{
    Storage::extend('dropbox', function ($app, $config) {
        $client = new DropboxClient(
            $config['accessToken'], $config['clientIdentifier']
        );

        return new Filesystem(new DropboxAdapter($client));
    });
}
```

Basic File Uploads and Manipulation

One of the more common usages for the `Storage` facade is accepting file uploads from your application's users. Let's look at a common workflow for that, in Example 14-3.

Example 14-3. Common user upload workflow

```
...
class DogsController
{
    public function updatePicture(Request $request, Dog $dog)
    {
        Storage::put(
            "dogs/{$dog->id}",
            file_get_contents($request->file('picture')->getRealPath())
        );
    }
}
```

We put() to a file named *dogs/id*, and we grab our contents from the uploaded file. Every uploaded file is a descendant of the SplFileInfo class, which provides a getRealPath() method that returns the path to the file's location. So, we get the temporary upload path for the user's uploaded file, read it with file_get_contents(), and pass it into Storage::put().

Since we have this file available to us here, we can do anything we want to the file before we store it—use an image manipulation package to resize it if it's an image, validate it and reject it if it doesn't meet our criteria, or whatever else we like.

If we wanted to upload this same file to S3 and we had our credentials stored in *config/filesystems.php*, we could just adjust Example 14-3 to call Storage::disk('s3')->put(); we'll now be uploading to S3. Take a look at Example 14-4 to see a more complex upload example.

Example 14-4. A more complex example of file uploads, using Intervention

```
...
class DogsController
{
    public function updatePicture(Request $request, Dog $dog)
    {
        $original = $request->file('picture');

        // Resize image to max width 150
        $image = Image::make($original)->resize(150, null, function ($constraint) {
            $constraint->aspectRatio();
        })->encode('jpg', 75);

        Storage::put(
            "dogs/thumbs/{$dog->id}",
            $image->getEncoded()
        );
    }
}
```

I used an image library called Intervention (*http://image.intervention.io*) in Example 14-4 just as an example; you can use any library you want. The important point is that you have the freedom to manipulate the files however you want before you store them.

Using store() and storeAs() on the Uploaded File

Laravel 5.3 introduced the ability to store an uploaded file using the file itself. Learn more in Example 7-12.

Simple File Downloads

Just like `Storage` makes it easy to accept uploads from users, it also simplifies the task of returning files to them. Take a look at Example 14-5 for the simplest example.

Example 14-5. Simple file downloads

```
public function downloadMyFile()
{
    return Storage::download('my-file.pdf');
}
```

Sessions

Session storage is the primary tool we use in web applications to store state between page requests. Laravel's session manager supports session drivers using files, cookies, a database, Memcached or Redis, or in-memory arrays (which expire after the page request and are only good for tests).

You can configure all of your session settings and drivers in *config/session.php*. You can choose whether or not to encrypt your session data, select which driver to use (`file` is the default), and specify more connection-specific details like the length of session storage and which files or database tables to use. Take a look at the session docs (*http://bit.ly/2HFXsW7*) to learn about specific dependencies and settings you need to prepare for whichever driver you choose to use.

The general API of the session tools allows you to save and retrieve data based on individual keys: `session()->put('user_id')` and `session()->get('user_id')`, for example. Make sure to avoid saving anything to a `flash` session key, since Laravel uses that internally for flash (only available for the next page request) session storage.

Accessing the Session

The most common way to access the session is using the `Session` facade:

```
session()->get('user_id');
```

But you can also use the `session()` method on any given Illuminate `Request` object, as in Example 14-6.

Example 14-6. Using the session() method on a Request object

```
Route::get('dashboard', function (Request $request) {
    $request->session()->get('user_id');
});
```

Or you can inject an instance of `Illuminate\Session\Store`, as in Example 14-7.

Example 14-7. Injecting the backing class for sessions

```
Route::get('dashboard', function (Illuminate\Session\Store $session) {
    return $session->get('user_id');
});
```

Finally, you can use the global `session()` helper. Use it with no parameters to get a session instance, with a single string parameter to "get" from the session, or with an array to "put" to the session, as demonstrated in Example 14-8.

Example 14-8. Using the global session() helper

```
// Get
$value = session()->get('key');
$value = session('key');
// Put
session()->put('key', 'value');
session(['key', 'value']);
```

If you're new to Laravel and not sure which to use, I'd recommend using the global helper.

Methods Available on Session Instances

The two most common methods are `get()` and `put()`, but let's take a look at each of the available methods and their parameters:

`session()->get($key, $fallbackValue)`

> `get()` pulls the value of the provided key out of the session. If there is no value attached to that key, it will return the fallback value instead (and if you don't pro-

vide a fallback, it will return null). The fallback value can be a string or a closure, as you can see in the following examples:

```
$points = session()->get('points');

$points = session()->get('points', 0);

$points = session()->get('points', function () {
    return (new PointGetterService)->getPoints();
});
```

session()->put($key, $value)

put() stores the provided value in the session at the provided key:

```
session()->put('points', 45);

$points = session()->get('points');
```

session()->push($key, $value)

If any of your session values are arrays, you can use push() to add a value to the array:

```
session()->put('friends', ['Saúl', 'Quang', 'Mechteld']);

session()->push('friends', 'Javier');
```

session()->has($key)

has() checks whether there's a value set at the provided key:

```
if (session()->has('points')) {
    // Do something
}
```

You can also pass an array of keys, and it only returns true if all of the keys exist.

session()->has() and Null Values

If a session value is set but the value is null, session()->has() will return false.

session()->exists($key)

exists() checks whether there's a value set at the provided key, like has(), but unlike has(), it will return true even if the set value is null:

```
if (session()->exists('points')) {
    // returns true even if 'points' is set to null
}
```

```
session()->all()
```
all() returns an array of everything that's in the session, including those values set by the framework. You'll likely see values under keys like _token (CSRF tokens), _previous (previous page, for back() redirects), and flash (for flash storage).

```
session()->forget($key) and session()->flush()
```
forget() removes a previously set session value. flush() removes every session value, even those set by the framework:

```
session()->put('a', 'awesome');
session()->put('b', 'bodacious');

session()->forget('a');
// a is no longer set; b is still set
session()->flush();
// Session is now empty
```

```
session()->pull($key, $fallbackValue)
```
pull() is the same as get(), except that it deletes the value from the session after pulling it.

```
session()->regenerate()
```
It's not common, but if you need to regenerate your session ID, regenerate() is there for you.

Flash Session Storage

There are three more methods we haven't covered yet, and they all have to do with something called "flash" session storage.

One very common pattern for session storage is to set a value that you only want available for the next page load. For example, you might want to store a message like "Updated post successfully." You could manually get that message and then wipe it on the next page load, but if you use this pattern a lot it can get wasteful. Enter flash session storage: keys that are expected to only last for a single page request.

Laravel handles the work for you, and all you need to do is use flash() instead of put(). These are the useful methods here:

```
session()->flash($key, $value)
```
flash() sets the session key to the provided value for just the next page request.

```
session()->reflash() and session()->keep($key)
```
If you need the previous page's flash session data to stick around for one more request, you can use reflash() to restore all of it for the next request or

keep($key) to just restore a single flash value for the next request. keep() can also accept an array of keys to reflash.

Cache

Caches are structured very similarly to sessions. You provide a key and Laravel stores it for you. The biggest difference is that the data in a cache is cached per application, and the data in a session is cached per user. That means caches are more commonly used for storing results from database queries, API calls, or other slow queries that can stand to get a little bit "stale."

The cache configuration settings are available at *config/cache.php*. Just like with a session, you can set the specific configuration details for any of your drivers, and also choose which will be your default. Laravel uses the file cache driver by default, but you can also use Memcached or Redis, APC, or a database, or write your own cache driver. Take a look at the cache docs (*http://bit.ly/2Yk60qV*) to learn about specific dependencies and settings you need to prepare for whichever driver you choose to use.

Example 14-9. Minutes or seconds for cache length

In versions of Laravel prior to 5.8, if you passed an integer to any cache methods to define the cache duration, it'd represent the number of minutes to cache the item. In 5.8+, as you'll learn in the following section, it represents seconds.

Accessing the Cache

Just like with sessions, there are a few different ways to access a cache. You can use the facade:

```
$users = Cache::get('users');
```

Or you can get an instance from the container, as in Example 14-10.

Example 14-10. Injecting an instance of the cache

```
Route::get('users', function (Illuminate\Contracts\Cache\Repository $cache) {
    return $cache->get('users');
});
```

You can also use the global cache() helper (introduced in Laravel 5.3), as in Example 14-11.

Example 14-11. Using the global cache() helper

```
// Get from cache
$users = cache('key', 'default value');
$users = cache()->get('key', 'default value');
// Put for $seconds duration
$users = cache(['key' => 'value'], $seconds);
$users = cache()->put('key', 'value', $seconds);
```

If you're new to Laravel and not sure which to use, I'd recommend using the global
helper.

Methods Available on Cache Instances

Let's take a look at the methods you can call on a Cache instance:

cache()->get(*$key*, *$fallbackValue*) *and*
cache()->pull(*$key*, *$fallbackValue*)
>   get() makes it easy to retrieve the value for any given key. pull() is the same as
>   get() except it removes the cached value after retrieving it.

cache()->put(*$key*, *$value*, *$secondsOrExpiration*)
>   put() sets the value of the specified key for a given number of seconds. If you'd
>   prefer setting an expiration date/time instead of a number of seconds, you can
>   pass a Carbon object as the third parameter:

```
    cache()->put('key', 'value', now()->addDay());
```

cache()->add(*$key*, *$value*)
>   add() is similar to put(), except if the value already exists, it won't set it. Also,
>   the method returns a Boolean indicating whether or not the value was actually
>   added:

```
    $someDate = now();
    cache()->add('someDate', $someDate); // returns true
    $someOtherDate = now()->addHour();
    cache()->add('someDate', $someOtherDate); // returns false
```

cache()->forever(*$key*, *$value*)
>   forever() saves a value to the cache for a specific key; it's the same as put(),
>   except the values will never expire (until they're removed with forget()).

cache()->has(*$key*)
>   has() returns a Boolean indicating whether or not there's a value at the provided
>   key.

```
cache()->remember($key, $seconds, $closure) and
cache()->rememberForever($key, $closure)
```
> remember() provides a single method to handle a very common flow: look up whether a value exists in the cache for a certain key, and if it doesn't, get that value somehow, save it to the cache, and return it.
>
> remember() lets you provide a key to look up, the number of seconds it should be saved for, and a closure to define how to look it up, in case the key has no value set. rememberForever() is the same, except it doesn't need you to set the number of seconds it should expire after. Take a look at the following example to see a common user scenario for remember():
>
> ```
> // Either returns the value cached at "users" or gets "User::all()",
> // caches it at "users", and returns it
> $users = cache()->remember('users', 7200, function () {
>     return User::all();
> });
> ```

```
cache()->increment($key, $amount) and cache()->decrement($key, $amount)
```
> increment() and decrement() allow you to increment and decrement integer values in the cache. If there is no value at the given key, it'll be treated as if it were 0, and if you pass a second parameter to increment or decrement, it'll increment or decrement by that amount instead of by 1.

```
cache()->forget($key) and cache()->flush()
```
> forget() works just like Session's forget() method: pass it a key and it'll wipe that key's value. flush() wipes the entire cache.

Cookies

You might expect cookies to work the same as sessions and the cache. A facade and a global helper are available for these too, and our mental models of all three are similar: you can get or set their values in the same way.

But because cookies are inherently attached to the requests and responses, you'll need to interact with cookies differently. Let's look really briefly at what makes cookies different.

Cookies in Laravel

Cookies can exist in three places in Laravel. They can come in via the request, which means the user had the cookie when they visited the page. You can read that with the Cookie facade, or you can read it off of the request object.

They can also be sent out with a response, which means the response will instruct the user's browser to save the cookie for future visits. You can do this by adding the cookie to your response object before returning it.

And lastly, a cookie can be *queued*. If you use the Cookie facade to set a cookie, you have put it into a "CookieJar" queue, and it will be removed and added to the response object by the AddQueuedCookiesToResponse middleware.

Accessing the Cookie Tools

You can get and set cookies in three places: the Cookie facade, the cookie() global helper, and the request and response objects.

The Cookie facade

The Cookie facade is the most full-featured option, allowing you to not only read and make cookies, but also to queue them to be added to the response. It provides the following methods:

Cookie::get($key)
: To pull the value of a cookie that came in with the request, you can just run Cookie::get('cookie-name'). This is the simplest option.

Cookie::has($key)
: You can check whether a cookie came in with the request using Cookie::has('cookie-name'), which returns a Boolean.

Cookie::make(...params)
: If you want to *make* a cookie without queueing it anywhere, you can use Cookie::make(). The most likely use for this would be to make a cookie and then manually attach it to the response object, which we'll cover in a bit.

Here are the parameters for make(), in order:

- $name is the name of the cookie.
- $value is the content of the cookie.
- $minutes specifies how many minutes the cookie should live.
- $path is the path under which your cookie should be valid.
- $domain lists the domains for which your cookie should work.
- $secure indicates whether the cookie should only be transmitted over a secure (HTTPS) connection.
- $httpOnly indicates whether the cookie will be made accessible only through the HTTP protocol.

- `$raw` indicates whether the cookie should be sent without URL encoding.

- `$sameSite` indicates whether the cookie should be available for cross-site requests; options are `lax`, `strict`, or `null`.

`Cookie::make()`
    Returns an instance of `Symfony\Component\HttpFoundation\Cookie`.

Default Settings for Cookies

The `CookieJar` that the `Cookie` facade instance uses reads its defaults from the session config. So, if you change any of the configuration values for the session cookie in *config/ session.php*, those same defaults will be applied to all of your cookies that you create using the `Cookie` facade.

`Cookie::queue(Cookie || params)`
    If you use `Cookie::make()`, you'll still need to attach the cookie to your response, which we'll cover shortly. `Cookie::queue()` has the same syntax as `Cookie::make()`, but it enqueues the created cookie to be automatically attached to the response by middleware.

    If you'd like, you can also just pass a cookie you've created yourself into `Cookie::queue()`.

    Here's the simplest possible way to add a cookie to the response in Laravel:

```
Cookie::queue('dismissed-popup', true, 15);
```

When Your Queued Cookies Won't Get Set

Cookies can only be returned as part of a response. So, if you enqueue cookies with the `Cookie` facade and then your response isn't returned correctly—for example, if you use PHP's `exit()` or something halts the execution of your script —your cookies won't be set.

The cookie() global helper

The `cookie()` global helper will return a `CookieJar` instance if you call it with no parameters. However, two of the most convenient methods on the `Cookie` facade— `has()` and `get()`—exist *only* on the facade, not on the `CookieJar`. So, in this context, I think the global helper is actually less useful than the other options.

The one task for which the `cookie()` global helper is useful is creating a cookie. If you pass parameters to `cookie()`, they'll be passed directly to the equivalent of `Cookie::make()`, so this is the fastest way to create a cookie:

```
$cookie = cookie('dismissed-popup', true, 15);
```

Injecting an Instance

You can also inject an instance of `Illuminate\Cookie\CookieJar` anywhere in the app, but you'll have the same limitations discussed here.

Cookies on Request and Response objects

Since cookies come in as a part of the request and are set as a part of the response, those Illuminate objects are the places they actually live. The `Cookie` facade's `get()`, `has()`, and `queue()` methods are just proxies to interact with the `Request` and `Response` objects.

So, the simplest way to interact with cookies is to pull cookies from the request and set them on the response.

Reading cookies from Request objects.   Once you have a copy of your `Request` object—if you don't know how to get one, just try `app('request')`—you can use the `Request` object's `cookie()` method to read its cookies, as shown in Example 14-12.

Example 14-12. Reading a cookie from a Request object

```
Route::get('dashboard', function (Illuminate\Http\Request $request) {
    $userDismissedPopup = $request->cookie('dismissed-popup', false);
});
```

As you can see in this example, the `cookie()` method has two parameters: the cookie's name and, optionally, the fallback value.

Setting cookies on Response objects.   Whenever you have your `Response` object ready, you can use the `cookie()` method (or the `withCookie()` method in Laravel prior to 5.3) on it to add a cookie to the response, like in Example 14-13.

Example 14-13. Setting a cookie on a Response object

```
Route::get('dashboard', function () {
    $cookie = cookie('saw-dashboard', true);

    return Response::view('dashboard')
```

```
        ->cookie($cookie);
});
```

If you're new to Laravel and not sure which option to use, I'd recommend setting cookies on the `Request` and `Response` objects. It's a bit more work, but will lead to fewer surprises if future developers don't understand the `CookieJar` queue.

Logging

We've seen a few really brief examples of logging so far in this book when we were talking about other concepts like the container and facades, but let's briefly look at what options you have with logging beyond just `Log::info('Message')`.

The purpose of logs is to increase "discoverability," or your ability to understand what's going on at any given moment in your application.

Logs are short messages, sometimes with some data embedded in a human-readable form, that your code will generate for the sake of understanding what was happening during the execution of the app. Each log must be captured at a specific *level*, which can vary from `emergency` (something very bad happened) to `debug` (something of almost no significance happened).

Without any modifications, your app will write any log statements to a file located at *storage/logs/laravel.log*, and each log statement will look a little bit like this:

```
[2018-09-22 21:34:38] local.ERROR: Something went wrong.
```

You can see we have the date, time, environment, error level, and message, all on one line. However, Laravel also (by default) logs any uncaught exceptions, and in that case you'll see the entire stack trace inline.

We'll cover how to log, why to log, and how to log elsewhere (for example, in Slack) in the following section.

When and Why to Use Logs

The most common use case for logs is to act as a semidisposable record of things that have happened that you *may* care about later, but to which you don't definitively need programmatic access. The logs are more about learning what's going on in the app and less about creating structured data your app can consume.

For example, if you want to have code that consumes a record of every user login and does something interesting with it, that's a use case for a *logins* database table. However, if you have a casual interest in those logins but you're not entirely certain whether you care or whether you need that information programmatically, you may just throw a `debug`- or `info`-level log on it and forget about it.

Logs are also common when you need to see the value of something at the moment it goes wrong, or at a certain time of day, or something else that means you want the data at a time when you're not around. Throw a log statement in the code, get the data you need out of the logs, and either keep it in the code for later usage or just delete it again.

Writing to the Logs

The simplest way to write a log entry in Laravel is to use the `Log` facade, and use the method on that facade that matches the severity level you'd like to record. The levels are the same as those defined in RFC 5424 (*http://bit.ly/2YltbAS*):

```
Log::emergency($message);
Log::alert($message);
Log::critical($message);
Log::error($message);
Log::warning($message);
Log::notice($message);
Log::info($message);
Log::debug($message);
```

You can also, optionally, pass a second parameter that's an array of connected data:

```
Log::error('Failed to upload user image.', ['user' => $user]);
```

This additional information may be captured differently by different log destinations, but here's how this looks in the default local log (although it will be just a single line in the log):

```
[2018-09-27 20:53:31] local.ERROR: Failed to upload user image. {
    "user":"[object] (App\\User: {
        \"id\":1,
        \"name\":\"Matt\",
        \"email\":\"matt@tighten.co\",
        \"email_verified_at\":null,
        \"api_token\":\"long-token-here\",
        \"created_at\":\"2018-09-22 21:39:55\",
        \"updated_at\":\"2018-09-22 21:40:08\"
    })"
}
```

Log Channels

In Laravel 5.6, the way we configure and capture logs was changed pretty significantly to introduce the idea of multiple *channels* and *drivers*. If you're working in 5.5 or earlier, you can skip on to "Full-Text Search with Laravel Scout" on page 396.

Like many other aspects of Laravel (file storage, database, mail, etc.), you can configure your logs to use one or more predefined log types, which you define in the config file. Using each type involves passing various configuration details to a specific log driver.

These log types are called channels, and out of the box you'll have options for `stack`, `single`, `daily`, `slack`, `stderr`, `syslog`, and `errorlog`. Each channel is connected to a single driver; the available drivers are `single`, `daily`, `slack`, `syslog`, `errorlog`, `mono log`, `custom`, or `stack`.

We'll cover the most common channels, here: `stack`, `single`, `daily`, and `slack`. To learn more about the drivers and the full list of channels available, take a look at the logging docs (*http://bit.ly/2TVgSwT*).

The single channel

The `single` channel writes every log entry to a single file, which you'll define in the `path` key. You can see its default configuration here in Example 14-14:

Example 14-14. Default configuration for the single channel

```
'single' => [
    'driver' => 'single',
    'path' => storage_path('logs/laravel.log'),
    'level' => 'debug',
],
```

This means it'll only log events at the `debug` level or higher, and it will write them all to a single file, *storage/logs/laravel.log*.

The daily channel

The `daily` channel splits out a new file for each day. You can see its default config here in Example 14-15.

Example 14-15. Default configuation for the daily channel

```
'daily' => [
    'driver' => 'daily',
    'path' => storage_path('logs/laravel.log'),
    'level' => 'debug',
    'days' => 7,
],
```

It's similar to `single`, but we now can set how many days of logs to keep before they're cleaned up, and the date will be appended to the filename we specify. For example, the preceding config will generate a file named *storage/logs/laravel-{yyyy-mm-dd}.log*.

The slack channel

The `slack` channel makes it easy to send your logs (or, more likely, only certain logs) over to Slack.

It also illustrates that you're not limited to just the handlers that come out of the box with Laravel. We'll cover this in a second, but this isn't a custom Slack implementation; it's just Laravel building a log driver that connects to the Monolog Slack handler, and if you can use any Monolog handler, you have a *lot* of options available to you.

The default configuration for this channel is shown in Example 14-16.

Example 14-16. Default configuation for the slack channel

```
'slack' => [
    'driver' => 'slack',
    'url' => env('LOG_SLACK_WEBHOOK_URL'),
    'username' => 'Laravel Log',
    'emoji' => ':boom:',
    'level' => 'critical',
],
```

The stack channel

The `stack` channel is the channel that's enabled by default on your application. Its default configuation in 5.7+ is shown in Example 14-17.

Example 14-17. Default configuration for the stack channel

```
'stack' => [
    'driver' => 'stack',
    'channels' => ['daily'],
    'ignore_exceptions' => false,
],
```

The `stack` channel allows you to send all your logs to more than one channel (listed in the `channels` array). So, while this is the channel that's configured by default on your Laravel apps, because its `channels` array is set to `daily` by default in 5.8+, in reality your app is just using the `daily` log channel.

But what if you wanted everything of the level `info` and above to go to the daily files, but you wanted `critical` and higher log messages to go to Slack? It's easy with the `stack` driver, as Example 14-18 demonstrates.

Example 14-18. Customizing the stack driver

```
'channels' => [
    'stack' => [
```

```
        'driver' => 'stack',
        'channels' => ['daily', 'slack'],
    ],

    'daily' => [
        'driver' => 'daily',
        'path' => storage_path('logs/laravel.log'),
        'level' => 'info',
        'days' => 14,
    ],

    'slack' => [
        'driver' => 'slack',
        'url' => env('LOG_SLACK_WEBHOOK_URL'),
        'username' => 'Laravel Log',
        'emoji' => ':boom:',
        'level' => 'critical',
    ],
```

Writing to specific log channels

There may also be times when you want to control exactly which log messages go
where. You can do that, too. Just specify the channel when you call the Log facade:

```
Log::channel('slack')->info("This message will go to Slack.");
```

Advanced Log Configuration

If you'd like to customize how each log is sent to each channel, or
implement custom Monolog handlers, check out the logging docs
(*http://bit.ly/2TVgSwT*) to learn more.

Full-Text Search with Laravel Scout

 Laravel Scout is a separate package that you can bring into your Laravel apps to add
full-text search to your Eloquent models. Scout makes it easy to index and search the
contents of your Eloquent models; it ships with an Algolia driver, but there are also
community packages for other providers. I'll assume you're using Algolia.

Installing Scout

First, pull in the package in any Laravel 5.3+ app:

```
composer require laravel/scout
```

Manually Registering Service Providers Prior to Laravel 5.5

If you're using a version of Laravel prior to 5.5, you will need to manually register the service provider by adding `Laravel\Scout\ScoutServiceProvider::class` to the providers section of *config/app.php*.

Next you'll want to set up your Scout configuration. Run this command:

```
php artisan vendor:publish --provider="Laravel\Scout\ScoutServiceProvider"
```

and paste your Algolia credentials in *config/scout.php*.

Finally, install the Algolia SDK:

```
composer require algolia/algoliasearch-client-php
```

Marking Your Model for Indexing

In your model (we'll use `Review`, for a book review, for this example), import the `Laravel\Scout\Searchable` trait.

You can define which properties are searchable using the `toSearchableArray()` method (it defaults to mirroring `toArray()`), and define the name of the model's index using the `searchableAs()` method (it defaults to the table name).

Scout subscribes to the create/delete/update events on your marked models. When you create, update, or delete any rows, Scout will sync those changes up to Algolia. It'll either make those changes synchronously with your updates or, if you configure Scout to use a queue, queue the updates.

Searching Your Index

Scout's syntax is simple. For example, to find any `Review` with the word `Llew` in it:

```
Review::search('Llew')->get();
```

You can also modify your queries as you would with regular Eloquent calls:

```
// Get all records from the Review that match the term "Llew",
// limited to 20 per page and reading the page query parameter,
// just like Eloquent pagination
Review::search('Llew')->paginate(20);

// Get all records from the Review that match the term "Llew"
// and have the account_id field set to 2
Review::search('Llew')->where('account_id', 2)->get();
```

What comes back from these searches? A collection of Eloquent models, rehydrated from your database. The IDs are stored in Algolia, which returns a list of matched

IDs; Scout then pulls the database records for those and returns them as Eloquent objects.

You don't have full access to the complexity of SQL WHERE commands, but it provides a basic framework for comparison checks like you can see in the code samples here.

Queues and Scout

At this point your app will be making HTTP requests to Algolia on every request that modifies any database records. This can slow down your application quickly, which is why Scout makes it easy to push all of its actions onto a queue.

In *config/scout.php*, set queue to true so that these updates are set to be indexed asynchronously. Your full-text index is now operating under "eventual consistency"; your database records will receive the updates immediately, and the updates to your search indexes will be queued and updated as fast as your queue worker allows.

Performing Operations Without Indexing

If you need to perform a set of operations and avoid triggering the indexing in response, wrap the operations in the withoutSyncingToSearch() method on your model:

```
Review::withoutSyncingToSearch(function () {
    // Make a bunch of reviews, e.g.
    factory(Review::class, 10)->create();
});
```

Conditionally Indexing Models

Sometimes you might only want to index records if they meet a certain condition. You may use the shouldBeSearchable() method on the model class to achieve this:

```
public function shouldBeSearchable()
{
    return $this->isApproved();
}
```

Manually Triggering Indexing via Code

If you want to manually trigger indexing your model, you can do it using code in your app or via the command line.

To manually trigger indexing from your code, add searchable() to the end of any Eloquent query and it will index all of the records that were found in that query:

```
Review::all()->searchable();
```

You can also choose to scope the query to only those records you want to index. However, Scout is smart enough to insert new records and update old records, so you may choose to just reindex the entire contents of the model's database table.

You can also run `searchable()` on relationship methods:

```
$user->reviews()->searchable();
```

If you want to unindex any records with the same sort of query chaining, just use `unsearchable()` instead:

```
Review::where('sucky', true)->unsearchable();
```

Manually Triggering Indexing via the CLI

You can also trigger indexing with an Artisan command:

```
php artisan scout:import "App\Review"
```

This will chunk all of the `Review` models and index them all.

Testing

Testing most of these features is as simple as using them in your tests; no need to mock or stub. The default configuration will already work—for example, take a look at *phpunit.xml* to see that your session driver and cache driver have been set to values appropriate for tests.

However, there are a few convenience methods and a few gotchas that you should know about before you attempt to test them all.

File Storage

Testing file uploads can be a bit of a pain, but follow these steps and it will be clear.

Uploading fake files

First, let's look at how to manually create an `Illuminate\Http\UploadedFile` object for use in our application testing (Example 14-19).

Example 14-19. Creating a fake UploadedFile for testing

```
public function test_file_should_be_stored()
{
    Storage::fake('public');

    $file = UploadedFile::fake()->image('avatar.jpg');

    $response = $this->postJson('/avatar', [
```

```
        'avatar' => $file,
    ]);

    // Assert the file was stored
    Storage::disk('public')->assertExists("avatars/{$file->hashName()}");

    // Assert a file does not exist
    Storage::disk('public')->assertMissing('missing.jpg');
}
```

We've created a new instance of `UploadedFile` that refers to our testing file, and we can now use it to test our routes.

Returning fake files

If your route is expecting a real file to exist, sometimes the best way to make it testable is to make that real file actually exist. Let's say every user must have a profile picture.

First, let's set up the model factory for the user to use Faker to make a copy of the picture, as in Example 14-20.

Example 14-20. Returning fake files with Faker

```
$factory->define(User::class, function (Faker\Generator $faker) {
    return [
        'picture' => $faker->file(
            storage_path('tests'), // Source directory
            storage_path('app'), // Target directory
            false // Return just filename, not full path
        ),
        'name' => $faker->name,
    ];
});
```

Faker's `file()` method picks a random file from the source directory and copies it to the target directory, and then returns the filename. So, we've just picked a random file from the *storage/tests* directory, copied it to the *storage/app* directory, and set its filename as the `picture` property on our `User`. At this point we can use a `User` in tests on routes that expect the `User` to have a picture, as seen in Example 14-21.

Example 14-21. Asserting that an image's URL is echoed

```
public function test_user_profile_picture_echoes_correctly()
{
    $user = factory(User::class)->create();

    $response = $this->get(route('users.show', $user->id));
```

```
    $response->assertSee($user->picture);
}
```

Of course, in many contexts you can just generate a random string there without even copying a file. But if your routes check for the file's existence or run any operations on the file, this is your best option.

Session

If you need to assert something has been set in the session, you can use some convenience methods Laravel makes available in every test. All of these methods are available in your tests on the Illuminate\Foundation\Testing\TestResponse object:

assertSessionHas($key, $value = null)
: Asserts that the session has a value for a particular key, and, if the second parameter is passed, that that key is a particular value:

```
public function test_some_thing()
{
    // Do stuff that ends up with a $response object...
    $response->assertSessionHas('key', 'value');
}
```

assertSessionHasAll(array $bindings)
: If passed an array of key/value pairs, asserts that all of the keys are equal to all of the values. If one or more of the array entries is just a value (with PHP's default numeric key), it will just be checked for existence in the session:

```
$check = [
    'has',
    'hasWithThisValue' => 'thisValue',
];

$response->assertSessionHasAll($check);
```

assertSessionMissing($key)
: Asserts that the session does *not* have a value for a particular key.

assertSessionHasErrors($bindings = [], $format = null)
: Asserts that the session has an errors value. This is the key Laravel uses to send errors back from validation failures.

    If the array contains just keys, it will check that errors are set with those keys:

```
$response = $this->post('test-route', ['failing' => 'data']);
$response->assertSessionHasErrors(['name', 'email']);
```

You can also pass values for those keys, and optionally a *$format*, to check that the messages for those errors came back the way you expected:

```
$response = $this->post('test-route', ['failing' => 'data']);
$response->assertSessionHasErrors([
    'email' => '<strong>The email field is required.</strong>',
], '<strong>:message</strong>');
```

Cache

There's nothing special about testing your features that use the cache—just do it:

```
Cache::put('key', 'value', 900);

$this->assertEquals('value', Cache::get('key'));
```

Laravel uses the `array` cache driver by default in your testing environment, which just stores your cache values in memory.

Cookies

What if you need to set a cookie before testing a route in your application tests? You can manually pass cookies to one of the parameters of the `call()` method. To learn more about `call()`, check out Chapter 12.

Excluding Your Cookie from Encryption During Testing

Your cookies won't work in your tests unless you exclude them from Laravel's cookie encryption middleware. You can do this by teaching the `EncryptCookies` middleware to temporarily disable itself for those cookies:

```
use Illuminate\Cookie\Middleware\EncryptCookies;
...

$this->app->resolving(
    EncryptCookies::class,
    function ($object) {
        $object->disableFor('cookie-name');
    }
);

// ...run test
```

That means you can set and check against a cookie with something like Example 14-22.

Example 14-22. Running unit tests against cookies

```
public function test_cookie()
{
    $this->app->resolving(EncryptCookies::class, function ($object) {
        $object->disableFor('my-cookie');
    });

    $response = $this->call(
        'get',
        'route-echoing-my-cookie-value',
        [],
        ['my-cookie' => 'baz']
    );
    $response->assertSee('baz');
}
```

If you want to test that a response has a cookie set, you can use `assertCookie()` to test for the cookie:

```
$response = $this->get('cookie-setting-route');
$response->assertCookie('cookie-name');
```

Or you could use `assertPlainCookie()` to test for the cookie and to assert that it's not encrypted.

Different Names for Testing Methods Prior to Laravel 5.4

In projects running versions of Laravel 5.4 `assertCookie()` should be replaced by `seeCookie()`, and `assertPlainCookie()` should be replaced by `seePlainCookie()`.

Log

The simplest way to test that a certain log was written is by making assertions against the `Log` facade (learn more in "Faking Other Facades" on page 321). Example 14-23 shows how this works.

Example 14-23. Making assertions against the Log facade

```
// Test file
public function test_new_accounts_generate_log_entries()
{
    Log::shouldReceive('info')
        ->once()
        ->with('New account created!');

    // Create a new account
    $this->post(route('accounts.store'), ['email' => 'matt@mattstauffer.com']);
```

```
}

// AccountsController
public function store()
{
    // Create account

    Log::info('New account created!');
}
```

There's also a package called Log Fake (*http://bit.ly/2JDI4vd*) that expands on what you can do with the facade testing shown here and allows you to write more customized assertions against your logs.

Scout

If you need to test code that uses Scout data, you're probably not going to want your tests triggering indexing actions or reading from Scout. Simply add an environment variable to your *phpunit.xml* to disable Scout's connection to Algolia:

```
<env name="SCOUT_DRIVER" value="null"/>
```

TL;DR

Laravel provides simple interfaces to many common storage operations: filesystem access, sessions, cookies, the cache, and search. Each of these APIs is the same regardless of which provider you use, which Laravel enables by allowing multiple "drivers" to serve the same public interface. This makes it simple to switch providers depending on the environment, or as the needs of the application change.

## CHAPTER 15

Mail and Notifications

Sending an application's users notifications via email, Slack, SMS, or another notification system is a common but surprisingly complex requirement. Laravel's mail and notification features provide consistent APIs that abstract away the need to pay too close attention to any particular provider. Just like in Chapter 14, you'll write your code once and choose at the configuration level which provider you'll use to send your email or notifications.

Mail

Laravel's mail functionality is a convenience layer on top of Swift Mailer (*http://swift mailer.org/*), and out of the box Laravel comes with drivers for Mailgun, Mandrill, Sparkpost, SES, SMTP, PHP Mail, and Sendmail.

For all of the cloud services, you'll set your authentication information in *config/services.php*. However, if you take a look you'll see there are already keys there —and in *config/mail.php*—that allow you to customize your application's mail functionality in *.env* using variables like MAIL_DRIVER and MAILGUN_SECRET.

Cloud-based API Driver Dependencies

If you're using any of the cloud-based API drivers, you'll need to bring Guzzle in with Composer. You can run the following command to add it:

```
composer require guzzlehttp/guzzle
```

If you use the SES driver, you'll need to run the following command:

```
composer require aws/aws-sdk-php:~3.0
```

"Classic" Mail

There are two different syntaxes in Laravel for sending mail: classic and mailable. The mailable syntax is the preferred syntax since 5.3, so we're going to focus on that in this book. But for those who are working in 5.2 or earlier, here's a quick look at how the classic syntax (Example 15-1) works.

Example 15-1. Basic "classic" mail syntax

```
Mail::send(
    'emails.assignment-created',
    ['trainer' => $trainer, 'trainee' => $trainee],
    function ($m) use ($trainer, $trainee) {
        $m->from($trainer->email, $trainer->name);
        $m->to($trainee->email, $trainee->name)->subject('A New Assignment!');
    }
);
```

The first parameter of `Mail::send()` is the name of the view. Keep in mind that `emails.assignment-created` means *resources/views/emails/assignment-created.blade.php* or *resources/views/emails/assignment-created.php*.

The second parameter is an array of data that you want to pass to the view.

The third parameter is a closure, in which you define how and where to send the email: from, to, CC, BCC, subject, and any other metadata. Make sure to `use` any variables you want access to within the closure. And note that the closure is passed one parameter, which we've named `$m`; this is the message object.

Take a look at the old docs (*http://bit.ly/2utCAZA*) to learn more about the classic mail syntax.

Basic "Mailable" Mail Usage

 Laravel 5.3 introduced a new mail syntax called the "mailable." It works the same as the classic mail syntax, but instead of defining your mail messages in a closure, you instead create a specific PHP class to represent each mail.

To make a mailable, use the `make:mail` Artisan command:

```
php artisan make:mail AssignmentCreated
```

Example 15-2 shows what that class looks like.

Example 15-2. An autogenerated mailable PHP class

```
<?php
```

```
namespace App\Mail;

use Illuminate\Bus\Queueable;
use Illuminate\Mail\Mailable;
use Illuminate\Queue\SerializesModels;
use Illuminate\Contracts\Queue\ShouldQueue;

class AssignmentCreated extends Mailable
{
    use Queueable, SerializesModels;

    /**
     * Create a new message instance
     *
     * @return void
     */
    public function __construct()
    {
        //
    }

    /**
     * Build the message
     *
     * @return $this
     */
    public function build()
    {
        return $this->view('view.name');
    }
}
```

This class probably looks familiar—it's shaped almost the same as a Job. It even imports the Queueable trait for queuing your mail and the SerializesModels trait so any Eloquent models you pass to the constructor will be serialized correctly.

So, how does this work? The build() method on a mailable is where you're going to define which view to use, what the subject is, and anything else you want to tweak about the mail *except who it's going to*. The constructor is the place where you'll pass in any data, and any public properties on your mailable class will be available to the template.

Take a look at Example 15-3 to see how we might update the autogenerated mailable for our assignment example.

Example 15-3. A sample mailable

```php
<?php

namespace App\Mail;

use Illuminate\Bus\Queueable;
use Illuminate\Mail\Mailable;
use Illuminate\Queue\SerializesModels;
use Illuminate\Contracts\Queue\ShouldQueue;

class AssignmentCreated extends Mailable
{
    use Queueable, SerializesModels;

    public $trainer;
    public $trainee;

    public function __construct($trainer, $trainee)
    {
        $this->trainer = $trainer;
        $this->trainee = $trainee;
    }

    public function build()
    {
        return $this->subject('New assignment from ' . $this->trainer->name)
            ->view('emails.assignment-created');
    }
}
```

Example 15-4 shows how to send a mailable.

Example 15-4. A few ways to send mailables

```php
// Simple send
Mail::to($user)->send(new AssignmentCreated($trainer, $trainee));

// With CC/BCC/etc.
Mail::to($user1))
    ->cc($user2)
    ->bcc($user3)
    ->send(new AssignmentCreated($trainer, $trainee));

// With collections
Mail::to('me@app.com')
    ->bcc(User::all())
    ->send(new AssignmentCreated($trainer, $trainee))
```

Mail Templates

Mail templates are just like any other template. They can extend other templates, use sections, parse variables, contain conditional or looping directives, and do anything else you can do in a normal Blade view.

Take a look at Example 15-5 to see a possible `emails.assignment-created` template for Example 15-3.

Example 15-5. Sample assignment created email template

```
<!-- resources/views/emails/assignment-created.blade.php -->
<p>Hey {{ $trainee->name }}!</p>

<p>You have received a new training assignment from <b>{{ $trainer->name }}</b>.
Check out your <a href="{{ route('training-dashboard') }}">training
dashboard</a> now!</p>
```

In Example 15-3, both `$trainer` and `$trainee` are public properties on your mailable, which makes them available to the template.

If you want to explicitly define which variables are passed to the template, you can chain the `with()` method onto your `build()` call as in Example 15-6.

Example 15-6. Customizing the template variables

```
public function build()
{
    return $this->subject('You have a new assignment!')
        ->view('emails.assignment')
        ->with(['assignment' => $this->event->name]);
}
```

HTML Versus Plain-text Emails

So far we've used the `view()` method in our `build()` call stacks. This expects the template we're referencing to pass back HTML. If you'd like to pass a plain-text version, the `text()` method defines your plain-text view:

```
public function build()
{
    return $this->view('emails.reminder')
        ->text('emails.reminder_plain');
}
```

Methods Available in build()

Here are a few of the methods available to you to customize your message in the build() method of your mailable:

from($address, $name = null)
    Sets the "from" name and address—represents the author

subject($subject)
    Sets the email subject

attach($file, array $options = [])
    Attaches a file; valid options are mime for MIME type and as for display name

attachData($data, $name, array $options = [])
    Attaches a file from a raw string; same options as attach()

attachFromStorage($path, $name = null, array $options = [])
    Attaches a file stored on any of your filesystem disks

priority($level = n)
    Set the email's priority, where 1 is the highest and 5 is the lowest

Finally, if you want to perform any manual modifications on the underlying Swift message, you can do that using withSwiftMessage(), as shown in Example 15-7.

Example 15-7. Modifying the underlying SwiftMessage object

```
public function build()
{
    return $this->subject('Howdy!')
        ->withSwiftMessage(function ($swift) {
            $swift->setReplyTo('noreply@email.com');
        })
        ->view('emails.howdy');
}
```

Attachments and Inline Images

Example 15-8 shows three options for how to attach files or raw data to your email.

Example 15-8. Attaching files or data to mailables

```
// Attach a file using the local filename
public function build()
{
    return $this->subject('Your whitepaper download')
        ->attach(storage_path('pdfs/whitepaper.pdf'), [
```

```
            'mime' => 'application/pdf', // Optional
            'as' => 'whitepaper-barasa.pdf', // Optional
        ])
        ->view('emails.whitepaper');
}


// Attach a file passing the raw data
public function build()
{
    return $this->subject('Your whitepaper download')
        ->attachData(
            file_get_contents(storage_path('pdfs/whitepaper.pdf')),
            'whitepaper-barasa.pdf',
            [
                'mime' => 'application/pdf', // Optional
            ]
        )
        ->view('emails.whitepaper');
}


// Attach a file stored on one of your filesystem disks, like S3
public function build()
{
    return $this->subject('Your whitepaper download')
        ->view('emails.whitepaper')
        ->attachFromStorage('/pdfs/whitepaper.pdf');
}
```

And you can see how to embed images directly into your email in Example 15-9.

Example 15-9. Inlining images

```
<!-- emails/image.blade.php -->
Here is an image:

<img src="{{ $message->embed(storage_path('embed.jpg')) }}">

Or, the same image embedding the data:

<img src="{{ $message->embedData(
    file_get_contents(storage_path('embed.jpg')), 'embed.jpg'
) }}">
```

Markdown Mailables

Markdown mailables allow you to write your email content in Markdown, after which it will be converted into full HTML (and plain-text) emails with Laravel's built-in, responsive HTML templates. You can also tweak these templates to make a customized email template that it's simple for your developers and nondevelopers to create content for.

First, run the make:mail Artisan command with the markdown flag:

```
php artisan make:mail AssignmentCreated --markdown=emails.assignment-created
```

You can see an example of what the mail file it'll generate looks like in Example 15-10.

Example 15-10. Generated Markdown mailable

```
class AssignmentCreated extends Mailable
{
    // ...

    public function build()
    {
        return $this->markdown('emails.assignment-created');
    }
}
```

As you can see, this is almost exactly the same as a normal mailable file in Laravel. The main difference is that you're calling the markdown() method instead of the view() method. Also note that the template you're referencing should represent a Markdown template, not a normal Blade template.

The difference is that, whereas a normal email template may be expected—with the use of includes and inheritance like any Blade file—to generate a full HTML email, Markdown templates simply pass Markdown content to a few predefined components. Framework and package-level components in Laravel are often nested with a *package::component* naming style, and as such the main body of your Markdown email should be passed into a component named mail::message. Take a look at Example 15-11 to see an example of a simple Markdown mail template.

Example 15-11. Simple assignment Markdown email

```
{{-- resources/views/emails/assignment-created.blade.php --}}
@component('mail::message')
# Hey {{ $trainee->name }}!

You have received a new training assignment from **{{ $trainer->name }}**

@component('mail::button', ['url' => route('training-dashboard')])
View Your Assigment
@endcomponent

Thanks,<br>
{{ config('app.name') }}
@endcomponent
```

As you can see in Example 15-11, there's a parent `mail::message` component to which you pass the body of your email, but you're also provided with other smaller components you can sprinkle into your emails. We used the `mail::button` component here, which takes a body ("View Your Assignment") but also requires parameters to be passed, as an array to the second parameter of the `@component` directive.

Markdown components

There are three types of components available:

Button
> Generates a centered button link. The button component requires a `url` attribute and allows an optional `color` attribute, to which you can pass `primary`, `success`, or `error`.

Panel
> Renders the provided text with a slightly lighter background than the rest of the message.

Table
> Converts the content passed into it via the Markdown table syntax.

> **Customizing the Components**
>
> These Markdown components are built into the core of the Laravel framework, but if you need to customize how they work, you can publish their files and edit them:
>
> ```
> php artisan vendor:publish --tag=laravel-mail
> ```

You can learn more about customizing these files and their themes in the Laravel docs (*http://bit.ly/2UUBUrF*).

Rendering Mailables to the Browser

When you're developing emails in your applications, it's helpful to be able to preview how they'll render. You can rely on a tool like Mailtrap for this, and that is a useful tool, but it can also be helpful to render the mails directly in your browser and see your changes made immediately.

Take a look at Example 15-12 to see a sample route you can add to your application to render a given mailable.

Example 15-12. Rendering a mailable to a route

```
Route::get('preview-assignment-created-mailable', function () {
    $trainer = Trainer::first();
```

```
$trainee = Trainee::first();

return new \App\Mail\AssignmentCreated($trainer, $trainee);
});
```

Queues

Sending email is a time-consuming task that can cause applications to slow down, so it's common to move it to a background queue. It's so common, in fact, that Laravel has a set of built-in tools to make it easier to queue your messages without writing queue jobs for each email:

queue()

To queue a mail object instead of sending it immediately, simply pass your mailable object to `Mail::queue()` instead of `Mail::send()`:

```
Mail::queue(new AssignmentCreated($trainer, $trainee));
```

later()

`Mail::later()` works the same as `Mail::queue()`, but it allows you to add a delay—either in minutes, or at a specific time by passing an instance of `DateTime` or `Carbon`—specifying when the email will be pulled from the queue and sent:

```
$when = now()->addMinutes(30);
Mail::later($when, new AssignmentCreated($trainer, $trainee));
```

 Configuring Queues

Your queues must be configured correctly for these methods to work. Take a look at Chapter 16 to learn more about how queues work and how to get them running in your application.

For both `queue()` and `later()`, if you'd like to specify which queue or queue connection your mail is added to, use the `onConnection()` and `onQueue()` methods on your mailable object:

```
$message = (new AssignmentCreated($trainer, $trainee))
    ->onConnection('sqs')
    ->onQueue('emails');

Mail::to($user)->queue($message);
```

If you'd like to direct that a given mailable should always be queued, you can make the mailable implement the `Illuminate\Contracts\Queue\ShouldQueue` interface.

Local Development

This is all well and good for sending mail in your production environments. But how do you test it all out? There are three primary tools you'll want to consider: Laravel's log driver, a Software as a Service (SaaS) app named Mailtrap, and the so-called "universal to" configuration option.

The log driver

Laravel provides a log driver that logs every email you try to send to your local *laravel.log* file (which is, by default, in *storage/logs*).

If you want to use this, edit *.env* and set MAIL_DRIVER to log. Now open up or tail *storage/logs/laravel.log* and send an email from your app. You'll see something like this:

```
Message-ID: <04ee2e97289c68f0c9191f4b04fc0de1@localhost>
Date: Tue, 17 May 2016 02:52:46 +0000
Subject: Welcome to our app!
From: Matt Stauffer <matt@mattstauffer.com>
To: freja@jensen.no
MIME-Version: 1.0
Content-Type: text/html; charset=utf-8
Content-Transfer-Encoding: quoted-printable

Welcome to our app!
```

In Laravel 5.7+, you can optionally specify that logged mail gets sent to a different log channel than the rest of your logs. Either modify *config/mail.php* or set the MAIL_LOG_CHANNEL variable in your *.env* file to the name of any existing log channel.

Mailtrap.io

Mailtrap (*https://mailtrap.io*) is a service for capturing and inspecting emails in development environments. You send your mail to the Mailtrap servers via SMTP, but instead of sending those emails off to the intended recipients, Mailtrap captures them all and provides you with a web-based email client for inspecting them, regardless of which email address is in the to field.

To set up Mailtrap, sign up for a free account and visit the base dashboard for your demo. Copy your username and password from the SMTP column.

Then edit your app's *.env* file and set the following values in the mail section:

```
MAIL_DRIVER=smtp
MAIL_HOST=mailtrap.io
MAIL_PORT=2525
MAIL_USERNAME=your_username_from_mailtrap_here
MAIL_PASSWORD=your_password_from_mailtrap_here
MAIL_ENCRYPTION=null
```

Now, any email you send from your app will show up in your Mailtrap inbox.

Universal to

If you'd like to inspect the emails in your preferred client, you can override the to field on each message with the "universal to" configuration setting. To set this up, add a to key to your *config/mail.php* file that looks something like this:

```
'to' => [
    'address' => 'matt@mattstauffer.com',
    'name' => 'Matt Testing My Application'
],
```

Note that you'll need to actually set up a real email driver with something like Mailgun or Sendmail in order to use this.

Notifications

Most of the mail that's sent from web apps really has the purpose of notifying users that a particular action has happened or needs to happen. As users' communication preferences grow more and more diverse, we gather ever more—and more disparate—packages to communicate via Slack, SMS, and other means.

Laravel 5.3 introduced a new concept in Laravel called, fittingly, *notifications*. Just like a mailable, a notification is a PHP class that represents a single communication that you might want to send to your users. For now, let's imagine we're notifying users of our physical training app that they have a new workout available.

Each class represents all of the information necessary to send notifications to your users *using one or many notification channels*. A single notification could send an email, send an SMS via Nexmo, send a WebSockets ping, add a record to a database, send a message to a Slack channel, and much more.

So, let's create our notification:

```
php artisan make:notification WorkoutAvailable
```

Example 15-13 shows what that gives us.

Example 15-13. An autogenerated notification class

```php
<?php

namespace App\Notifications;

use Illuminate\Bus\Queueable;
use Illuminate\Notifications\Notification;
use Illuminate\Contracts\Queue\ShouldQueue;
use Illuminate\Notifications\Messages\MailMessage;
```

```php
class WorkoutAvailable extends Notification
{
    use Queueable;

    /**
     * Create a new notification instance
     *
     * @return void
     */
    public function __construct()
    {
        //
    }

    /**
     * Get the notification's delivery channels
     *
     * @param  mixed  $notifiable
     * @return array
     */
    public function via($notifiable)
    {
        return ['mail'];
    }

    /**
     * Get the mail representation of the notification
     *
     * @param  mixed  $notifiable
     * @return \Illuminate\Notifications\Messages\MailMessage
     */
    public function toMail($notifiable)
    {
        return (new MailMessage)
                    ->line('The introduction to the notification.')
                    ->action('Notification Action', url('/'))
                    ->line('Thank you for using our application!');
    }

    /**
     * Get the array representation of the notification
     *
     * @param  mixed  $notifiable
     * @return array
     */
    public function toArray($notifiable)
    {
        return [
            //
        ];
```

```
        }
}
```

We can learn a few things here. First, we're going to pass relevant data into the constructor. Second, there's a `via()` method that allows us to define, for a given user, which notification channels to use (`$notifiable` represents whatever entities you want to notify in your system; for most apps, it'll be a user, but that's not always the case). And third, there are individual methods for each notification channel that allow us to specifically define how to send one of these notifications through that channel.

 When Would a $notifiable Not Be a User?

While the most common notification targets will be users, it's possible you may want to notify something else. This may simply be because your application has multiple user types—so, you might want to be able to notify both trainers and trainees. But you also might find yourself wanting to notify a group, a company, or a server.

So, let's modify this class for our `WorkoutAvailable` example. Take a look at Example 15-14.

Example 15-14. Our WorkoutAvailable notification class

```
...
class WorkoutAvailable extends Notification
{
    use Queueable;

    public $workout;

    public function __construct($workout)
    {
        $this->workout = $workout;
    }

    public function via($notifiable)
    {
        // This method doesn't exist on the User... we're going to make it up
        return $notifiable->preferredNotificationChannels();
    }

    public function toMail($notifiable)
    {
        return (new MailMessage)
            ->line('You have a new workout available!')
            ->action('Check it out now', route('workout.show', [$this->workout]))
```

```
        ->line('Thank you for training with us!');
    }

    public function toArray($notifiable)
    {
        return [];
    }
}
```

Defining the via() Method for Your Notifiables

As you can see in Example 15-14, we're somehow responsible for deciding, for each notification and each notifiable, which notification channels we're going to use.

You could just send everything as mail or just send everything as an SMS (Example 15-15).

Example 15-15. Simplest possible via() method

```
public function via($notifiable)
{
    return 'nexmo';
}
```

You could also let each user choose their one preferred method and save that on the User itself (Example 15-16).

Example 15-16. Customizing the via() method per user

```
public function via($notifiable)
{
    return $notifiable->preferred_notification_channel;
}
```

Or, as we imagined in Example 15-14, you could create a method on each notifiable that allows for some complex notification logic. For example, you could notify the user over certain channels during work hours and other channels in the evening. What is important is that via() is a PHP class method, so you can do whatever complex logic you want there.

Sending Notifications

There are two ways to send a notification: by using the Notification facade, or by adding the Notifiable trait to an Eloquent class (likely your User class).

Sending notifications using the Notifiable trait

Any model that imports the `Laravel\Notifications\Notifiable` trait (which the `App\User` class does by default) has a `notify()` method that can be passed a notification, which will look like Example 15-17.

Example 15-17. Sending a notification using the Notifiable trait

```
use App\Notifications\WorkoutAvailable;
...
$user->notify(new WorkoutAvailable($workout));
```

Sending notifications with the Notification facade

The `Notification` facade is the clumsier of the two methods, since you have to pass both the notifiable and the notification. However, it's helpful because you can choose to pass more than one notifiable in at the same time, like you can see in Example 15-18.

Example 15-18. Sending notifications using the Notification facade

```
use App\Notifications\WorkoutAvailable;
...
Notification::send($users, new WorkoutAvailable($workout));
```

Queueing Notifications

Most of the notification drivers need to send HTTP requests to send their notifications, which could slow down your user experience, so you probably want to queue your notifications. All notifications import the `Queueable` trait by default, so all you need to do is add `implements ShouldQueue` to your notification and Laravel will instantly move it to a queue.

As with any other queued features, you'll need to make sure you have your queue settings configured correctly and a queue worker running.

If you'd like to delay the delivery of a notification, you can run the `delay()` method on the notification:

```
$delayUntil = now()->addMinutes(15);

$user->notify((new WorkoutAvailable($workout))->delay($delayUntil));
```

Out-of-the-Box Notification Types

Out of the box, Laravel comes with notification drivers for email, database, broadcast, Nexmo SMS, and Slack. I'll cover each briefly, but I'd recommend referring to the docs (*http://bit.ly/2JC2TqQ*) for more thorough introductions to each.

It's also easy to create your own notification drivers, and dozens of people already have; you can find them at the Laravel Notification Channels website (*http://bit.ly/2YmpHOF*).

Email notifications

Let's take a look at how the email from our earlier example, Example 15-14, is built:

```
public function toMail($notifiable)
{
    return (new MailMessage)
        ->line('You have a new workout available!')
        ->action('Check it out now', route('workouts.show', [$this->workout]))
        ->line('Thank you for training with us!');
}
```

The result is shown in Figure 15-1. The email notification system puts your application's name in the header of the email; you can customize that app name in the name key of *config/app.php*.

This email is automatically sent to the email property on the notifiable, but you can customize this behavior by adding a method to your notifiable class named routeNotificationForMail() that returns the email address you'd like email notifications sent to.

The email's subject is set by parsing the notification class name and converting it to words. So, our WorkoutAvailable notification would have the default subject of "Workout Available". You can also customize this by chaining the subject() method on the MailMessage in the toMail() method.

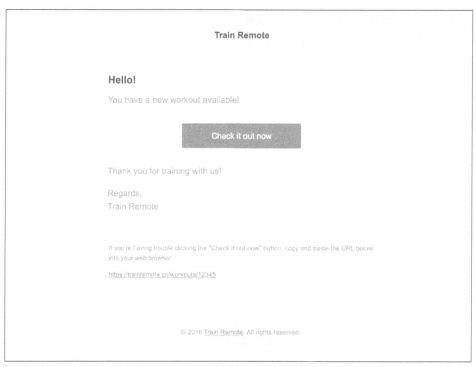

Figure 15-1. An email sent with the default notification template

If you want to modify the templates, publish them and edit to your heart's content:

```
php artisan vendor:publish --tag=laravel-notifications
```

Markdown mail notifications. If you like working with Markdown emails (see "Markdown Mailables" on page 411), you can also use the same `markdown()` method in your notifications, as shown in Example 15-19:

Example 15-19. Using the markdown() method with notifications

```
public function toMail($notifiable)
{
    return (new MailMessage)
        ->subject('Workout Available')
        ->markdown('emails.workout-available', ['workout' => $this->workout]);
}
```

You can also change the style of the default template to be an "error" message, which uses a bit of different language and changes the primary button color to red. Just add a call to the `error()` method to your `MailMessage` call chain in the `toMail()` method.

Database notifications

You can send notifications to a database table using the `database` notification channel. First, create your table with `php artisan notifications:table`. Next, create a `toDatabase()` method on your notification and return an array of data there. This data will be encoded as JSON and stored in the database table's `data` column.

The `Notifiable` trait adds a `notifications` relationship to any model it's imported in, allowing you to easily access records in the notifications table. So if you're using database notifications, you could so something like Example 15-20:

Example 15-20. Iterating over a user's database notifications

```
User::first()->notifications->each(function ($notification) {
    // Do something
});
```

The `database` notification channel also has the concept of whether or not a notification is "read." You can scope to only the "unread" notifications as shown in Example 15-21:

Example 15-21. Iterating over a user's unread database notifications

```
User::first()->unreadNotifications->each(function ($notification) {
    // Do something
});
```

And you can mark one or all notifications as read, as Example 15-22 demonstrates:

Example 15-22. Marking database notifications as read

```
// Individual
User::first()->unreadNotifications->each(function ($notification) {
    if ($condition) {
        $notification->markAsRead();
    }
});

// All
User::first()->unreadNotifications->markAsRead();
```

Broadcast notifications

The `broadcast` channel sends notifications out using Laravel's event broadcasting features, which are powered by WebSockets (we'll learn more about these in "Broadcasting Events over WebSockets, and Laravel Echo" on page 442).

Create a `toBroadcast()` method on your notification and return array of data, and if your app is correctly configured for event broadcasting, that data will be broadcast on a private channel named *notifiable.id*. The *id* will be the ID of the notifiable, and *notifiable* will be the notifiable's fully qualified class name, with the slashes replaced by periods—for example, the private channel for the `App\User` with the ID of 1 will be `App.User.1`.

SMS notifications

SMS notifications are sent via Nexmo (*https://www.nexmo.com*), so if you want to send SMS notifications, sign up for a Nexmo account and follow the instructions in the docs (*http://bit.ly/2JC2TqQ*). Like with the other channels, you'll be setting up a `toNexmo()` method and customizing the SMS message there.

SMS Notification Package Extracted in 5.8+

In Laravel 5.8+, the SMS notification channel is a first-party package. If you want to use Nexmo SMS notifications, simply require this package with Composer:

```
composer require laravel/nexmo-notification-channel
```

Slack notifications

The `slack` notification channel allows you to customize the appearance of your notifications and even attach files to your notifications. Like with the other channels, you'll set up a `toSlack()` method and customize the message there.

Slack notification package extracted in 5.8+

In Laravel 5.8+, the Slack notification channel is a first-party package. If you want to use Slack notifications, simply require this package with Composer.

```
composer require laravel/slack-notification-channel
```

Other notifications

Looking to send your notifications through other channels than those that come out of the box? There's a robust community effort to provide an incredible variety of notification channels; check out what's on offer at the Laravel Notifications Channels website (*http://bit.ly/2YmpHOF*).

Testing

Let's take a look at how to test mail and notifications.

Mail

There are two options for testing mail in Laravel. If you're using the traditional mail syntax (which is, by the way, not the preferred method in Laravel 5.3 and later), I'd recommend using a tool called MailThief (*http://bit.ly/2CCJ4K6*), which Adam Wathan wrote for Tighten. Once you bring MailThief into your application with Composer, you can use `MailThief::hijack()` in your tests to make MailThief capture any calls to the `Mail` facade or any mailer classes.

MailThief then makes it possible to make assertions against the senders, recipients, CC and BCC values, and even content and attachments of your mail. Take a look at the GitHub repo to learn more, or bring it into your app:

```
composer require tightenco/mailthief --dev
```

If you're using mailables, there's a simple syntax for writing assertions against your sent mail (Example 15-23).

Example 15-23. Asserting against mailables

```
public function test_signup_triggers_welcome_email()
{
    Mail::fake();

    Mail::assertSent(WelcomeEmail::class, function ($mail) {
        return $mail->subject == 'Welcome!';
    });

    // You can also use assertSentTo() to explicitly test the recipients, and
    // you can use assertNotSent() to test that a specific mail wasn't sent.
}
```

Notifications

Laravel provides a built-in set of assertions for testing your notifications. Example 15-24 demonstrates.

Example 15-24. Asserting notifications were sent

```
public function test_new_signups_triggers_admin_notification()
{
    Notification::fake();

    Notification::assertSentTo($user, NewUsersSignedup::class,
        function ($notification, $channels) {
            return $notification->user->email == 'user-who-signed-up@gmail.com'
            && $channels == ['mail'];
    });
```

```
    // Assert that the email was sent to a given user
    Notification::assertSentTo(
        [$user],
        NewUsersSignedup::class
    );

    // You can also use assertNotSentTo()
    Notification::assertNotSentTo(
        [$userDidntSignUp], NewUsersSignedup::class
    );
}
```

TL;DR

Laravel's mail and notification features provide simple, consistent interfaces to a variety of messaging systems. Laravel's mail system uses "mailables," PHP classes that represent emails, to provide a consistent syntax to different mail drivers. The notification system makes it easy to build a single notification that can be delivered in many different media—from emails to SMS messages to physical postcards.

Queues, Jobs, Events, Broadcasting, and the Scheduler

So far we've covered some of the most common structures that power web applications: databases, mail, filesystems, and more. All of these are common across a majority of applications and frameworks.

Laravel also provides facilities for some less common architecture patterns and application structures. In this chapter we'll cover Laravel's tools for implementing queues, queued jobs, events, and WebSocket event publishing. We'll also cover Laravel's scheduler, which makes manually edited cron schedules a thing of the past.

Queues

To understand what a queue is, just think about the idea of "queueing up" in a line at the bank. Even if there are multiple lines—queues—only one person is being served at a time from each queue, and each person will eventually reach the front and be served. In some banks, it's a strict first-in-first-out sort of policy, but in other banks, there's not an exact guarantee that someone won't cut ahead of you in line at some point. Essentially, someone can get added to the queue, be removed from the queue prematurely, or be successfully "processed" and then removed. Someone might even hit the front of the queue, not be able to be served correctly, return to the queue for a time, and then be processed again.

Queues in programming are very similar. Your application adds a "job" to a queue, which is a chunk of code that tells the application how to perform a particular behavior. Then some other separate application structure, usually a "queue worker," takes the responsibility for pulling jobs off of the queue one at a time and performing the appropriate behavior. Queue workers can delete the jobs, return them to the queue with a delay, or mark them as successfully processed.

Laravel makes it easy to serve your queues using Redis, *beanstalkd*, Amazon's Simple Queue Service (SQS), or a database table. You can also choose the sync driver to have the jobs run right in your application without actually being queued, or the null driver for jobs to just be discarded; these two are usually used in local development or testing environments.

Why Queues?

Queues make it easy to remove a costly or slow process from any synchronous call. The most common example is sending mail—doing so can be slow, and you don't want your users to have to wait for mail to send in response to their actions. Instead, you can trigger a "send mail" queued job and let the users get on with their day. And sometimes you may not be worried about saving your users time, but you might have a process like a cron job or a webhook that has a lot of work to get through; rather than letting it all run at once (and potentially time out), you may choose to queue its individual pieces and let the queue worker process them one at a time.

Additionally, if you have some heavy processing that's more than your server can handle, you can spin up more than one queue worker to work through your queue faster than your normal application server could on its own.

Basic Queue Configuration

Like many other Laravel features that abstract multiple providers, queues have their own dedicated config file (*config/queue.php*) that allows you to set up multiple drivers and define which will be the default. This is also where you'll store your SQS, Redis, or *beanstalkd* authentication information.

Simple Redis Queues on Laravel Forge

Laravel Forge (*http://forge.laravel.com/*) is a hosting management service provided by Taylor Otwell, the creator of Laravel, that makes serving queues with Redis a breeze. Every server you create has Redis configured automatically, so if you visit any site's Forge console, you can just go to the Queue tab and hit Start Worker and you're ready to use Redis as your queue driver; you can leave all the default settings, and no other work is necessary.

Queued Jobs

Remember our bank analogy? Each person in the bank's *queue* (line) is, in programming terms, a *job*. Queued jobs can, depending on the environment, take many shapes, like arrays of data or simple strings. In Laravel, they will each be a collection of information containing the job name, the data payload, the number of attempts that have been made so far to process this job, and some other simple metadata.

But you don't need to worry about any of that in your interactions with Laravel. Laravel provides a structure called a Job, which is intended to encapsulate a single task—a behavior that your application can be commanded to do—and allow it to be added to and pulled from a queue. There are also simple helpers to make it easy to queue Artisan commands and mail.

Let's start with an example where, every time a user changes their plan with your SaaS app, you want to rerun some calculations about your overall profit.

Creating a job

As always, there's an Artisan command for that:

```
php artisan make:job CrunchReports
```

Take a look at Example 16-1 to see what you'll get.

Example 16-1. The default template for jobs in Laravel

```php
<?php

namespace App\Jobs;

use Illuminate\Bus\Queueable;
use Illuminate\Queue\SerializesModels;
use Illuminate\Queue\InteractsWithQueue;
use Illuminate\Contracts\Queue\ShouldQueue;
use Illuminate\Foundation\Bus\Dispatchable;

class CrunchReports implements ShouldQueue
{
    use Dispatchable, InteractsWithQueue, Queueable, SerializesModels;

    /**
     * Create a new job instance
     *
     * @return void
     */
    public function __construct()
    {
        //
    }

    /**
     * Execute the job
     *
     * @return void
```

```
    */
    public function handle()
    {
        //
    }
}
```

As you can see, this template imports the `Dispatchable`, `Queueable`, `InteractsWith Queue`, and `SerializesModels` traits, and implements the `ShouldQueue` interface. Prior to Laravel 5.3, some of this functionality came in through the parent `App\Jobs` class.

We also get two methods from this template: the constructor, which you'll want to use to attach data to the job, and the `handle()` method, which is where the job's logic should reside (and is also the method signature you'll use to inject dependencies).

The traits and interface provide the class with the ability to be added to, and interact with, the queue. `Dispatchable` gives it methods to dispatch itself; `Queueable` allows you to specify how Laravel should push this job to the queue; `InteractsWithQueue` allows each job, while being handled, to control its relationship with the queue, including deleting or requeueing itself; and `SerializesModels` gives the job the ability to serialize and deserialize Eloquent models.

Serializing Models

The `SerializesModels` trait gives jobs the ability to serialize (convert to a flatter format that can be stored in a data store like a database or queue system) injected models so that your job's `handle()` method will have access to them. However, because it's too difficult to reliably serialize an entire Eloquent object, the trait ensures that just the primary keys of any attached Eloquent objects are serialized when the job is pushed onto the queue. When the job is deserialized and handled, the trait pulls those Eloquent models fresh from the database by their primary key. This means that when your job runs, it will be pulling a fresh instance of this model, not whatever state it was in when you queued the job.

Let's fill out the methods for our sample class, as in Example 16-2.

Example 16-2. An example job

```
...
use App\ReportGenerator;

class CrunchReports implements ShouldQueue
{
    use Dispatchable, InteractsWithQueue, Queueable, SerializesModels;
```

```
    protected $user;

    public function __construct($user)
    {
        $this->user = $user;
    }

    public function handle(ReportGenerator $generator)
    {
        $generator->generateReportsForUser($this->user);

        Log::info('Generated reports.');
    }
}
```

We're expecting the User instance to be injected when we create the job, and then when it's handled we're typehinting a ReportGenerator class (which we presumably wrote) and a Logger (which Laravel provides). Laravel will read both typehints and inject those dependencies automatically.

Pushing a job onto a queue

There are multiple methods by which you can dispatch a job, including some methods available to every controller and a global dispatch() helper. But since Laravel 5.5, we've had a simpler and preferred method: calling the dispatch() method on the job itself. So, if you're running Laravel 5.5+, just ignore the other options, as we'll do for the rest of this chapter.

In order to dispatch your job, you can just create an instance of it and then call its dispatch() method, passing any necessary data directly into that method. Take a look at Example 16-3 for an example.

Example 16-3. Dispatching jobs

```
$user = auth()->user();
$daysToCrunch = 7;
\App\Jobs\CrunchReports::dispatch($user, $daysToCrunch);
```

There are three settings you can control in order to customize exactly how you dispatch a job: the connection, the queue, and the delay.

Customizing the connection. If you ever have multiple queue connections in place at once, you can customize the connection by chaining onConnection() after the dispatch() method:

```
    DoThingJob::dispatch()->onConnection('redis');
```

Customizing the queue. Within queue servers, you can specify which named queue you're pushing a job onto. For example, you may differentiate your queues based on their importance, naming one `low` and one `high`.

You can customize which queue you're pushing a job onto with the `onQueue()` method:

```
DoThingJob::dispatch()->onQueue('high');
```

Customizing the delay. You can customize the amount of time your queue workers should wait before processing a job with the `delay()` method, which accepts either an integer representing the number of seconds to delay a job or a *DateTime/Carbon* instance:

```
// Delays five minutes before releasing the job to queue workers
$delay = now()->addMinutes(5);
DoThingJob::dispatch()->delay($delay);
```

Note that Amazon SQS doesn't allow delays longer than 15 minutes.

Running a Queue Worker

So what is a queue worker, and how does it work? In Laravel, it's an Artisan command that stays running forever (until it's stopped manually) and takes the responsibility for pulling down jobs from your queue and running them:

```
php artisan queue:work
```

This command starts a daemon "listening" to your queue; every time there are jobs on the queue, it will pull down the first job, handle it, delete it, and move on to the next. If at any point there are no jobs, it "sleeps" for a configurable amount of time before checking again to see if there are any more jobs.

You can define how many seconds a job should be able to run before the queue listener stops it (`--timeout`), how many seconds the listener should "sleep" when there are no jobs left (`--sleep`), how many tries each job should be allowed before being deleted (`--tries`), which connection the worker should listen to (the first parameter after `queue:work`), and which queues it should listen to (`--queue=`):

```
php artisan queue:work redis --timeout=60 --sleep=15 --tries=3
  --queue=high,medium
```

You can also process just a single job with `php artisan queue:work`.

Handling Errors

So, what happens when something goes wrong with your job when it's in the middle of processing?

Exceptions in handling

If an exception is thrown, the queue listener will release that job back onto the queue. The job will be rereleased to be processed again and again until it is able to finish successfully or until it has been attempted the maximum number of times allowed by your queue listener.

Limiting the number of tries

The maximum number of tries is defined by the `--tries` switch passed to the `queue:listen` or `queue:work` Artisan command.

> **The Danger of Infinite Retries**
>
> If you don't set `--tries`, or if you set it to 0, the queue listener will allow infinite retries. That means if there are any circumstances in which a job can just *never* be completed—for example, if it relies on a tweet that has since been deleted—your app will slowly crawl to a halt as it retries forever.
>
> The documentation (*http://bit.ly/2TWQHpq*) and Laravel Forge both show 3 as the recommended starting point for the maximum number of retries. So, in case of confusion, start there and adjust:
>
> ```
> php artisan queue:work --tries=3
> ```

If at any point you'd like to check how many times a job has been attempted already, use the `attempts()` method on the job itself, as in Example 16-4.

Example 16-4. Checking how many times a job has already been tried

```
public function handle()
{
    ...
    if ($this->attempts() > 3) {
        //
    }
}
```

Handling failed jobs

Once a job has exceeded its allowable number of retries, it's considered a "failed" job. Before you do anything else—even if all you want to do is limit the number of times a job can be tried—you'll need to create the "failed jobs" database table.

There's an Artisan command to create the migration (and you'll then want to migrate):

```
php artisan queue:failed-table
php artisan migrate
```

Any job that has surpassed its maximum number of allowed attempts will be dumped there. But there are quite a few things you can do with your failed jobs.

First, you can define a `failed()` method on the job itself, which will run when that job fails (see Example 16-5).

Example 16-5. Defining a method to run when a job fails

```
...
class CrunchReports implements ShouldQueue
{
    ...

    public function failed()
    {
        // Do whatever you want, like notify an admin
    }
}
```

Next, you can register a global handler for failed jobs. Somewhere in the application's bootstrap—if you don't know where to put it, just put it in the `boot()` method of `AppServiceProvider`—place the code in Example 16-6 to define a listener.

Example 16-6. Registering a global handler to handle failed jobs

```
// Some service provider
use Illuminate\Support\Facades\Queue;
use Illuminate\Queue\Events\JobFailed;
...
    public function boot()
    {
        Queue::failing(function (JobFailed $event) {
            // $event->connectionName
            // $event->job
            // $event->exception
        });
    }
```

There is also a suite of Artisan tools for interacting with the failed jobs table.

queue:failed shows you a list of your failed jobs:

```
php artisan queue:failed
```

The list will look something like this:

```
+----+------------+---------+--------------------+---------------------+
| ID | Connection | Queue   | Class              | Failed At           |
+----+------------+---------+--------------------+---------------------+
| 9  | database   | default | App\Jobs\AlwaysFails | 2018-08-26 03:42:55 |
+----+------------+---------+--------------------+---------------------+
```

From there, you can grab the ID of any individual failed job and retry it with queue:retry:

```
php artisan queue:retry 9
```

If you'd rather retry all of the jobs, pass all instead of an ID:

```
php artisan queue:retry all
```

You can delete an individual failed job with queue:forget:

```
php artisan queue:forget 5
```

And you can delete all of your failed jobs with queue:flush:

```
php artisan queue:flush
```

Controlling the Queue

Sometimes, from within the handling of a job, you'll want to add conditions that will potentially either release the job to be restarted later or delete the job forever.

To release a job back into the queue, use the release() method, as in Example 16-7.

Example 16-7. Releasing a job back onto the queue

```
public function handle()
{
    ...
    if (condition) {
        $this->release($numberOfSecondsToDelayBeforeRetrying);
    }
}
```

If you want to delete a job during its handling, you can just return at any point, as seen in Example 16-8; that's the signal to the queue that the job was handled appropriately and should not be returned to the queue.

Example 16-8. Deleting a job

```
public function handle()
{
    ...
    if ($jobShouldBeDeleted) {
        return;
    }
}
```

Queues Supporting Other Functions

The primary use for queues is to push jobs onto them, but you can also queue mail using the `Mail::queue` functionality. You can learn more about this in "Queues" on page 414. You can also queue Artisan commands, which we covered in Chapter 8.

Laravel Horizon

Laravel Horizon, like some of the other tools we've covered (Scout, Passport, etc.), is a tool provided by Laravel that doesn't come bundled with the core.

Horizon provides insight into the status of your Redis queued jobs. You can see which jobs have failed, how many are queued, and how fast they're working, and you can even get notifications when any of your queues are overloaded or failing. The Horizon dashboard is shown in Figure 16-1.

Figure 16-1. A preview of the Horizon dashboard

Installing and running Horizon is pretty straightforward and the documentation is thorough, so if you're interested, take a look at the Horizon docs (*https://laravel.com/docs/horizon*) to learn how to install, configure, and deploy it.

 Please note that you will need to have Laravel 5.5+ and PHP 7.1+ in order to run Horizon.

Events

With jobs, the calling code informs the application that it should *do something*: `CrunchReports`, or `NotifyAdminOfNewSignup`.

With an event, the calling code instead informs the application that *something happened*: `UserSubscribed`, or `UserSignedUp`, or `ContactWasAdded`. Events are notifications that something has taken place.

Some of these events may be "fired" by the framework itself. For example, Eloquent models fire events when they are saved, or created, or deleted. But some events can also be manually triggered by the application's code.

An event being fired doesn't do anything on its own. However, you can bind *event listeners*, whose sole purpose is to listen for the broadcasting of specific events and to act in response. Any event can have anywhere from zero to many event listeners.

Laravel's events are structured like the observer, or "pub/sub," pattern. Many events are fired out into the application; some may never be listened for, and others may have a dozen listeners. The events don't know or care.

Firing an Event

There are three ways to fire an event. You can use the `Event` facade, inject the `Dispatcher`, or use the `event()` global helper, as illustrated in Example 16-9.

Example 16-9. Three ways to fire an event

```
Event::fire(new UserSubscribed($user, $plan));
// or
$dispatcher = app(Illuminate\Contracts\Events\Dispatcher::class);
$dispatcher->fire(new UserSubscribed($user, $plan));
// or
event(new UserSubscribed($user, $plan));
```

If in doubt, I'd recommend using the global helper function.

To create an event to fire, use the `make:event` Artisan command:

```
php artisan make:event UserSubscribed
```

That'll make a file that looks something like Example 16-10.

Example 16-10. The default template for a Laravel event

```php
<?php

namespace App\Events;

use Illuminate\Broadcasting\Channel;
use Illuminate\Queue\SerializesModels;
use Illuminate\Broadcasting\PrivateChannel;
use Illuminate\Broadcasting\PresenceChannel;
use Illuminate\Foundation\Events\Dispatchable;
use Illuminate\Broadcasting\InteractsWithSockets;
use Illuminate\Contracts\Broadcasting\ShouldBroadcast;

class UserSubscribed
{
    use Dispatchable, InteractsWithSockets, SerializesModels;

    /**
     * Create a new event instance
     *
     * @return void
     */
    public function __construct()
    {
        //
    }

    /**
     * Get the channels the event should be broadcast on
     *
     * @return \Illuminate\Broadcasting\Channel|array
     */
    public function broadcastOn()
    {
        return new PrivateChannel('channel-name');
    }
}
```

Let's take a look at what we get here. SerializesModels works just like with jobs; it allows you to accept Eloquent models as parameters. InteractsWithSockets, Should Broadcast, and the broadcastOn() method provide the backing functionality for broadcasting events using WebSockets, which we'll cover in a bit.

It might seem strange that there's no handle() or fire() method here. But remember, this object exists not to determine a particular action, but just to encapsulate some data. The first piece of data is its name; UserSubscribed tells us that a particu-

---

lar event happened (a user subscribed). The rest of the data is any data we pass into the constructor and associate with this entity.

Example 16-11 shows what we might want to do with our UserSubscribed event.

Example 16-11. Injecting data into an event

```
...
class UserSubscribed
{
    use InteractsWithSockets, SerializesModels;

    public $user;
    public $plan;

    public function __construct($user, $plan)
    {
        $this->user = $user;
        $this->plan = $plan;
    }
}
```

Now we have an object that appropriately represents the event that happened: $event->user subscribed to the $event->plan plan. Remember, firing this event is as simple as event(new UserSubscribed($user, $plan)).

Listening for an Event

We have an event, and the ability to fire it. Now let's look at how to listen for it.

First, we'll create an event listener. Let's say we want to email the app's owner every time a new user subscribes:

```
php artisan make:listener EmailOwnerAboutSubscription --event=UserSubscribed
```

That gives us the file in Example 16-12.

Example 16-12. The default template for a Laravel event listener

```
<?php

namespace App\Listeners;

use App\Events\UserSubscribed;
use Illuminate\Queue\InteractsWithQueue;
use Illuminate\Contracts\Queue\ShouldQueue;

class EmailOwnerAboutSubscription
{
    /**
```

```
 * Create the event listener
 *
 * @return void
 */
public function __construct()
{
    //
}

/**
 * Handle the event
 *
 * @param  UserSubscribed  $event
 * @return void
 */
public function handle(UserSubscribed $event)
{
    //
}
}
```

This is where the action happens—where the `handle()` method lives. This method expects to be passed an event of type `UserSubscribed` and act in response to it.

So, let's make it send an email (Example 16-13).

Example 16-13. A sample event listener

```
...
use App\Mail\UserSubscribed as UserSubscribedMessage;

class EmailOwnerAboutSubscription
{
    public function handle(UserSubscribed $event)
    {
        Log::info('Emailed owner about new user: ' . $event->user->email);

        Mail::to(config('app.owner-email'))
            ->send(new UserSubscribedMessage($event->user, $event->plan));
    }
}
```

Now, one last task: we need to set this listener to listen to the `UserSubscribed` event. We'll do that in the `$listen` property of the `EventServiceProvider` class (see Example 16-14).

Example 16-14. Binding listeners to events in EventServiceProvider

```
class EventServiceProvider extends ServiceProvider
{
```

```
    protected $listen = [
        \App\Events\UserSubscribed::class => [
            \App\Listeners\EmailOwnerAboutSubscription::class,
        ],
    ];
```

As you can see, the key of each array entry is the class name of the event, and the value is an array of listener class names. We can add as many class names as we want under the `UserSubscribed` key and they will all listen and respond to each `User Subscribed` event.

Event subscribers

There's one more structure you can use to define the relationship between your events and their listeners. Laravel has a concept called an *event subscriber*, which is a class that contains a collection of methods that act as separate listeners to unique events, and also contains the mapping of which method should handle which event. In this case it's easier to show than to tell, so take a look at Example 16-15. Note that event subscribers are not a particularly commonly used tool.

Example 16-15. A sample event subscriber

```php
<?php

namespace App\Listeners;

class UserEventSubscriber
{
    public function onUserSubscription($event)
    {
        // Handles the UserSubscribed event
    }

    public function onUserCancellation($event)
    {
        // Handles the UserCanceled event
    }

    public function subscribe($events)
    {
        $events->listen(
            \App\Events\UserSubscribed::class,
            'App\Listeners\UserEventSubscriber@onUserSubscription'
        );

        $events->listen(
            \App\Events\UserCanceled::class,
            'App\Listeners\UserEventSubscriber@onUserCancellation'
        );
```

```
    }
}
```

Subscribers need to define a `subscribe()` method, which is passed an instance of the event dispatcher. We'll use that to pair events with their listeners, but in this case, those are methods on this class, instead of entire classes.

As a refresher, any time you see an @ inline like this means the class name is to the left of the @ and the method name is to the right. So, in Example 16-15, we're defining that the `onUserSubscription()` method of this subscriber will listen to any `UserSub scribed` events.

There's one last thing we need to do: in `App\Providers\EventServiceProvider`, we need to add our subscriber's class name to the `$subscribe` property, as seen in Example 16-16.

Example 16-16. Registering an event subscriber

```
...
class EventServiceProvider extends ServiceProvider
{
    ...
    protected $subscribe = [
        \App\Listeners\UserEventSubscriber::class
    ];
}
```

Broadcasting Events over WebSockets, and Laravel Echo

WebSocket (often called WebSockets) is a protocol, popularized by Pusher (a hosted WebSocket SaaS), that makes it simple to provide near-real-time communication between web devices. Rather than relying on information passing via HTTP requests, WebSockets libraries open a direct connection between the client and the server. WebSockets are behind tools like the chat boxes in Gmail and Facebook, where you don't have to wait for the page to reload or for Ajax requests to receive or send data; instead, data is both sent and received in real time.

WebSockets work best with small pieces of data passed in a pub/sub structure—just like Laravel's events. Laravel has a built-in set of tools that make it easy to define that one or more of your events should be broadcast to a WebSocket server; it's straightforward, for example, to have a `MessageWasReceived` event that is published to the notifications box of a certain user or set of users the instant a message arrives at your application.

Configuration and Setup

Take a look at *config/broadcasting.php* to find the configuration settings for your event broadcasting. Laravel supports three drivers for broadcasting: Pusher, a paid SaaS offering; Redis, for locally running WebSocket servers; and log, for local development and debugging.

Queue Listeners

In order for event broadcasting to move quickly, Laravel pushes the instruction to broadcast them onto a queue. That means you'll need to have a queue worker running (or use the sync queue driver for local development). See "Running a Queue Worker" on page 432 to learn how to run a queue worker.

Laravel suggests a default delay of three seconds before the queue worker looks for new jobs. However, with event broadcasting, you may notice some events take a second or two to broadcast. To speed this up, update your queue settings to only wait one second before looking for new jobs.

Broadcasting an Event

To broadcast an event, you need to mark that event as a broadcast event by having it implement the Illuminate\Contracts\Broadcasting\ShouldBroadcast interface. This interface requires you to add the broadcastOn() method, which will return an array of either strings or Channel objects, each representing a WebSocket channel.

The Structure of WebSocket Events

Every event you send with WebSockets can have three primary characteristics: the name, the channel, and the data.

The *name* of an event might be something like user-was-subscribed, but Laravel's default is to use the fully qualified class name of the event; that is something like App \Events\UserSubscribed. You can customize this by passing the name to the optional broadcastAs() method in your event class.

The *channel* is the way of describing which clients should receive this message. It's a very common pattern to have a channel for each user (e.g., users.1, users.2, etc.), and possibly a channel for all users (e.g., users), and maybe one for just users who are members of a certain account (accounts.1).

If the channel you're targeting is a private channel, preface the channel name with private-, and if it's a presence channel, preface the channel name with presence-. So, a private Pusher channel named groups.5 should be, instead, private-groups.5. If you use Laravel's PrivateChannel and PresenceChannel objects in your broadcastOn() method, they'll take care of adding those prefaces to your channel names for you.

If you're not familiar with public, private, and presence channels, see the note in "The broadcast service provider" on page 449.

The *data* is a payload, usually JSON, of information relevant to the event—the message, maybe, or information about the user or plan that can be acted upon by the consuming JavaScript.

Example 16-17 shows our UserSubscribed event, modified to broadcast on two channels: one for the user (to confirm the user's subscription) and one for admins (to notify them of a new subscription).

Example 16-17. An event broadcasting on multiple channels

```
...
use Illuminate\Contracts\Broadcasting\ShouldBroadcast;

class UserSubscribed implements ShouldBroadcast
{
    use Dispatchable, InteractsWithSockets, SerializesModels;

    public $user;
    public $plan;

    public function __construct($user, $plan)
    {
```

```
        $this->user = $user;
        $this->plan = $plan;
    }

    public function broadcastOn()
    {
        // String syntax
        return [
            'users.' . $this->user->id,
            'admins'
        ];

        // Channel object syntax
        return [
            new Channel('users.' . $this->user->id),
            new Channel('admins'),
            // If it were a private channel: new PrivateChannel('admins'),
            // If it were a presence channel: new PresenceChannel('admins'),
        ];
    }
}
```

By default, any public properties of your event will be serialized as JSON and sent along as the data of your broadcast event. That means the data of one of our broadcast UserSubscribed events might look like Example 16-18.

Example 16-18. Sample broadcast event data

```
{
    'user': {
        'id': 5,
        'name': 'Fred McFeely',
        ...
    },
    'plan': 'silver'
}
```

You can override this by returning an array of data from the broadcastWith() method on your event, as in Example 16-19.

Example 16-19. Customizing the broadcast event data

```
public function broadcastWith()
{
    return [
        'userId' => $this->user->id,
        'plan' => $this->plan
    ];
}
```

You can customize which queue your event is pushed onto by setting the $broadcast
Queue property on the event class:

```
public $broadcastQueue = 'websockets-for-faster-processing';
```

You may choose to do this so you can keep other queue items from slowing down
your event broadcast; real-time WebSockets aren't much fun if a long-running job
that's higher in the queue keeps the events from going out in time.

You can also force a given event to skip the queue entirely (using the "sync" queue
driver, which is processed by the current PHP thread), by having it implement the
ShouldBroadcastNow contract (Example 16-20).

Example 16-20. Forcing an event to skip the broadcast queue

```
use Illuminate\Contracts\Broadcasting\ShouldBroadcastNow;

class UserSubscribed implements ShouldBroadcastNow
{
    //
}
```

And, finally, you can choose to customize whether a given event should be broadcast
at all by giving it a broadcastWhen() method as in Example 16-21:

Example 16-21. Conditionally determining whether an event should be broadcast

```
public function broadcastWhen()
{
    // Notify me only when users sign up from the White House
    return str_contains($this->user->email, 'whitehouse.gov');
}
```

Receiving the Message

If you choose to host your own Redis WebSockets server, the Laravel docs (*http://
bit.ly/2VApJBb*) have a great walkthrough on how to set that up using socket.io and
ioredis.

As of this book's publication, the most common solution Laravel developers use is
Pusher (*https://pusher.com/*). Plans over a certain size cost money, but there's a gener-
ous free plan. Pusher makes it incredibly easy to set up a simple WebSocket server,
and its JavaScript SDK handles all of the authentication and channel management
with almost no work on your part. SDKs are available for iOS, Android, and many
more platforms, languages, and frameworks.

There's also a new tool announced just before the publication of this book called Laravel WebSockets (*http://bit.ly/2HS4rur*) that lets you host your own Laravel-based,

Pusher-compatible WebSockets server. You can install the package into your current Laravel app (the same app you're broadcasting from) or into a separate microservice.

If you choose to work with a Laravel WebSockets server, you'll follow all of the directions in this book as if you were working with Pusher, but your configuration settings will be a bit different.

Simple WebSockets listening with Pusher

It's helpful to understand how to listen to Laravel's broadcast events without Echo even if you choose to use Echo in the end, but because much of the code here is not necessary if you use Echo, I'd recommend reading this section, and then reading "Laravel Echo (the JavaScript Side)" on page 452 before you start implementing any of it; you can decide which way you prefer and then write your code from there.

To get started, pull in Pusher's library, get an API key from your Pusher account, and subscribe to any events on any channels with code like that in Example 16-22.

Example 16-22. Basic usage of Pusher

```
...
<script src="https://js.pusher.com/4.3/pusher.min.js"></script>
<script>
// Enable Pusher logging - don't include this in production
Pusher.logToConsole = true;

// Globally, perhaps; just a sample of how to get data in
var App = {
    'userId': {{ auth()->id() }},
    'pusherKey': '{{ config('broadcasting.connections.pusher.key') }}'
};

// Locally
var pusher = new Pusher(App.pusherKey, {
    cluster: '{{ config('broadcasting.connections.pusher.options.cluster') }}',
    encrypted: {{ config('broadcasting.connections.pusher.options.encrypted') }}
});

var pusherChannel = pusher.subscribe('users.' + App.userId);

pusherChannel.bind('App\\Events\\UserSubscribed', (data) => {
    console.log(data.user, data.plan);
});
</script>
```

Escaping Backslashes in JavaScript

Since \ is a control character in JavaScript, you need to write \\ to represent a backslash in your strings, which is why there are two backslashes between each namespace segment in Example 16-22.

To publish to Pusher from Laravel, get your Pusher key, secret, cluster, and app ID from your Pusher account dashboard, and then set them in your *.env* file under the keys PUSHER_KEY, PUSHER_SECRET, PUSHER_APP_CLUSTER, and PUSHER_APP_ID.

If you serve your app, visit a page with the JavaScript from Example 16-22 embedded in it in one window, push a broadcast event in another window or from your terminal, have a queue listener running or are using the sync driver, and all of your authentication information is set up correctly, you should see event logs popping up in your JavaScript window's console in near real time.

With this power, it's now easy for you to keep your users up to date with what's happening with their data any time they're in your app. You can notify users of the actions of other users, of long-running processes that have just finished, or of your application's responses to external actions like incoming emails or webhooks. The possibilities are endless.

Requirements

If you want to broadcast with Pusher or Redis, you'll need to bring in these dependencies:

- Pusher: pusher/pusher-php-server "~3.0"
- Redis: predis/predis

Advanced Broadcasting Tools

Laravel has a few more tools to make it possible to perform more complex interactions in event broadcasting. These tools, a combination of framework features and a JavaScript library, are called *Laravel Echo*.

These framework features work best when you use Laravel Echo in your JavaScript frontend (which we'll cover in "Laravel Echo (the JavaScript Side)" on page 452), but you can still enjoy some of the benefits of Echo without using the JavaScript components. Echo will work with both Pusher and Redis, but I'm going to use Pusher for any examples.

Excluding the current user from broadcast events

Every connection to Pusher is assigned a unique "socket ID" identifying that socket connection. And it's easy to define that any given socket (user) should be excluded from receiving a specified broadcast event.

This feature makes it possible to define that certain events should not be broadcast to the user who fired them. Let's say every user in a team gets notified when other users create a task; would you want to be notified of a task you just created? No, and that's why we have the `toOthers()` method.

To implement this, there are two steps to follow. First, you need to set up your Java‐Script to send a certain `POST` to `/broadcasting/socket` when your WebSocket con‐nection is initialized. This attaches your `socket_id` to your Laravel session. Echo does this for you, but you can also do it manually—take a look at the Echo source (*http://bit.ly/2CAM89w*) to see how it works.

Next, you'll want to update every request that your JavaScript makes to have an X-Socket-ID header that contains that `socket_id`. Example 16-23 shows how to do that with Axios or in jQuery. Note that your event must use the `Illuminate\Broadcast ing\InteractsWithSockets` trait in order to call the `toOthers()` method.

Example 16-23. Sending the socket ID along with each Ajax request with Axios or in jQuery

```
// Run this right after you initialize Echo
// With Axios
window.axios.defaults.headers.common['X-Socket-Id'] = Echo.socketId();

// With jQuery
$.ajaxSetup({
    headers: {
        'X-Socket-Id': Echo.socketId()
    }
});
```

Once you've handled this, you can exclude any event from being broadcast to the user who triggered it by using the `broadcast()` global helper instead of the `event()` global helper and then chaining `toOthers()` after it:

```
broadcast(new UserSubscribed($user, $plan))->toOthers();
```

The broadcast service provider

All of the other features that Echo provides require your JavaScript to authenticate with the server. Take a look at `App\Providers\BroadcastServiceProvider`, where you'll define how to authorize users' access to your private and presence channels.

The two primary actions you can take are to define the middleware that will be used on your broadcasting auth routes, and to define the authorization settings for your channels.

If you're going to use these features, you'll need to uncomment the `App\Providers\BroadcastServiceProvider::class` line in *config/app.php*.

And if you'll be using these features *without* Laravel Echo, you'll either need to manually handle sending CSRF tokens along with your authentication requests, or exclude `/broadcasting/auth` and `/broadcasting/socket` from CSRF protection by adding them to the `$except` property of the `VerifyCsrfToken` middleware.

Binding authorization definitions for WebSocket channels. Private and presence WebSocket channels need to be able to ping your application to learn whether the current user is authorized for that channel. You'll use the `Broadcast::channel()` method to define the rules for this authorization in your *routes/channels.php* file.

Public, Private, and Presence Channels

There are three types of channels in WebSockets: public, private, and presence.

Public channels can be subscribed to by any user, authenticated or not.

Private channels require the end user's JavaScript to authenticate against the application to prove that the user is both authenticated and authorized to join this channel.

Presence channels are a type of private channel, but instead of allowing for message passing, they simply keep track of which users join and leave the channel, and make this information available to the application's frontend.

`Broadcast::channel()` takes two parameters: first, a string representing the channel(s) you want it to match, and second, a closure that defines how to authorize users for any channel matching that string. The closure will be passed an Eloquent model of the current user as its first parameter, and any matched *variableNameHere* segments as additional parameters. For example, a channel authorization definition with a string of `teams.teamId`, when matched against the channel `teams.5`, will pass its closure `$user` as the first parameter and 5 as the second parameter.

If you're defining the rules for a private channel, your `Broadcast::channel()` closure will need to return a Boolean: is this user authorized for this channel or not? If you're defining the rules for a presence channel, your closure should return an array of data you want available to the presence channel for any users that you want to show up in the channel. Example 16-24 illustrates defining rules for both kinds of channel.

Example 16-24. Defining authorization rules for private and presence WebSocket channels

```
...
// routes/channels.php

// Define how to authenticate a private channel
Broadcast::channel('teams.{teamId}', function ($user, $teamId) {
    return (int) $user->team_id === (int) $teamId;
});

// Define how to authenticate a presence channel; return any data
// you want the app to have about the user in the channel
Broadcast::channel('rooms.{roomId}', function ($user, $roomId) {
    if ($user->rooms->contains($roomId)) {
        return [
            'name' => $user->name
        ];
    }
});
```

You might be wondering how this information gets from your Laravel application to your JavaScript frontend. Pusher's JavaScript library sends a POST to your application; by default it will hit /pusher/auth, but you can customize that (and Echo customizes it for you) to hit Laravel's authentication route, /broadcasting/auth:

```
var pusher = new Pusher(App.pusherKey, {
    authEndpoint: '/broadcasting/auth'
});
```

Example 16-25 shows how we can tweak Example 16-22 for private and presence channels, *without* Echo's frontend components.

Example 16-25. Basic use of Pusher for private and presence channels

```
...
<script src="https://js.pusher.com/4.3/pusher.min.js"></script>
<script>
    // Enable Pusher logging - don't include this in production
    Pusher.logToConsole = true;

    // Globally, perhaps; just a sample of how to get data in
    var App = {
        'userId': {{ auth()->id() }},
        'pusherKey': '{{ config('broadcasting.connections.pusher.key') }}'
    };

    // Locally
    var pusher = new Pusher(App.pusherKey, {
        cluster: '{{ config('broadcasting.connections.pusher.options.cluster') }}',
        encrypted: {{ config('broadcasting.connections.pusher.options.encrypted') }},
```

```
        authEndpoint: '/broadcasting/auth'
    });

    // Private channel
    var privateChannel = pusher.subscribe('private-teams.1');

    privateChannel.bind('App\\Events\\UserSubscribed', (data) => {
        console.log(data.user, data.plan);
    });

    // Presence channel
    var presenceChannel = pusher.subscribe('presence-rooms.5');

    console.log(presenceChannel.members);
</script>
```

We now have the ability to send WebSocket messages to users depending on whether they pass a given channel's authorization rules. We can also keep track of which users are active in a particular group or section of the site, and display relevant information to each user about other users in the same group.

Laravel Echo (the JavaScript Side)

Laravel Echo is comprised of two pieces: the advanced framework features we just covered, and a JavaScript package that takes advantage of those features and drastically reduces the amount of boilerplate code you need to write powerful WebSocket-based frontends. The Echo JavaScript package makes it easy to handle authentication, authorization, and subscribing to private and presence channels. Echo can be used with the SDKs for either Pusher (for Pusher or a custom Pusher-compatible server) or socket.io (for Redis).

Bringing Echo into your project

To use Echo in your project's JavaScript, add it to *package.json* using npm install --save (be sure to bring in the appropriate Pusher or socket.io SDK as well):

```
npm install pusher-js laravel-echo --save
```

Let's assume you have a basic Laravel Mix file compiling your *app.js* file with Webpack, like in Example 16-26.

Example 16-26. Compiling app.js with Laravel Mix

```
let mix = require('laravel-mix');

mix.js('resources/assets/js/app.js', 'public/js');
```

Laravel's default *resources/js/app.js* structure has a great example of how best to initialize your Echo install. Take a look at Example 16-27 to see how that works between that file and *resources/js/bootstrap.js*.

Example 16-27. Initializing Echo in app.js and bootstrap.js

```
// app.js
require('./bootstrap');

// ... lots of Vue stuff ...

// Add your Echo bindings here
```

```
// bootstrap.js
import Echo from "laravel-echo";

window.Echo = new Echo({
    broadcaster: 'pusher',
    key: process.env.MIX_PUSHER_APP_KEY,
    cluster: process.env.MIX_PUSHER_APP_CLUSTER
});
```

For CSRF protection, you'll also need to add a `csrf-token` `<meta>` tag to your HTML template:

```
<meta name="csrf-token" content="{{ csrf_token() }}">
```

And, of course, remember to link to your compiled *app.js* in your HTML template:

```
<script src="{{ asset('js/app.js') }}"></script>
```

Now we're ready to get started.

Changes to the Configuration When Using the Laravel WebSockets Server Package

If you're working with a Laravel WebSockets server (using the package discussed earlier in "Receiving the Message" on page 446), the configuration details in Example 16-27 will be a little bit different. See the Laravel WebSockets package docs (*http://bit.ly/2Txh2Wv*) for more info.

Using Echo for basic event broadcasting

This is nothing different from what we've already used Pusher for, but Example 16-28 is a simple code sample to show how to use Echo to listen to public channels for basic event information.

Example 16-28. Listening to a public channel with Echo

```
var currentTeamId = 5; // Likely set elsewhere

Echo.channel(`teams.${currentTeamId}`)
    .listen('UserSubscribed', (data) => {
        console.log(data);
    });
```

Echo provides a few methods for subscribing to various types of channels; `channel()` will subscribe you to a public channel. Note that when you listen to an event with Echo, you can ignore the full event namespace and just listen for the unique class name of this event.

We now have access to the public data that's passed along with our event, represented in the `data` object. We can also chain `listen()` handlers, as in Example 16-29.

Example 16-29. Chaining event listeners in Echo

```
Echo.channel(`teams.${currentTeamId}`)
    .listen('UserSubscribed', (data) => {
        console.log(data);
    })
    .listen('UserCanceled', (data) => {
        console.log(data);
    });
```

Remember to Compile and Include!

Did you try these code samples and not see anything change in your browser? Make sure to run `npm run dev` (if you're running it once) or `npm run watch` (to run a listener) to compile your code. And, if you haven't yet, be sure to actually include *app.js* in your template somewhere.

Private channels and basic authentication

Echo also has a method for subscribing to private channels: `private()`. It works the same as `channel()`, but it requires you to have set up channel authorization definitions in *routes/channel.php*, like we covered earlier. Additionally, unlike with the SDKs, you don't need to put `private-` in front of your channel name.

Example 16-30 shows what it looks like to listen to a private channel named `private-teams.5`.

Example 16-30. Listening to a private channel with Echo

```
var currentTeamId = 5; // Likely set elsewhere

Echo.private(`teams.${currentTeamId}`)
    .listen('UserSubscribed', (data) => {
        console.log(data);
    });
```

Presence channels

Echo makes it much simpler to join and listen to events in presence channels. This time you'll want to use the `join()` method to bind to the channel, as in Example 16-31.

Example 16-31. Joining a presence channel

```
var currentTeamId = 5; // Likely set elsewhere

Echo.join(`teams.${currentTeamId}`)
    .here((members) => {
        console.log(members);
    });
```

`join()` subscribes to the presence channel, and `here()` allows you to define the behavior when the user joins and also when any other users join or leave the presence channel.

You can think of a presence channel like a "who's online" sidebar in a chat room. When you first join a presence channel, your `here()` callback will be called and provided a list of all the members at that time. And any time any members join or leave, that callback will be called again with the updated list. There's no messaging happening here, but you can play sounds, update the on-page list of members, or do whatever else you want in response to these actions.

There are also specific methods for individual events, which you can use individually or chained (see Example 16-32).

Example 16-32. Listening for specific presence events

```
var currentTeamId = 5; // Likely set elsewhere

Echo.join('teams.' + currentTeamId)
    .here((members) => {
        // Runs when you join
        console.table(members);
    })
    .joining((joiningMember, members) => {
```

```
    // Runs when another member joins
    console.table(joiningMember);
})
.leaving((leavingMember, members) => {
    // Runs when another member leaves
    console.table(leavingMember);
});
```

Excluding the current user

We covered this previously in the chapter, but if you want to exclude the current user, you can use the `broadcast()` global helper instead of the `event()` global helper and then chain the `toOthers()` method after your broadcast call. But with Echo, the JavaScript side of this is already handled for you. It'll just work.

As you can see, the Echo JavaScript library doesn't do anything you couldn't do on your own—but it makes a lot of common tasks much simpler, and provides a cleaner, more expressive syntax for common WebSocket tasks.

Subscribing to notifications with Echo

Laravel's notifications come with a broadcast driver out of the box that pushes notifications out as broadcast events. You can subscribe to these notifications with Echo using `Echo.notification()`, as in Example 16-33.

Example 16-33. Subscribing to a notification with Echo

```
Echo.private(`App.User.${userId}`)
    .notification((notification) => {
        console.log(notification.type);
    });
```

Client events

If you'd like to send quick, performant messages between your users without the messages even hitting your Laravel application—for example, to send "typing…" notifications—you can use Echo's `whisper()` method, as shown in Example 16-34.

Example 16-34. Bypassing the Laravel server using Echo's whisper() method

```
Echo.private('room')
    .whisper('typing', {
        name: this.user.name
    });
```

And then use `listenForWhisper()` to listen, as in Example 16-35.:

Example 16-35. Listening for whisper events with Echo

```
Echo.private('room')
    .listenForWhisper('typing', (e) => {
        console.log(e.name);
    });
```

Scheduler

If you've ever written a cron job before, you likely already wish for a better tool. Not only is the syntax onerous and frustratingly difficult to remember, but it's one significant aspect of your application that can't be stored in version control.

Laravel's scheduler makes handling scheduled tasks simple. You'll write your scheduled tasks in code, and then point one cron job at your app: once per minute, run `php artisan schedule:run`. Every time this Artisan command is run, Laravel checks your schedule definitions to find out if any scheduled tasks should run.

Here's the cron job to define that command:

```
* * * * * cd /home/myapp.com && php artisan schedule:run >> /dev/null 2>&1
```

There are many task types you can schedule and many time frames you can use to schedule them.

app/Console/Kernel.php has a method named `schedule()`, which is where you'll define any tasks you'd like to schedule.

Available Task Types

First, let's take a look at the simplest option: a closure, run every minute (Example 16-36). Every time the cron job hits the `schedule:run` command, it will call this closure.

Example 16-36. Scheduling a closure to run once every minute

```
// app/Console/Kernel.php
public function schedule(Schedule $schedule)
{
    $schedule->call(function () {
        CalculateTotals::dispatch();
    })->everyMinute();
}
```

There are two other types of tasks you can schedule: Artisan and shell commands.

You can schedule Artisan commands by passing their syntax exactly as you would call them from the command line:

```
$schedule->command('scores:tally --reset-cache')->everyMinute();
```

And you can run any shell commands that you could run with PHP's `exec()` method:

```
$schedule->exec('/home/myapp.com/bin/build.sh')->everyMinute();
```

Available Time Frames

The beauty of the scheduler isn't just that you can define your tasks in code; it's that you can schedule them in code, too. Laravel keeps track of time passing and evaluates whether it's time for any given task to run. That's easy with `everyMinute()` because the answer is always simple: run the task. But Laravel keeps the rest simple for you, too, even for the most complex of requests.

Let's take a look at your options by starting with a monstrous definition that's simple in Laravel:

```
$schedule->call(function () {
    // Runs once a week on Sunday at 23:50
})->weekly()->sundays()->at('23:50');
```

Notice that we can chain times together: we can define frequency and specify the day of the week and the time, and of course we can do much more.

Table 16-1 shows a list of potential date/time modifiers for use when scheduling a job.

Table 16-1. Date/time modifiers for use with the scheduler

Command	Description
`->timezone('America/Detroit')`	Set the time zone for schedules
`->cron('* * * * *')`	Define the schedule using the traditional cron notation
`->everyMinute()`	Run every minute
`->everyFiveMinutes()`	Run every 5 minutes
`->everyTenMinutes()`	Run every 10 minutes
`->everyThirtyMinutes()`	Run every 30 minutes
`->hourly()`	Run every hour
`->daily()`	Run every day at midnight
`->dailyAt('14:00')`	Run every day at 14:00
`->twiceDaily(1, 14)`	Run every day at 1:00 and 14:00
`->weekly()`	Run every week (midnight on Sunday)
`->weeklyOn(5, '10:00')`	Run every week on Friday at 10:00
`->monthly()`	Run every month (midnight on the 1st)
`->monthlyOn(15, '23:00')`	Run every month on the 15th at 23:00
`->quarterly()`	Run every quarter (midnight on the 1st of January, April, July, and October)

Command	Description
`->yearly()`	Run every year (midnight on the 1st of January)
`->when(closure)`	Limit the task to when the closure returns `true`
`->skip(closure)`	Limit the task to when the closure returns `false`
`->between('8:00', '12:00')`	Limit the task to between the given times
`->unlessBetween('8:00', '12:00')`	Limit the task to any time except between the given times
`->weekdays()`	Limit to weekdays
`->sundays()`	Limit to Sundays
`->mondays()`	Limit to Mondays
`->tuesdays()`	Limit to Tuesdays
`->wednesdays()`	Limit to Wednesdays
`->thursdays()`	Limit to Thursdays
`->fridays()`	Limit to Fridays
`->saturdays()`	Limit to Saturdays

Most of these can be chained one after another, but of course, any combinations that don't make sense chained can't be chained.

Example 16-37 shows a few combinations you could consider.

Example 16-37. Some sample scheduled events

```php
// Both run weekly on Sunday at 23:50
$schedule->command('do:thing')->weeklyOn(0, '23:50');
$schedule->command('do:thing')->weekly()->sundays()->at('23:50');

// Run once per hour, weekdays, 8am-5pm
$schedule->command('do:thing')->weekdays()->hourly()->when(function () {
    return date('H') >= 8 && date('H') <= 17;
});

// Run once per hour, weekdays, 8am-5pm using the "between" method
$schedule->command('do:thing')->weekdays()->hourly()->between('8:00', '17:00');

// Run every 30 minutes except when directed not to by the SkipDetector
$schedule->command('do:thing')->everyThirtyMinutes()->skip(function () {
    return app('SkipDetector')->shouldSkip();
});
```

Defining Time Zones for Scheduled Commands

You can define the time zone on a specific scheduled command, using the `time zone()` method:

```php
$schedule->command('do:it')->weeklyOn(0, '23:50')->timezone('America/Chicago');
```

And in apps running Laravel 5.8+, you can also set a default time zone (separate from the application timezone) that all of your scheduled times will be defined in, by defining the scheduleTimezone() method in App\Console\Kernel:

```
protected function scheduleTimezone()
{
    return 'America/Chicago';
}
```

Blocking and Overlap

If you want to avoid your tasks overlapping each other—for example, if you have a task running every minute that may sometimes take longer than a minute to run—end the schedule chain with the withoutOverlapping() method. This method skips a task if the previous instance of that task is still running:

```
$schedule->command('do:thing')->everyMinute()->withoutOverlapping();
```

Handling Task Output

Sometimes the output from your scheduled task is important, whether for logging, notifications, or just ensuring that the task ran.

If you want to write the returned output of a task to a file, use sendOutputTo():

```
$schedule->command('do:thing')->daily()->sendOutputTo($filePath);
```

If you want to append it to a file instead, use appendOutputTo():

```
$schedule->command('do:thing')->daily()->appendOutputTo($filePath);
```

And if you want to email the output to a designated recipient, write it to a file first and then add emailOutputTo():

```
$schedule->command('do:thing')
    ->daily()
    ->sendOutputTo($filePath)
    ->emailOutputTo('me@myapp.com');
```

Make sure that your email settings are configured correctly in Laravel's basic email configuration.

Closure Scheduled Events Can't Send Output

The sendOutputTo(), appendOutputTo(), and emailOutputTo() methods only work for command()- scheduled tasks. You can't use them for closures, unfortunately.

You may also want to send some output to a webhook to verify that your tasks ran correctly. There are a few services that provide this sort of uptime monitoring, most

significantly Laravel Envoyer (*https://envoyer.io*), a zero-downtime deployment service that also provides cron uptime monitoring, and Dead Man's Snitch (*https://dead
manssnitch.com/*), a tool designed purely for monitoring cron job uptime.

These services don't expect something to be emailed to them, but rather expect an
HTTP "ping," so Laravel makes that easy with `pingBefore()` and `thenPing()`:

```
$schedule->command('do:thing')
    ->daily()
    ->pingBefore($beforeUrl)
    ->thenPing($afterUrl);
```

If you want to use the ping features, you'll need to pull in Guzzle using Composer:

```
composer require guzzlehttp/guzzle
```

Task Hooks

Speaking of running something *before* and *after* your task, there are hooks for that,
with `before()` and `after()`:

```
$schedule->command('do_thing')
    ->daily()
    ->before(function () {
        // Prepare
    })
    ->after(function () {
        // Cleanup
    });
```

Testing

Testing queued jobs (or anything else in the queue) is easy. In *phpunit.xml*, which is
the configuration file for your tests, the `QUEUE_DRIVER` environment variable is set to
sync by default. That means your tests will run your jobs or other queued tasks synchronously, directly in your code, without relying on a queue system of any sort. You
can test them just like any other code.

However, if you'd just like to check that a job was fired, you can do that with the
`expectsJobs()` method, as in Example 16-38.

Example 16-38. Asserting that a job of the specified class was dispatched

```
public function test_changing_number_of_subscriptions_crunches_reports()
{
    $this->expectsJobs(\App\Jobs\CrunchReports::class);

    ...
}
```

Or, in projects running Laravel 5.3 and above, you can assert against the specific job itself, as in Example 16-39.

Example 16-39. Using a closure to verify that a dispatched job meets given criteria

```
use Illuminate\Support\Facades\Bus;
...
public function test_changing_subscriptions_triggers_crunch_job()
{
    ...
    Bus::fake();

    Bus::assertDispatched(CrunchReports::class, function ($job) {
        return $job->subscriptions->contains(5);
    });

    // Also can use assertNotDispatched()
}
```

To test that an event fired, you have three options. First, you can just test that the behavior you expected happened, without concerning yourself with the event itself.

Second, in Laravel 5.2 and above, you can explicitly assert that the event fired, as in Example 16-40.

Example 16-40. Asserting that an event of the specified class was fired

```
public function test_usersubscribed_event_fires()
{
    $this->expectsEvents(\App\Events\UserSubscribed::class);

    ...
}
```

Finally, you can run a test against the event that was fired, as in Example 16-41. This is available in Laravel 5.3 and above.

Example 16-41. Using a closure to verify that a fired event meets given criteria

```
use Illuminate\Support\Facades\Event;
...
public function test_usersubscribed_event_fires()
{
    Event::fake();

    ...

    Event::assertDispatched(UserSubscribed::class, function ($e) {
        return $e->user->email = 'user-who-subscribed@mail.com';
```

```
    });

    // Also can use assertNotDispatched()
}
```

Another common scenario is that you're testing code that incidentally fires events, and you want to disable the event listeners during that test. You can disable the event system with the `withoutEvents()` method, as in Example 16-42.

Example 16-42. Disabling event listeners during a test

```
public function test_something_subscription_related()
{
    $this->withoutEvents();

    ...
}
```

TL;DR

Queues allow you to separate chunks of your application's code from the synchronous flow of user interactions out to a list of commands to be processed by a "queue worker." This allows your users to resume interactions with your application while slower processes are handled asynchronously in the background.

Jobs are classes that are structured with the intention of encapsulating a chunk of application behavior so that it can be pushed onto a queue.

Laravel's event system follows the pub/sub or observer pattern, allowing you to send out notifications of an event from one part of your application, and elsewhere bind listeners to those notifications to define what behavior should happen in response to them. Using WebSockets, events can also be broadcast to frontend clients.

Laravel's scheduler simplifies scheduling tasks. Point an every-minute cron job to `php artisan schedule:run` and then schedule your tasks with even the most complex of time requirements using the scheduler, and Laravel will handle all the timings for you.

## CHAPTER 17

Helpers and Collections

We've already covered many global functions throughout the book: these are little helpers that make it easier to perform common tasks, like `dispatch()` for jobs, `event()` for events, and `app()` for dependency resolution. We also talked a bit about Laravel's collections, or arrays on steroids, in Chapter 5.

In this chapter we'll cover some of the more common and powerful helpers and some of the basics of programming with collections.

Helpers

You can find a full list of the helpers Laravel offers in the docs (*http://bit.ly/2HQKaFC*), but we're going to cover a few of the most useful functions here.

 Laravel 5.8 deprecated all global helpers that start with `array_` or `str_`. The helpers will be removed in Laravel 5.9 but will be made available in a package for backward compatibility. Each of these helpers is backed by a method on the `Arr` or `Str` facades, so you can prepare for this future either by using Facade calls or just planning to pull in the first-party package when it's made available.

Arrays

PHP's native array manipulation functions give us a lot of power, but sometimes there are standard manipulations we want to make that require unwieldy loops and logic checks. Laravel's array helpers make a few common array manipulations much simpler:

`array_first($array, $callback, $default = null)`

Returns the first array value that passes a test, defined in a callback closure. You can optionally set the default value as the third parameter. Here's an example:

```
$people = [
    [
        'email' => 'm@me.com',
        'name' => 'Malcolm Me'
    ],
    [
        'email' => 'j@jo.com',
        'name' => 'James Jo'
    ],
];

$value = array_first($people, function ($person, $key) {
    return $person['email'] == 'j@jo.com';
});
```

`array_get($array, $key, $default = null)`

Makes it easy to get values out of an array, with two added benefits: it won't throw an error if you ask for a key that doesn't exist (and you can provide defaults with the third parameter), and you can use dot notation to traverse nested arrays. For example:

```
$array = ['owner' => ['address' => ['line1' => '123 Main St.']]];

$line1 = array_get($array, 'owner.address.line1', 'No address');
$line2 = array_get($array, 'owner.address.line2');
```

`array_has($array, $keys)`

Makes it easy to check whether an array has a particular value set using dot notation for traversing nested arrays. The $keys parameter can be a single entry or an array of entries, which will check whether every entry in the array exists:

```
$array = ['owner' => ['address' => ['line1' => '123 Main St.']]];

if (array_has($array, 'owner.address.line2')) {
    // Do stuff
}
```

`array_pluck($array, $value, $key = null)`

Returns an array of the values corresponding to the provided key:

```
$array = [
    ['owner' => ['id' => 4, 'name' => 'Tricia']],
    ['owner' => ['id' => 7, 'name' => 'Kimberly']],
];

$array = array_pluck($array, 'owner.name');
```

```
// Returns ['Tricia', 'Kimberly'];
```

If you want the returned array to be keyed by another value from the source array, you can pass that value's dot-notated reference as the third parameter:

```
$array = array_pluck($array, 'owner.name', 'owner.id');

// Returns [4 => 'Tricia', 7 => 'Kimberly'];
```

array_random(*$array*, *$num = null*)

Returns a random item from the provided array. If you provide a *$num* parameter, it will pull an array of that many results, randomly selected:

```
$array = [
    ['owner' => ['id' => 4, 'name' => 'Tricia']],
    ['owner' => ['id' => 7, 'name' => 'Kimberly']],
];

$randomOwner = array_random($array);
```

Strings

Just like with arrays, there are some string manipulations and checks that are possible with native PHP functions, but can be cumbersome. Laravel's helpers make a few common string operations faster and simpler:

e(*$string*)

An alias to htmlentities(); prepares a (often user-provided) string for safe echoing on an HTML page. For example:

```
e('<script>do something nefarious</script>');

// Returns &lt;script&gt;do something nefarious&lt;/script&gt;
```

starts_with(*$haystack, $needle*), ends_with(*$haystack, $needle*), *and*
str_contains(*$haystack, $needle*)

Return a Boolean indicating whether the provided *$haystack* string starts with, ends with, or contains the provided *$needle* string:

```
if (starts_with($url, 'https')) {
    // Do something
}

if (ends_with($abstract, '...')) {
    // Do something
}

if (str_contains($description, '1337 h4x0r')) {
    // Run away
}
```

`str_limit($value, $limit = 100, $end = '...')`
Limits a string to the provided number of characters. If the string's length is less than the limit, just returns the string; if it's greater, trims to the number of characters provided and then appends either ... or the provided *$end* string. For example:

```
$abstract = str_limit($loremIpsum, 30);

// Returns "Lorem ipsum dolor sit amet, co..."

$abstract = str_limit($loremIpsum, 30, "&hellip;");

// Returns "Lorem ipsum dolor sit amet, co&hellip;"
```

`str_is($pattern, $value)`
Returns a Boolean indicating whether or not a given string matches a given pattern. The pattern can be a regex pattern, or you can use asterisks to indicate wildcard positions:

```
str_is('*.dev', 'myapp.dev');        // true
str_is('*.dev', 'myapp.dev.co.uk');  // false
str_is('*dev*', 'myapp.dev');        // true
str_is('*myapp*', 'www.myapp.dev');  // true
str_is('my*app', 'myfantasticapp');  // true
str_is('my*app', 'myapp');           // true
```

 How to Pass a Regex to str_is()

If you're curious about what regex patterns are acceptable to pass to `str_is()`, check out the function definition here (shortened for space) to see how it works. Note that it's an alias of `Illuminate\Support\Str::is()`:

```
public function is($pattern, $value)
{
    if ($pattern == $value) return true;

    $pattern = preg_quote($pattern, '#');
    $pattern = str_replace('\*', '.*', $pattern);
    if (preg_match('#^'.$pattern.'\z#u', $value) === 1) {
        return true;
    }

    return false;
}
```

`str_random($length = n)`
Returns a random string of alphanumeric mixed-case characters of the length specified:

```
$hash = str_random(64);

// Sample: J40uNWAvY60wE4BPEWxu7BZFQEmxEHmGiLmQncj0ThMGJK705Kfgptyb9ulwspmh
```

str_slug($title, $separator = '-', $language = 'en')
    Returns a URL-friendly slug from a string—often used for creating a URL seg-
    ment for a name or title:

```
str_slug('How to Win Friends and Influence People');

// Returns 'how-to-win-friends-and-influence-people'
```

str_plural($value, $count = n)
    Converts a string to its plural form. This function currently only supports the
    English language:

```
str_plural('book');

// Returns books

str_plural('person');

// Returns people

str_plural('person', 1);

// Returns person
```

__($key, $replace = [], $locale = null)
    Translates the given translation string or translation key using your localization
    files:

```
echo __('Welcome to your dashboard');

echo __('messages.welcome');
```

Application Paths

When you're dealing with the filesystem, it can often be tedious to make links to certain directories for getting and saving files. These helpers give you quick access to
find the fully qualified paths to some of the most important directories in your app.

Note that each of these can be called with no parameters, but if a parameter is passed,
it will be appended to the normal directory string and returned as a whole:

app_path($append = '')
    Returns the path for the *app* directory:

```
app_path();

// Returns /home/forge/myapp.com/app
```

`base_path($path = '')`

Returns the path for the root directory of your app:

```
base_path();

// Returns /home/forge/myapp.com
```

`config_path($path = '')`

Returns the path for configuration files in your app:

```
config_path();

// Returns /home/forge/myapp.com/config
```

`database_path($path = '')`

Returns the path for database files in your app:

```
database_path();

// Returns /home/forge/myapp.com/database
```

`storage_path($path = '')`

Returns the path for the *storage* directory in your app:

```
storage_path();

// Returns /home/forge/myapp.com/storage
```

URLs

Some frontend file paths are consistent but at times annoying to type—for example, paths to assets—and it's helpful to have convenient shortcuts to them, which we'll cover here. But some can actually vary as route definitions move or new files are versioned with Mix, so some of these helpers are vital in making sure all of your links and assets work correctly:

`action($action, $parameters = [], $absolute = true)`

Assuming a controller method has a single URL mapped to it, returns the correct URL given a controller and method name pair (separated by @) or using tuple notation:

```
<a href="{{ action('PeopleController@index') }}">See all People</a>
// Or, using tuple notation:
<a href=
    "{{ action([App\Http\Controllers\PeopleController::class, 'index']) }}">
    See all People
</a>

// Returns <a href="http://myapp.com/people">See all People</a>
```

If the controller method requires parameters, you can pass them in as the second parameter (as an array, if there's more than one required parameter). You can key them if you want for clarity, but what matters is just that they're in the right order:

```
<a href="{{ action('PeopleController@show', ['id' => 3] }}">See Person #3</a>
// or
<a href="{{ action('PeopleController@show', [3] }}">See Person #3</a>

// Returns <a href="http://myapp.com/people/3">See Person #3</a>
```

If you pass `false` to the third parameter, your links will generate as relative (*/people/3*) instead of absolute (*http://myapp.com/people/3*).

route($name, $parameters = [], $absolute = true)
If a route has a name, returns the URL for that route:

```
// routes/web.php
Route::get('people', 'PeopleController@index')->name('people.index');

// A view somewhere
<a href="{{ route('people.index') }}">See all People</a>

// Returns <a href="http://myapp.com/people">See all People</a>
```

If the route definition requires parameters, you can pass them in as the second parameter (as an array if more than one parameter is required). Again, you can key them if you want for clarity, but what matters is just that they're in the right order:

```
<a href="{{ route('people.show', ['id' => 3]) }}">See Person #3</a>
// or
<a href="{{ route('people.show', [3]) }}">See Person #3</a>

// Returns <a href="http://myapp.com/people/3">See Person #3</a>
```

If you pass `false` to the third parameter, your links will generate as relative instead of absolute.

url($string) *and* secure_url($string)
Given any path string, converts to a fully qualified URL. (secure_url() is the same as url() but forces HTTPS):

```
url('people/3');

// Returns http://myapp.com/people/3
```

If no parameters are passed, this instead gives an instance of Illuminate \Routing\UrlGenerator, which makes method chaining possible:

```
url()->current();
// Returns http://myapp.com/abc

url()->full();
// Returns http://myapp.com/abc?order=reverse

url()->previous();
// Returns http://myapp.com/login

// And many more methods available on the UrlGenerator...
```

mix($path, $manifestDirectory = ' ')

If assets are versioned with Elixir's versioning system, given the nonversioned path name, returns the fully qualified URL for the versioned file:

```
<link rel="stylesheet" href="{{ mix('css/app.css') }}">

// Returns something like /build/css/app-eb555e38.css
```

 Using the elixir() Helper Prior to Laravel 5.4

In projects running versions of Laravel prior to 5.4, you'll want to use the `elixir()` helper instead of the `mix()` helper. Check the docs (*http://bit.ly/2ACcHu1*) for more info.

Miscellaneous

There are a few other global helpers that I'd recommend getting familiar with. Of course, you should check out the whole list (*http://bit.ly/2HQKaFC*), but the ones mentioned here are definitely worth taking a look at:

abort($code, $message, $headers), abort_unless($boolean, $code, $message, $headers), and abort_if($boolean, $code, $message, $headers)

Throw HTTP exceptions. `abort()` throws the exception defined, `abort_unless()` throws it if the first parameter is `false`, and `abort_if()` throws it if the first parameter is `true`:

```
public function controllerMethod(Request $request)
{
    abort(403, 'You shall not pass');
    abort_unless(request()->filled('magicToken'), 403);
    abort_if(request()->user()->isBanned, 403);
}
```

auth()

Returns an instance of the Laravel authenticator. Like the `Auth` facade, you can use this to get the current user, to check for login state, and more:

```
$user = auth()->user();
$userId = auth()->id();
```

```
if (auth()->check()) {
    // Do something
}
```

back()

Generates a "redirect back" response, sending the user to the previous location:

```
Route::get('post', function () {
    ...

    if ($condition) {
        return back();
    }
});
```

collect(*$array*)

Takes an array and returns the same data, converted to a collection:

```
$collection = collect(['Rachel', 'Hototo']);
```

We'll cover collections in just a bit.

config(*$key*)

Returns the value for any dot-notated configuration item:

```
$defaultDbConnection = config('database.default');
```

csrf_field() *and* csrf_token()

Return a full HTML hidden input field (csrf_field()) or just the appropriate token value (csrf_token()) for adding CSRF verification to your form submission:

```
<form>
    {{ csrf_field() }}
</form>

// or

<form>
    <input type="hidden" name="_token" value="{{ csrf_token() }}">
</form>
```

dd(*$variable...*)

Short for "dump and die," runs var_dump() on all provided parameters and then exit() to quit the application (this is used for debugging):

```
...
dd($var1, $var2, $state); // Why is this not working???
```

env(*$key, $default = null*)

Returns the environment variable for the given key:

```
$key = env('API_KEY', '');
```

Remember not to ever use +env()+ outside of config files.

dispatch(*$job*)

Dispatches a job:

```
dispatch(new EmailAdminAboutNewUser($user));
```

event(*$event*)

Fires an event:

```
event(new ContactAdded($contact));
```

factory(*$entityClass*)

Returns an instance of the factory builder for the given class:

```
$contact = factory(App\Contact::class)->make();
```

old(*$key = null, $default = null*)

Returns the old value (from the last user form submission) for this form key, if
it exists:

```
<input name="name" value="{{ old('value', 'Your name here') }}"
```

redirect(*$path*)

Returns a redirect response to the given path:

```
Route::get('post', function () {
    ...

    return redirect('home');
});
```

Without parameters, this generates an instance of the Illuminate\Routing
\Redirector class.

response(*$content, $status = 200, $headers*)

If passed with parameters, returns a prebuilt instance of Response. If passed with
no response, it returns an instance of the Response factory:

```
return response('OK', 200, ['X-Header-Greatness' => 'Super great']);

return response()->json(['status' => 'success']);
```

view(*$viewPath*)

Returns a view instance:

```
Route::get('home', function () {
    return view('home'); // Gets /resources/views/home.blade.php
});
```

Collections

Collections are one of the most powerful yet underappreciated tools Laravel provides. We covered them a bit in "Eloquent Collections" on page 135, but here's a quick recap.

Collections are essentially arrays with superpowers. The array-traversing methods you normally have to pass arrays into (`array_walk()`, `array_map()`, `array_reduce()`, etc.), all of which have confusingly inconsistent method signatures, are available as consistent, clean, chainable methods on every collection. You can get a taste of functional programming and map, reduce, and filter your way to cleaner code.

We'll cover some of the basics of Laravel's collections and collection pipeline programming here, but for a much deeper overview, check out Adam Wathan's book *Refactoring to Collections* (Gumroad).

The Basics

Collections are not a new idea within Laravel. Many languages make collection-style programming available on arrays out of the box, but with PHP we're not quite so lucky.

Using PHP's `array*()` functions, we can take the monstrosity shown in Example 17-1 and turn it into the slightly less monstrous monstrosity shown in Example 17-2.

Example 17-1. A common, but ugly, foreach loop

```
$users = [...];

$admins = [];

foreach ($users as $user) {
    if ($user['status'] == 'admin') {
        $user['name'] = $user['first'] . ' ' . $user['last'];
        $admins[] = $user;
    }
}

return $admins;
```

Example 17-2. Refactoring the foreach loop with native PHP functions

```
$users = [...];

return array_map(function ($user) {
    $user['name'] = $user['first'] . ' ' . $user['last'];
    return $user;
}, array_filter($users, function ($user) {
```

```
    return $user['status'] == 'admin';
}));
```

Here, we've gotten rid of a temporary variable ($admins) and converted one confusing foreach loop into two distinct actions: map and filter.

The problem is, PHP's array manipulation functions are awful and confusing. Just look at this example; array_map() takes the closure first and the array second, but array_filter() takes the array first and the closure second. In addition, if we added any complexity to this, we'd have functions wrapping functions wrapping functions. It's a mess.

Laravel's collections take the power of PHP's array manipulation methods and give them a clean, fluent syntax—and they add many methods that don't even exist in PHP's array manipulation toolbox. Using the collect() helper method that turns an array into a Laravel collection, we can do what's shown in Example 17-3.

Example 17-3. Refactoring the foreach loop with Laravel's collections

```
$users = collect([...]);

return $users->filter(function ($user) {
    return $user['status'] == 'admin';
})->map(function ($user) {
    $user['name'] = $user['first'] . ' ' . $user['last'];
    return $user;
});
```

This isn't the most extreme of examples. There are plenty where the reduction in lines of code and the increased simplicity would make an even stronger case. But this right here is *so common*.

Look at the original example and how muddy it is. It's not entirely clear until you understand the entire code sample what any given piece is there for.

The biggest benefit collections provide, over anything else, is breaking the actions you're taking to manipulate an array into simple, discrete, understandable tasks. You can now do something like this:

```
    $users = [...]
    $countAdmins = collect($users)->filter(function ($user) {
        return $user['status'] == 'admin';
    })->count();
```

or something like this:

```
    $users = [...];
    $greenTeamPoints = collect($users)->filter(function ($user) {
        return $user['team'] == 'green';
    })->sum('points');
```

Many of the examples we'll look at in the rest of this chapter operate on this mythical `$users` collection we've started imagining here. Each entry in the `$users` array will represent a single human; they'll likely all be array-accessible. The specific properties each user will have may vary a bit depending on the example. But any time you see this `$users` variable, know that that's what we're working with.

A Few Methods

There's much more you can do than what we've covered so far. I recommend you take a look at the Laravel collections (*http://bit.ly/2FwS1VN*) to learn more about all the methods you can use, but to get you started, here are just a few of the core methods:

`all()` *and* `toArray()`

If you'd like to convert your collection to an array, you can do so with either `all()` or `toArray()`. `toArray()` flattens to arrays not just the collection, but also any Eloquent objects underneath it. `all()` *only* converts the collection to an array; any Eloquent objects contained within the collection will be preserved as Eloquent objects. Here are a few examples:

```
$users = User::all();

$users->toArray();

/* Returns
    [
        ['id' => '1', 'name' => 'Agouhanna'],
        ...
    ]
*/

$users->all();

/* Returns
    [
        Eloquent object { id : 1, name: 'Agouhanna' },
        ...
    ]
*/
```

`filter()` *and* `reject()`

When you want to get a subset of your original collection by checking each item against a closure, you'll use `filter()` (which keeps an item if the closure returns `true`) or `reject()` (which keeps an item if the closure returns `false`):

```
$users = collect([...]);
$admins = $users->filter(function ($user) {
    return $user->isAdmin;
});
```

```
$paidUsers = $user->reject(function ($user) {
    return $user->isTrial;
});
```

where()

where() makes it easy to provide a subset of your original collection where a
given key is equal to a given value. Anything you can do with where() you can
also do with filter(), but it's a shortcut for a common scenario:

```
$users = collect([...]);
$admins = $users->where('role', 'admin');
```

first() *and* last()

If you want just a single item from your collection, you can use first() to pull
from the beginning of the list or last() to pull from the end.

If you call first() or last() with no parameters, they'll just give you the first or
last item in the collection, respectively. But if you pass either a closure, they'll
instead give you the first or last item in the collection *that returns true when
passed to that closure.*

Sometimes you'll do this because you want the actual first or last item. But sometimes it's the easiest way to get one item even if you only expect there to be one:

```
$users = collect([...]);
$owner = $users->first(function ($user) {
    return $user->isOwner;
});

$firstUser = $users->first();
$lastUser = $users->last();
```

You can also pass a second parameter to each method, which is the default value
and will be provided as a fallback if the closure doesn't provide any results.

each()

If you'd like to do something with each item of a collection, but it doesn't include
modifying the items or the collection itself, you can use each():

```
$users = collect([...]);
$users->each(function ($user) {
    EmailUserAThing::dispatch($user);
});
```

map()

If you'd like to iterate over all the items in a collection, make changes to them,
and return a new collection with all of your changes, you'll want to use map():

```
$users = collect([...]);
$users = $users->map(function ($user) {
    return [
        'name' => $user['first'] . ' ' . $user['last'],
        'email' => $user['email'],
    ];
});
```

reduce()

If you'd like to get a single result from your collection, like a count or a string, you'll probably want to use reduce(). This method works by taking an initial value (called the "carry") and then allowing each item in the collection to change that value somehow. You can define an initial value for the carry, and a closure that accepts the current state of the carry and then each item as parameters:

```
$users = collect([...]);

$points = $users->reduce(function ($carry, $user) {
    return $carry + $user['points'];
}, 0); // Start with a carry of 0
```

pluck()

If you want to pull out just the values for a given key under each item in a collection, you can use pluck() ((lists(), in Laravel 5.1 and earlier):

```
$users = collect([...]);

$emails = $users->pluck('email')->toArray();
```

chunk() *and* take()

chunk() makes it easy to split your collection into groups of a predefined size, and take() pulls just the provided number of items:

```
$users = collect([...]);

$rowsOfUsers = $users->chunk(3); // Separates into groups of 3

$topThree = $users->take(3); // Pulls the first 3
```

groupBy()

If you want to group all of the items in your collection by the value of one of their properties, you can use groupBy():

```
$users = collect([...]);

$usersByRole = $users->groupBy('role');

/* Returns:
    [
        'member' => [...],
```

```
            'admin' => [...],
        ]
    */
```

You can also pass a closure, and whatever you return from the closure will be what's used to group the records:

```
$heroes = collect([...]);

$heroesByAbilityType = $heroes->groupBy(function ($hero) {
    if ($hero->canFly() && $hero->isInvulnerable()) {
        return 'Kryptonian';
    }

    if ($hero->bitByARadioactiveSpider()) {
        return 'Spidermanesque';
    }

    if ($hero->color === 'green' && $hero->likesSmashing()) {
        return 'Hulk-like';
    }

    return 'Generic';
});
```

reverse() *and* shuffle()

reverse() reverses the order of the items in your collection, and shuffle() randomizes them:

```
$numbers = collect([1, 2, 3]);

$numbers->reverse()->toArray(); // [3, 2, 1]
$numbers->shuffle()->toArray(); // [2, 3, 1]
```

sort(), sortBy(), *and* sortByDesc()

If your items are simple strings or integers, you can use sort() to sort them:

```
$sortedNumbers = collect([1, 7, 6])->sort()->toArray(); // [1, 6, 7]
```

If they're more complex, you can pass a string (representing the property) or a closure to sortBy() or sortByDesc() to define your sorting behavior:

```
$users = collect([...]);

// Sort an array of users by their 'email' property
$users->sort('email');

// Sort an array of users by their 'email' property
$users->sortBy(function ($user, $key) {
    return $user['email'];
});
```

count(), isEmpty(), *and* isNotEmpty()

You can see how many items there are in your collection using count(), isEmpty(), or isNotEmpty():

```
$numbers = collect([1, 2, 3]);

$numbers->count();    // 3
$numbers->isEmpty(); // false
$numbers->isNotEmpty() // true
```

avg() *and* sum()

If you're working with a collection of numbers, avg() and sum() do what their method names say and don't require any parameters:

```
collect([1, 2, 3])->sum(); // 6
collect([1, 2, 3])->avg(); // 2
```

But if you're working with arrays, you can pass the key of the property you'd like to pull from each array to operate on:

```
$users = collect([...]);

$sumPoints = $users->sum('points');
$avgPoints = $users->avg('points');
```

Using Collections Outside of Laravel

Have you fallen in love with collections, and do you want to use them on your non-Laravel projects? With Taylor's blessing, I split out just the collections functionality from Laravel into a separate project called Collect (*http://bit.ly/2f1It7n*), and developers at my company keep it up to date with Laravel's releases.

Just use the composer require tightenco/collect command and you'll have the Illuminate\Support\Collection class ready to use in your code—along with the collect() helper.

TL;DR

Laravel provides a suite of global helper functions that make it simpler to do all sorts of tasks. They make it easier to manipulate and inspect arrays and strings, they facilitate generating paths and URLs, and they provide simple access to some consistent and vital functionality.

Laravel's collections are powerful tools that bring the possibility of collection pipelines to PHP.

## CHAPTER 18

The Laravel Ecosystem

As Laravel has grown, Taylor has built a suite of tools to support and simplify the lives and workflows of Laravel developers. Much of the new work has gone straight into the core, but there are quite a few packages and SaaS offerings that aren't part of the core but are still very much a part of the Laravel experience.

We've already covered quite a few of them, and for those I'll provide pointers to where to go in the book for more information. For the tools we haven't covered, I'll give each a quick description and a link to the relevant website.

Tools Covered in This Book

We've already taken a look at these, but here are some brief reminders of what they are and links to where you can find the relevant sources in the book.

Valet

Valet is a local development server (for Mac, but with forks for Windows and Linux) that makes it quick and easy to serve all of your projects to your browser with almost no effort. You'll install Valet globally on your local development machine via Composer.

With a few commands you can have Nginx, MySQL, Redis, and more serving every Laravel app on your machine at a *.test* domain.

Valet is covered in "Laravel Valet" on page 12.

Homestead

Homestead is a configuration layer on top of Vagrant that makes it simple to serve multiple Laravel applications from a Laravel-friendly Vagrant setup.

Horizon was introduced briefly in "Laravel Homestead" on page 13.

The Laravel Installer

The Laravel installer is a package installed globally on your local development machine (via Composer) that makes it easy and quick to set up a new Laravel project.

The installer is covered in "Installing Laravel with the Laravel Installer Tool" on page 14.

Mix

Mix is a Webpack-based frontend build system. It can run Babel, Browsersync, and your favorite CSS pre- and post-processors, and provides Hot Module Replacement, code splitting, versioning, and much more. Mix replaced Elixir, a Gulp-based tool used for the same purposes, in Laravel.

Mix is covered in "Laravel Mix" on page 159.

Dusk

Dusk is a frontend testing framework built for testing your entire application, JavaScript and all. It's a powerful package you can pull into your application via Composer and that drives actual browsers with ChromeDriver.

Dusk is covered in "Testing with Dusk" on page 324.

Passport

Passport is a powerful, simple-to-set-up OAuth2 server for authenticating clients to your APIs. You'll install it in each application as a Composer package, and with very little work you can have a full OAuth2 flow accessible to your users.

Passport is covered in "API Authentication with Laravel Passport" on page 357.

Horizon

Horizon is a queue monitoring package you can install into each application via Composer. It exposes a full user interface for monitoring the health, performance, failures, and history of your Redis queued jobs.

Horizon is introduced briefly in "Laravel Horizon" on page 436.

Echo

Echo is a JavaScript library (introduced along with a series of improvements to Laravel's notification system) that makes it simple to subscribe to events and channels broadcast from your Laravel app via WebSockets.

Echo is covered in "Laravel Echo (the JavaScript Side)" on page 452.

Tools Not Covered in This Book

These are a few tools that I did not cover because they are beyond the scope of this book. Some of these are just for use in special circumstances (Cashier for taking payments, Socialite for social login, etc.) but some I use every day (Forge, especially).

Here's a brief introduction, beginning with the ones you're most likely to encounter in your work. Note that this list is not exhaustive!

Forge

Forge (*https://forge.laravel.com/*) is a paid SaaS tool for creating and managing virtual servers on hosts like DigitalOcean, Linode, AWS, and more. It provisions Laravel-ready servers (and individual sites on those servers) with all the tools you need to run them, from queues and queue workers to Let's Encrypt SSL certs. It can also set up simple shell scripts to autodeploy your sites when you push up new code to GitHub or Bitbucket.

Forge is incredibly useful for spinning up sites quickly and easily, but it's not so minimal that you can't also run your apps on it in the longer term or at larger scale. You can scale up your server sizes, add load balancers, and manage private networking between your servers, all within Forge.

Envoyer

Envoyer (*https://envoyer.io/*) is paid SaaS tool that's branded as offering "zero downtime PHP deployment." Unlike Forge, Envoyer doesn't spin up your servers or manage them. Its primary job is to listen to triggers—usually when you push new code, but you can also manually trigger deploys or trigger them with webhooks—and perform your deploy steps in response.

There are three ways that Envoyer does this much better than Forge's push-to-deploy tool and most other push-to-deploy solutions:

1. It has a robust toolset for building out your deploy pipeline as a simple but powerful multistage process.

2. It deploys your app using Capistrano-style zero-downtime deploys; each new deploy is built into its own folder, and only once the build process has completed successfully is that deploy folder symlinked to your actual web root. Because of this, there's no moment when your server is broken while Composer installs or NPM builds.

3. Because of this folder-based system, it's easy and quick to roll back any breaking changes to a previous release; Envoyer just updates the symlink back to a previous deploy folder and it's immediately serving an older build.

You can also set up regular health checks (pings against your servers that report errors to you if the pings don't get back a 200 HTTP response), expectations that your cron jobs will ping Envoyer on a regular schedule, and chat-based notifications of any significant events.

Envoyer is more of a niche tool than Forge. I don't know many Laravel developers who don't use Forge, but those who pay for Envoyer are more likely to have websites that will suffer if they can't immediately roll back a problematic commit, or who get enough traffic (or important enough traffic) that 10 seconds of downtime here and there can be a big issue. If your site is in that category, Envoyer will feel like magic.

Cashier

Cashier (*http://bit.ly/2Or9V0r*) is a free package that provides a simple interface in front of Stripe's and Braintree's subscription billing offerings. Cashier handles much of the basic functionality of subscribing users, changing their plans, giving them access to invoices, handling webhook callbacks from the billing service, managing cancellation grace periods, and more.

If you want to allow your users to sign up for subscriptions using Stripe or Braintree, Cashier will make your life a lot easier.

Socialite

Socialite (*http://bit.ly/2TVjmvd*) is a free package that makes it incredibly simple to add social login (for example, via GitHub or Facebook) to your apps.

Nova

Nova (*https://nova.laravel.com/*) is a paid package for building admin panels. If you imagine your average complex Laravel app, it may have a few parts: the public-facing website or customer view, the administration section for making changes to the core data or customer list, and maybe an API.

Nova drastically simplifies the process of building the admin panel part of the site using Vue and a Laravel API. It makes it easy to generate CRUD (create, read, update, delete) pages for all of your resources, together with more complex custom views for your data, custom actions and relationships on each of your resources, and even custom tools for adding non-CRUD tooling to the same general admin space.

Spark

Spark (*https://spark.laravel.com/*) is a paid package for generating a SaaS that accepts payments and makes it easy to manage users, teams, and subscriptions. It provides Stripe integration, invoices, two-factor authentication, profile photos for your users, team management and billing, password resets, announcements, API token authentication, and more.

Spark is both a series of routes and a series of Vue components. You'll use Spark to scaffold the basis of a new project, so don't plan to add it to your existing apps after the fact.

Lumen

Lumen (*https://lumen.laravel.com/*) is a free API-focused microframework built from Laravel parts. Because it's for APIs, many of the conveniences Laravel offers that target non-API calls (for example, Blade templating) have been stripped out.

That makes for a leaner framework with a few less of the niceties, but with the benefit of speed improvements.

My general approach to Lumen is that, unless you have built APIs in Laravel and found them too slow, or unless you're *definitely* building a microservice-style API that will absolutely never have need for any views or any of the other niceties Laravel offers, you should stick with Laravel.

But when you find yourself developing microservice-style APIs in Laravel and you need to eke out more speed at the millisecond level, that's the right time to look at Lumen.

Envoy

Envoy (*http://bit.ly/2CDa9Ns*) is a local task runner that makes it easy to define common tasks that will run on your remote servers, commit those tasks' definitions to version control, and run them simply and predictably.

Take a look at Example 18-1 to get a sense of what a common Envoy task looks like.

Example 18-1. A common Envoy task

```
@servers(['web-1' => '192.168.1.1', 'web-2' => '192.168.1.2'])

@task('deploy', ['on' => ['web-1', 'web-2']])
```

```
    cd mysite.com
    git pull origin {{ $branch }}
    php artisan migrate
    php artisan route:cache
@endtask
```

To run Example 18-1, you'd run the following command from your local terminal:

```
envoy run deploy --branch=master
```

Telescope

Telescope (*http://bit.ly/2HQPg4B*) is a free debugging tool, installable as a package, for Laravel applications running version 5.7.7+. It generates a dashboard where you can dig into the current status of jobs, queue workers, HTTP requests, database queries, and much more.

Other Resources

I've mentioned many of these already, but here's a nonexhaustive list of resources folks often turn to to learn Laravel:

- Laravel News (*https://laravel-news.com/*)
- Laracasts (*https://laracasts.com/*)
- @TaylorOtwell (*https://twitter.com/taylorotwell*) and @LaravelPHP (*https://twitter.com/laravelphp*) on Twitter
- Adam Wathan's courses (*https://adamwathan.me/*)
- Chris Fidao's courses (*https://fideloper.com/*)
- The Laravel Podcast (*http://www.laravelpodcast.com/*)
- The many Laravel chats; at the time of writing, the Laravel Discord server (*https://laravel.com/discord*) is the primary location where Taylor and other contributors are accessible, but there are also unofficial channels on Slack (*https://larachat.co/*) and IRC (#laravel on Freenode)

There are many blogs (I have one at *mattstauffer.com* and Tighten has one at *tighten.co*, and there are plenty of others that are incredibly useful), many excellent Twitter-ers, many superb package authors, and far too many Laravel practitioners who I respect to fit into a list here. This is a rich, diverse, and giving community, full of developers who love to share everything they're learning; the hard part is not finding good content but finding the time to consume it all.

I can't list every person or resource you should look to in your journey as a Laravel developer, but if you start with the resources and folks listed here, you will be off to a great start in getting up and running with Laravel.

Glossary

Accessor

A method defined on an Eloquent model that customizes how a given property will be returned. Accessors make it possible to define that getting a given property from a model will return a different (or, more likely, differently formatted) value than what is stored in the database for that property.

ActiveRecord

A common database ORM pattern, and also the pattern that Laravel's Eloquent uses. In ActiveRecord the same model class defines both how to retrieve and persist database records *and* how to represent them. Additionally, each database record is represented by a single entity in the application, and each entity in the application is mapped to a single database record.

API

Technically *application programming interface*, but most commonly used to refer to a series of endpoints (and instructions on how to use them) that can be used to make HTTP-based calls to read and modify data from outside of a system. Sometimes, the term API is also used to describe the set of interfaces, or affordances, any given package or library or class exposes to its consumers.

Application test

Often called acceptance or functional tests, application tests test the entire behavior of the application, usually at an outer boundary, by employing something like a DOM crawler—which is exactly what Laravel's application test suite offers.

Argument (Artisan)

Arguments are parameters that can be passed to Artisan console commands. Arguments aren't prefaced with -- or followed by =, but instead just accept a single value.

Artisan

The tool that makes it possible to interact with Laravel applications from the command line.

Assertion

In testing, an assertion is the core of the test: you are *asserting* that something should be equal to (or less than or greater than) something else, or that it should have a given count, or whatever else you like. Assertions are the things that can either pass or fail.

Authentication

Correctly identifying oneself as a member/user of an application is the act of authentication. Authentication doesn't define *what* you may do, but simply *who* you are (or aren't).

Authorization

Assuming you've either succeeded or failed at authenticating yourself, authorization defines what you're *allowed* to do given your particular identification. Authorization is about access and control.

Autowiring

When a dependency injection container will inject an instance of a resolvable class without a developer having explicitly taught it how to resolve that class, that's called autowiring. With a container that doesn't have autowiring, you can't even inject a plain PHP object with no dependencies until you have explicitly bound it to the container. With autowiring, you only have to explicitly bind something to the container if its dependencies are too complex or vague for the container to figure out on its own.

beanstalkd

Beanstalk is a work queue. It's simple and excels at running multiple asynchronous tasks—which makes it a common driver for Laravel's queues. *beanstalkd* is its daemon.

Blade

Laravel's templating engine.

BrowserKit

Laravel's pre-5.4 testing facilities for DOM-based interactions, available as a Composer package for 5.4+ apps.

Carbon

A PHP package that makes working with dates much easier and more expressive.

Cashier

A Laravel package that makes billing with Stripe or Braintree, especially in subscription contexts, easier and more consistent and powerful.

Closure

Closures are PHP's version of anonymous functions. A closure is a function that you can pass around as an object, assign to a variable, pass as a parameter to other functions and methods, or even serialize.

CodeIgniter

An older PHP framework that Laravel was inspired by.

Collection

The name of a development pattern and also Laravel's tool that implements it. Like arrays on steroids, collections provide map, reduce, filter, and many other powerful operations that PHP's native arrays don't.

Command

The name for a custom Artisan console task.

Composer

PHP's dependency manager. Like Ruby Gems or NPM.

Container

Somewhat of a catchall word, in Laravel "container" refers to the application container that's responsible for dependency injection. Accessible via `app()` and also responsible for resolving calls to controllers, events, jobs, and commands, the container is the glue that holds each Laravel app together.

Contract

Another name for an interface.

Controller

A class that is responsible for routing user requests through to the application's services and data, and returning some form of useful response back to the user.

CSRF (cross-site request forgery)

A malicious attack where an external site makes requests against your application by hijacking your users' browsers (with JavaScript, likely) while they're still logged in to your site. Protected against by adding a token (and a check for that token on the `POST` side) to every form on the site.

Dependency injection

A development pattern where dependencies are injected in from the outside—usually through the constructor—instead of being instantiated in the class.

Directive

Blade syntax options like `@if`, `@unless`, etc.

Dot notation

Navigating down inheritance trees using `.` to reference a jump down to a new level. If you have an array like `['owner' => ['address' => ['line1' => '123 Main St.']]]`, you have three levels of nesting. Using dot notation, you would represent "123 Main St." as `"owner.address.line1"`.

Dusk

Laravel's frontend testing package that can test JavaScript (primarily Vue) and DOM interactions by spinning up Chrome-Driver to run the tests.

Eager loading

Avoiding $N+1$ problems by adding a second smart query to your first query to get a set of related items. Usually you have a first query that gets a collection of thing A. But each A has many Bs, and so every time you get the Bs from an A, you need a new query. Eager loading means doing two queries: first you get all the As, and then you get *all* the Bs related to all those As, in a single query. Two queries, and you're done.

Echo

A Laravel product that makes WebSocket authentication and syncing of data simple.

Elixir

Laravel's old build tool, since replaced by Mix; a wrapper around Gulp.

Eloquent

Laravel's ActiveRecord ORM. The tool you'll use to define and query something like a `User` model.

Environment variables

Variables that are defined in an *.env* file that is expected to be excluded from version control. This means that they don't sync between environments and that they're also kept safe.

Envoy

A Laravel package for writing scripts to run common tasks on remote servers. Envoy provides a syntax for defining tasks and servers and a command-line utility for running the tasks.

Envoyer

A Laravel SaaS product for zero-downtime deployment, multiserver deploys, and server and cron health checks.

Event

Laravel's tool for implementing a pub/sub or observer pattern. Each event represents that an event happened: the name of the event describes what happened (e.g., `User Subscribed`) and the payload allows for attaching relevant information. Designed to be "fired" and then "listened" for (or published and subscribed, if you prefer the pub/sub concept).

Facade

A tool in Laravel for simplifying access to complex tools. Facades provide static access to core services in Laravel. Since every facade is backed by a class in the container, you could replace any call to something like `Cache::put();` with a two-line call to something like `$cache = app('cache'); $cache->put();`.

Faker

A PHP package that makes it easy to generate random data. You can request data in different categories, like names, addresses, and timestamps.

Flag

A parameter anywhere that is on or off (Boolean).

Fluent

Methods that can be chained one after another are said to be fluent. In order to provide a fluent syntax, each method must return the instance, preparing it to be chained again. This allows for something like `People::where('age', '>', 14)->orderBy('name')->get()`.

Flysystem

The package that Laravel uses to facilitate its local and cloud file access.

Forge

A Laravel product that makes it easy to spin up and manage virtual servers on major cloud providers like DigitalOcean and AWS.

FQCN (fully qualified class name)

The full namespaced name of any given class, trait, or interface. `Controller` is the class name; `Illuminate\Routing\Controller` is the FQCN.

Gulp

A JavaScript-based build tool.

Helper

A globally accessible PHP function that makes some other functionality easier—for example, `array_get()` simplifies the logic of looking up results from arrays.

HMR (Hot Module Replacement)

A technology that makes it possible to reload just pieces of an active website's frontend dependencies without reloading the entire file.

Homestead

A Laravel tool that wraps Vagrant and makes it easier to spin up Forge-parallel virtual servers for local Laravel development.

Horizon

A Laravel package that provides tooling for managing queues with greater nuance than Laravel's defaults, and also provides insight into the current and historic operating state of the queue workers and their jobs.

Illuminate

The top-level namespace of all Laravel components.

Integration test

Integration tests test the way individual units work together and pass messages.

IoC (inversion of control)

The concept of giving "control" over how to make a concrete instance of an interface to the higher-level code of the package age instead of the lower-level code. Without IoC, each individual controller and class might decide what instance of `Mailer` it wanted to create. IoC makes it so that the low-level code—those controllers and classes—just get to ask for a `Mailer`, and some high-level configuration code defines *once* per application which instance should be provided to satisfy that request.

Job

A class that intends to encapsulate a single task. Jobs are intended to be able to be pushed onto a queue and run asynchronously.

JSON (JavaScript Object Notation)

A syntax for data representation.

JWT (JSON Web Token)

A JSON object containing all of the information necessary to determine a user's authentication state and access permissions. This JSON object is digitally signed, which is what makes it trustworthy, using HMAC or RSA. Usually delivered in the header.

Mailable

An architectural pattern designed to encompass the functionality of sending mail into a single "sendable" class.

Markdown

A formatting language designed for formatting plain text and outputting to multiple output formats. Commonly used for formatting text that has a good chance of being processed by a script or read by humans in its raw form—for example, Git READMEs.

Mass assignment
The ability to pass many parameters at once to create or update an Eloquent model, using a keyed array.

Memcached
An in-memory data store designed to provide simple but fast data storage. Memcached only supports basic key/value storage.

Middleware
A series of wrappers around an application that filter and decorate its inputs and outputs.

Migration
A manipulation to the state of the database, stored in and run from code.

Mix
A frontend build tool based on Webpack. Replaced Elixir in Laravel 5.4 and can be used to concatenate, minify, and preprocess your frontend assets, and much more.

Mockery
A library included with Laravel that makes it easy to mock PHP classes in your tests.

Model
A class used to represent a given database table in your system. In ActiveRecord ORMs like Laravel's Eloquent, this class is used both to represent a single record from the system, and to interact with the database table.

Model factory
A tool for defining how the application can generate an instance of your model if needed for testing or seeding. Usually paired with a fake data generator like Faker.

Multitenancy
A single app serving multiple clients, each of which has its customers. Multitenancy often suggests that each client of your application gets its own theming and domain name with which to differentiate its service to its customers vis-à-vis your other clients' potential services.

Mutator
A tool in Eloquent that allows you to manipulate the data being saved to a model property before it is saved to the database.

Nginx
A web server similar to Apache.

Notification
A Laravel framework tool allowing a single message to be sent via myriad notification channels (e.g., email, Slack, SMS) to one or more recipients.

Nova
A paid Laravel package for building admin panels for your Laravel apps.

NPM (Node Package Manager)
A central web-based repository for Node packages, at *npmjs.org*; also a utility used on your local machine to install a project's frontend dependencies into the *node_modules* directory based on the specifications of *package.json*.

OAuth
The most common authentication framework for APIs. OAuth has multiple grant types, each of which describes a different flow of how consumers retrieve, use, and refresh the "tokens" that identify them after the initial authentication handshake.

Option (Artisan)
Like arguments, options are parameters that can be passed to Artisan commands. They're prefaced with `--` and can be used as a flag (`--force`) or to provide data (`--userId=5`).

ORM (object-relational mapper)
A design pattern that is centered around using objects in a programming language to represent data, and its relationships, in a relational database.

Passport

A Laravel package that can be used to easily add an OAuth authentication server to your Laravel app.

PHPSpec

A PHP testing framework.

PHPUnit

A PHP testing framework. The most common and connected to the most of Laravel's custom testing code.

Polymorphic

In database terms, able to interact with multiple database tables with similar characteristics. A polymorphic relationship will allow entities of multiple models to be attached in the same way.

Preprocessor

A build tool that takes in a special form of a language (for CSS, one special form is LESS) and generates code with just the normal language (CSS). Preprocessors build in tools and features that are not in the core language.

Primary key

Most database tables have a single column that is intended to represent each row. This is called the primary key and is commonly named id.

Queue

A stack onto which jobs can be added. Usually associated with a queue worker, which pulls jobs one at a time from a queue, works on them, and then discards them.

React

A JavaScript framework. Created and maintained by Facebook.

Real-time facades

Similar to facades, but without requiring a separate class. Real-time facades can be used to make any class's methods callable as static methods by importing that class with Facades\ in front of its namespace.

Redis

Like Memcached, a data store simpler than most relational databases but powerful and fast. Redis supports a very limited set of structures and data types but makes up for it in speed and scalability.

REST (Representational State Transfer)

The most common format for APIs these days. Usually suggests that interactions with an API should each authenticate separately and should be "stateless"; also usually suggests that the HTTP verbs are used for basic differentiation of requests.

Route

A definition of a way or ways the user might visit a web application. A route is a pattern definition; it can be something like /users/5, or /users, or /users/id.

S3 (Simple Storage Service)

Amazon's "object storage" service, which makes it easy to use AWS's incredible computing power to store and serve files.

SaaS (Software as a Service)

Web-based applications that you pay money to use.

Scope

In Eloquent, a tool for defining how to consistently and simply narrow down a query.

Scout

A Laravel package for full-text search on Eloquent models.

Serialization

The process of converting more complex data (usually an Eloquent model) to something simpler (in Laravel, usually an array or JSON).

Service provider

A structure in Laravel that registers and boots classes and container bindings.

Socialite

A Laravel package making it simple to add social authentication (e.g., login via Facebook) to Laravel apps.

Soft delete

Marking a database row as "deleted" without actually deleting it; usually paired with an ORM that by default hides all "deleted" rows.

Spark

A Laravel tool that makes it easy to spin up a new subscription-based SaaS app.

Symfony

A PHP framework that focuses on building excellent components and making them accessible to others. Symfony's HTTP Foundation is at the core of Laravel and every other modern PHP framework.

Telescope

A Laravel package for adding a debugging assistant to Laravel apps.

Tinker

Laravel's REPL, or read–evaluate–print loop. It's a tool that allows you to perform complex PHP operations within the full context of your app from the command line.

TL;DR

Too long; didn't read. "Summary."

Typehinting

Prefacing a variable name in a method signature with a class or interface name. Tells PHP (and Laravel, and other developers) that the only thing that's allowed to be passed in that parameter is an object with the given class or interface.

Unit test

Unit tests target small, relatively isolated units—a class or method, usually.

Vagrant

A command-line tool that makes it easy to build virtual machines on your local computer using predefined images.

Valet

A Laravel package (for Mac OS users, but there are forks for macOS and Windows) that makes it easy to serve your applications from your development folder of choice, without worrying about Vagrant or virtual machines.

Validation

Ensuring that user input matches expected patterns.

View

An individual file that takes data from the backend system or framework and converts it into HTML.

View composer

A tool that defines that, every time a given view is loaded, it will be provided a certain set of data.

Vue

A JavaScript framework. Preferred by Laravel. Written by Evan You.

Webpack

Technically a "module bundler," Webpack is a tool commonly used to run frontend build tasks, especially those that involve processing CSS and JavaScript and other frontend source files and outputting them in a more production-ready format.

Index

Symbols

* (asterisk), following array arguments or options, 210

- - (hyphen, double), preceding Artisan command options, 210

-> ,=> (arrow)

    -> chaining methods, 31, 36

    -> traversing JSON structure, 116

    => preceding Tinker responses, 217

. (period), dot notation, 491

/ (slash), escaping in Artisan commands, 339

:: (colon, double), in facades, 289

= (equal sign), in Artisan argument definition, 210

? (question mark)

    following optional Artisan command arguments, 209

    following optional parameters, 29

    query parameters, 107

@ (at sign)

    preceding Blade directives, 63

    preceding Blade echo syntax, 64

\ (backslash), escaping in Artisan commands, 448

__() helper, 469

{ } (braces)

    enclosing Artisan command arguments, 209

    enclosing route parameters, 50, 186

    { !! !!}, Blade echo syntax, not escaped, 64, 197

    { { }}, Blade echo syntax, escaped, 64, 197

A

abilities (rules) for authorization, 240

abort() helper, 59, 472

abort_if() helper, 59, 472

abort_unless() helper, 59, 472

acceptance tests (see application tests)

accepts() method, Request, 261

accessors, 131, 139, 156, 489

ACL (access control list), 240, 242

    (see also authorization)

actingAs() method, 309, 375

action() helper, 57, 470

ActiveRecord pattern, 117, 489

    (see also Eloquent)

add() method, Cache, 387

addGlobalScope() method, 130

after() method, Blueprint, 94

after() method, tasks, 461

Ajax, 55

Algolia SDK, 397

aliases, binding to, 285

aliasing, of component, 75

all() method, collection, 477

all() method, Eloquent, 121

all() method, ParameterBag, 259

all() method, Request, 182, 197, 259

all() method, Session, 385

allDirectories() method, Storage, 380

allFiles() method, Request, 261

allFiles() method, Storage, 379

anonymous functions (see closures)

anticipate() method, 213

api guard, 236

api middleware group, 274

API resource controllers, 49

API routes, 26

(see also routes)
api.php file, 26
APIs, 337-376
    authentication with API tokens, 373
    authentication with Passport, 358-373
    customizing 404 responses, 374
    defined, 489
    Eloquent API resources, 352-357
    fallback route, 374
    filtering results, 347
    JSON for, 338, 341, 345
    Lumen for, 487
    nesting relationships between resources,
        350-352
    paginating results, 344
    request headers, reading, 342, 343
    resource controllers, 339-342
    response headers, sending, 342
    REST style of, 337-338
    sorting results, 345-347
    testing, 374
    transforming results, 348-352
app commands, Artisan, 204
app folder, 16
app() helper, 258, 281
app.js file, 452
app.php file in config, 397, 450
append() method, Storage, 379
appendOutputTo() method, tasks, 460
application
    bootstrapping, 254
    exiting, 473
    kernel, 254
    lifecycle, 253-256
application container (see container)
application tests, 304
    defined, 296, 489
    exception handling, 310
    TestCase class, 304
AppServiceProvider, 292
app_path() helper, 469
argument()/arguments() methods, Artisan, 211,
    489
arrays
    as Artisan arguments or options, 210
    collections as alternative to, 136
    collections compared to, 475
    converting to collections, 473
    helpers for, 465-467

array_filter() method, 476
array_first() helper, 466
array_get() helper, 466
array_has() helper, 466
array_map() method, 476
array_pluck() helper, 466
array_random() function, 467
arrow
    -> chaining methods, 31, 36
    -> traversing JSON structure, 116
    => preceding Tinker responses, 217
Artisan commands, 201-217
    asserting against Artisan command syntax,
        322
    basic commands, 202
    calling from code, 209, 216
    custom, 206-215
    defined, 490
    escaping slashes in, 339
    options for, 203
    output during execution of, 214-215
    progress bars for, 215
    prompting for user input, 213
    queueing, 205, 436
    sample command, 208
    scheduling as tasks, 457
    testing, 219, 322-323
    using input from, 211-213
Artisan facade, 216
artisan file, 17
artisan() method, 219
artisan() method, TestCase, 322
Artisan, defined, 489
as() method, Eloquent, 146
ask() method, 213
assert() method, Dusk, 332
assertCookie() method, TestCase, 308, 403
assertCookieExpired() method, TestCase, 308
assertCookieNotExpired() method, TestCase,
    308
assertDatabaseHas() method, TestCase, 311
assertDatabaseMissing() method, TestCase, 311
assertDispatched() method, TestCase, 313
assertDontSee() method, TestCase, 307
assertion, defined, 489
assertJson() method, TestCase, 307
assertNotDispatched() method, TestCase, 313
assertNothingSent() method, TestCase, 316
assertNotSent() method, notification, 425

assertOk() method, TestCase, 306
assertPlainCookie() method, TestCase, 403
assertRedirect() method, TestCase, 308
assertSee() method, TestCase, 307
assertSent() method, notification, 425
assertSentTo() method, TestCase, 316
assertSessionHas() method, TestCase, 307, 401
assertSessionHasAll() method, TestCase, 401
assertSessionHasErrors() method, TestCase,
    307, 401
assertSessionMissing() method, TestCase, 401
assertStatus() method, TestCase, 307
assertViewHas() method, TestCase, 84, 307
assets folder, 161
associate() method, Eloquent, 143
asterisk (*), following array arguments or
    options, 210
at sign (@)
    preceding Blade directives, 63
    preceding Blade echo syntax, 64
attach() method, Dusk, 328
attach() method, Eloquent, 147
attach() method, mailable, 410
attachData() method, mailable, 410
attachFromStorage() method, mailable, 410
attempt() method, authentication, 232
attempts() method, jobs, 433
attribute casting, 133
attribute() method, Dusk, 327
auth commands, Artisan, 204
@auth directive, 236
Auth facade, 225
auth middleware, 234
auth scaffold, 231
auth scaffolding, 170
auth() helper, 225, 472
auth.basic middleware, 234
auth.php file, 237, 359
Auth::routes() facade, 229, 230, 235
AuthController, 221
Authenticatable contract, 224
AuthenticateSession middleware, 233
authentication, 221-240
    APIs for, 358-373
    Blade directives, 236
    contracts, 224
    defined, 222, 489
    Dusk and, 327
    events, 239

ForgotPasswordController, 229
guards for, 236-238
invalidating sessions on other devices, 233
LoginController, 227-228
manual authentication, 233
manually logging out a user, 233
MustVerifyEmail trait, 235
RegisterController, 226-227
RegistersUsers trait, 227
remember me access token, 232
ResetPasswordController, 229
route middleware for, 234
routes for, 229
testing, 249-252, 309
VerificationController, 229
views for, 231
WebSocket (see Echo)
Authorizable contract, 225
Authorizable trait, 245
authorization, 240-249
    Authorizable contract, 225
    AuthorizesRequests trait, 243
    Blade checks, 246
    checking user capabilities, 245
    defined, 222, 489
    defining rules for, 240
    Gate facade, 241
    intercepting checks, 246
    policies, 247-249
    resource gates, 242
    route middleware for, 243
    testing, 249-252
authorization code grant, Passport, 362-366
authorize() method, AuthorizesRequests trait,
    243
authorize() method, form request, 194
authorizeForUser() method, AuthorizesRe-
    quests trait, 243
authorizeResource() method, AuthorizesRe-
    quests trait, 243
AuthorizesRequests trait, 243
AuthServiceProvider, 240, 246, 255, 371
autowiring, 282, 490
avg() method, collection, 481
avg() method, DB, 114
away() method, redirects, 57

B

back() helper, 57, 266, 473

backslash (\), escaping in Artisan commands, 448

base_path() helper, 470

be() method, TestCase, 250

beanstalkd queues, 428, 490

before() method, tasks, 461

beginTransaction() method, DB, 117

belongsTo() method, Eloquent, 140, 142, 149

belongsToMany() method, Eloquent, 145

bigIncrements() method, Blueprint, 93

bigInteger() method, Blueprint, 92

billing (see Cashier)

binary() method, Blueprint, 92

bind() method, 284, 284

binding
    API resource controllers, 49
    classes to container, 283-286
    data to views, 76-79
    PDO parameter binding, 107
    route model binding, 50-51

Blade, 63-85
    authentication directives, 236
    basics, 63
    checks using, 246
    components and slots, 73-75
    conditionals, 65
    control structures, 65-67
    custom directives, 80-83
    defined, 490
    directives for, 63
    echoing PHP in, 64
    included view partials, 70-72
    loops, 65-67, 71
    multitenancy using, 82
    sections, 68-70
    service injection, 79-80
    stacks, 72
    template inheritance, 68-75
    templates, 40
    view composers, 76-79

Blade::if() method, 83

Blueprint class, 92-94

boolean() method, Blueprint, 92

boot() method, Eloquent model, 130

boot() method, service providers, 51, 238, 240, 255, 371

bootstrap folder, 16

bootstrapping application, 254

braces ({ })

enclosing Artisan command arguments, 209

enclosing route parameters, 50, 186

{ !! !!}, Blade echo syntax, not escaped, 64, 197

{{ }}, Blade echo syntax, escaped, 64, 197

broadcast notifications, 423

broadcast() helper, 449, 456

broadcastAs() method, events, 444

broadcasting events (see WebSockets)

broadcasting.php file, 443

broadcastOn() method, events, 438, 443

BroadcastServiceProvider, 449

broadcastWith() method, events, 445

browse() method, Dusk, 326

browser tests, 323-335
    BrowserKit Testing package, 324
    Dusk for, 324-335
        (see also Dusk)
    tool choice, 324

BrowserKit testing package, 198, 324, 490

build() method, mailable, 407, 410

Bus facade
    testing, 314

C

cache commands, Artisan, 204

Cache facade, 386

cache() helper, 386

caches
    accessing, 204, 386-388
    data stores used by, 89
    for custom directive results, 81
    for routes, 52
    testing, 402

call() method, Artisan, 216

call() method, container, 288

call() method, TestCase, 402

camel_case() helper, 175

@can directive, 246

can() method, Authorizable, 245

@cannot directive, 246

cannot() method, Authorizable, 245

CanResetPassword contract, 225

cant() method, Authorizable, 245

capture() method, Request, 257

Carbon package, 387, 490

Carbon::now(), 40

Cashier, 486, 490

chaining methods, 31, 36

channel() method, Broadcast, 450
channel() method, Echo, 454
channels, log, 393-396
char() method, Blueprint, 92
check() method, authorization, 225
check() method, Dusk, 328
choice() method, 213
chunk() method, collection, 479
chunk() method, Eloquent, 122
classes
     FQCN for, 492
     view composers using, 78
clear-compiled command, Artisan, 202
click() method, Dusk, 328
clickLink() method, Dusk, 328
closure request guard, 238
closures
     binding to, 283
     defined, 26, 490
     defining Artisan commands as, 215
     defining routes using, 26
     view composers using, 77
Cloud storage (see storage)
cloud-based mail, 405
CodeIgniter, 490
collect() helper, 135, 473, 476
Collection class, 106, 135-137
collection() method, API resource, 354
collections, 475-481
     compared to arrays, 475
     converting to arrays, 476
     defined, 490
     returned by Eloquent, 135-137
     serialization, 137
     using outside Laravel, 481
colon, double (::), in facades, 289
columns, creating, 92-94
commands, Artisan (see Artisan commands)
comment() method, Artisan, 214
commit() method, DB, 117
@component directive, Blade, 74
components, Blade, 73-75
components, Dusk, 333-335
Composer, 12, 254
     commands for, 14
     creating new projects, 14
     defined, 490
     service provider features with, 256
composer.json file, 17

composer.lock file, 17
conditionals (Blade), 65
config commands, Artisan, 204
config folder, 16, 18
config() helper, 473
config/app.php file, 397, 450
config/cache.php file, 386
config/scout.php file, 397
config/session.php file, 382
configuration files, 16, 18, 236, 470
config_path() helper, 470
confirm() method, Artisan, 213
Console component, Symfony, 201
constructor injection, 279, 281, 287
container, 46
     accessing facade backing class from, 290
     accessing objects from, 281
     autowiring, 282
     binding classes to, 283-286
     constructor injection, 287
     defined, 490
     dependency injection, 279-281
     method injection, 287
     registering bindings for, 291
contextual binding, 286
contracts, 490
     (see also interfaces)
Contracts namespace, 224
controllers, 42-49
     API resource controllers, 49
     applying middleware using, 34
     controller/method reference syntax, 29
     creating, 43-45
     defined, 490
     getting and handling user input, 45-46
     handling routes using, 28
     in MVC, 24
     injecting dependencies into, 46
     namespaces for, 44
     resource controllers, 47-49, 339-342
     single action, 49
Cookie facade, 389
cookie() helper, Cookies, 390
cookie() method, Request, 262, 391
cookie() method, Response, 391
CookieJar class, 390
cookies, 388-392
     accessing with Cookie facade, 389
     accessing with cookie() helper, 390

accessing with Request and Response, 391

configuring, 390

encryption for, 402

locations of, 388

testing, 402

copy() method, Mix, 164

copy() method, Storage, 379

copyDirectory() method, Mix, 164

count() method, collection, 481

count() method, DB, 114

count() method, ParameterBag, 259

create() method, model factories, 102, 123, 124

create() method, resource controllers, 25

create() method, Schema, 91

create, read, update, delete (see CRUD)

CreateFreshApiToken middleware, 367, 368

create_users_table migration, 90, 222

cron jobs, scheduler as alternative to, 457

CRUD (create, read, update, delete), 42

(see also resource controllers)

CSRF (cross-site request forgery), 53-55, 453, 490

csrf_field() helper, 473

csrf_token() helper, 473

CSS

Blade stacks for, 72

postprocessor for, 163

preprocessor for, 160, 163

preprocessorless, in Mix, 163

custom route model binding, 51

D

daily log channel, 394

database folder, 16

database notifications, 423

database tests, 311, 327

DatabaseMigrations trait, 302

databases, 87-157

(see also Eloquent)

configuring connections to, 87-89

custom guard providers for, 239

migrations, 89-98

paginating results from, 170

query builder, 105-117

seeders, 98-105

testing, 155-157

Tinker interacting with, 217

DatabaseSeeder class, 98

DatabaseTransactions trait, 302

database_path() helper, 470

date mutators, 134

dates and times (see Carbon package) (see scheduler) (see timestamps)

datetime() method, Blueprint, 92

db commands, Artisan, 204

DB facade, 105

dd() helper, 473

Dead Man's Snitch, 460

debugging

dump server for, 218

Telescope for, 488

decimal() method, Blueprint, 92

decrement() method, Cache, 388

decrement() method, DB, 115

default() method, Blueprint, 94

$defer property, 255

DeferrableProvider interface, 255

define() method, model factories, 100

delay() method, jobs, 432

delay() method, notification, 420

DELETE method, 25

for resource controllers, 25

routes based on, 28

delete() method, DB, 107, 116

delete() method, Eloquent, 126-128

delete() method, Storage, 379

deleteDirectory() method, Storage, 380

deleted_at column, 127

deleteFileAfterSend() method, Response, 265

dependency injection, 279-281

constructor injection, 279, 281, 287

defined, 490

method injection, 279, 287

setter injection, 279-279

testing using, 292

destroy() method, resource controllers, 25

detach() method, Eloquent, 147

development environments, 12-17

DI (dependency injection) container (see container)

directives (Blade), 63

aliasing components to be, 75

defined, 491

directories() method, Storage, 380

disk() method, Storage, 378, 381

dispatch() helper, 431, 474

Dispatchable trait, 430

dissociate() method, Eloquent, 143

distinct() method, DB, 111
dnsmasq tool, 13
dot notation, 491
double() method, Blueprint, 92
down command, Artisan, 202
down() method, migrations, 90
download responses, 264
download() method, Response, 60, 264
downloads, 382
drag() method, Dusk, 328
dragDown() method, Dusk, 328
dragLeft() method, Dusk, 328
dragRight() method, Dusk, 328
dragUp() method, Dusk, 328
dump server, 218
dump() helper, 218
dump-server command, Artisan, 202, 218
Dusk, 324-335
    as part of Laravel ecosystem, 484
    assertions, 330
    authentication and databases, 327
    components, 333-335
    customizing environment variables, 325
    defined, 491
    installing, 325
    interactions with page, 327-329
    page class, 331-333
    selector matching order, 328
    waiting methods, 329
    writing tests, 325
dynamic rate limiting, 35

E
e() helper, 174, 467
@each directive, Blade, 71
each() method, collection, 478
eager loading, 152, 491
Echo, 443, 447-448
    as part of Laravel ecosystem, 485
    authorization for channels, 450-452
    client events, 456
    defined, 491
    event broadcasting, 453
    excluding user from events, 449, 456
    JavaScript package for, 452-456
    listening for events, 453
    presence channels, 455
    private channels, 454
    service provider configuration, 449-452

subscribing to channels, 454
subscribing to notifications, 456
ecosystem, Laravel, 483-488
edit() method, resource controllers, 25
elements() method, Dusk, 332
Elixer, 484
    (see also Mix build tool)
Elixir
    compiling Passport frontend components,
        370
    defined, 491
elixir() helper, 472
Eloquent, 36, 87, 117-155
    accessors, 131
    aggregates, 122
    API resources, 352-357
    attribute casting, 133
    child records updating parent record time-
        stamps, 152-154
    collections returned by, 135-137
    customizing route key for, 51
    date mutators, 134
    defined, 491
    deletes, 126-128
    eager loading, 152
    events, 154-155
    exceptions thrown by, 121
    filtering API results, 347
    full-text search for, 396-399
    inserts, 122
    JSON results for APIs, 341
    mass assignment, 124, 196
    migration, creating with model, 119
    model creation, 119
    mutators, 132
    pagination for, 170-172, 344
    primary keys, 119
    relationships, 139-151
    retrieving data, 120-122
    scopes (filters), 128-131
    serialization, 137-139
    sorting results, 345-347
    table names, 119
    timestamps, 120, 152-154
    transforming results, 348-352
    updates, 123-125
    user input from, 196
Eloquent API resources
    conditionally applying attributes, 357

creating a resource class, 352
nesting relationships, 355
pagination, 356
resource collections, 354
@else directive, Blade, 65, 246
@elseif directive, Blade, 65
email notifications, 419
email verification
migrations and, 91
MustVerifyEmail trait, 235
VerificationController, 229
emailOutputTo() method, tasks, 460
EncryptCookies middleware, 402
encryption
for cookies, 402
generating keys for OAuth server, 358
key:generate and, 204
of session data, 382
@endcan directive, 246
@endcannot directive, 246
@endif directive, Blade, 65
@endsection directive, Blade, 69
ends_with() helper, 175, 467
@endunless directive, Blade, 65
enum() method, Blueprint, 93
env command, Artisan, 202
.env file, 17, 18, 19, 168
env() helper, 18, 473
.env.example file, 17
.env.test file, 301
environment variables
defined, 491
Mix, 168
returning, 473
setting for tests, 301
environment() method, 301
Envoy, 487, 491
Envoyer, 460, 485, 491
equal sign (=), in Artisan argument definition, 210
error bags, 174, 179
error() method, 214
error() method, notification, 422
errors and exceptions
from Eloquent, 121
from HTTP, 472
from jobs in queue, 433-435
from session, testing for, 401
from user input, 193

in message and error bags, 174, 179
$errors variable, 174
ES6, JavaScript, 164
event commands, Artisan, 204
Event facade, 437
event fakes, 312
event() helper, 437, 474
Event::fake() method, Eloquent, 313
events, 437-442
authentication, 239
broadcasting over WebSockets (see Web-
Sockets)
creating, 437-439
creating listeners for, 439-442
defined, 491
Eloquent, 154-155
firing, 437-439, 474
pub/sub pattern used by, 437
subscribers for, 441
testing, 462
ExampleTest.php file, 296
except() method, Request, 182, 259
exception handling, HTTP tests, 310
exceptions (see errors and exceptions)
exists() method, Request, 259
exists() method, Session, 384
exists() method, Storage, 379
expectsOutput() method, TestCase, 322
expectsQuestion() method, TestCase, 322
$expression parameter, Blade, 81
@extends directive, Blade, 69
extract() method, 167

F
facades, 289-291
accessing backing class of, 290
creating, 291
defined, 491
importing, 75
importing namespaces for, 289
injecting backing class of, 290
namespaces for, 185
static calls using, 27
factory() helper, 101, 474
failed() method, jobs, 434
fake() method, 312
Faker, 295, 400, 491
fallback routes, 36
feature tests, 296

File facade, 380
file responses, 265
file() method, Faker, 400
file() method, Request, 187, 261
file() method, Response, 60, 265
files() method, Storage, 379
filesystem storage (see storage)
filesystems.php file, 377
file_get_contents() function, 381
filled() method, Request, 259
filter() method, collection, 477
filtering API results, 347
filters (see scopes)
find() method, DB, 113
find() method, Eloquent, 120
findOrFail() method, DB, 113
findOrFail() method, Eloquent, 120
first() method, Blueprint, 94
first() method, collection, 478
first() method, DB, 113
first() method, Eloquent, 120
firstOrCreate() method, Eloquent, 125
firstOrFail() method, DB, 113
firstOrFail() method, Eloquent, 120
firstOrNew() method, Eloquent, 125
flag, defined, 491
flash session storage, 385
flash() method, Request, 262
flash() method, Session, 385
flashExcept() method, Request, 262
flashOnly() method, Request, 262
float() method, Blueprint, 93
fluent interface, 105
fluent, defined, 491
flush() method, Cache, 388
flush() method, Request, 262
flush() method, Session, 385
Flysystem package, 377, 380, 492
@for directive, Blade, 66
forceDelete() method, Eloquent, 128
@foreach directive, Blade, 66
@forelse directive, Blade, 66
forever() method, Cache, 387
Forge, 428, 485, 492
forget() method, Cache, 388
forget() method, Session, 385
ForgotPasswordController, 229
form encoding, 189
form method spoofing, 52

form requests, 194-196, 276
forUser() method, Gate, 242
FQCN (fully qualified class name), 492
Fractal package, 349
frameworks, 1-4
    (see also Laravel)
from() method, mailable, 410
frontend components, 169
    (see also Mix build tool)
full-text search, Scout package for, 396-399
functional tests (see application tests)
functions (see helper functions)

G

Gate facade, 241
GET method, 24
    for resource controllers, 25
    routes based on, 28
get() method, Cache, 387
get() method, Cookie, 389
get() method, DB, 108, 113
get() method, Eloquent, 121
get() method, ParameterBag, 259
get() method, Route, 31
get() method, Session, 383
get() method, Storage, 379
get() method, TestCase, 305
getFacadeAccessor() method, 290
getJson() method, 306
getRealPath() method, SplFileInfo, 381
getVisibility() method, Storage, 379
.gitignore file, 17
global scopes, 129-131
grant types, Passport, 360-368
groupBy() method, collection, 479
groupBy() method, DB, 112
Grunt, 159
guard() method, 237
guards, 236-238
    adding, 237
    changing default, 237
    closure request guards, 238
    custom user providers, 238
    driver for, 236, 238
    provider for, 236-238
@guest directive, 236
guest middleware, 234
guest() method, 225
guest() method, redirects, 57

Gulp, 159, 492
gulpfile.js file, 15

H

handle() method, events, 440
handle() method, jobs, 430
handle() method, requests, 255, 270-272, 275
has() method, Cache, 387
has() method, Cookie, 389
has() method, Eloquent, 143
has() method, ParameterBag, 259
has() method, Request, 183
has() method, Session, 384
HasApiTokens trait, 359
hasCookie() method, Request, 262
hasFile() method, Request, 188, 261
hasMany() method, Eloquent, 142
hasManyThrough() method, Eloquent, 144
hasOne() method, Eloquent, 140
hasOneThrough() method, Eloquent, 144
having() method, DB, 112
havingRaw() method, DB, 112
HEAD method, 24
header() method, Request, 260, 343
header() method, Response, 343
headers (see request headers) (see response
    headers)
$headers array, 277
help command, Artisan, 202
helper functions, 465-474
    (see also specific helpers)
    defined, 492
    for arrays, 465-467
    for paths, 469
    for strings, 467-469
    for URLs, 470-472
here() method, Echo, 455
$hidden property, 348
HMR (Hot Module Replacement; hot reload-
    ing), 167, 492
home() method, redirects, 57
Homestead, 13, 484, 492
Horizon, 436, 484, 492
Hot Module Replacement (HMR), 166, 492
.htaccess file, 254
htmlentities() function, 64, 467
HTTP method spoofing, 53
HTTP methods (verbs), 24, 28, 52
HTTP redirects, 55-59, 473, 474

HTTP requests, 59, 253-262, 276-277
    (see also Request object)
HTTP responses, 60, 262-269, 474
    (see also Response object)
HTTP tests, 305-311
    authenticating responses, 309
    basic page, 305
    customizations, 310
    exception handling, 310
    JSON testing, 306
    $response object assertions, 306
HttpFoundation classes, 257
HTTPS requests, 276-277
hyphen, double (- -), preceding Artisan com-
    mand options, 210

I

id() method, 225
@if directive, Blade, 65
if statements, 83
illuminate collections, 106
illuminate namespace, 492
implicit route model binding, 50
@include directive, Blade, 70
increment() method, Cache, 388
increment() method, DB, 115
increments() method, Blueprint, 93
index() method, Blueprint, 94
index() method, resource controllers, 25
index.php file, 254
info() method, 214
@inject directive, Blade, 80
input() method, Request, 183, 185, 259
inRandomOrder() method, DB, 112
insert() method, DB, 107, 115
insertGetId() method, DB, 115
installer tool, 14, 21, 484
instance() method, Mockery, 320
instances, binding to, 285
integer() method, Blueprint, 92
integration tests, 303, 492
intended() method, redirects, 57
InteractsWithQueue trait, 430
InteractsWithSockets trait, 449
interfaces (contracts), 224, 285
Intervention library, 381
invoke() method, 49
IoC (inversion of control), 280, 292, 492
IoC container (see container)

ip() method, Request, 260
is() method, Request, 260
isEmpty() method, collection, 481
isJson() method, Request, 261
isMethod() method, Request, 184
isNotEmpty() method, collection, 481
isValid() method, File, 188

J

JavaScript
    concatenating, in Mix, 163
    Echo JavaScript package, 452-456
        (see also Echo)
    escaping backslashes in, 448
    processing, in Mix, 164
    vendor extraction, in Mix, 167
JavaScript ES6, 164
JavaScript files, Blade stacks for, 72
JavaScript Object Notation (see JSON)
jobs, 428-432
    (see also queues)
    creating, 429-431
    defined, 427, 492
    deleting, 435
    dispatching, 474
    failed, 433-435
    number of tries for, 433
    pushing onto queue, 431
    releasing back to queue, 435
join() method, DB, 114
join() method, Echo, 455
js() method, Mix, 166
JSON (JavaScript Object Notation)
    API pattern for, 338
    API spec for, 345
    defined, 492
    operations, 116, 137-139
    responses, 265
    storing default string as key with, 178
    testing, 306
JSON Web Token (JWT), 367, 492
json() method, Blueprint, 93
json() method, Request, 185, 259
json() method, Response, 60, 265
jsonb() method, Blueprint, 93
jsonp() method, Response, 60
JWT (JSON Web Token), 367, 492

K

kebab_case() helper, 175
keep() method, Session, 385
kernel, 254
Kernel.php file, 272
key commands, Artisan, 204
key, storing default string as, 178
keys() method, Dusk, 328
keys() method, ParameterBag, 259

L

Lambo package, 14
Laravel
    advantages of, 4-6
    community for, 6
    documentation for, xviii
    ecosystem for, 483-488
    installer, 14, 21, 484
    local development environments for, 12-17
    online resources, 488
    PHP versions and extensions for, 11
    starting, 21
    system requirements, xviii, 11
    versions of (see versions of Laravel)
Laravel Cashier, 486, 490
Laravel Dusk (see Dusk)
Laravel Echo (see Echo)
Laravel Envoy, 487
Laravel Envoyer (see Envoyer)
Laravel Forge (see Forge)
Laravel Homestead (see Homestead)
Laravel Horizon (see Horizon)
Laravel Lumen, 487
Laravel Mix (see Mix build tool)
laravel new command (Laravel installer), 14, 21
Laravel Nova, 486, 493
Laravel Passport (see Passport package)
Laravel Socialite, 486, 494
Laravel Spark, 487, 495
Laravel Telescope, 488, 495
Laravel Valet (see Valet package)
laravel.log file, 415
last() method, collection, 478
lastModified() method, Storage, 379
later() method, Mail, 414
latest() method, DB, 112
lazy loading, 152, 153
LengthAwarePaginator class, 171
lifecycle of application, 253-256

line() method, 214
links() method, 170
listen() method, Echo, 454
listeners, for events, 439-443
listenForWhisper() method, Echo, 456
loadMissing() method, Eloquent, 154
local development environments, 12-17
local disk, 378
local scopes, 128
localization, 175-179
    basic, 176
    parameters in, 177
    pluralization in, 177
    storing default string as key with JSON, 178
Log facade, 289-291
Log Fake package, 404
logging, 289-291, 392-396, 415
    channels, 393-396
    daily channel, 394
    reasons to use, 392
    single channel, 394
    slack channel, 395
    stack channel, 395
    testing, 403
    writing to logs, 393
logging out, manually, 233
login() method, 228, 233
loginAs() method, Dusk, 327
LoginController, 227-228
loginUsingId() method, 233
logoutOtherDevices() method, 233
longText() method, Blueprint, 93
$loop variable, 67
loops (Blade), 65-67, 71
Lumen, 487

M

mail, 405-426
    attachments, 410
    capturing, 415
    classic mail, 406
    configuring, 405
    creating, 406-408
    customizing, 410
    drivers supported, 405
    HTML vs. plain-text, 409
    inline images, 410
    local development, 415
    logging, 415

    mailable mail, 406-408
    manually modifying, 410
    Markdown mailables, 411-413
    notifications, 416-424
    queues for, 414, 436
    rendering mailables to the browser, 413
    sending, 408
    templates, 409
    testing, 415, 425
    universal to, 416
Mail facade, testing, 315
mail.php file, 405, 416
mailables, 492
    (see also Markdown)
MailThief, 425
Mailtrap, 415
make commands, Artisan, 204, 207
make() method, app, 282
make() method, Cookie, 389
make() method, model factories, 102
make() method, Response, 60
make:auth command, Artisan, 231
make:controller command, Artisan, 43, 45, 47
make:event command, Artisan, 437
make:factory command, Artisan, 100
make:job command, Artisan, 429
make:mail command, Artisan, 406, 412
make:middleware command, Artisan, 270
make:migration command, Artisan, 91
make:model command, Artisan, 119, 340
make:policy command, Artisan, 247
make:resource command, Artisan, 352
make:seeder command, Artisan, 98
makeDirectory() method, Storage, 380
makeVisible() method, Eloquent, 138
makeWith() method, app, 288
many to many polymorphic relationships, 150
many-to-many relationships, 139, 145-148
map() method, collection, 478
mapApiRoutes() method, RouteServiceProvider, 274
mapWebRoutes() method, RouteServiceProvider, 274
Markdown
    components, 413
    defined, 492
    mailables, 411-413
    notifications, 422
markdown() method, 412, 422

mass assignment, 124, 196, 493
max() method, DB, 114
Mbstring PHP extension, 11
mediumInteger() method, Blueprint, 92
mediumText() method, Blueprint, 93
Memcached data store, 89, 493
message bags, 172-174, 179
message() method, Request, 192
MessageBag class, 172-174
method injection, 279, 287
method() method, Request, 184, 260
methods, 31
    (see also specific methods)
    chaining, 31, 36
    controller/method reference syntax, 29
    HTTP methods (verbs), 24, 28
middleware, 27, 269-276
    binding, 272-275
    custom, 270-272
    defined, 493
    for authentication, 234
    for authorization, 243
    groups, 273
    passing parameters to, 275
    route groups for, 34-36
    trusted proxies, 276-277
middleware() method, 34, 274
migrate command, Artisan, 97, 202, 205, 340
migrate:fresh command, Artisan, 302
migrations, 89-98
    columns, creating, 92-94
    columns, modifying, 94-97
    creating with Eloquent model, 119
    defined, 493
    defining, 90-97
    field properties, 93
    foreign keys, 96
    indexes, adding, 96
    indexes, removing, 96
    running, 97
    tables, creating, 91
    tables, dropping, 94
min() method, DB, 114
Mix build tool, 159-168
    as part of Laravel ecosystem, 484
    copying files or directories, 164
    defined, 493
    directory structure for, 161
    environment variables, 168

HMR, 166
    JavaScript, concatenating, 163
    JavaScript, processing, 164
    pre- and post-processors, 163
    preprocessorless CSS, 163
    running, 161
    source maps, generating, 162
    vendor extraction, 167
    versioning, 164-166
    Vue and React components, 166
mix() helper, 165, 167
mix.version() method, 165
Mockery library, 295, 318-321, 493
mocking, 318-321
model
    defined, 493
    in MVC, 23
model factories, 99-104, 312, 493
Model-View-Controller (MVC) pattern (see
    MVC pattern)
modelKeys() method, collection, 136
morphs() method, Blueprint, 93
move() method, Storage, 379
multitenancy, 82, 493
mutators, 132, 493
MVC (Model-View-Controller) pattern, 23
    (see also controllers; views)
    primary concepts, 23
    views in, 40

N

name prefixes, route groups for, 38
name() method, 31
namespace prefixes, route groups for, 37
namespaces
    default App namespace, replacing, 204
    escaping backslashes in JavaScript, 448
    facades for namespaced classes, 75
    for contracts, 224
    for controllers, 44
    for facades, 185, 289
    Illuminate, 254
    make namespace, for Artisan, 207
Nexmo, 424
Nginx, 493
Node.js, installing, 161
Notifiable trait, 419
Notification facade, 316, 419
notifications, 416-424

broadcast notifications, 423
    channels for, 418
    creating, 416-418
    database notifications, 423
    defined, 493
    drivers supported, 421
    Markdown, 422
    queueing, 420
    sending, 419
    Slack notifications, 424
    SMS notifications, 424
    subscribing to, 456
    testing, 425
notifications commands, Artisan, 205
notify() method, Notifiable, 420
Nova, 486, 493
now() helper, 40
NPM (Node Package Manager), 493
npm install command, 452
nullable() method, Blueprint, 94
nullableTimestamps() method, Blueprint, 93

O

OAuth 2.0, 358, 493
    (see also Passport package)
object-relational mapper (ORM), 36, 493
    (see also Eloquent)
old() helper, 58, 474
old() method, Request, 262
oldest() method, DB, 112
once() method, 233
onceUsingId() method, 233
onConnection() method, jobs, 431
onConnection() method, mailable, 414
one-to-many relationships, 139, 141-143
one-to-one relationships, 140-141
online resources
    facades documentation, 290
    Laravel documentation, xviii
    Valet documentation, 13
only() method, Request, 125, 182, 197, 259
onlyTrashed() method, Eloquent, 128
onQueue() method, events, 432
onQueue() method, jobs, 432
onQueue() method, mailable, 414
onUserSubscription() method, events, 442
OpenSSL PHP extension, 11
operating system requirements, xviii, 11
optimize command, Artisan, 202

option()/options() methods, Artisan, 211, 493
OPTIONS method, 25
orderBy() method, DB, 111
orderBy() method, Eloquent, 120
ORM (object-relational mapper), 36, 493
    (see also Eloquent)
orWhere() method, DB, 109

P

package commands, Artisan, 205
package.json file, 17
Package::make() method, Eloquent, 303
page class, Dusk, 331-333
page tests, 305
paginate() method, 170, 344
pagination, 170-172, 356
Paginator class, 172
parameter binding, PDO, 107
ParameterBag class, 259
@parent directive, Blade, 70
passes() method, Request, 192
Passport package, 358-373
    as part of Laravel ecosystem, 484
    defined, 494
    deploying, 373
    grant types for, 360-368
    installing, 358
    routes for, 359, 369
    scopes, 371-372
    Vue components, 369-370
passport:keys command, Artisan, 373
PassportServiceProvider, 358
password grant, Passport, 360
PATCH method, 25
path prefixes, route groups for, 36
path() method, Request, 260
paths
    for facades, 185
    helpers for, 469
pause() method, Dusk, 329
PDO parameter binding, 107
PDO PHP extension, 11
personal access client, 366
personal access tokens, Passport, 366
PHP
    versions and extensions for, 11
    views rendered with, 40
PHPSpec, 494
PHPUnit testing framework, 21, 295, 494

assertions syntax, 297
  method naming, 300
phpunit.xml file, 17, 301
pingBefore() method, tasks, 461
pivot table, 145-148
pjax() method, Request, 261
pluck() method, collection, 479
pluralization, 174, 177
polymorphic relationships, 139, 148-151, 494
POST method, 24
  for resource controllers, 25
  getting user input from, 45
  routes based on, 28
prepend() method, Storage, 379
preprocessor, 494
preset command, Artisan, 202
primary key, 494
primary() method, Blueprint, 94
priority() method, mailable, 410
private() method, Echo, 454
progress bars, 215
progressAdvance() method, 215
progressFinish() method, 215
projects
  configuring, 18
  creating, 14
  directory structure for, 15-17
provides() method, service providers, 256
$proxies array, 276
proxies, trusted, 276-277
pub/sub pattern, 437, 442
public disk, 378
public folder, 16
pull() method, Cache, 387
pull() method, Session, 385
push() method, Session, 384
Pusher, 442, 446-452
PUT method, 25
  for resource controllers, 25
  routes based on, 28
put() method, Cache, 387
put() method, Session, 384
put() method, Storage, 379, 381
putFile() method, Storage, 379

Q

query builder, 105-117
  (see also Eloquent)
  aggregates, 122

chaining methods with, 107-116
conditional methods, 112
constraining queries, 108-111
DB facade for, 105
deletes, 116
inserts, 115
joins, 114
JSON operations, 116
modifying queries, 111
multiple query results, format for, 106
pagination for, 170, 344
parameter binding, 107
raw SQL queries, 106, 114
relationships as, 143
returning results, 113
transactions, 116
unions, 115
updates, 115
query parameters, versioning assets with, 165
question mark (?)
  following optional Artisan command arguments, 209
  following optional parameters, 29
  query parameters, 107
question() method, 214
queue commands, Artisan, 205
Queue facade, testing, 314
queue() method, Cookie, 390
queue() method, Mail, 414
queue.php file, 428
queue:failed command, Artisan, 435
queue:failed-table command, Artisan, 434
queue:flush command, Artisan, 435
queue:forget command, Artisan, 435
queue:listen command, Artisan, 433
queue:retry all command, Artisan, 435
queue:retry command, Artisan, 435
queue:work command, Artisan, 432, 433
Queueable trait, 430
queues, 427-436
  benefits of, 428
  configuring, 428
  creating jobs in, 429-431
  defined, 494
  deleting jobs in, 435
  dispatching jobs in, 474
  error handling, 433-435
  for Artisan commands, 205, 436
  for jobs, 428-432

for mail, 414, 436
number of tries for jobs, 433
providers and drivers for, 428
pushing jobs onto, 431
releasing jobs back to, 435
testing, 461-463
workers, 432

R

radio() method, Dusk, 328
randomly generated data, 101
rate limiting, 35
raw() method, DB, 114
React, 166, 494
react() method, Mix, 166
read-evaluate-print-loop (REPL) (see Tinker)
readme.md file, 17
real-time facades, 291, 494
redirect() helper, 55-59, 266, 474
redirectPath() method, 227
redirects, 55-59
Redis, 89, 436, 446, 448, 494
reduce() method, collection, 479
reflash() method, Session, 385
refresh tokens, 365
refresh() method, redirects, 57
RefreshDatabase trait, 302
regenerate() method, Session, 385
register() method, RegisterUsers, 227
register() method, service providers, 255, 283, 291
RegisterController, 226-227
RegistersUsers trait, 227
regression tests, 296
(see also Dusk)
regular expressions
passing to str_is(), 468
route constraints using, 30
reject() method, collection, 477
relationships, 139-151
as query builders, 143
eager loading, 152
inserting related items, 141
lazy eager loading, 153
serialization of, 138
when defining model factories, 103
release() method, jobs, 435
remember me access token, 232
remember() method, Cache, 388

rememberForever() method, Cache, 388
rememberToken() method, Blueprint, 93
render() method, pagination, 170
REPL (read-evaluate-print-loop) (see Tinker)
Representational State Transfer (REST), 337-338
Request facade, 181
request headers, 342, 343
Request object, 181-186, 257-262
accessing, 257-262
array input, accessing, 184
capturing directly, 257
file handling methods, 261
form requests, 276
headers for, 342, 343
JSON input, accessing, 185
lifecycle of, 253-255
persistence of, for session interaction, 262
reading cookies from, 391
testing, 277-278
typehinting in constructors, 47
user and request state methods, 260
user input methods, 258
validate() on, 189
request() helper, 181, 185, 258, 348
reset() method, 229
resetPassword() method, 229
ResetPasswordController, 229
resource controller binding, 48
resource controllers, 47-49, 339-342
resource gates, 242
resource() method, 242
resources folder, 16, 161
resources, API, 337, 350-352
resources, online (see online resources)
respondWithRoute() method, API resource, 374
Responsable interface, 268-269
response headers, 343
Response object, 262-269
creating, 263
custom, 60
custom response macros, 267
download responses, 264
file responses, 265
headers for, 343
JSON responses, 265
lifecycle of, 253-255
redirect responses, 266-267

Responsable interface, 268-269
  setting cookies on, 391
  testing, 277-278
  view responses, 264
$response object, 305-308
response() helper, 60, 266, 474
REST (Representational State Transfer), 25,
  337-338, 494
restore() method, Eloquent, 128
reverse() method, collection, 480
right angle bracket, triple (> > >), Tinker
  prompt, 217
rollBack() method, DB, 117
route commands, Artisan, 205
route groups, 33-38
  (see also controllers)
  defining, 33
  fallback routes, 36
  middleware applied to, 34-36
  name prefixes, 38
  namespace prefixes using, 37
  path prefixes using, 36
  rate limiting, 35
  subdomain routing using, 37
route middleware, 234, 243, 273
route model binding, 50-51
route() helper, 32, 471
route() method, 56
Route::apiResource() method, 342
Route::fallback() method, 374
Route::view(), 41
route:cache command, Artisan, 52
route:list command, Artisan, 48
routes
  caching, 52
  data from URL, 186
  defined, 494
  defining, 26-33
  exiting, 59
  fluent definitions of, 31
  handling, 28
  modifying to allow signed links, 40
  naming, 31
  parameters for, 29, 50-51, 186
  signed, 38-40
  testing, 61
  verbs for, 28
routes folder, 16
routes() method, Auth, 229

routes.php file, 26, 274
RouteServiceProvider, 255, 274
rules (abilities) for authorization, 240
rules() method, form request, 194

S

S3 cloud storage, 378, 494
s3 disk, 378
SaaS (Software as a Service), 494
Sass, 160
save() method, Eloquent, 122
schedule commands, Artisan, 206
schedule:run command, Artisan, 457
scheduler, 457-461
  Artisan commands as tasks, 457
  avoiding tasks overlapping, 460
  closures as tasks, 457, 460
  defining time zones for scheduled com-
    mands, 460
  shell commands as tasks, 457
  task output, handling, 460
  task types, 457
  time frames for, setting, 458
scheduleTimezone() method, tasks, 460
scopes (filters), Eloquent, 128-131, 494
scopes (privileges), OAuth, 371-372
Scout package, 396-399
  conditional indexing, 398
  defined, 494
  drivers supported, 396
  installing and configuring, 396
  manually triggering, 398
  marking model for indexing, 397
  performing operations without indexing,
    398
  queuing actions of, 398
  searching index, 397
  testing, 404
ScoutServiceProvider, 397
script injection, 197
Searchable trait, 397
searchable() method, 398
searchableAs() method, 397
secret() method, 213
@section directive, Blade, 68-70
sections, Blade, 68-70
secure() method, redirects, 57
secure() method, Request, 261
security

authentication (see authentication)

authorization (see authorization)

CSRF (cross-site request forgery), 53-55, 453

encryption (see encryption)

mass assignment, 124, 196

script injection, 197

seeCookie() method, TestCase, 403

seeders, 98-105

    creating, 98

    model factories for, 99-104

seeding, 312

seePlainCookie() method, TestCase, 403

segment() method, Request, 186

segments() method, Request, 186

select() method, DB, 106, 108

select() method, Dusk, 328

selectRaw() method, DB, 114

send() method, Mail, 406

sendOutputTo() method, tasks, 460

serialization, 137-139, 494

SerializesModels trait, 430

serve command, Artisan, 202

server() method, Request, 261

server.php file, 17

service container (see container)

service providers, 255-256, 291, 494

    (see also specific service providers)

services, injecting into a view, 79-80

services.php file, 405

session commands, Artisan, 206

Session facade, 383

session() helper, 383

session() method, Request, 383

sessions, 382-386

    accessing, 383

    configuring, 382

    drivers supported, 382

    flash session storage, 385

    testing, 401

setter injection, 279-279

setUp() method, 292

setVisibility() method, Storage, 379

share() method, 77

shell commands, scheduling as tasks, 457

shouldBeSearchable() method, 398

ShouldBroadcast interface, 443

ShouldBroadcastNow contract, 446

shouldHaveReceived() method, Mockery, 321

shouldIgnoreMissing() method, Mockery, 319

shouldReceive() method, Mockery, 320

@show directive, Blade, 68

show() method, resource controllers, 25

showLinkRequestForm() method, 229

showLoginForm() method, 228

showRegistrationForm() method, 227

showResetForm() method, 229

shuffle() method, collection, 480

signed routes, 38-40

signed URLs, 39

signedRoute() method, 39

single action controllers, 49

single log channel, 394

singleton() method, 284

singletons, binding to, 284

size() method, Storage, 379

skip() method, DB, 112

slack log channel, 395

Slack notifications, 424

slash (/), escaping in Artisan commands, 339

@slot directive, Blade, 74

slots, Blade, 73-75

smallInteger() method, Blueprint, 92

SMS notifications, 424

snake_case() helper, 175

Socialite, 486, 494

soft deletes, 126-128, 495

softDeletes() method, Blueprint, 93, 127

sort() method, collection, 480

sortBy() method, collection, 480

sortByDesc() method, collection, 480

sorting API results, 345-347

source maps, Mix, 162

Spark, 487, 495

SplFileInfo class, 381

SQL queries, raw, 106

    (see also query builder)

SQLite

    dependencies for, 94

    modifying multiple columns, 95

stack log channel, 395

stacks, Blade, 72

starts_with() helper, 175, 467

state() method, model factories, 104

stateless APIs, 337

statement() method, DB, 106

static calls, 27

stdClass object

returned by DB facade, 106
returned by loops, 67
storage, 377-404
    (see also databases)
    adding providers, 380
    cache, 386-388
    configuring file access, 377
    cookies, 388-392
    downloads, 382
    file managers, 377-380
    flash session storage, 385
    injecting instance for, 380
    logging, 392-396
    session storage, 382-386
    Storage facade methods for, 378-380
    testing, 399-404
    uploads and manipulation, 380-382
storage commands, Artisan, 206
Storage facade, 317, 378-380
storage folder, 16
storage:link command, Artisan, 378
storage_path() helper, 378, 470
Store class, 383
store() method, resource controllers, 25
store() method, UploadedFile, 189, 382
storeAs() method, UploadedFile, 189, 382
streamDownload() method, Response, 60
string() method, Blueprint, 92
strings
    helpers for, 467-469
    localization, 175-179
    pluralization, 174, 177
    string helpers, 174
str_contains() helper, 175, 467
str_is() helper, 175, 468
str_limit() helper, 468
str_plural() helper, 175, 469
str_random() helper, 468
str_singular() helper, 175
str_slug() helper, 175, 469
studly_case() helper, 175
subdomain routing, 37
subject() method, mailable, 410
subscribe() method, events, 442
sum() method, collection, 481
sum() method, DB, 114
Symfony, 4, 495
    Console component, 201
    HttpFoundation classes, 257

    Translation component, 178
sync() method, Eloquent, 148
synchronizer tokens, Passport, 367-368
system requirements, xviii, 11

T

table() method, 214
take() method, collection, 479
take() method, DB, 112
Task::all() query, 41, 44
tasks, scheduling (see scheduler)
Telescope, 488, 495
templates (see Blade) (see views)
temporarySignedRoute() method, 39
@test docblock, 300
TestCase class, 304
TestCase.php file, 296
testing, 295-336
    APIs, 374
    Artisan commands, 219, 322-323
    authentication and authorization, 249-252
    basics, 296-300
    browsers, 323-335
    bus fakes, 314
    cache, 402
    cookies, 402
    database operations, 155-157
    database tests, 311
    dependency injection in, 292
    environment for, 301
    event fakes, 312
    failed test results, 299
    frontend components, 179
    HTTP tests, 305-311
    inversion of control in, 292
    log, 403
    mail, 425
    mail fakes, 315
    mocking, 318-321
    model factories in, 312
    names for methods prior to Laravel 5.4, 252
    naming tests, 300
    notification fakes, 316
    notifications, 425
    queue fakes, 314
    queues, 461-463
    requests and responses, 277-278
    routes, 61
    running tests, 21

Scout, 404
seeding in, 312
sessions, 401
storage, 399-404
Storage fakes, 317
traits for, 301-302
user input, 197
views, 83-84
writing tests, 21
tests folder, 16, 296
text() method, Blueprint, 93
text() method, Dusk, 327
text() method, mailable, 409
thenPing() method, tasks, 461
time() method, Blueprint, 93
times and dates (see Carbon package) (see
    scheduler) (see timestamps)
timestamp() method, Blueprint, 93
timestamps, 93, 124
    child records updating parent record time-
        stamps, 152-154
    data mutators and, 134
timestamps() method, Blueprint, 93
timezone() method, tasks, 459
Tinker, 217, 495
tinker command, Artisan, 202
tinyInteger() method, Blueprint, 92
title_case() helper, 175
TL;DR, xviii, 495
to() method, 56
toArray() method, API resource, 352
toArray() method, collection, 477
toArray() method, Eloquent, 137
toBroadcast() method, notification, 424
toDatabase() method, notification, 423
toJson() method, Eloquent, 137
Tokenizer PHP extension, 11
tokens, CSRF, 53-55
toMail() method, notification, 421
toNexmo() method, notification, 424
toOthers() method, events, 449, 456
toResponse() method, Response, 268
toSearchableArray() method, 397
toSlack() method, notification, 424
trans() helper, 177
transaction() method, DB, 117
transactions, 116
translation (see localization)
Translation component, Symfony, 178

trashed() method, Eloquent, 128
truncate() method, DB, 116
TrustedProxy package, 276-277
Twig Bridge package, 64
    (see also Blade)
type() method, Dusk, 328
typehint, 46, 495
typehinting, 285

U

uncheck() method, Dusk, 328
union() method, DB, 115
unionAll() method, DB, 115
unique() method, Blueprint, 94
unique() method, Faker, 101
unit tests
    defined, 296, 495
    generating in PHPUnit, 299
    simple, 303
universal to, for mail, 416
@unless directive, Blade, 65
unless() parameter, DB, 113
unsearchable() method, 399
unsigned() method, Blueprint, 94
up command, Artisan, 202
up() method, migrations, 90
update() method, DB, 107, 115
update() method, Eloquent, 123-125
update() method, resource controllers, 25
updateExistingPivot() method, Eloquent, 148
uploaded files, 187-189, 380-382, 399
UploadedFile class, 188, 261, 399
url() helper, 31, 471
url() method, Dusk, 332
url() method, Request, 260
URLs
    helpers for, 470-472
    user input from route parameters, 186
    user input from URL segments, 186
user authentication (see authentication)
user authorization (see authorization)
user input
    Artisan commands, 211-213
    custom rule objects, 192
    Eloquent model, 196
    form requests, 194-196
    getting and handling with controllers, 45-46
    Request object, 181-186, 258
    route parameters, 186

testing, 197
uploaded files, 187-189
URLs, 186
validating, 189-191
User model, 222
user() method, 225, 237
username() method, 228
uuid() method, Blueprint, 93

V

Vagrant, 98
(see also Homestead)
defined, 495
migrations with, 98
Valet package, 12, 483, 495
validate() method, 59
validate() method, controller, 189-193
validateLogin() method, 228
validation of user input, 189-191
custom rule objects, 192
defined, 495
displaying error messages, 193
manual validation, 192
validate() method, controller, 189-193
validation rules, 191
Validator class, 192
validator() method, 227
validators, 173
value() method, DB, 113
value() method, Dusk, 327
vendor commands, Artisan, 206
vendor folder, 16
vendor.js file, 167
VerificationController, 229
VerifiesEmails, 229
versioning, in Mix, 164-166
versions of Laravel, xix
versions of Laravel, after 5.1
ACL (access control list), 240
versions of Laravel, after 5.2
policy methods, 248
versions of Laravel, after 5.3
real-time facades, 291
versions of Laravel, after 5.4
API resources, 349
Browserkit, 198
RefreshDatabase trait, 302
testing method nomenclature, 198
versions of Laravel, after 5.5

invalidating sessions on other devices, 233
TrustedProxy package, 276
versions of Laravel, after 5.6
Artisan command testing, 218
Auth::routes() in, 230
email verification, 230, 235
mail logging, 415
versions of Laravel, after 5.7
assertions against $response, 306
binding Mockery instances to the container, 320
calling Artisan commands, 216
DeferrableProvider interface, 255
defining cache duration, 386
defining time zones for scheduled commands, 460
helper functions, 465
policy auto-discovery, 247
SMS notifications, 424
stack log channel, 395
versions of Laravel, prior to 5.2
authentication guards, 237
conditional query modifications, 348
.env testing, 301
fluent route definitions, 31
middleware groups, 273
render() method, pagination, 170
versions of Laravel, prior to 5.3
API token authentication, 373
assertViewHas() method, 84
authentication controllers, 221
classic mail, 406
DB facade results, 106
Eloquent results, 121
$expression parameter, 81
factory states, 104
form requests, 195
generating resource controllers, 45
$loop variable, 67
PHP and extensions, 11
policy methods, 248
routes file, 26
withCookie() method, Response, 391
versions of Laravel, prior to 5.4
elixir() helper, 472
route group modifications, 34
testing, 297
testing method names, 84, 157, 252, 403
testing methods, 62

translation helper, 177
versions of Laravel, prior to 5.5
    calling validate() method on controller, 190
    manual package registration, 205
    manually binding commands, 208
    model factory file, 100
    resource controllers/routes in, 339
    service provider registration, 397
versions of Laravel, prior to 5.6
    CSREF helpers in, 54
    fallback routes, 36
versions of Laravel, prior to 5.7
    Artisan tests, 322
    assets folder, 161
versions of Laravel, prior to 5.8
    changes to Artisan commands, 203
via() method, notification, 418, 419
viaRemember() method, 232
viaRequest() auth method, 238
view commands, Artisan, 206
view composers, 42, 76-79, 495
view partials, 70-72
view responses, 264
view() helper, 77, 264, 474
view() method, Response, 264
views, 40-42
    binding data to, 76-79
    defined, 495
    in MVC, 23, 40
    loading, 41
    passing variables to, 41, 75
    testing, 83-84
$visible property, 348
Vue, 166, 369-370, 495
Vue Resource, 55

W

waitFor() method, Dusk, 329
waitForLink() method, Dusk, 330
waitForLocation() method, Dusk, 330
waitForMissing() method, Dusk, 329
waitForReload() method, Dusk, 330
waitForRoute() method, Dusk, 330
waitForText() method, Dusk, 330
waitUntil() method, Dusk, 330
wantsJson() method, Request, 261
web guard, 236
web middleware group, 274
web routes, 26

    (see also routes)
web.php file, 26
Webpack, 159, 164, 495
webpack.mix.js file, 17, 159
website resources (see online resources)
WebSocket authentication (see Echo)
WebSockets, 442-456
    authorization for channels, 450-452
    broadcasting events, 443-446
    channels for, 444, 450-452
    configuring, 443
    drivers supported, 443
    Echo for, 447
    event structure for, 444
    excluding user from events, 449
    pub/sub pattern used by, 442
    receiving event messages, 446-456
    service provider configuration, 449-452
when() parameter, DB, 112
whenAvailable() method, Dusk, 329
where() method, collection, 478
where() method, DB, 108
where() method, Eloquent, 121
whereBetween() method, DB, 110
whereExists() method, DB, 111
whereIn() method, DB, 110
whereNull() method, DB, 111
whereRaw() method, DB, 111
@while directive, Blade, 66
whisper() method, Echo, 456
with() method, 57-59, 77
with() method, Eloquent, 153
withCookie() method, Response, 391
withcount() method, Eloquent, 154
withErrors() method, 174
withExceptionHandling() method, 311
withHeaders() method, 310
withInput() method, 58
withoutExceptionHandling() method, 310
withoutGlobalScope() method, 131
withoutGlobalScopes() method, 131
WithoutMiddleware trait, 302
withoutOverlapping() method, tasks, 460
withoutSyncingToSearch() method, 398
withPivot() method, Eloquent, 146
withSession() method, 310
withSwiftMessage() method, mailable, 410
withTrashed() method, Eloquent, 127
workers for queues, 432

X

X- preceding header names, 342

Y

@yield directive, Blade, 68

About the Author

Matt Stauffer is a developer and a teacher. He is a partner and technical director at Tighten (*https://tighten.co/*), blogs at *mattstauffer.com*, and hosts the Laravel Podcast and the Five-Minute Geek Show.

Colophon

The animal on the cover of *Laravel: Up & Running* is a gemsbok (*Oryx gazella*). This large antelope is native to the deserts of South Africa, Botswana, Zimbabwe, and Namibia, where it is featured on the country's coat of arms.

Gemsbok measure about 5 feet 7 inches tall at the shoulder and can weigh from 250 to 390 pounds. They are typically pale gray or brown, with black and white facial markings and long black tails. A black stripe extends from the chin to the lower edge of the neck. The gemsbok's impressive straight horns, used in defensive maneuvers, average 33 inches in length and are regarded as charms in many cultures. In medieval England, they were often marketed as unicorn horns.

Although these horns make the gemsbok a highly sought trophy animal, the population remains stable throughout Southern Africa. In 1969, gemsbok were introduced to southern New Mexico, where their current population is around 3,000.

Gemsbok are well suited to such desert environments, with the ability to survive without drinking water for most of the year. To achieve this, they do not pant or sweat, allowing their body temperature to rise several degrees above normal on hot days. Their lifespan is approximately 18 years in the wild.

Many of the animals on O'Reilly covers are endangered; all of them are important to the world. To learn more about how you can help, go to *animals.oreilly.com*.

The cover illustration is by Karen Montgomery, based on a black and white engraving from *Riverside Natural History*. The cover fonts are Gilroy Semibold and Guardian Sans. The text font is Adobe Minion Pro; the heading font is Adobe Myriad Condensed; and the code font is Dalton Maag's Ubuntu Mono.

O'REILLY®

There's much more where this came from.

Experience books, videos, live online training courses, and more from O'Reilly and our 200+ partners—all in one place.

Learn more at oreilly.com/online-learning

CPSIA information can be obtained
at www.ICGtesting.com
Printed in the USA
BVHW081041040419
544543BV00012B/55/P